GALVESTON

ARCHITECTURE GUIDEBOOK

GALVESTON

ARCHITECTURE GUIDEBOOK

Ellen Beasley and Stephen Fox

Photographs by Ellen Beasley

Rice University Press Houston
Galveston Historical Foundation

Copyright © 1996 Galveston Historical Foundation

Library of Congress Cataloging-In-Publication Data

Beasley, Ellen.
    Galveston architecture guidebook / by Ellen Beasley & Stephen Fox.
    p. cm.
    Includes bibliographical reference and index.
    ISBN 0-89263-345-X. — ISBN 0-89263-346-8 (pbk.)
    1. Architecture —Texas—Galveston—Guidebooks. 2. Galveston
    (Tex.)—Buildings, structures, etc.—Guidebooks. 3. Galveston
    (Tex.)—Guidebooks. I. Fox, Stephen. II. Title.
NA735.G35B43 1996
720'.9764'139—dc20

96–9889
CIP

CONTENTS

Preface vii

Dedication viii

Using the Guidebook 2

Introduction 4

Tour A: Downtown and Central Park 13

Tour B: East End 61

Tour C: UTMB–East End Flats 119

Tour D: San Jacinto 131

Tour E: West End 161

Tour F: Factory District 197

Tour G: Denver Resurvey 209

Tour H: Seawall Boulevard 225

Tour I: Offatt's Bayou and West Beach 237

Galveston Building Types 250

Glossary of Selected Terms 253

Selected Bibliography 255

Acknowledgements 257

Index 258

When 25 local businessmen chartered the Galveston Historical Society on 3 August 1871, preserving papers and artifacts documenting the history of Galveston Island was the group's primary purpose. After the organization changed its focus to the preservation of Galveston's architectural heritage in 1954, it was incorporated as Galveston Historical Foundation (GHF). In 1994 GHF began to look for a way to commemorate its 125th anniversary that would be appropriate to both the history of the organization and the future of the city. Glenn Kirk and Pat Burns, co-chairmen of the anniversary committee, and their fellow volunteers, Gleaves James, John Gorman, Sally Wallace, and Frances St. John, hoped to "leave something behind" that would reflect GHF's expanded role in the community and its place as Texas's oldest historic preservation group.

In a happy coincidence, historic preservationist Ellen Beasley and architectural historian Stephen Fox were negotiating with Rice University Press to produce an architecture guidebook for Galveston. While much has been written about Galveston, and architectural inventories have been conducted, a city-wide guidebook has never been published. The GHF anniversary committee discussed a myriad of possibilities including the restoration of a historic building or erecting a monument, but, in the end, the committee recommended to GHF's Board of Directors that the *Galveston Architecture Guidebook* be designated the official remembrance of the 125th anniversary. The board unanimously approved the project and the Harris and Eliza Kempner Fund, through its Program-Related Investment Program provided funding to enable GHF to support this project.

The preservation of Galveston's architecture, as well as the documentation of its history is at the heart of Galveston Historical Foundation's mission. We are pleased that the *Galveston Architecture Guidebook* is another key element in fulfilling that mission.

Betty Massey

Executive Director
Galveston Historical Foundation

For all those who have

worked to preserve Galveston's

architectural riches

especially

Peter H. Brink

first executive director

1973-1989

Galveston Historical Foundation

The *Galveston Architecture Guidebook* is divided into nine geographical and thematic tours. The names for most of the tours have a historic precedent, at least for the general area defined by tour boundaries. San Jacinto is the one exception. Although Galveston's City Planning Department and residents now call this section of the city the San Jacinto neighborhood (after San Jacinto Elementary School), it seems to have had no inclusive historic name such as the East End.

Each of the nine tours is introduced by a summary description of the area. This is followed by a map on which the buildings and sites in that tour are identified numerically. These numbers correspond to the listing of entries and photographs within the tour text, which is arranged to aid the reader in walking or driving the tour route.

Individual entries are identified first by street address, then the historic name of the building (if there is one), the date of construction, and the name of the original architect and/or builder, if documented. In some instances, the date(s) and architect(s) of later major additions or alterations have been listed. This information is followed by a description of the building or site. Most buildings listed are not open to the public, and inclusion in the book is not an invitation to trespass.

A few points regarding the entries. Many streets are known to Galvestonians by names other than their numerical or alphabetical names; e.g., Avenue B is the Strand, 23rd Street is Tremont. In the entries, the addresses for buildings on these streets are identified by the names used by Galvestonians. Both names are included on the maps so the reader can always use the numerical listing to locate an entry if confused by a street address.

Most entries include a photograph that illustrates one building, but there are exceptions. In instances where more than one building is pictured, the addresses for the entry read from left to right in the order in which the buildings appear in the photograph.

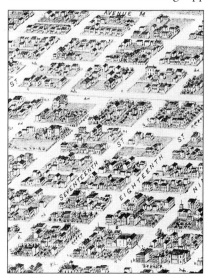

Detail of C. Drie's 1871 bird's-eye view of Galveston.

The entry for some buildings includes references to other buildings. If the latter still exist, the names or addresses of the buildings appear in boldface.

When researching the history of buildings in Galveston, certain documents are used repeatedly and, therefore, are frequently referenced in the entries. One of the most important documents for dating early buildings in Galveston is an 1871 bird's-eye, or perspective, view made by lithographer C. Drie. A second bird's-eye view was produced in 1885 by Augustus Koch.

Insurance records are another valuable source. Beginning in the late 19th century, forms were filled out for the Galveston Insurance Board for all insured properties. Information such as the date of construction, additions or alterations, ownership, and size was recorded. The Sanborn Map & Publishing Company, originally based in New York City, prepared insurance maps for cities and towns throughout the United States, the first one for Galveston in 1876. By using colors and symbols, these maps detailed the buildings in a city.

A word about the selection of entries. Galveston's architectural riches make it difficult, in a guidebook such as this, to narrow the number of entries even to 720. Emphasis has been placed on structures dating from the late 19th and early 20th centuries, representative examples of later periods and local architects, buildings designed by important architects, and examples of building typologies characteristic of Galveston. It is hoped that, when moving from one listed entry to another, the reader will notice the many architecturally interesting buildings in-between.

Galveston's reputation for having one of the most important and intact collections of late-19th-century architecture in the country is secure. For obvious reasons, these buildings are the focus of this guidebook. But Galveston's architectural legacy spans the 20th century as well, and the guidebook is intended to stir a greater interest in the city's later buildings and streetscapes.

Specific references to individual rehabilitation efforts are confined primarily to commercial properties, in part because those records tend to be more complete. Many buildings, especially dwellings, have experienced a second, even a third, generation of rehabilitation since the early 1970s when preservation activity began in earnest, but trying to list all of those becomes unmanageable. And then there are those properties whose owners have simply taken care of them—long before preservation had ever become a part of Galveston's vocabulary.

Tour Name ——————————— **Tour A**   **Downtown and Central Park** ——— Geographic Section

Building Address ——————— **2202-2206 Strand**   **A–13** ——— Map Code

Original Name ——————— W. L. Moody Building (now Strand Surplus Center) ——— Current Name

Date ——————— 1883, N. J. Clayton ——— Architect/Builder

Description ——————— The Storm of 1900 knocked the cornice and top floor off the building that Colonel William L. Moody built to contain his cotton commission and banking operations. Even so, it retains the finely finished dark red brick surfaces and subtle detailing with which Clayton organized its Strand and 22nd Street elevations.

1 ——————— Page Number

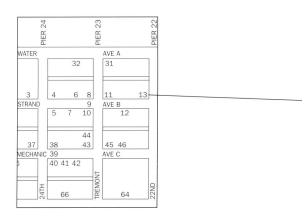

Building Location

For every building that's in this book, at least two others could be added—which is another way of saying that Galveston is a city with incredibly rich architectural resources.

The rewards for taking a walk or a drive through the city are not confined to the first-time visitor. Even for the longtime resident, the buildings and streetscapes in Galveston offer constant surprises, depending on the time of day and year you wander about the city.

Galveston beach scene, 1894.

The architectural history—the history—of Galveston begins with water. The plentiful harvests of the bay provided sustenance for the Akokisa Indians, thought to be the first residents of the sand-barrier island. Once discovered and mapped by European explorers, Galveston Island became a frequent destination.

It is hard to imagine how those who came to live on the island in the 1830s reacted when they saw, for the first time, their newly adopted landscape—a sandy, narrow slip of land, two miles at its widest point, flat, very flat, and virtually treeless, except, according to earliest reports, for three live oak trees.

Obviously, the city's founders were visionaries. They had to be. That vision, of course, was defined by the economic and commercial lure of Galveston Bay. Entered from the Gulf of Mexico, the bay formed a natural harbor and an ideal port for trading with the interior of the southwest territory, and became even more strategic after Texas won its independence in 1836. Location clearly compensated for any disadvantages that might be caused by climate and topography.

Galveston wharves in 1861. Photograph taken from the rooftop of a building at 20th Street and Strand looking west. The backsides of the buildings open directly onto the bay. Retouched photograph.

In 1838, the newly formed Galveston City Company hired New York surveyor John D. Groesbeck (already in the area for health reasons) to survey the eastern tip of the island. The resulting city plan was a very precise grid pattern with most blocks in the core area divided into 14 narrow lots (42'10" x 120') oriented north/south, and split by a 20-foot-wide alley. Public uses were assigned to specific blocks.

The primary system for naming

streets was simple and direct: East-west streets were given alphabetical names, north-south streets numerical names. The land south of Avenue M was sectioned into outlots that were the equivalent of four undivided blocks, thereby lending themselves initially to countrylike estates and, then, to later subdivision.

Groesbeck's plan accommodated the island's difficult configuration and scarcity of land, characteristics complicated even further by the ever-shifting tides that made for a very slippery, sometimes even vanishing, cityscape. The plan, however, has endured and shaped the city's physical and architectural face.

It was the importance of the port, and all its attendant businesses, that bought the city's architectural glory. Cotton was the primary export throughout the 19th and well into the 20th centuries. Imports included human commodities who would have an impact on the city's architecture. Galveston became the port of entry for thousands of European immigrants, many of whom—most particularly, German artisans—chose to stay in the coastal city rather than move inland. And prior to the Civil War, Galveston's slave trade supplied labor not only to cotton planters in eastern and central Texas but also to Galveston's urban slaveholders.

German traveller Dr. Ferdinand Roemer described the Galveston Island of his first visit in 1838 as having only one or two houses (perhaps a slight understatement), but when he returned in 1845, there were "five thousand inhabitants, a number of wholesale mercantile houses, three churches and several hotels." By 1860 when the census recorded 6,127 whites, 1,178 slaves, and 2 free blacks, Galveston was claiming some semblance to refined,

View of Galveston looking south toward the Gulf in 1861. The building to the left with the cupola is the first City Market House (1847), which was also the City Hall. The steeples of St. Mary's Cathedral are in the center background.

even elegant living, including buildings that were architecturally distinguished and stylistically up-to-date, of which fewer than a dozen survive.

The period that defined the city architecturally, and for which Galveston is most noted today, is 1870 to 1900. "The sound of the hammer and saw" and "the ring of the trowel" were phrases oft-repeated in the local newspapers, as mechanics, builders, and architects kept pace with a rapidly expanding commercial and shipping center, and a population that, according to one observer, "changed as often as the sands upon our beach," a reference as much to the transient nature, as to the number, of inhabitants. The official census count for Galveston in 1870 was 13,818 residents; 22,248 in 1880; 29,084 in 1890; and 37,789 in 1900.

The buildings and streetscapes that evolved in late-19th-century Galveston—most especially the commercial and public buildings, and larger residential structures—made some deference to national

The Strand, looking east from 22nd Street, 1894. The First National Bank Building, now the Galveston Arts Center, is on the right. On the left is the Moore, Stratton & Company Building.

architectural styles and trends, but usually there was a Galveston or regional, i.e., Gulf Coast, twist—or both. Consequently, there are few structures that can be classified stylistically as picture-book examples. Rather, most buildings, especially the residential structures, are more expressive of climate and topography than style. People speak of a vernacular building: Galveston could be described as a vernacular city.

The major buildings were usually architect-designed. In the 1881-82 Galveston City Directory five architectural firms and architects were listed, a respectable number for a city with a population of 22,000. One of those names—Nicholas J. Clayton—appears again and again in the inventory of buildings in this guidebook. Clayton's buildings, most of them built from 1875 to 1902, were astounding both in number and design. Without question, Clayton shaped the city's architecture more than any other individual in its history.

Galveston developed with greater density than did many cities its size because land, and therefore housing, were always at a premium. Most people lived in detached houses, many residential block fronts having the prescribed seven structures—one per lot—if not more, which meant that neighbors

were *very* close together. In addition, many blocks had an alley population, individuals and families—frequently African-American—who lived in a back building separated from the front house and built either as a support building, with slave quarters before the Civil War or servants quarters afterwards, or as rental housing. Galveston was a city of layers, both architecturally and sociologically, for many properties, both front and back, large and small, and black and white, housed a

Residential streetscape in the East End, 16th Street looking east on Sealy (Avenue I), late 19th century.

combination of immediate and extended family members, boarders, employees, and servants.

Wherever Galvestonians lived or worked, there were constant reminders that the city's livelihood was defined by water. Throughout the 1890s, the flat terrain of the north-south cross-streets terminated with views of the Gulf of Mexico on the south and Galveston Bay, with its ship masts, on the north.

Aftermath of hurricane on September 8, 1900.

If water is the defining element in the development of Galveston, the defining event in the city's history (and psyche) is the hurricane of 8 September 1900. It remains the deadliest natural disaster in North America: over six thousand people killed, one-third of the buildings totally destroyed, and some damage to every structure in the city, not to mention the psychological suffering that must have been experienced to some degree by every storm survivor.

Galveston resolved to rebuild, and rebuild it did in an extraordinary way. First the Seawall was built—a 17-foot-high concrete wall that extended four miles on the Gulf side of the island (and later lengthened another six-and-a-half miles). Then the elevation of the island's populated area was literally raised. For seven years, residents in sections of the city took their turn being leveed off, their buildings raised on stilts or blocks, and their area pumped with damp and sandy fill dredged from the bay. Once the grade-raising project was completed, Galvestonians believed they were on higher, safer, and more valuable ground.

The building of the Seawall and the raising of the island both altered and influenced Galveston architecturally. The lower level of many structures was partially filled, especially where houses were set on raised basements or masonry piers. This explains the half-buried foundations that can be seen on some of the larger structures.

With the island buffered from the Gulf and flooding from storm surges controlled (but far from ever eliminated), Galvestonians had much more latitude in the use and development of their properties. Many owners, especially of smaller structures, could now raise their buildings to a height that created another level, even a separate living unit if they met the flooring requirements subsequently specified in city codes.

Understandably, there was little new construction early in the 20th century—the primary public exception being Rosenberg Library, built in 1901–2. But once the city returned to normal and survived, relatively intact, a hurricane in 1915, the impact of the Seawall and

Galveston during the grade-raising, circa 1907. Fill is being pumped into an area where the buildings and appurtenances (including outhouses and fences) have been raised on stilts. A dredge boat is pumping the fill as it moves through a canal connected to the bay.

the grade-raising project on new development became apparent, most especially in boosting tourist and beach facilities along the Seawall itself and in the residential subdivisions established in the southwest section of the city.

A packed Seawall and beach at Tremont (23rd Street), circa 1920. The large building on the left is the Galvez Hotel; Murdoch's Bath House is on the right. In center foreground are the granite piers commemorating the Seawall and the grade-raising project.

Although Galveston made a miraculous recovery from the storm, other forces were altering the city's economic future even before 1900. Since the mid-19th century, Houston and Galveston had competed for port commerce, but Houston's location proved to have the advantage, as the transportation of goods relied more heavily on a rail-harbor combination. The storm gave Houston the opportunity to secure its trade supremacy: While Galveston focused on its massive rebuilding efforts, Houston built the 50-mile-long Houston Ship Channel.

Ironically, Galveston's economic woes are what saved its architectural riches. Had the Galveston wharves been expanded, much of the east end of the island would eventually have been swallowed by port-related industries and development. There is, after all, little space for expansion on such a narrow strip of land.

The Galveston scene, including its architecture, was no longer dominated, as in the past, by port activities and wholesale trade. Throughout the 1920s, major new buildings, including the larger residences, reflected a mix of interests: cotton, banking, insurance, retail, tourism, and gambling. Galveston still supported an architectural profession but not to the degree that it had in the late 19th century. The more lucrative commissions usually went to outside architects, including a growing number of out-of-state practitioners.

Following World War II, downtown Galveston resumed its place as a retail center, another economic base that soon began to dwindle. With their new automobiles, shoppers shifted their loyalties to new and/or relocated stores in outlying areas, and eventually to the mainland.

By the 1950s, Galveston's defining image was that of a city where gambling was illegal but allowed. In 1957, the Texas Attorney General closed down the gambling operations, and Galveston became a city in limbo, fitting even more Edna Ferber's description that it was "a remnant of haunted beauty—gray, shrouded, crumbling," a description written in 1939.

It is cities like Galveston that were waiting for the invention of the historic preservation movement—and helped create it. Any architecture guidebook of this Gulf Coast city must also acknowledge the parallel tale of the many individual and organizational efforts that make it possible to celebrate the city that we see today.

Houston architect Howard Barnstone is listed as architect for only two buildings in the guidebook. His name, however, is frequently mentioned in the text because he had as profound an impact on Galveston's architecture as did N. J. Clayton. It was Barnstone who conceived the book *The Galveston That Was,* a collection of photographs by famed photographers Ezra Stoller and Henri Cartier-Bresson, that has become an icon in the city's preservation movement. The book was an eloquent, moody, and lyrical homage to the city's rich but decaying—and disappearing—architectural heritage, which, at the time of its publication in 1966, was appreciated by a very small but dedicated band of citizens.

In the 30 years since publication of *The Galveston That Was,* Galveston has, quite literally, experienced a transformation. It is a change that can be measured by passage of a local preservation ordinance; designation of four locally protected historic districts, two of which are also National Historic Landmark Districts; restoration of hundreds of buildings, both public and private, large and small; the activation of numerous neighborhood associations; and national, even international, recognition of its preservation program.

Ezra Stoller photograph published in The Galveston That Was, *1966. In the foreground is the Trueheart Building, designed by N. J. Clayton. (The Museum of Fine Arts, Houston)*

To use a water analogy, not all, of course, has been smooth sailing—a situation not unique to preservation in Galveston. For those with the longer memories, it may be hard to forget some of the bitter and not always successful struggles to save the city's architectural riches. And it is obvious, as you walk and drive about the city, that there is still much to be done. Galveston, like all cities with a sizeable older building stock, has more buildings that need renovation than people to renovate them, which means that both the public and the private sectors are, as in other cities, always searching for new and creative ways to enlarge its preservation circle. The survival of the city depends upon it—along with a little luck each hurricane season.

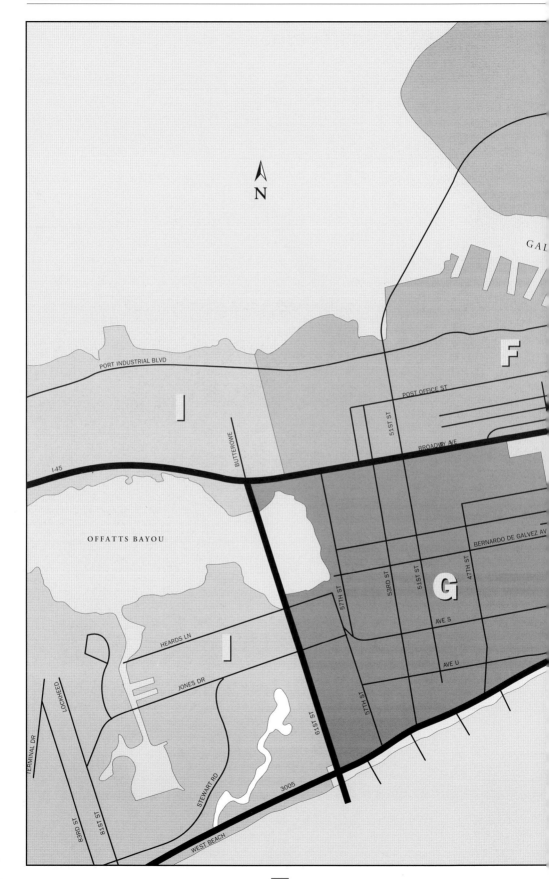

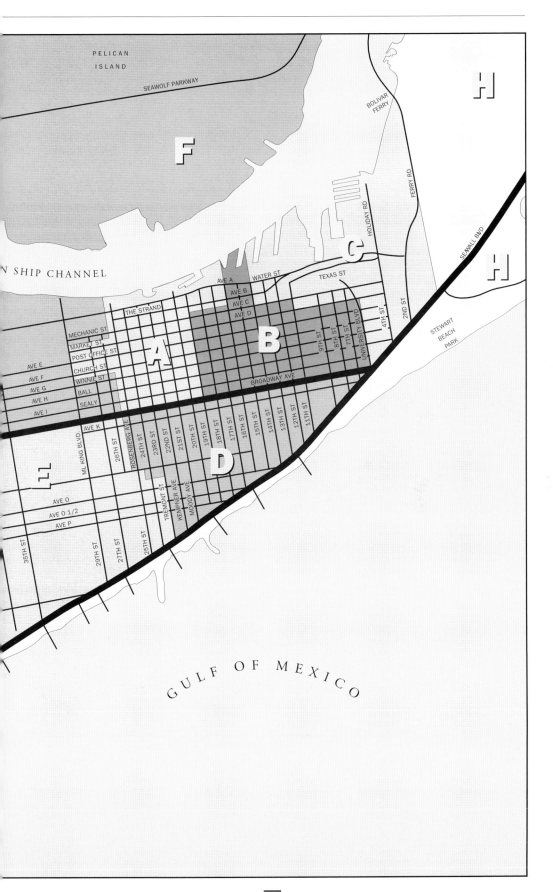

T he heart of Galveston has always been Downtown and the Central Park area. Here is found the largest concentration of singularly important buildings in the city, as well as one of the most significant assemblages of late-19th-century commercial buildings in the country.    The buildings in the area reflect the city's patterns of development and shifts in economic fortunes. From the beginning, port-related interests dominated the streets on the bay side of the island, specifically Water, Strand, and

Hendley Buildings, corner 20th and Strand. Photograph circa 1875.

Mechanic between 20th and 24th Streets. With the division between water and land considerably more scraggly in the mid-19th century than what you see today, and Water Street, or Avenue A, even partially submerged, it was Strand Street, or Avenue B, that became what Galveston historian Virginia Eisenhour called "the Wall Street of the Southwest." It was here that financial good fortune was equated with architectural display. As the city developed, businesses along Market and Postoffice Streets catered to the local trade. By the late 19th century, substantial brick structures had replaced almost all the early wooden buildings along these streets, an architectural refinement brought about by the city's adoption of stricter building codes in response to the devastating fires that had periodically swept through downtown. The more sophisticated look had an added benefit: It promoted Galveston's role as a regional retail center. Some of the most architecturally imposing structures in the area have always been identified with governmental offices, but Galveston County is the only governmental entity still functioning at its original location. Although the Galveston County Courthouse has been replaced three times, each time with an ever-larger building, the courthouse continues to face Central Park, the only block near downtown to be designated a public space in the original city plan. The blocks south of Church Street were dominated by residential and institutional, specifically religious, buildings. Along the southern boundary, *now* the most scraggly edge of the area, there are occasional pockets and lone survivors of residential buildings, including three Broadway "palaces"—Ashton Villa, the Open Gates, and the Moody Mansion and Museum. Downtown and the Central

Park area has its share of vacant lots, the most obvious legacy of changing economic times. With the opening of auto-oriented shopping centers and the removal of businesses to Broadway and outlying areas, Galveston's downtown merchants struggled to keep up-to-date by "modernizing" building façades and providing surface parking. The closing

The Galveston port looking east from Pier 22, late 19th century.

of gambling activities in 1957 resulted in the eventual demolition of many buildings, especially west of Tremont Street: No longer was it possible for property owners to collect high rents, even in derelict buildings, for illegal uses. ⋂ ⋂ ⋂ Although commercial enterprises on the Strand also suffered economic decline, the streetscape and buildings remained essentially intact. Strand businesses never relied on a predominantly retail market, which meant that property owners felt little pressure to update their buildings and therefore left them in a relatively untouched state. ⋂ ⋂ ⋂ The Strand became the focus of the city's revitalization efforts in the early 1970s. Under the tutelage of the Galveston Historical Foundation, the last quarter of the 20th century has witnessed a remarkable change in what became the Strand Historic District, now a National Historic Landmark District. It is a change that reflects not only a fiercely intense and successful preservation program but also the explosive growth of the travel industry in this country. ⋂ ⋂ ⋂ In

Looking south on Tremont (23rd) from Market (Avenue D) as the Akron passes overhead, circa 1932.

recent years, redevelopment activity has spilled over into other sections of Downtown and the Central Park area, most particularly Postoffice Street, where "the sound of the hammer and saw" has been especially audible. ⋂ ⋂ ⋂ Interesting—keeping up-to-date has taken on a very 19th-century look.

1. 123 Rosenberg Avenue
2. Rosenberg Avenue and Strand
3. 2410–2412 Strand
4. 2326–2328 Strand
5. 2317–2319 and 2321–2323 Strand
6. 2310–2314 Strand
7. 2309–2311 and 2313–2315 Strand
8. 2302 Strand
9. Tremont and Strand
10. 2301–2307 Strand
11. 2222–2228 Strand
12. 2211–2223 Strand
13. 2202–2206 Strand
14. 2118–2128 Strand
15. 2127 Strand
16. 2117–2119 and 2121 Strand
17. 2114–2116 Strand
18. 2109, 2111, and 2115 Strand
19. 2101–2107 Strand
20. 2025 Strand
21. 2021–2023 Strand
22. 2001–2011 Strand
23. 2002–2016 Strand
24. 1601 Strand
25. 1700 Strand
26. 101 21st Street
27. 108 22nd Street
28. Pier 21: Harbor House
29. Pier 21: Texas Seaport Museum
30. Pier 22
31. 2223–2227 Harborside Drive
32. 2307–2309 Harborside Drive
33. Pier 23–26
34. 206 Rosenberg Avenue

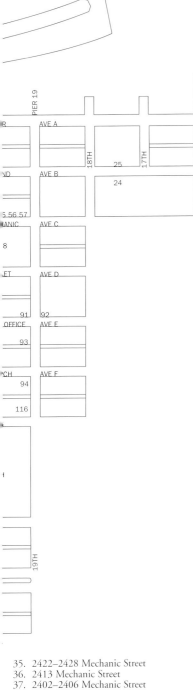

35. 2422–2428 Mechanic Street
36. 2413 Mechanic Street
37. 2402–2406 Mechanic Street
38. 2300 Mechanic Street
39. 24th Street and Mechanic Street
40. 2325–2327 Mechanic Street
41. 2317 Mechanic Street
42. 2309–2315 Mechanic Street
43. 219–223 Tremont Street
44. 213–217 Tremont Street
45. 2222–2228 Mechanic Street
46. 2220 Mechanic Street
47. 220 22nd Street
48. 212 22nd Street
49. 306 22nd Street
50. 2108 Mechanic Street
51. 2102 Mechanic Street

52. 305 21st Street
53. 308 21st Street
54. 221 20th Street
55. 1922 and 1918 Mechanic Street
56. 1914–1916 Mechanic Street
57. 1902 Mechanic Street
58. 1902–1928 Market Street
59. 1921 Market Street and 402–410 20th Street
60. 2121 Market Street
61. 2201 Market Street
62. 2219 Market Street
63. 2221 Market Street
64. 2200 Market Street
65. 401–403 Tremont Street
66. 2326–2328, 2322–2324, 2318–2320, and 2314–2316 Market Street
67. 2401 Market Street
68. 2415 and 2419 Market Street
69. 2425–2427 Market Street
70. 2501–2503, 2509–2511, and 2513–2515 Market Street
71. 2523 Market Street
72. 2528, 2526, and 2522–2524 Market Street
73. 2626–2628 Market Street
74. 2828 Market Street
75. 2528 Postoffice Street
76. 2302 Postoffice Street
77. 512 Tremont Street
78. 2221–2227 Postoffice Street
79. 2218 Postoffice Street
80. 2213–2215 Postoffice Street
81. 2214–2216 Postoffice Street
82. 2208 Postoffice Street
83. 2202–2204 Postoffice Street
84. 2205 Postoffice Street
85. 2128 Postoffice Street
86. 2118–2120 Postoffice Street
87. 2109 Postoffice Street
88. 2102–2104 Postoffice Street
89. 2012–2020 Postoffice Street
90. 1927 Postoffice Street
91. 1902 Postoffice Street
92. 424 19th Street
93. 509 19th Street
94. 1903 Church Street
95. 2010 and 2006 Church Street
96. 2011 Church Street
97. 2105 Church Street
98. 2116 Church Street
99. 2128 Church Street
100. 2202–2206 Church Street
101. 2401 Church Street
102. 2406 Church Street
103. 513–525 Rosenberg Avenue
104. 601 Rosenberg Avenue
105. 2401 Winnie Avenue
106. 2310 Ball Avenue
107. 823 Tremont Street
108. 902–912 Tremont Street
109. 906 22nd Street
110. 816 22nd Street
111. 2117 Ball Avenue
112. 721 22nd Street
113. 701 22nd Street
114. 621 21st Street
115. 722 21st Street
116. 615 19th Street
117. 1923 Sealy Avenue
118. 2017, 2019, 2021, and 2023 Sealy Avenue
119. 2102 Sealy Avenue
120. 2020 Broadway
121. 2013 Broadway
122. 2217 Broadway
123. 2328 Broadway
124. 2424 Broadway
125. Broadway and Rosenberg Avenue
126. 823 Rosenberg Avenue
127. 2618 Broadway
128. 2628 Broadway

123 Rosenberg Avenue　　　　　　　　　　A-1
Santa Fe Building (now Shearn Moody Plaza)
1913, Dalbert Simpson
1932, E. A. Harrison

Terminating the vista at the head of the Strand is the imposing 11-story Santa Fe Building, Galveston's ex-railroad passenger station. Clad in white terra cotta, it is noticeably off the center line of the Strand axis, a testimony to its episodic construction.

The Gulf, Colorado & Santa Fe Railway (a railroad corporation organized in Galveston in 1873 and sold to the Atcheson, Topeka & Santa Fe Railway in 1886) joined with the International & Great Northern Railway in the 1890s in an ambitious program to modernize and rationalize Galveston's railroad network. One important goal was to separate passenger traffic from freight traffic, and replace the 1876 passenger station with a new union station whose location would not conflict with traffic on the waterfront. In 1897 a ponderous, castellated, Victorian Romanesque-style terminal and office building was constructed at Strand and 25th Street, built across the right-of-way of the Strand, along which, farther west, the new passenger-line tracks were routed. The growth of the Santa Fe Railway's regional branch office in Galveston in the early 20th century occasioned construction of an eight-story annex to the south side of the 1897 terminal. This annex is the south wing of the present building. Designed by the Santa Fe's Topeka-based corporate architect Dalbert Simpson, its rational distribution of large-scale windows and gleaming white terra cotta could not have been more at variance with the architecture of the Victorian terminal.

Nearly two decades later, the Santa Fe Railway demolished the 1897 terminal. E. A. Harrison, Santa Fe's Chicago-based corporate architect, designed the center bay, with its distinctive tiered top, and the north wing of the present building, updating the Modern French cartouche-style of the 1913 wing (and its 1932 twin) with the Art Deco modernistic massing and detail of the central bay.

By the time the Santa Fe closed its Galveston office in 1965 and discontinued passenger service in 1967, the building was almost vacant. In 1976, the building was purchased by the Moody Foundation. It was rehabilitated by Ford, Powell & Carson and reopened as Shearn Moody Plaza in 1981. The **Center for Transportation and Commerce (the Railroad Museum)** occupies the ex-concourse and

passenger loading areas inside and behind the building. Ford, Powell & Carson worked with Barry Howard & Associates of New York on the museum's exhibition design, which includes a series of life-sized genre figures modeled by the New York sculptors Elliott and Ivan Schwartz.

As an urban anchor, the Santa Fe Building is of immeasurable importance, although it shares neither the architectural attributes nor scale of the Strand National Historic Landmark District's Victorian buildings. It gives the district spatial closure and monumentalizes the crucial economic role of railroad transportation in linking the rich cotton-producing country of central Texas to the port of Galveston in the 19th century.

Rosenberg Avenue and Strand　　　　　　　A-2
Mardi Gras Arch
1990, Aldo Rossi with Morris Adjmi and Cisneros Architects

Commissioned by Cynthia and George Mitchell, this "arch" was one of the first architectural projects by Aldo Rossi, Italy's most internationally celebrated architect, to be built in the United States. Rossi produced two pairs of conical turrets whose shapes evoke maritime lighthouses and recall Galveston's historic role in the 19th and early 20th centuries as the gateway through which many foreign immigrants entered Texas. The combination of big scale and whimsical simplicity gives the lighthouses both an urban presence and a nostalgic allure. Rossi was touched by this allure when he first visited Galveston in the late 1970s, and he made his Mardi Gras Arch a memento of the sentiments the city aroused in him. The Rossi lighthouses show signs of advancing age, accurately depicting the long-term effects of Galveston's extreme combination of sunlight, moisture, and salt air on local architecture.

In 1985 Cynthia and George Mitchell revived Mardi Gras as an annual civic carnival at the recommendation of Susan Silverman Brink. In the late 19th century, Mardi Gras had been celebrated in Galveston in grand style, but by the late 1970s it had become the exclusive province of O'Connell High School. To attract widespread attention to the Mardi Gras revival, temporary ceremonial arches were solicited from some of the most celebrated postmodern architects of the 1980s by Mr. and Mrs. Mitchell's publicist, Dancie Perugini Ware. Stanley Tigerman and Helmut Jahn of Chicago, Michael Graves of Princeton, Charles Moore of Los Angeles, César Pelli of New Haven, and Texans Boone Powell of San Antonio and Eugene Aubry of Houston joined to produce these bits of festive ephemera. Rossi's arch was constructed four years after the first episode of ceremonial arch building.

2410-2412 Strand   **A–3**

James Fadden Building

1898, N. J. Clayton & Company

Although modest in comparison to some of Clayton's other downtown buildings, the Fadden Building illustrates the clarity of proportion that characterized his work and the skill with which he deployed decoration to give a sense of textural richness and depth to his architecture. It housed James Fadden's wholesale wine, liquor, and cigar business, which Rosa Fadden managed after her husband's death, about the time the building was completed. Across the street, at 2411 Strand, is what remains of the **Wallis, Landes & Company Building** by Clayton & Lynch of 1877. Once a three-story building, it now consists only of a Victorian Gothic sidewalk-level arcade. The sidewalk in front does retain its Galvestonian red-and-black tile paving.

2326-2328 Strand   **A–4**

Ball, Hutchings & Company–John Sealy Office Buildings

1896, N. J. Clayton & Company

Although best known for his High Victorian buildings, N. J. Clayton was one of the first Texas architects whose work reflected the return to classical order that occurred in American architecture in the 1890s. Here, in the pair of buildings familiarly known as the Hutchings-Sealy Building, he gave full sway to this classical revival. Yet like other architects of his generation who attempted this transition,

Clayton could never quite part with the aggressive rhythms of Victorian architecture. As a result, his principal essay in monumental classicism—with its layered base of gray and pink granite and red sandstone, its piano nobile of buff brick, and its creamy terra-cotta decoration—is tawny in color rather than pristinely white. It is bold in scale and asymmetrical in organization, because it is two separate buildings rather than one.

In 1856, the dry goods wholesale and cotton commission house of Ball, Hutchings & Co., organized by George Ball, John H. Hutchings, and John Sealy, built a three-story building on the 31-foot-wide lot at 24th and Strand to house its operations. The firm expanded into banking in 1860 and in 1867 made John Sealy's younger brother, George Sealy, its partner in charge of banking. John Sealy built a building adjacent to the Ball, Hutchings & Co. Building in 1870, which extended the façade of the earlier building along the Strand. These two buildings were demolished in 1895 by J. H. Hutchings and George Sealy, the surviving partners, for replacement with Clayton's new construction. The buildings' terra-cotta-encased steel frame was one of the earliest examples of steel-framed construction in Texas, and was engineered to permit the addition of two extra floors. The banking hall at 2328 Strand retains some of its original finishes. The most impressive interior space is in the Sealy portion of the building, a two-story-high skylit court with a glass floor light on the second floor of the building.

In 1897, Ball, Hutchings & Co. was reorganized as Hutchings, Sealy & Co. It remained a private bank until 1930 when it was chartered as the Hutchings-Sealy National Bank. In 1935 the bank left this building for a new, and smaller, structure that it built on Market Street. After a number of uses, including a moving and storage warehouse, the Hutchings-Sealy Building was bought by Cynthia and George Mitchell in 1985. Ford, Powell & Carson were architects for its rehabilitation (1987). Dallas architect Michael Malone designed the **Discovery Channel Store** (1994).

2317-2319 Strand   **A–5**

Merchants Mutual Insurance Company Building

1870, P. N. Comegys

2321-2323 Strand

Bolton Estate Building

1877, Clayton & Lynch

When Clayton's Bolton Building was restored in 1976 for La

King's Confectionery, a new sidewalk canopy was built. The sidewalk canopy was a standard fixture of Texas downtowns during the 19th and well into the 20th centuries, a welcome feature in a climate of unpredictable extremes.

During the Civil War era, American insurance companies commenced using architecture to distinguish themselves from the rank and file of downtown commercial loft buildings. What made the Strand's first example of this phenomenon singular was Comegys's application of a "French roof" (the steeply sloped mansard cap sporting a pedimented central dormer window flanked by a pair of round "bull's-eye" windows) to what would otherwise appear to be a loft building. Comegys completed the Merchants Mutual building in 1869 in what the *Galveston Daily News* referred to as "insurance square." The building was destroyed by fire, along with all others on this side of Strand, just months later. The Merchants Mutual Insurance Company was rebuilt as a *"fac simile"* of its predecessor, according to the *News,* under the direction of architect and supervisor B. O. Hamilton. In 1978 the building was rehabilitated for Lee Trentham and Craig Lazzari. This entailed the reconstruction of the long-vanished cornice.

2310-2314 Strand   **A–6**
Greenleve, Block & Company Building
1882, N. J. Clayton

The Greenleve-Block building lost its top floor and cornice, one of the most overwrought that Clayton ever designed, to demolition in 1953. Even so, it remains a powerful presence at sidewalk level thanks to Clayton's skill at emphasizing the sculptural and spatial potential of cast-iron construction. In contrast to more conservative iron fronts on the Strand, with their thick paneled piers reproducing the appearance of masonry, Clayton pulled his iron supports apart. Thin cylindrical columns stand well forward of the door frames, to which they are linked by thin webs pierced by oval and quatrefoil cutouts. The transparency of the extremely tall glass doors reinforces a feeling of delicacy. Yet at the same time, the monumental scale of the doors, and the way that the impost blocks atop the columns terminate in triangular wedges emphasize the compressive thrust of the structural work that is being performed here. Clayton's ability to make urban theater out of commercial construction is strongly evident at the Greenleve-Block Building. It affords an insight into the characteristics that make his architecture so compelling.

2309-2311 Strand   **A–7**
Rosenberg Building
1870, P. N. Comegys

2313-2315 Strand
Magale Building
1870, B. O. Hamilton

Although contemporary Galveston newspaper reports identified Comegys (one of a number of architect-builders who had short-lived practices in Galveston just before the Panic of 1873, then disappeared) and Hamilton (who more often seems to have worked as a construction supervisor) as the architects of these adjoining buildings, they are virtually identical. Both are built of dark red brick laid with the narrow mortar joints typical of late-19th-century construction. Both feature galvanized cast-iron storefronts, window sills, and arcuated lintels above the windows. Both have lost their galvanized cast-iron cornices. And both have been handsomely rehabilitated. The Magale Building is notable for its Strand-front sidewalk, surfaced with large slabs of weathered stone. Taft Architects not only restored the exterior of the Rosenberg Building for Robert L. K. Lynch in 1977 but turned the upper floors into ingeniously designed apartments that took advantage of the building's generous ceiling heights to introduce double-level lofts within apartments. It is difficult to imagine today that when Henri Cartier-Bresson photographed this block in 1962 for *The Galveston That Was,* weeds were growing in profusion through the brick sidewalk in front of the Rosenberg Building.

2302 Strand   **A–8**
Saengerfest Park
1994, Eubanks/Bohnn Associates

As was typical of 19th-century American commercial streets,

the Strand was all business. Its real estate was too valuable to be set aside as public open space. When, in the 20th century, space opened up, it was usually in the form of asphalt-topped parking lots replacing burned-down (or torn-down) Victorian buildings. Therefore, Cynthia and George Mitchell's transformation of one such parking lot into an open plaza, with provision for seating, casual meandering, and occasional festivities, is a spatial novelty. It bespeaks the evolution of this commercial street in response to the business of leisure at the turn of the 21st century. The Saengerfest designation refers to an annual convention of German men's choral societies that rotated among various Texas cities during the last quarter of the 19th century. It was for one such meeting in Galveston, held in 1881, that the temporary ceremonial arches which inspired the Mardi Gras arches were erected.

Accessible from Saengerfest Plaza is the ex-**Armour & Company Building** at 2201 Water (1916, R. C. Clark), rehabilitated and expanded by Eubanks/Bohnn Associates as the Strand Brewery for Cynthia and George Mitchell in 1995. Its second- and third-floor decks afford spectacular views of the Galveston Ship Channel and waterfront.

Tremont and Strand   A–9
Mardi Gras Arch
1986, Michael Graves
Michael Graves's Mardi Gras Arch—built by the Houston developer J. R. McConnell—was one of the most imposing and substantial of the seven built in 1986. Its striped base and openwork wood pediment look to some of the Italian sources favored a hundred years earlier by N. J. Clayton. The Lone Star medallion, another favorite Clayton icon, is featured prominently. As a close look at its surfaces reveals, the arch was clearly not intended to be permanent.

2301-2307 Strand   A–10
T. J. League Building
1872
One of the worst fires in downtown Galveston occurred on 2 December 1869. A north wind propelled flames southward, burning out the 2300 block of Strand and blocks south as far as 24th and Church Streets. The League Building was constructed on the site of Moro Castle, Galveston's most famous saloon, where the fire had begun. The League Building is representative of Strand commercial houses of the late 1860s and early 1870s, with its street walls of segmentally arched windows evenly spaced above

sidewalk-level storefronts of galvanized cast iron and glass. The *Galveston Daily News* in March 1872 identified the Southern Ornamental Iron Works of New Orleans as fabricators of the League Building's cast-iron storefront, window lintels, and a no-longer-extant cornice.

The League Building was in shabby condition in 1976 when it became the first Strand property to be acquired by Cynthia and George Mitchell from the Galveston Historical Foundation, which had bought the building to ensure its preservation. Mr. and Mrs. Mitchell worked with Ford, Powell & Carson's Boone Powell to reconfigure the League Building's interior loft spaces for a restaurant and shops. Raising the ground floor several feet above sidewalk level to protect the interiors from minor street flooding and introducing sky light from a newly inserted top-lit internal court were features repeated in subsequent Mitchell-Powell rehabilitations.

2222-2228 Strand   A–11
Dargan & Tobyn and Frosh Buildings
1870
These three-story buildings, although built for different owners, were originally part of a group of five buildings, the three westernmost of which were destroyed in 1882 in one of the many fires that plagued downtown Galveston in the 19th century. Architecturally, the Dargan & Tobyn and Frosh Buildings mark the interim architectural stage that occurred during Galveston's Reconstruction-era building boom. This stage separated the flat, planar building fronts of the 1850s from the much more assertive façades of the late 1870s. The segmentally arched door and window openings and heavy decorative brick cornices of the Dargan & Tobyn and Frosh Buildings were characteristic of this transitional period in the architectural evolution of the Strand.

Gotsdiner Architects of Houston rehabilitated the exteriors of these buildings for Mr. and Mrs. George Mitchell (1992).

2211-2223 Strand   **A–12**

Blum Hardware Company Building (now Old Galveston
Square)

1858, 1871, 1911

Like the Dargan & Tobyn and Frosh Buildings across the
street, this row is a composite. Now organized as one
building, it consists of four separate structures. The six
window bays closest to Tremont Street belonged to the
Berlocher Building. The next four window bays originally
faced the coffee importer Henry Runge's building. The next
eight windows were the T. W. House Building. All three of
these buildings were built in 1871 to replace predecessors
destroyed by fire in February 1870.

The four windows closest to the 22nd Street corner—
which are the most widely spaced—belong to the E. S.
Wood Building. Built in 1858 by the hardware merchant E.
S. Wood, it survived the fire of 1870. The Wood Building
was originally faced with a full iron front, one of seven
fabricated by Sanson & Farrand of Philadelphia and
installed on different downtown Galveston buildings
between 1856 and 1860.

During the early 20th century, the Blum Hardware
Company combined these structures into a single building,
remodeling the façade to advertise architectural unity. In
1986 the row was rehabilitated as a shopping arcade by
Melton Henry Architects of Houston for the Houston real
estate developer J. R. McConnell and re-christened Old
Galveston Square. McConnell installed the steel and
concrete **cornet** fabricated by Houston artist David Adickes
outside the postmodern version of a Victorian conservatory,
which Melton Henry designed on the corner of Tremont
and Strand. McConnell also retained Joe Pehoski of Salado,
Texas, to fabricate the decorative ironwork in the newly
created interior court.

Following acquisition of the complex by Mr. and Mrs.
George Mitchell in 1987, Eubanks/Bohnn Associates of
Houston rehabilitated Old Galveston Square and designed a
number of the shop interiors. They are also responsible for
designing the **Mardi Gras Museum,** located on the third
floor of Old Galveston Square.

2202-2206 Strand   **A–13**

W. L. Moody Building (now Strand Surplus Center)

1883, N. J. Clayton

The Storm of 1900 knocked the cornice and top floor off
the building that Colonel William L. Moody built to
contain his cotton commission and banking operations.
Even so, it retains the finely finished dark red brick surfaces
and subtle detailing with which Clayton organized its
Strand and 22nd Street elevations. As on his other Strand
commercial buildings, Clayton treated the street walls of the
Moody Building as shallow layered planes. Triple windows
are framed with brick surrounds and bands of sparkling
yellow tile. Along 22nd Street, windows are stacked in
vertical bays marked off by ribbed and incised brick piers.
Inset panels of tile and yellow brick enhance the illusion
that the street walls are composed of deeply receding layers.
Upholding these bravura displays of ornamental brickwork
are cast-iron storefronts, which have lost their double-leaf
doors and column capitals.

Moody, a lawyer and wholesale merchant, moved to
Galveston from central Texas in 1866 and embarked on an
extremely successful career as a cotton factor and banker. He
built this building to replace a four-story structure that
burned in 1882. Moody was joined in business in 1881 by
his eldest son, W. L. Moody, Jr., who would surpass his
father to become Galveston's richest entrepreneur in the
early 20th century. This building remained the headquarters
for the Moody businesses until construction of the 11-story
American National Insurance Company Building on
Market Street in 1913. N. J. Clayton repaired the Moody
Building following the 1900 storm, although the fourth
story was never rebuilt.

Stationed on the sidewalk in front of the Moody
Building is a shaped aluminum **Building Information Sign**
(Taft Architects, 1978), displaying a historic photograph of
the Moody Building on one side and an information text
panel on the other. This was the prototype for similar signs
installed by the Galveston Historical Foundation
throughout the Strand Historic District in accordance with
the Venturi & Rauch Strand Action Plan of 1975.

2118-2128 Strand   **A–14**

Moore, Stratton & Company Building

1882

One of the most imposing commercial buildings along Strand, the Moore, Stratton & Company Building is an essay in surface richness, achieved economically with stuccoed brick. Generously scaled, continuous ground-floor arcades on both the Strand and 22nd Street fronts are complemented by tall, segmentally arched second-floor windows encased between paneled piers and scored spandrels that simulate the scale and density of dressed stone. The stucco has weathered to a mottled Galveston gray (wisely left in this condition when the building was rehabilitated for Daniel K. Thorne by architects Louis L. Oliver & Tibor Beerman in 1976), which becomes animated in sunlight. The upper register of the Moore, Stratton & Company Building has lost an unusual feature, an architecturally integrated canopy that shaded second-floor windows, as well as a concluding layer of bracketed cornice and arched frontispieces that exuberantly topped off the parapet. Unfortunately, the identity of the architect of the Moore, Stratton & Company Building has yet to come to light.

2127 Strand   **A–15**

First National Bank Building (now the Galveston Arts Center)

1878

At the midpoint of the 19th century, the American banking house emerged as a specialized urban building type, distinguished from commercial loft buildings by its aspirations to monumentality, even though it was often smaller in size than surrounding commercial buildings. The First National Bank Building (home to Texas's oldest chartered bank, an ancestor of the present NationsBank Galveston) exemplifies these attributes. It is a freestanding building, with a screen of cast-iron Corinthian columns affixed to the Strand front, as though to underscore the point that this is not just another in the row of commercial storefronts. The red-and-brown tile paving outside the building constituted the prestige sidewalk of late-19th-century Galveston: this is a rare survivor downtown. Although newspaper accounts of the period reported on the First National Bank Building's construction, no architect was identified. Stylistic evidence suggests N. Tobey, Jr., as the most likely candidate. Tobey was a Galveston Victorian

architect whose work is not as well documented as N. J. Clayton's. Although his few known buildings lack the singularity of Clayton's work, they are dignified contributions to the commercial district's streetscape.

The angled rear door added to the 22nd Street side of the building documents the Strand's decline in prominence. This new portal was oriented toward Market Street, which supplanted the Strand as the city's banking corridor in the 1920s. After the First National Bank merged with the Hutchings-Sealy National Bank in 1958, it vacated this building. In 1969 the building was acquired by the Junior League of Galveston County and converted into the Galveston County Cultural Arts Council's Galveston Arts Center, the city's major public art gallery, which features regular exhibitions of painting, sculpture, works on paper, and photography.

The south side of the entire 2100 block of Strand was reconstructed following a devastating fire on 8 June 1877. Therefore its buildings exemplify the changes introduced to the Strand by American High Victorian architecture in the late 1870s.

2117-2119 Strand and 2121 Strand   **A–16**

Marx & Kempner Building and Mrs. Clara Lang Building

1878, John Moser

Mural, 1976, Richard Haas, artist

These two buildings lost their top floors during the Storm of 1900 and what remained of Moser's original architectural countenances to subsequent 20th-century effacement. In

1976 the Galveston Historical Foundation commissioned the New York painter Richard Haas to "restore" their façades with murals that evoke American High Victorian architecture but do not pretend to literal replication. Haas first visited Galveston in 1972 in order to prepare a set of drawings based on the city's Victorian buildings. He had only recently launched himself as an architectural illusionist when called upon to paint these full-scale façades, which had to incorporate existing door and window openings.

Taft Architects carried the spirit of Haas's façades into the interiors of these buildings, when they were rehabilitated for shops and compact studio apartments for Robert L. K. Lynch in 1982. The wit and sophistication that Haas and Taft Architects brought to the problem posed by these genuinely old but architecturally degraded buildings exemplify the inventiveness that won Galveston preservationists and the Strand Historic District national recognition in the early 1980s.

2114-2116 Strand   **A–17**
Mallory Building
1879
The Mallory Building was one of the first Strand buildings to undergo rehabilitation as Bill H. Fullen's Old Strand Emporium. The sign suspended above the sidewalk advertising the Old Strand Emporium was designed in 1975 by the Philadelphia architects Venturi & Rauch as a prototype for appropriately scaled new advertising graphics in the Strand Historic District. The second-story loft space above the Emporium served as studios and apartments for the painters Michael Tracy and Joe Glasco during the 1970s. Fullen was also responsible for installing the Waterwall terrace at 2110-2112 Strand.

2109 Strand   **A–18**
Clara Lang Building
1878, John Moser

2111 Strand
J. S. Brown & Company Building
1878, Clayton & Lynch

2115 Strand
Oppermann Building
1878, John Moser
The Fire of 1877 gave rise to these midblock commercial buildings. The Storm of 1900 laid them low. And the historic

preservation movement of the 1970s and 1980s brought them back to life. These three façades, their relatively narrow widths notwithstanding, were vigorously built-out with shallow layers of brick and cast iron, imbuing each building with a distinct presence in the parade of building fronts along the Strand. The Oppermann Building at 2115, designed by the German-born and -trained architect John Moser for the real estate investor Gustav Oppermann, was only two stories high to begin with. It, however, has lost an elaborately detailed cornice, which originally projected forward of the blank panel above the second-story windows. Like Clayton & Lynch's J. S. Brown & Company Building at 2111 (originally three stories tall), the Lang Building lost its upper floors to the Storm of 1900. What remained of both were cast-iron storefronts at ground level, now painted to accentuate their stylized High Victorian detail. Above the storefronts, paneled brick walls frame pairs of windows decorated with more High Victorian detail. The building at 2109 was one of two narrow four-story commercial houses designed by Moser as investment properties for Mrs. Clara Lang.

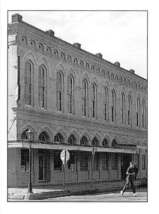

2101-2107 Strand   **A–19**
George Schneider & Company Building
1878, Clayton & Lynch
The Schneider Building, constructed as an investment by Ball, Hutchings & Company following the Fire of 1877, was not only larger than pre–Civil War business houses, but was also more intensively decorated. N. J. Clayton grouped ground-floor doors and tall pairs of second-story windows beneath pointed arch openings, then outlined these with High Victorian Gothic molding. Above these windows,

Clayton produced a frieze and cornice composed of advancing and recessed brick panels. The building's stuccoed brick walls highlight the play of light and shadow. Through such means, Clayton invested the wall surfaces of his commercial buildings with a sense of depth, plasticity, and big scale that made earlier Galveston buildings of the 1850s look taut, even fragile, by comparison. It is interesting to observe that "architecture" was applied only to the Strand front of the Schneider Building. The side flank along 21st Street is bare of architectural detail.

exposed the heavy timber structural frame inside the building and installed a polished concrete floor, wood stair, and wood-framed glass partitions to give the interior a distinctive Austin look.

2025 Strand   A–20
Nichols Building
1860
This building, built by the commission merchant Ebenezer B. Nichols, is one of the oldest commercial houses on the Strand. The destruction of original surfaces, and alterations to the ground floor, disguise the venerability of the Nichols Building. The six-pane-over-six-pane sash windows and the horizontal belt course at the top of the Strand front were elements common to the brick commercial buildings that began to replace Galveston's original wood commercial houses after Texas was admitted to the United States in 1845–46. The rear wall of the Nichols Building (visible across the parking lot at 21st and Mechanic) displays the dark red brick characteristic of buildings of this era. The change in brick color from red (midway up the wall) to yellow suggests the reconstruction of the building's upper portion. Next door at 2027 Strand, the **Jockusch Building** (1866) has also been effaced. Painting the street fronts of both buildings in subdued colors emphasizes their measured proportions, compensating for the loss of architectural detail.

2021-2023 Strand   A–21
J. D. Rogers Building
1894
It is the file of thick piers and semicircular arches along its sidewalk arcade that gives the Rogers Building its urban presence. The extent to which the Strand's brick-bearing-wall commercial houses could be opened up to the street is especially evident in the remodeling of the building's interior as an arcade of shops by the Austin architects Black, Atkinson & Vernooy in 1983. Sinclair Black and his partner Simon Atkinson, who bought the building in 1982,

2001-2011 Strand   A–22
Rosenberg Building
1876, N. Tobey, Jr.
This is one of three buildings that the Swiss-born banker, investor, and philanthropist Henry Rosenberg built as investment properties in downtown Galveston in the 1870s. Deep-set arcaded doorways give the Rosenberg Building a strong urban presence at sidewalk level that is the more powerful for being understated. Because the sidewalk canopies cut off the view of the upper part of the building, it is the repetition of tall, thick piers, molded archways, and inset openings that makes the experience of walking alongside the building rhythmic and elevating. The design of the second story and cornice exemplifies Tobey's style.

2002-2016 Strand   A–23
Hendley Buildings
1859
Hendley Wall, 1979, Taft Architects
The Hendley Buildings represent the entrepreneurial success achieved by Galveston commission merchants on the eve of the Civil War. These constituted one of the largest and most substantial business houses built in Texas in the 1850s. Although cast-iron fronts were introduced to Galveston in 1856, the Hendley Buildings' ground-floor storefronts were built according to more conservative techniques. The piers, sills, and lintels are solid gray granite. Granite quoins at the corners of the building and at six-bay intervals along the Strand façade indicate the internal division of the row into four separate buildings. (Note that the names of the buildings' four investors are inscribed on plaques centered

above the third-floor windows.) With the corbeled brick banding near the top of the walls, these quoins give the Hendley Buildings a subdued decorative touch. Historic photographs indicate that the beautifully proportioned second-floor windows once opened onto a continuous balcony, rimmed with ornamental cast-iron rails. At street level, louvered shutters screened the bottom half of openings between piers, so that during business hours the tall double-leaf doors could remain open, allowing the prevailing breeze to penetrate the interior, yet inhibiting access from the sidewalk.

The west half of the Hendley Buildings (2010-2016) was bought in 1968 by pioneer preservationists Sally B. and Jack Wallace to ensure its preservation. The Wallaces presented 2014-2016 to the Galveston Historical Foundation, which commissioned Taft Architects of Houston to rehabilitate it. Faced with the necessity of installing modern plumbing and a fire stair, as well as shoring the exposed west-side wall (originally a shared party wall rather than an exterior wall), Taft and the Houston engineer R. George Cunningham imaginatively added a five-foot-wide steel-framed sliver to buttress the side of the building and incorporate restrooms and the stair.

At 2014-2016 is the Galveston Historical Foundation's **Strand Visitors Center,** rehabilitated by Galveston architect David Watson (1993). Above it are the offices of the Galveston Historical Foundation. Here, 19th-century mercantile austerity is tempered by spatial generosity and the delightful insertion of interior windows between rooms.

The ground-floor interior at **Hendley Market** (2010-2012) is accessible and largely intact. What one sees here is how simply commercial lofts were finished inside: a grid of cast-iron columns supporting heavy timber beams, beaded wood ceilings, and a gridded wood-and-glass ceiling light that brought sky light down into the interior. Such ceiling lights were standard features of larger Strand business buildings into the early 20th century. The floors above Hendley Market have been converted into apartments.

1601 Strand   A–24
Magnolia Homes
1953, R. R. Rapp, Fred B. Stafford, and Thomas M. Price;
Arne G. Engberg, consulting architect
Magnolia Homes was one of a number of low-income public housing complexes built by the Housing Authority of

the City of Galveston in the early 1950s. The Housing Authority cleared three city blocks of all existing structures, replacing them with rows of two-story apartments built to the standards of the U.S. Public Housing Administration. Magnolia Homes was the housing authority's complex for Mexican-American families. It was well planned and solidly constructed but, typical of public housing of the time, had little landscaping and inadequate community spaces. After residents successfully resisted attempts by public and private interests to close the complex and sell the property, it was rehabilitated (1992, C. S. Gilbert). New postmodern façades relieve the uniformity of Engberg's apartment blocks, but the lack of landscape improvements means that the complex has not been reintegrated with the adjacent historic neighborhood to the extent that it might be.

1700 Strand   A–25
United States Custom House (now 1700 Strand Building, University of Texas Medical Branch)
1933, Bottomley, Wagner & White
The Custom House is the only Texas building designed by the celebrated New York architect William Lawrence Bottomley, best remembered for Manhattan's River House and his impeccable country houses. The high-raised building occupies a full city block, just outside the downtown business district. Its classical architectural decoration pays homage to Texas's Spanish past, but the flat, planar, rigorously simplified historical detail has a distinctive 1930s feel. The third-floor windows at each end of the central block represent academic versions of the streamlined-modernistic corner window. The Custom House is now owned and occupied by the University of Texas Medical Branch at Galveston, which maintains it with respectfulness.

At 2013 Water Street (now called Harborside Drive) is a tall, freestanding, brick-and-tile smokestack. This was part of the **Galveston Ice & Cold Storage Company plant,** a portion of which remains at 102-104 21st Street. The complex was built in 1913 to the designs of the St. Louis architects Widman & Walsh. The smokestack figures as a strong vertical element on the downtown skyline, especially from the waterfront. Other waterfront industrial installations attained heights that caused them to tower over the two-, three-, and four-story commercial houses along the Strand. The most imposing was the Texas Star Flour Mills and Elevator, which rose at the northeast corner of 21st and Water Streets, where a parking lot is now located. Completed in 1887, it dominated the downtown wharf front until its demolition in 1974.

101 21st Street   A–26
Heffron Building
1906, Charles W. Bulger
1907, Donald N. McKenzie
United States Appraiser's Stores Building, 1915
This two-story brick building was constructed in three phases, the first two by the concrete contractor Isaac Heffron, the third by the U.S. Appraiser's Stores after it bought the warehouse from Heffron. The most notable external features of the building are its sliding steel fire shutters, visible on the Water Street front. Such shutters were a standard item on Galveston commercial buildings in the late 19th and early 20th centuries. They usually were installed on alley windows, however, rather than facing the street. In 1984 the building was rehabilitated. It now contains a skylit passageway connecting 21st Street and Water Street, onto which shop spaces face.

108 22nd Street   A–27
Harbor Square
1986, Ochsner Associates
This three-story retail center, begun by developer J. R.

McConnell, is one of the few new buildings constructed in the Strand Historic District. Houston architects Jeffrey Karl Ochsner and Eduardo Robles conscientiously analyzed the architecture of the Strand in developing its design, which was intended to be deferential without being imitative. McConnell's sensational bankruptcy brought construction to a halt. Thus the Historic District's newest building has become the one most conspicuously in need of restoration.

Pier 21   A–28
Pier 21 and Harbor House
1993, Ford, Powell & Carson
The decline of Galveston as a shipping port has made it feasible to redevelop the harbor front with recreational amenities. Cynthia and George Mitchell's Pier 21 comprises a pair of wood-framed, gable-roofed buildings containing restaurants, retail space, and a small hotel. San Antonio architect Boone Powell faced the buildings with brick bases and ribbed concrete panels to evoke the waterfront tradition of utilitarian construction. Wood storm shutters and operable windows give the complex a 19th-century scale. Inside, structural wood posts and trusses are exposed, contributing to the complex's light, airy feel.

Pier 21   A–29
Texas Seaport Museum
1991, Ray Bailey Architects
The Seaport Museum is a small building that projects out onto Pier 21 adjacent to the Galveston Historical Foundation's tall ship, *Elissa*. A square-rigged iron barque launched in 1877 in Aberdeen, Scotland, *Elissa* was a merchant ship, originally under British ownership, that, twice during her long career, called at Galveston. In 1975 the Galveston Historical Foundation purchased the ship from an American archeologist who had bought *Elissa* to save her from destruction. *Elissa* was partially restored in

Greece, then brought back across the Atlantic to Galveston in 1979, where a corps of professionals and volunteers completed restoration in 1982. Since then she has functioned as a floating museum and is one of the oldest tall ships still capable of sailing. Several times a year, *Elissa* is taken out into the Gulf of Mexico. The Seaport Museum was designed to serve as an interpretive center for visitors to *Elissa*. It was refaced (1993) to harmonize with the adjacent Pier 21 development.

2307-2309 Harborside Drive　　　　　**A–32**
J. Mayrant Smith Building
1876, H. Lowell, builder
Although the Galveston City Company, which developed the Galveston townsite, illustrated a "Water Street" on its maps, it was not until the mid-1870s that land was reclaimed from the bay to make this designation a reality. Until 1874 the buildings on the north side of the Strand backed up to the bay. During the mid-1870s, the Galveston Wharf Company, the privately owned corporation enfranchised by the City of Galveston to operate the public wharves, expanded the waterfront into the harbor on reclaimed land to provide buildable lots on the south side of Water Street, as well as broad aprons onto which the Galveston, Houston & Henderson Railroad and the Gulf, Colorado & Santa Fe Railway could extend their tracks to integrate rail and shipping transportation. The brick Smith Building, part of a row that once extended to Tremont Street, dates from this period of improvement. Across Water Street from 1876 until 1898 stood the original Union Depot. The Smith Building was acquired by Mr. and Mrs. George Mitchell in 1988 and rehabilitated externally by Ford, Powell & Carson.

Pier 22　　　　　　　　　　　　　　　　**A–30**
Fisherman's Wharf at Pier 22
1995, Eubanks/Bohnn Associates
Fisherman's Wharf is a conversion and expansion of an authentic metal-clad wharf warehouse, the ex-Liberty Fish & Oyster Company market. Despite decoration that clashes with its architecture, Fisherman's Wharf preserves the feel of the working waterfront in a way that other new recreational installations along the wharves do not. This is also true of **Hill's Pier 19 Restaurant** and **Sampson & Son's** fish market, both at Pier 20. These two established businesses back up to Pier 19, home of the Mosquito Fleet, as Galveston's flotilla of shrimp trawlers is affectionately known.

2223-2227 Harborside Drive　　　　　**A–31**
Wolston, Wells & Vidor Warehouse
1877, N. Tobey, Jr.
The cotton merchants Wolston, Wells & Vidor retained Nathaniel W. Tobey to design their two-story brick warehouse. After being acquired by Mr. and Mrs. George Mitchell in 1992, the Wolston, Wells & Vidor building was rehabilitated externally by the Houston architects Hall Merriman, who inserted a sidewalk arcade behind its Water Street front, continuing the arcades from the Smith Building to the west.

Pier 23-26　　　　　　　　　　　　　　**A–33**
Mallory Line Warehouse (now Cruise Terminal)
1927
The Mallory Line Warehouse is an immense, cast-in-place concrete wharf warehouse that stretches for four blocks along the waterfront. Apart from the two-story central bay, with its scalloped Spanish-style gable, it consists of repeating bays of what were originally cotton and general cargo storage. The scalloped central bay gives the warehouse a civic dimension, enabling it to play an urban role as the architectural terminus of Rosenberg Avenue.

Portions of the building were converted into a passenger terminal for cruise ships by Rapp Partners (1990).

206 Rosenberg Avenue   A–34
Panama Hotel
1913, Green & Finger

The Panama (its name celebrating Galveston's boast that it was the closest U.S. port to the newly constructed Panama Canal) is a typical early-20th-century railroad hotel. Aimed primarily at business travelers, it was respectable rather than prestigious. The Houston architects Lewis Sterling Green and Joseph Finger produced a stolid composition in brownish red brick with a weighty two-bay portico that faced the Santa Fe station, a color scheme perhaps more compatible with the 1897 terminal building than with its Art Deco successor. Green-and-yellow tile spandrels give the Panama a welcome sparkle.

2422-2428 Mechanic Street   A–35
Sergeant Building
c. 1874

The Sergeant Building shows how effective stucco-faced brick construction is in creating surfaces that take on density and shape in Galveston's strong sunlight. The repetitive rhythm of brick pilasters, brick belt courses that tie the arched second-floor window heads together, and corbeled brick ornament give the building its uninsistent measure. The eastern bays along Mechanic Street retain their double-leaf wood doors with wrought-iron door pulls and a melancholy faded green color that evokes the Galveston that was.

2413 Mechanic Street   A–36
Hanretta Building
c. 1874

This simple, two-story, stucco-surfaced brick building sustains the somewhat tattered fabric of the old wholesale and manufacturing sector in this corner of downtown. The Hanretta Building was rehabilitated by Taft Architects in 1985, when its upper floor was converted into apartments.

2402-2406 Mechanic Street   A–37
Clarke & Courts Building
1890, N. J. Clayton & Company

The Clarke & Courts Building was the largest downtown business building that Clayton designed. Until 1900, it was the tallest building in Galveston. It is of brick and heavy timber frame construction, carried, according to news reports at the time it was built, on an innovative system of isolated pier foundations. The five-story building was built to contain the "Texas House," as printer Robert Clarke and stationer George M. Courts advertised their business, which specialized in the production of printed forms, government record forms, and bank checks and had a statewide clientele. Perhaps because it was envisioned primarily as a production plant rather than an office building, the Clarke & Courts Building was more simply detailed than many of Clayton's Strand buildings. It is this attribute that distinguishes the Clarke & Courts Building as Clayton's contribution to a series of British and American warehouses that constituted some of the noblest architecture of the 19th century.

In 1893, Robert M. Hutchings, a son of the banker John H. Hutchings, bought a controlling interest in Clarke & Courts. Under the direction of Hutchings and his brother, Sealy Hutchings, Clarke & Courts expanded its operations beyond Texas and opened new branch offices. Sealy Hutchings transferred the corporation's headquarters to Houston in 1935. But until 1989, when Clarke & Courts closed its Galveston operation, the corporation was the sole occupant of this building.

In 1904 the one-story wing at 2410-2416 Mechanic was added by the architect C. W. Bulger. The Clarke & Courts Building was bought in 1993 by Houston developer Randall Davis, who, in 1995, remodeled it for conversion to apartments.

2300 Mechanic Street   A–38
Leon & H. Blum Building (now The Tremont House)
1879, 1882, Eugene T. Heiner
Rehabilitation and additions, 1985, Ford, Powell & Carson
The cousins Leon and Hyman Blum, and Leon Blum's brother Sylvain, were Alsatian Jews who immigrated to Texas in the 1850s. In 1865 they moved to Galveston to open the dry goods wholesale and mercantile house of Leon & H. Blum, which became one of the largest wholesalers in Texas in the 1870s and 1880s. Following the loss of its building on the Strand in the fire of June 1877, the firm acquired this site and in 1879 had the Houston architect Eugene T. Heiner design a substantial three-story building of stucco-faced brick at the corner of 24th and Mechanic. In 1882, the Blum firm recalled Heiner to expand the building farther east along Mechanic Street. Heiner cleverly turned what had been the east end bay of the 1879 building into the middle bay of the expanded building, emphasizing the center of the long Mechanic front with a pediment-crowned frontispiece that breaks through the long horizontal line of the bracketed galvanized iron cornice. An illustration published at the time of the 1882 expansion depicted the building with a mansard-roofed attic that was perhaps anticipated for a future phase of expansion, but never built. The Leon & H. Blum Building had the most extensive street frontage of any of the downtown Galveston wholesale houses. However, as happened to a number of other important mercantile houses in the aftermath of the

Panic of 1893, the firm went bankrupt in 1896. Increasing competition from Dallas, San Antonio, and a fast-rising Houston exposed the vulnerability of Galveston's established wholesale businesses, which found themselves no longer at the maritime gateway to Texas but at the wrong end of the railroad network that connected Texas cities to Kansas City, St. Louis, and Chicago by the late 1880s.

In 1981 Cynthia and George Mitchell bought the Blum Building, which was in shabby condition but largely intact externally. Working with Ford, Powell & Carson's Boone Powell and Carolyn Peterson and Chicago interior designer Ann Miller Gray, they restored the exterior of the building and transformed the interior into a 124-room hotel, the first major hotel in downtown Galveston in nearly sixty years. Mr. and Mrs. Mitchell named it after the Tremont Hotel, Galveston's most famous Victorian hotel, which had opened in 1877 at Tremont and Church, and was demolished in 1928. In order to secure adequate space to make the hotel financially feasible and still qualify for federal tax credits for certified rehabilitation of a listed historic property, Mr. and Mrs. Mitchell won permission from the National Park Service to add a fourth floor to the building—in the form of the never-built mansard-roofed attic. The tranquil public spaces of the hotel are forecast by the quiet authority of the ranks of double-leaf wood-and-glass doors in the building's sidewalk arcade. Street trees and the muted gray flagstone paving of the sidewalk underscore the Tremont House's urbanity. Preservation and rehabilitation have meant a radical change in the Blum Building's use and its demeanor. Ford, Powell & Carson, and their clients, have effected these changes with tact and assurance.

24th Street and Mechanic Street   A–39
Mardi Gras Arch
1986, Ford, Powell & Carson
Boone Powell's contribution to the lineup of celebrity arches is a schematic tribute to the Victorian version of Renaissance classical decoration that Heiner incorporated in the façades of the Leon & H. Blum Building. In contrast to the density of Michael Graves's arch on the Strand, Powell's celebrates ephemerality in its lightness, thinness, and transparency.

2325-2327 Mechanic Street   **A–40**

Marx & Blum Building

1890, N. J. Clayton & Company

Reconstruction, 1904, C. W. Bulger

The Marx & Blum Building was originally four stories high, slender in profile, and exhibited the elegant Néo-Grec classical detail that Clayton frequently applied in the 1890s. Its graceful profile may have contributed to its undoing. The Storm of 1900 brought down the top three floors. Yet rather than demolish the wrecked building, its subsequent owner, the dry goods merchants Mistrot Brothers & Company, retained C. W. Bulger to restore it, although as two floors rather than four. As was the case when Bulger simultaneously added to the Clarke & Courts Building, he respectfully preserved the character of Clayton's architecture.

By the early 1990s the building was vacant and boarded up. Cynthia and George Mitchell bought the Marx & Blum Building and, in 1995, had the Houston architects Merriman Holt restore its exteriors and consolidate it with the building next door to contain public function rooms for the Tremont House across the street. This restoration has rescued and restored to visual prominence, for the second time in the 20th century, Clayton's fine classical decor.

2317 Mechanic Street   **A–41**

John Berlocher Building

1870, P. N. Comegys

1993, Strand Street Theatre addition, Ford, Powell & Carson

The Strand Street Theatre, a theatrical performance company, commissioned Ford, Powell & Carson to reconstruct the interior of this building to contain a 200-seat theater with support facilities. Ford, Powell & Carson added a new sliver building to contain the public entrance, detailing it with unobtrusive, modern accoutrements, such as the glass-roofed canopy.

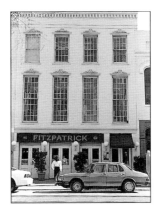

2309-2315 Mechanic Street   **A–42**

John Berlocher Building

1858, 1859, James Brown, builder

Berlocher was a Swiss immigrant and commission merchant who was especially active in improving downtown Galveston real estate during the 1850s, 1860s, and 1870s. This pair of buildings is notable for the 16-pane-over-16-pane double-hung windows with which the second floor is lit. Their elongated proportions imbue this otherwise typical 1850s' brick storefront with an especially graceful aspect, to which the scroll-topped cast-iron architraves above the windows contribute. The exterior of 2315 was restored in 1985 by Ford, Powell & Carson for Mr. and Mrs. George Mitchell and that of 2309-2311 by David Watson (1993). Ford, Powell & Carson was able to replicate what paint analysis revealed to be the historic colors of the buildings. The interiors of 2315 were rehabilitated by Ford, Powell & Carson (1991), and those of 2309-11 were rehabilitated by David Watson (1993). Eubanks/Bohnn Associates designed the interiors of **Made in France.**

219-223 Tremont Street   **A–43**

McDonnell Building

1873

The rehabilitation of the McDonnell Building entailed de-construction of several layers of additions piled on top of it in the early 20th century. In 1990, Ford, Powell & Carson removed the fifth and sixth floors, added in 1909 when this was the Royal Hotel. They retained a fourth floor added to the original in 1907 by Galveston architect Donald N. McKenzie and rehabilitated the interior to serve as public function and conference rooms for the Tremont House. As the architectural treatment of the building's two street fronts demonstrates, the Tremont elevation was the main façade. Tremont Street was downtown's principal north-south thoroughfare. From at least the 1850s, corner buildings faced it rather than the alphabetical avenues.

213-217 Tremont Street   **A–44**

Rice, Baulard & Company Building

1870

The pioneer conversion of commercial loft space to residential use downtown occurred with Ford, Powell & Carson's 1975 rehabilitation of 217 Tremont as expansive "town flats" for Emily Whiteside, the first director of the Galveston County Cultural Arts Council. Her initial tenant was the Galveston Historical Foundation's first executive director, Peter H. Brink. In 1978 Taft Architects rehabilitated the two stucco-faced bays at 213-15 as loft apartments for Daniel K. Thorne. Like Ford, Powell & Carson at 217, Taft Architects organized apartments around a newly inserted skylit stair well. But their design intervention was more formally assertive, contrasting the existing historic fabric with white-painted sculptural shapes. Although erected at the same time by the paint and glass suppliers Joseph W. Rice and Victor J. Baulard and sharing a common architectural vocabulary, these buildings were built as separate structures.

The **alley** alongside the Rice-Baulard Building, like others downtown, has a distinct character that differentiates it from the street fronts of blocks. Paved with brick, it is spatially framed by plain, undecorated building walls. Window openings are shuttered with metal fire shutters, either hinged folding shutters or, in some cases, shutters that slide to one side on exposed rods. This particular alley now does double duty as a pedestrian shortcut between the Mitchell-owned properties on either side.

2222-2228 Mechanic Street   **A–45**

The Washington Building

1987, Ford, Powell & Carson

Cynthia and George Mitchell were poised to begin rehabilitation of the ex-Washington Hotel (built in 1873 by the hardware supplier J. P. Davie and originally known as the Cosmopolitan Hotel) when it burned in an electrical fire caused by Hurricane Alicia in 1983. All that was left

standing was the east-side party wall and one bay facing Mechanic Street. Because Ford, Powell & Carson had already prepared construction drawings for rehabilitation of the historic building, they were able to convert these into construction documents for a new reinforced concrete–framed building that faithfully reproduces the exterior elevations of the Washington Hotel. Rather than replacing an adjoining 1940s' building facing Tremont that was also destroyed in the 1983 fire, Mr. and Mrs. Mitchell created a rear courtyard, which gives access to the **Phoenix Bakery and Coffee House,** designed by David Watson (1989).

2220 Mechanic Street   **A–46**

J. P. Davie Building

1860

J. P. Davie's four-story office and warehouse building is almost identical to his later Washington Hotel next door, except that here face brick was exposed rather than finished with stucco and scored, as on the Washington, and window openings are more closely spaced. Davie's building is in the conservative style typical of Galveston business houses of the 1850s. A photograph, taken from the roof of the Hendley Buildings, probably in the early 1860s, shows Davie's building facing a row of two-story, gable-fronted wood buildings of the type that the *Galveston Daily News* in the late 19th century routinely dismissed as "rookeries." The photograph indicates how tall, solid, and progressive this building must have seemed when new. Next door, at **2214-16 Mechanic,** is a three-story building constructed as an investment by John Sealy in 1873. At 2202-10 Mechanic is the sadly defaced **J. Reymershoffer's Sons Building** (1877) by Duhamel & Lawler. It has been shorn of its original architectural detail and its unusual multiple-gabled roof.

220 22nd Street   **A–47**
Kauffman & Runge Building (now Stewart Title Building)
1882, Eugene T. Heiner

The Kauffman & Runge Building represents the scale that was typical of Galveston's wholesale and financial district in the 1880s. That Eugene T. Heiner had the opportunity to design much larger business buildings in Galveston than he did in Houston, where his practice was based, was an expression of Galveston's commercial supremacy. As a measure of how short-lived this supremacy proved to be, the grocery wholesaling and cotton exporting firm of Kauffman & Runge went bankrupt in 1887 and was dissolved. Heiner designed the Kauffman & Runge Building in the "modern" High Victorian version of Italian Renaissance classical architecture that he frequently used. Its ribbed and paneled brick walls, varying arch shapes, and contrasting trim colors are evidence of how anticlassical American High Victorian architects' approach to the revival of classical architecture was.

In 1905 the building was acquired by the lawyer Maco Stewart and remodeled by C. W. Bulger to serve as an office building and headquarters for what became the Stewart Title Company, one of the major real estate service corporations in Texas. Bulger inserted the toplit central court around which offices are organized. Although the Stewart Title Company moved its headquarters to Houston, it continues to occupy the building, which was rehabilitated by Galveston architect David V. Barker in 1977. Barker restored the long-lost cornice but maintained the exterior painted surfaces, a 20th-century alteration.

212 22nd Street   **A–48**
H. M. Trueheart & Company Building
1882, N. J. Clayton

Although the real estate office building of H. M. Trueheart & Co. is diminutive when compared to the Kauffman & Runge Building next door, it holds its own urbanistically, thanks to Clayton's skill at composition and detail. Symmetry, authoritative proportions, and a dexterous use of sunken panels and bands of multicolored brick and tile ornament animate the street front of this infill building. At the time the Trueheart Building was built, the *Galveston Daily News* characterized it as an example of the "polychromatic architecture of the cities of central Italy,"

referring to High Victorian architects' fascination with using the materials from which their buildings were built to provide ornamental richness and color, a trait they had observed in the medieval urban architecture of parts of Italy. The Trueheart Building's luster had dimmed considerably when Cartier-Bresson and Ezra Stoller photographed it in 1962 for *The Galveston That Was*. But thanks in part to the attention it received, the building was bought by the Junior League of Galveston County in 1969 and rehabilitated in 1971.

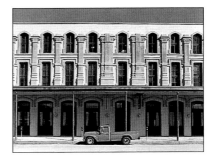

306 22nd Street   **A–49**
H. Marwitz & Company Building
1878, John Moser

Like many other 19th-century Galveston business buildings, the Marwitz Building has lost its original cornice. In rehabilitating the building in 1982, Houston architect Graham B. Luhn compensated for this loss by emphasizing the plasticity of the building's exterior surfaces. These energize the experience of walking past the Marwitz Building and demonstrate how successful American Victorian architects were at creating a sense of spatial excitement with the most ordinary means. The Marwitz Building was one of several built in this block in the 1870s by the commission merchant, importer, and exporter Sampson Heidenheimer, although it bore the name of the wholesale and retail grocers and ship stores firm, H. Marwitz & Company, Heidenheimer's tenant. In 1874 Heidenheimer had built what was to have been Galveston's most imposing Victorian hotel, the four-story Grand Southern (designed by the Chicago architects Sherwin & Overmire), at this corner. It was destroyed in the fire of June 1877, which decimated both sides of the 2100 block of Mechanic Street.

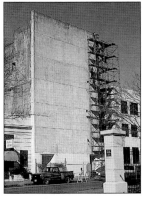

Galveston News Building, photographed spring 1995.

Galveston News Building, photographed spring 1996.

2108 Mechanic Street   **A–50**
Galveston News Building
1884, N. J. Clayton

The Galveston News Building is one of Clayton's masterpieces. It consists of a complexly conceived front façade of pressed brick and cast stone affixed to a tall, three-story, iron-framed and brick-caged building built to contain the offices and production facilities of the *Galveston Daily News,* then the most widely circulated newspaper in Texas. Clayton compacted brick arcades within larger-scaled arcades, as though the Mechanic Street front were a Roman aqueduct. Howard Barnstone suggested that this intense expression of compressive strength was related to the location of the newspaper's heavy printing equipment on the building's top floor. The framing of third-floor windows repeats the divided center motif of the lower part of the building. Clayton brilliantly resolved the visual tension this organization induced by projecting a central, undivided frontispiece above the roof line of the News Building (a feature that no longer exists). Just as impressive as this counterplay of line and rhythm was Clayton's extraordinary ornamental repertoire, carried out in molded brick, tile, and cast stone. Here, one sees the characteristics that distinguish Clayton's architecture from that of so many of his Victorian

contemporaries. Decoration is not simply overlaid on the building's surfaces to achieve visual distraction, but absorbed into its fabric. The result is best described not in visual terms but musically: It is symphonic. Definition, shading, nuance, harmonic variation, crescendo—the architectural elements of the News Building swell into a full-bodied, romantic composition.

Clayton's client was the publisher A. H. Belo, who, two years after completion of the News Building, founded the *Dallas Morning News* in a sort of territorial expansion of the *News's* journalistic empire. The impressive growth of Dallas in the last decades of the 19th century led Belo to move his operations there. In 1923 the Galveston newspaper was acquired by W. L. Moody, Jr., and remained under Moody ownership until 1963. The sale of the newspaper to the *Houston Post* led to construction of a new, suburban office and production plant, designed by Howard Barnstone & Eugene Aubry. After the *News* left this building, it became a warehouse. In 1970, the entire street front of the building was refaced with plaster cement panels. These were removed in early 1995 by new owners, Mr. and Mrs. John Saracco, who had damaged ornamental detail reconstructed and the exterior rehabilitated, restoring the News Building to its deserved position of prominence in Galveston's architectural pantheon.

2102 Mechanic Street   **A–51**
Galveston Cotton Exchange and Board of Trade Building
1940, Ben Milam

As the sociologist Joe R. Feagin observed, the cotton trade integrated 19th-century Texas with world financial markets, a process that the Galveston cotton exchange, the first in Texas, was organized to facilitate. John Moser designed a swaggering, three-and-one-half-story, red pressed brick and limestone-trimmed building for the Cotton Exchange, which was completed in 1879. It was the first Galveston building to be illustrated in a national architectural periodical, and its dedication was the subject of a feature article in *Frank Leslie's Illustrated Weekly.*

By the second quarter of the 20th century, Galveston's importance as a cotton trading center had so declined that the Cotton Exchange decided to replace its Victorian exchange building with a smaller structure. In 1938, Moser's building was demolished. Its replacement was this unassuming white office block, decorated with polished granite banding and mildly modernistic detail (note the wrought iron panels of cotton-related imagery). Milam's rather fussy exteriors were improved when architect Charles L. Zwiener re-glazed the windows with sheets of solar gray glass. The simple rhythms, serene scale, and white façades of the Cotton Exchange Building provide a restrained backdrop for the richly surfaced and colored Victorian buildings that surround it.

305 21st Street   A–52
Heidenheimer & Company Building (now Marine Building)
1875, 1877

Sampson Heidenheimer built this building in two stages. He then added a three-story annex where the Mechanic Street entrance to the parking garage is located. The now-demolished three-story building, of 1879, was designed by John Moser. Newspaper reports of the period do not identify an architect for the Heidenheimer-Marine Building. It is disappointing not to know the architect, for the Heidenheimer Building is a particularly good example of how stucco surfaces can be manipulated to produce rich light-and-shadow effects in Galveston's strong sunlight. The shaped parapets above the center lines of the two street fronts and the Victorian Gothic arcades of the ground-floor openings give the Heidenheimer Building an extra lilt. In 1984, the building was rehabilitated by Ford, Powell & Carson for Mr. and Mrs. George Mitchell.

308 21st Street   A–53
Medical Arts Building
1929, Andrew Fraser

Andrew Fraser, an architect and engineer born and trained in Scotland, came to Galveston in 1926. He was particularly identified with the Moody interests, for whom he designed this 11-story "skyscraper," decorated with modernistic detail. The Medical Arts Building was an annex to the American National Insurance Company Building of 1913, which occupied the rest of the 21st Street front of this block until its demolition in 1972.

221 20th Street   A–54
Bennison Building (now Seaman's Center)
1871

The minimal ornamental detail of the Bennison Building's brick cornice and its flat-headed windows must have appeared very conservative as increasingly aggressive ornament and scale were introduced into Galveston commercial architecture in the early 1870s. Today, the Bennison Building, built by the grocer Hugh Bennison on what had been the premises of his family-owned blacksmith operations, possesses a quiet dignity, enhanced by its rehabilitation in 1978 as the Seaman's Center.

1922 Mechanic Street   A–55
Dolson-Horn Furniture Company Warehouse
1911

1918 Mechanic Street
David Taylor Classic Car Museum
1990, Cannady, Jackson & Ryan

Houston architect William T. Cannady provided a snappy streamlined refacing of an existing storefront to accommodate expansion of the Houston car dealer David Taylor's classic automobile museum on the right.

Next door, at 1922 Mechanic (now part of the Taylor complex), is the former Dolson-Horn Furniture Company Warehouse. Despite its prosaic use, the building's classical countenance gave it a strong urban presence on what was an adjunct to the downtown financial and retail district.

1914-1916 Mechanic Street   **A–56**

C. F. Marschner Building (now David Taylor Classic Car Museum)

1905, Otto Haas, builder

Although spatially compact, downtown Galveston in the 19th and early 20th centuries consisted of numerous subdistricts, each with its own character. Built to house C. F. Marschner's bottling plant, this handsome, architecturally conservative late Victorian building contributed to the light industrial sector that lay east of 20th Street. Research by the Galveston Historical Foundation indicates that the Marschner family not only ran their business from this building, but lived on the second floor. In 1990, the building was rehabilitated by architect David Watson to contain the David Taylor car museum.

1902 Mechanic Street   **A–57**

National Maritime Union of America Building (now United Way of Galveston)

1954, R. R. Rapp

As a glance at the west-side party wall indicates, the street fronts here are simply skins. But they are deftly articulated skins, as the planar composition of polished granite, thin Roman brick, common brick, corrugated spandrel, and green-tinted corrugated window glass attests.

1902-1928 Market Street   **A–58**

One Moody Plaza

1971, Neuhaus & Taylor

The American National Insurance Company built this 20-story, 358-foot-high tower as its corporate headquarters, clearing two blocks of 19th-century buildings in the

process. For maximum visibility on the skyline, Neuhaus & Taylor of Houston rotated the tower diagonally atop a block-square, brick-paved plateau that caps two levels of parking. They further heightened the building's assertion of corporate superiority with a grandiose colonnade and entrance lobby 50 feet high. Despite the vacancy of the ground-floor level and the overweening exception to prior conventions of urban siting and spatiality that it registers, One Moody Plaza makes a place for itself by reflecting Galveston light and sky. In treating the exterior of the tower as a dense file of intensely white, precast concrete piers, overlaid with cast-in-place horizontal concrete spandrels, and infilled with silver, reflective window panes, Neuhaus & Taylor let the sun imbue the tower with the depth and plasticity that earlier generations of Galveston architects also knew how to manipulate.

Because Galveston Island is a sandbar and the water table is only one foot below grade, the engineering of One Moody Plaza required considerable ingenuity. Ellisor Engineers of Houston specified bearing piles as deep as 120 feet to support the tower. The below-grade parking garage, which was designed to be flooded on occasion, represented the reverse problem. It had to be anchored with tension piles to resist the tendency of the moisture-laden ground to push it upward.

One Moody Plaza represents an attitude characteristic of mid-20th-century modern architecture in the United States. "Old" buildings (and "old" cities) were tolerated as a mute backdrop to dramatic feats of heroic, engineering-inspired design that proclaimed newness and a liberation from history. During the late 1960s and 1970s, Market Street was where this spatial narrative was played out in downtown Galveston. Ultimately, it was not modern architecture so much as the cut-and-clear imperative of the car—achieved by street-widening and by demolishing commercially redundant buildings to provide surface parking lots—that resulted in the "Houstonization" of Market Street.

1921 Market Street   **A–59**

Wegner Brothers Building

1889

402-410 20th Street

Catholic Building

1888, N. J. Clayton

Market Street was the principal retail street of late-19th and early-20th-century Galveston. Grocers, butchers, bakers, and other food trades clustered in the 1900 and 2000 blocks because of their proximity to the City Market, located at 20th and Market since the 1840s, and from which, of course, Avenue D takes its name. When Alfred Muller's deliciously overwrought Victorian City Hall and Market House was built at this corner in 1888 (on the long, slender esplanade in the middle of 20th Street between Market and Mechanic), it bestowed an aura of civic dignity that the market square had previously lacked. This pair of buildings figured in the ensuing real estate boost. Wegner Brothers sold groceries and liquors. The Catholic Building was built by Bishop Nicholas A. Gallagher to provide meeting rooms on its second floor for Catholic lay organizations and income-producing rental space down below. In 1995 architect David Watson bought and rehabilitated the Wegner Building, with its plastically assertive second-story façade. The Catholic Building, one of Clayton's most undemonstrative designs, was rehabilitated in 1987 by the Lone Star Property Management company. It is notable for its two-story-high piers, which give the street faces a modest monumentality.

2121 Market Street   **A–60**
Guaranty Federal Savings & Loan Association Building (now Guaranty Federal Bank)
1973, Rapp Tackett Fash
The Guaranty Bank Building demonstrates that modern architecture can contribute to the texture of older, more traditionally organized downtowns. The building's broad, simple wall planes, surfaced in travertine, contrast with dark glass voids. Rapp Tackett Fash's design partner, Gerald Tackett, shaped the low building to frame a raised terrace, whose steps hold the sidewalk line and thus respect the space

of the street. Across the street, the **2100 Market Street Garage** (1975) contributes to the Houstonization of Market Street by occupying an entire block front. The Market Street sidewalk was pulled under the trays of parking, which replicate the feel of a canopy covering. The decision to install plantings in the sidewalk reserve added to the suburbanized softening of Market Street's once firm urban edges.

2201 Market Street   **A–61**
United States National Bank Building
1925, Alfred C. Bossom with Sanguinet, Staats & Hedrick
The architect Alfred C. Bossom worked in New York from 1903 until 1926, when he returned to England, where he had been born and trained. Thanks to connections made by his father-in-law, a New York banker, Bossom had a lively Texas practice in the 1920s, designing tall office buildings in Houston and Dallas, where, for the Galvestonian John H. Sealy, he designed the Magnolia Petroleum Building (1921), the tallest in Texas until the mid-1920s. The 11-story United States National Bank Building, with its dark granite base, smooth limestone facing, and tall arched windows separated by Corinthian pilasters, is representative of Bossom's work. It is notable for the urbane way that it shapes space on Market and 22nd Streets with its elegant chamfered corner. The clock face, above the pediment-capped corner entrance, was an urban amenity especially associated with banks. The building was rehabilitated in 1990 by David Watson.

The United States National Bank was the outgrowth of a savings bank in which the wholesale grocer, cotton factor, and real estate investor H. Kempner acquired an interest in 1885. Kempner's sons bought controlling interest in the bank in 1902, and in 1923, one of them, Daniel W. Kempner, directed the planning and construction of this modern office building. The height of the U.S. National Bank Building signaled to W. L. Moody, Jr., the Kempner brothers' business rival, their determination not to take second place to his 11-story American National Insurance Company Building at 21st and Market.

2219 Market Street   **A–62**

City National Bank Building (now Galveston County Historical Museum)

1920, Weary & Alford

The Chicago architects Weary & Alford sandwiched a monumental Corinthian temple-front onto this midblock lot to contain W. L. Moody, Jr.'s City National Bank. To compensate for the site's narrow frontage, the architects emphasized scale and vertical rise. A steep flight of narrow steps leads from the sidewalk up to the long, tunnel-vaulted banking hall. Filtered skylight illuminates the hall's intricately decorated plaster ceiling panels and its marble interior finishes. The exterior is surfaced in terra cotta, a thrifty substitute for limestone. With the construction of this imposing building, W. L. Moody, Jr., initiated the transfer of Galveston's financial district from the Strand to Market Street. The City National Bank (subsequently renamed the Moody National Bank) occupied this building until 1962. In 1972, Moody's daughter, Mary Moody Northen, gave it to Galveston County for use as the county's historical museum, which opened in 1976.

2221 Market Street   **A–63**

E. S. Levy Building

1896, 1900, C. W. Bulger

Charles W. Bulger was one of a number of architects who began practice in Galveston in the 1890s. He had previously worked in Colorado and would move his practice a final time, to Dallas, in 1904. This retail and office block was his first major building in downtown Galveston. It marks his transition away from the red brick and intensively ornamented surfaces of Galveston's Victorian commercial architecture to the tawny-hued brick and relative restraint

that Clayton introduced with the classically ornamented Hutchings-Sealy Buildings on the Strand. Bulger added the top floor in 1900, which gives the Levy Building its thick, top-heavy aspect. After 1908 the Levy Building was owned and occupied by various business interests of W. L. Moody, Jr., first the City National Bank, and subsequently the National Hotel Company.

2200 Market Street   **A–64**

First Hutchings-Sealy National Bank Building (now NationsBank Building)

1972, Caudill Rowlett Scott with Thomas M. Price

Further contributing to the Houstonization of Market Street is the visually arresting 10-story slab designed for Galveston's oldest bank by the Houston architects CRS. Unlike older generations of tall buildings (such as the U.S. National Bank Building), First Hutchings-Sealy does not reinforce the space of the street and sidewalk. Instead, its designer, CRS's Paul A. Kennon, Jr., declared the building's exceptional status by locating it in the middle of a cleared block (although in order to build around the bank's 1935 building at 22nd and Market, it was pushed weakly off the center line of the block). Kennon tried to Galvestonize the building by raising it above street level and by deeply recessing its glass curtain wall to create porchlike balconies on the Market Street face of the building. These efforts, however, tend to emphasize its remoteness, except along Mechanic Street, where the desired contrast with older surrounding buildings does occur. Were First Hutchings-Sealy not so isolated, it might achieve the sense of monumentality that was clearly sought. But deference to parking lots and driveways condemns the building to float in suburbanized space, even though it stands at the heart of downtown Galveston.

401-403 Tremont Street   **A–65**

T. E. Thompson Building

1869, P. N. Comegys

Befitting its location in the downtown retail district, the Thompson Building, with its arched windows and bracketed cornice, was more elaborately detailed than Comegys's other buildings on the Strand. Above Thompson's jewelry store were the Thompson Flats. The *Galveston Daily News* wrote at the time of the building's

construction that it was not to be surpassed by anything in New Orleans. An amusing feature of the Thompson Building was the clock (now gone) stationed on the parapet above the Tremont-Market corner, flanked by lions rampant. The Thompson Building has suffered from effacement.

2326-2328 Market Street   A–66

Dubie Building
1874

2322-2324 Market Street

Schulte Building
1874

2318-2320 Market Street

A. Flake & Company Building
1874

2314-2316 Market Street

Engelke Building
1874

Partial restoration (1996, Robert Robinowitz) has uncovered nearly a block of commercial houses long masked with undistinguished modern façades. It is the urban impact of this row of buildings, rather than the architecture of its component parts, that makes it such a forceful presence.

2401 Market Street   A–67

Central Hotel
1870

This very ordinary-looking building is an exceptional survivor. It is the replacement of a similarly built wood building destroyed in the Fire of 1869. The owner of the property, Judge J. L. Darragh, skirted the city's new fire code, which required that construction be in noncombustible materials, by claiming that he was merely repairing the Central Hotel's predecessor. Thus the Central Hotel preserves what was a very characteristic shape (as well as the wooden construction) of Galveston commercial houses of the 1840s and 1850s.

2415 Market Street   A–68

Trube Building
1894

2419 Market Street

Lalor Building
1894

Rehabilitation has disclosed the textural strength of the three-story Trube Building. It is notable not only for its fine molded brick decoration but also for its delicate cast-iron storefront, which resembles N. J. Clayton's distinctive cast-iron storefront designs.

The composition of the second-story façade of the Lalor Building next door closely resembles that of the Wegner Brothers Building at 1921 Market Street. Bifurcating the center was a Victorian Mannerist technique that N. J. Clayton, among other architects, used with considerable panache on occasion. There is no documentary evidence to connect either of these buildings to Clayton, nor does either much look like his work. What the Claytonesque details of both suggest is the extent to which Clayton influenced other Galveston architects by the 1890s.

2425-2427 Market Street A–69

R. F. Martin & Company Building
1878

By the time Market Street reached 25th Street (Rosenberg Avenue), its respectability began to diminish. Although Galveston's red-light zone, the Restricted District, lay on the west side of Rosenberg, this sober brick building with its tiers of round and segmental arched openings housed the Variety Saloon on its ground floor by 1885 and "female boarding" (a euphemism for a bordello) on its second.

2501-2503 Market Street A–70

Hall-Scott Buildings
1906, George B. Stowe

2509-2511 Market Street

Levi Building
1917

2513-2515 Market Street

Hughes Building
1907, George B. Stowe

Like every Southern city, Galveston had two downtowns. One was mainstream; the other was a parallel downtown where retail and entertainment establishments that catered to African-Americans and working-class immigrants were situated. Typically located near the railroad station, this "other" downtown was off-limits to middle-class white women and girls because it was also where businesses that did not conform to middle-class standards of propriety tended to concentrate. Galveston, as a port city, had an expanded

clientele for the diversions such businesses offered. The Restricted District, as this segment of downtown was designated by the early 20th century, combined vice specialties (saloons, gambling, and prostitution) with more mundane businesses oriented toward African-American and immigrant patrons. Reflecting the specialized role this area played in downtown, one strip of buildings identified with Irish immigrants was called "Smoky Row" as early as the 1860s.

One of the ways that Galveston compensated for its decline in the early 20th century was to resist public morality campaigns that succeeded in criminalizing gambling, prostitution, and the consumption of drugs and alcohol. Therefore, "the district" remained an urban locale where such activities were tolerated until 1957, when the Attorney General of Texas, Will Wilson, in a celebrated series of raids, closed down the "Free State of Galveston" (as historian David McComb referred to the city in his book *Galveston, A History*) and forced vice to go underground. The end of legal racial segregation in the 1960s, coupled with the decline of the port, has left the district the most deteriorated portion of downtown.

This row of buildings, bookended with blocks designed by Stowe for a series of investors, gives the district an architectural façade that is almost disappointing in its respectability. Rehabilitation of the Levi Building in 1996 entailed reconstruction of its long-lost sidewalk canopy.

2523 Market Street A–71

Carver Theater
1948

The Galveston theater entrepreneur Giosue Martini built both the Carver and the no-longer-extant Booker T. Theater at 2601 Market (1948) for African-American audiences. During the middle decades of the 20th century, these blocks were the business and entertainment center for black Galveston and Mexican-American Galveston.

2528 and 2526 Market Street A–72

Scott Buildings
c. 1870; c. 1876

2522-2524 Market Street

Scott Building
1891

The real estate investor Mitchell L. Scott owned these adjoining lots for most of the last quarter of the 19th century. He built the stucco-faced brick building at 2522-

2524 Market in 1891. As historic photographs and Augustus Koch's bird's-eye panorama "Galveston, Texas, 1885" illustrate, West Market Street was built up with similar two-story business blocks as far west as 29th Street. The pair of buildings at 2526 and 2528 Market are harder to date from existing records. The narrow stucco-faced building at 2526 originally wrapped around the corner building at 2528 Market. This corner building, which appears in C. Drie's "Bird's Eye View of the City of Galveston, Texas, 1871," is a survivor of the type of gable-fronted wooden business house also represented by the Central Hotel at 2401 Market Street. The weathered look of all three buildings is a reminder of how the Strand and Mechanic Street appeared in the 1960s and early 1970s.

2626-2628 Market Street   A–73
Cotton Compress Workers, Inc. Building
1957, Ben J. Kotin & Associates
Working-class culture was at home in this "other" downtown. A modern addition to the district was this office and retail building, built by a union local. Despite hard times, its crisp tile revetment (combined with stucco bands and horizontal strip windows along 27th Street) gives it a pert profile.

A block away at 2801 Market Street is the **International Longshoremen's Association Local Union 851 Building** (1969, John S. Chase), the last new building on the west end of Market Street. It is home to an AFL-CIO affiliate that began in 1898 as the Lone Star Cotton Jammers of Texas, a union composed of African-American workers skilled at tightly "jamming" cotton bales into the holds of ships. The ILA Building was designed by the Houston architect John Chase, the first African American to be licensed to practice architecture in Texas.

2828 Market Street   A–74
Fire Station Number 3
1903
Terminating the western extension of the downtown business district is the ex-Fire Station #3. It possesses the archaic look that stucco-faced Galveston buildings acquire through intensive weathering. The white marble plaque centered beneath the parapet line commemorates the Star State Fire Company, originally organized in 1859 as the city's third volunteer fire-fighting company.

2528 Postoffice Street   A–75
1886
Postoffice Street was the portion of the district where the houses of prostitution clustered. This sober, two-bay-wide, clapboard "house" with a low-pitched hipped roof and boxed eaves is the last survivor. It was built and owned by Miss Mollie Walters, one of the district's most celebrated madams.

2302 Postoffice Street   A–76
Moody National Bank Building
1962, Golemon & Rolfe with John A. Greeson II
1969, Golemon & Rolfe with Ben J. Kotin & Tibor Beerman
The Moody National Bank left the City National Bank's

classical temple on Market Street for what was the preferred bank building type of the 1960s: a one-story, flat-roofed, glass-walled pavilion, raised on a low podium. When the Houston architects Golemon & Rolfe were called back at the end of the decade to add the bank's rear office slab, they registered the influence of *The Galveston That Was* by paying respectful attention to Bulger's Levy Building across Tremont Street and detailing their five-story block with emphatic horizontal belt courses and an overhanging cornice.

512 Tremont Street   **A–77**
Star Drug Store Company Building
1909, N. J. Clayton
Clayton's client for the Star Drug Store job was Houston's foremost female real estate investor of the period, Miss Kate Scanlan, whose family firm owned this and other properties on Tremont Street. Against all odds, Miss Scanlan's tenant, the Star Drug Store, has hung onto the interiors it installed in 1917. The elegant exterior, detailed with Néo-Grec classical decoration, was a continuation of the street façade of the Star Drug Store's next-door neighbor, which Clayton had designed over twenty years earlier for Mrs. Olympia Freybe.

2221-2227 Postoffice Street   **A–78**
Mrs. Olympia Freybe Building
1886, N. J. Clayton
The exterior of Mrs. Freybe's building has not fared as well as the Star Drug Store. Occupied by the Galveston retail firm of E. S. Levy & Company from 1917 until 1979, Mrs. Freybe's building suffered the fate of many Main Street storefronts: owners scraped off as much architectural detail as feasible, then slapped up blank stucco panels to efface

what little was left. In 1993, the Needville, Texas, contractor Earl Barbin removed the stucco panels from the Freybe Building, exposing the remains of Clayton's rhythmic second-floor arcade and distinctive perforated iron columns along the ground floor.

Postoffice Street began to be redeveloped with overflow from the Market Street retail district in the late 1880s. After Market Street acceded to the Strand's historic role as a financial corridor, Postoffice Street became downtown Galveston's primary shopping street, a function it fulfilled into the early 1970s. But the street's primacy was already being challenged in 1970 when the 2100 and 2200 blocks were closed to automobile traffic and a landscaped pedestrian mall, Central Plaza, was installed (Raymond R. Rapp & Associates). As was often the case in American downtowns in the 1950s and 1960s, the mall proved to be more of an obstacle than a help. By the time the street was reopened to traffic in 1990, its stores were almost deserted.

Although the buildings of Postoffice Street are not as monumental as those of the Strand, the 2000 through 2200 blocks retain their spatial integrity to a greater degree. One important element that has been lost are the canopies that extended out in front of buildings to shade sidewalks, a standard amenity in Southern cities. The loss of many sidewalk canopies in downtown Galveston occurred during the 1970s and 1980s, almost without notice, sometimes in conjunction with the rehabilitation of run-down buildings.

2218 Postoffice Street   **A–79**
Chapman & Duffield Bar & Billiard Saloon Building
1868
This two-story brick infill building, with its distinctive corbeled brick cornice, is representative of Postoffice Street's status prior to its absorption into the downtown shopping district in the 1880s. It was originally the Chapman & Duffield Bar & Billiard Saloon, one of a number of saloons and livery establishments that collected on what, in the late 1860s, was the periphery of downtown Galveston.

2213-2215 Postoffice Street   **A–80**
Salzmann-Houlahan Building
1885
This curious two-story building is extremely unusual for

was added in 1930 when the Thompson Building was leased to the J. C. Penney Company. The Postoffice Street front is very simple, relying on the proportions and detailing of the steel-framed window sash and the discreet terra-cotta cartouches above the third-floor windows. It was rehabilitated in 1996.

being built of wood. It was erected just before the disastrous Fire of 1885 caused the City Council to expand the fire district. The upper floor of 2215 was originally the residence of William J. Houlahan, a house painter. Numa Salzmann, a watchmaker and jeweler, lived upstairs above his shop at 2213, which is still occupied by Salzmann's.

2202-2204 Postoffice Street　　　　A–83
Fellman Dry Goods Company Building
1906, Charles W. Bulger
Bulger's touch was not light, nor was his mastery of classical detail beyond reproach. But because he suffered from few architectural inhibitions, he made the most of this commission for Fellman's dry goods store, which occupied all five floors of the building. With this building, Fellman's signaled that Postoffice Street was no longer prepared to subordinate itself to Market Street.

2214-2216 Postoffice Street　　　　A–81
Nathan's
1949, Irving R. Klein & Associates
Nathan's clothing store, which occupied this building until its dissolution in 1975, exemplifies the sleek look of late modernistic retail architecture. Its planar front, the work of Houston architect Irving Klein, is elegantly veneered in limestone slabs and pierced by thin horizontal window slots.

2205 Postoffice Street　　　　A–84
Garbade, Eiband & Company Building
1914, L.S. Green
Eiband's clothing store represents the consolidation of several buildings into a new retail complex, which was refaced and expanded in size with the addition of a fourth floor by the Houston architect Lewis Sterling Green. The middle segment facing Postoffice Street was originally the Ballinger & Jack Building (1870, P. M. Comegys), a three-story professional building erected by Galveston's most prominent law firm. From 1875 until 1890, the Supreme Court of Texas sat in this building. It became part of the core of Eiband's in 1900. The Eiband Building was rehabilitated by Mr. and Mrs. James B. Earthman (1995).

2208 Postoffice Street　　　　A–82
Clark W. Thompson Company Building
1923, 1930
Clark Thompson, the son-in-law of W. L. Moody, Jr., bought out the Fellman Dry Goods Company in 1920 and added this building to its existing complex. The top floor

2128 Postoffice Street　　　　　　　　　　　**A–85**
Pix Building
1859
The Pix Building is a handsome survivor of the pre–Civil War period, when its brick construction, three-story height, and cast-iron window sills and lintels made it a major addition to the landscape of downtown. It was built by Charles H. Pix, an English-born merchant and ship's broker.

2118-2120 Postoffice Street　　　　　　　**A–86**
Knights of Columbus Building
1908, 1916
This building was built as the Peoples Theater, as the rear brick fly tower, visible from the alley, attests. In 1916 it was acquired by the Knights of Columbus fraternal organization and remodeled to provide rental retail space at sidewalk level and lofty upper-floor meeting rooms for the Knights of Columbus. Tall second-story windows and an unusual sloped-roof hood, framed between scroll-topped piers, give the Knights of Columbus Building a pronounced urban presence. The building was rehabilitated in 1996.

Across the street, at 2115 Postoffice, the ex-**S. H. Kress & Company Building** (1924), was rehabilitated in 1994. Its upper floor was converted into residential apartments.

2109 Postoffice Street　　　　　　　　　　**A–87**
Harmony Club Building
1895, N. J. Clayton & Company
This midblock three-story storefront, with its raised central frontispiece, is the modest successor to one of Clayton's most ebullient public buildings, Harmony Hall of 1883 (subsequently the Scottish Rite Temple), located a block away at 2128 Church Street. When the Harmony Club, 19th-century Galveston's most elite Jewish social club, could no longer afford its opulent quarters in Harmony Hall, it had to vacate. The livery stable, carriage depository, and

undertaking firm of J. Levy & Brother built this three-story building as a replacement. The Harmony Club occupied rooms on the upper floors. The sidewalk-level space was rented as income-producing property.

2102-2104 Postoffice Street　　　　　　　**A–88**
Ikelheimer & Company Building (now St. Germain Place)
1898, George B. Stowe
The Galveston-born architect George B. Stowe contributed to the transformation of Postoffice Street in the 1890s with this three-story building for the investor Marx Marx. It was Stowe's first major downtown building, and it led Marx to commission him the next year to design Galveston's first "skyscraper," the six-story Improvement Loan & Trust Company Building (1900, demolished 1955) at 2228 Postoffice and Tremont. Tan brick and classical colonnettes mark Stowe's academic aspirations. But the chamfered corner tower with its conical cap is a vestige of Victorian picturesqueness. The building was remodeled for use as residential apartments in the early 1990s. New ground-floor façades were installed that were intended to be compatible with the historic fabric of the building.

Diagonally across the 21st-Postoffice intersection, another of N. J. Clayton's imposing public buildings of the 1880s once stood, the Masonic Temple (1884). Situated at this intersection today is one of the **Rosenberg Fountains** (1898, J. Massey Rhind, sculptor; installed 1995, Richard C. Ainslie), once located throughout the city. The elaborate public fountains, meant to provide drinking water for both people and animals, were part of the bequest of Henry

Rosenberg. Almost all of the 17 fountains were dismantled between the 1930s and the 1950s, but 10 of them escaped destruction. These were reassembled and reinstalled in various parts of the city beginning in 1965. This fountain, originally located at 20th Street and Mechanic Street in the city market, was installed by Lyda Ann Q. Thomas as a tribute to her parents, Mr. and Mrs. Arthur W. Quinn.

2012-2020 Postoffice Street　　　　　　　**A-89**
Galveston Opera House–Hotel Grand (now 1894 Grand Opera House)
1894–95, Frank Cox with N. Tobey, Jr.

Postoffice Street's fortunes received a boost when the New Orleans–based theatrical impresario Henry Greenwall abandoned the 23-year-old Tremont Opera House (on the site of the Levy Building at 23rd and Market) in 1894 and persuaded a group of Galveston businessmen to invest in the construction of this 1,500-seat theater, with which Greenwall combined a 56-room hotel. Frank Cox, a little-known New Orleans architect and scene painter, designed the building in the round-arched style associated with the great 19th-century Boston architect H. H. Richardson. The fine red pressed brick, the similarly colored panels of terra-cotta ornament distributed across the front façade, and the great, round-arched entrance portal (a partial reconstruction of the original) were all elements of the Richardsonian Romanesque, as H. H. Richardson's personal version of medieval Romanesque architecture came to be known in the 1890s. The Grand operated continuously, first as a venue for live performances, then as a movie theater, until 1974, undergoing inappropriate alterations and suffering from insufficient maintenance along the way. When the theater closed in 1974, it was acquired by the recently organized Galveston County Cultural Arts Council, whose first director, Emily Whiteside, launched the effort to rehabilitate the Grand. The restoration of the stage was carried out by Hardy Holzman Pfeiffer & Associates of New York (1981). The second phase, restoration of the auditorium, lobby, and exterior, was the work of San Antonio architect Killis Almond & Associates (1986). Houston artist Earl Staley is responsible for the florid stage curtain, which was based on photographs of the original, and decorative artist Mary Canales Jary of San Antonio restored the interior stencilwork.

Although the design of the theater's public spaces was even less architecturally advanced than that of its exterior, restoration has performed an important task of preserving

an eminently usable, intimately proportioned, Victorian urban theater. It is the only one of Henry Greenwall's theaters that remains in existence. The 1894 Grand Opera House programs popular entertainment year-round.

1927 Postoffice Street　　　　　　　**A-90**
United States Custom House, Post Office and Court Room
1861, A. B. Young, Supervising Architect of the Treasury

The Custom House was the first civil building constructed by the U.S. government in Texas. Historian Donald J. Lehman, in his book *Lucky Landmark* (1973), sorted out the complicated history of the design of the building. Ammi B. Young, then official U.S. government architect in Washington, D.C., prepared three sets of plans between 1856 and 1860, as the building's contractor, the ex-Savannah architect Charles B. Cluskey, schemed successfully to have Congress adopt modifications based on Cluskey's own designs. After four years of intrigue, the building was built in only four and a half months' time by the experienced Boston contractors Blaisdell & Emerson in order to ensure its completion (and their payment) before Texas seceded from the Union in March 1861.

Young's built design was in the Renaissance revival style, thoughtfully adapted to the humid climate of the Gulf coast with inset loggias on the long north and south sides of the building and an honorific two-story portico on the west-facing 20th Street side. Elongated casement windows set in architrave-capped, paneled frames hint at the developing Victorian taste for verticality, although these are countered by the horizontal belt course that separates the first and second floors. This exhibits very refined detailing. The same observation can be made of the building's materials—the gray granite plinth and the walls of sand-surfaced salmon-colored brick. It was in the realm of materials that the Custom House was most innovative. Young specified extensive use of galvanized cast iron for architectural detail (as rust spots make evident) and, even more notably, of wrought-iron structural beams and cast-iron columns to support the building's interior.

The Custom House narrowly escaped destruction in the great East End fire of November 1885, which scorched its east side and consumed the buildings that surrounded it. Following efforts by U.S. District Judge and Mrs. James L. Noel to ensure that the General Services Administration neither sell nor demolish the building, it was rehabilitated in phases between 1967 and 1972. Further rehabilitation was completed in 1985 (Graham B. Luhn, architect) to repair extensive damage incurred when a boiler exploded. In 1977, the Custom House was illustrated on a U.S. Postal Service commemorative postcard. Although long supplemented by additional federal office buildings in Galveston, the Custom House remains a property of the U.S. government.

1902 Postoffice Street   A–91
1890

What makes this five-bay-wide, raised cottage with front porch and double-window dormers unusual is that it was built of brick rather than wood, the nearly universal material for residential construction in 19th-century Galveston. The explanation is probably linked to the devastating fire of 13 November 1885, the greatest urban disaster to befall Galveston prior to the Storm of 1900. The fire burned buildings as far west as 20th Street north of Broadway. In response, the City Council adopted new protective ordinances, including a "fire limit" zone encompassing downtown and its surroundings, where use of noncombustible materials for new construction was mandatory. This cottage, built for the bookkeeper James S. DeForest, sat just inside the fire limit zone. Hence its brick construction.

424 19th Street   A–92
Salvation Army Chapel (now Galveston Bible Church)
1924

This small chapel is a particularly graceful building, combining Spanish Mission–style profiling with an arched Palladian window on its Postoffice Street side. It deftly marks the transition from downtown to the residential East End.

509 19th Street   A–93
1888, John Hourigan, builder

Like the raised brick cottage at 1902 Postoffice, this gable-fronted two-story dwelling house represents a building type constructed almost exclusively in wood in Galveston, but executed here in brick because it lay inside the newly mandated fire limit. Exterior surfaces were not only stuccoed and scored but marbleized, an unusual treatment in Galveston. What makes this house, built for Mrs. Eliza Moser, doubly unusual is that the type it represents was associated primarily with commercial houses (such as the Central Hotel) rather than with dwelling houses, which is the purpose Mrs. Moser's house was built to serve. Mrs. Moser's building was handsomely restored in 1996 by the Dallas designer Ron Bryan.

1903 Church Street   A–94
First Presbyterian Church
1876, 1889, Jones & Baldwin with N. J. Clayton
1912, T. William English Memorial Building, Donald N. McKenzie

The First Presbyterian Church is one of the landmarks of Victorian architecture in Texas. Designed by the Memphis architects Edward C. Jones and Matthias H. Baldwin, it transmitted the influence of the 19th-century French architectural theorist Eugène Emmanuel Viollet-le-Duc to the shores of the Gulf of Mexico. Viollet-le-Duc's impact is visible in the masterful shaping of the church's exterior wall surfaces as planar masses, from which piers, labels, and moldings seem to have been extruded, so that the white painted stucco surfaces (scored to simulate stone blocks) display plastic vigor yet are rigorously simple.

Despite its assured appearance, the First Presbyterian Church had a complicated building history. During the post–Civil War boom, the congregation called a new pastor, the Rev. R. F. Bunting, who commissioned what was described at the time as a Norman-style church ("Norman" was a favored 19th-century stylistic term for medieval English Romanesque architecture) from E. C. Jones, a major Charleston architect who relocated his practice to Memphis after the Civil War. Jones was a Presbyterian and had designed several Presbyterian churches in Charleston. Published descriptions at the time the cornerstone was laid in 1872 stated that the First Presbyterian Church would seat 800 and would be faced with two towers, one 80 feet high, the other 190 feet high. N. J. Clayton, who had only recently arrived in Houston from Cincinnati, where he grew up, moved to Galveston to supervise construction of the church building.

The Panic of 1873 deflated the Gilded Age economic boom, and the congregation had to struggle to complete the shell of the building and roof it by mid-1876, when the chapel (facing Church Street) was dedicated. Not until 1887 did the *Galveston Daily News* report the resumption of construction. The towers were completed to Clayton's design (neither achieved the originally planned height), and in 1888–89 the interior of the church was built according to the designs of the Houston architect George E. Dickey, who was a Presbyterian. Despite its protracted construction, the First Presbyterian Church presents itself as a powerfully integrated work of architecture, not the result of piecemeal changes by different architects.

Projecting from the south side of the building, abutting the alley, is the T. William English Memorial Building by Donald N. McKenzie (1912). Both McKenzie and his contemporaries, the architects George B. and Elwood E. Stowe, were members of the congregation. The First Presbyterian Church was restored in 1994 by architect David Watson.

2010 Church Street   **A–95**
c. 1867

2006 Church Street
1912

This row of houses is a fragment of the neighborhood that, well into the 20th century, signified the predominantly residential character of Church Street. Despite the

conservative appearance resulting from its raised, two-story veranda, the Miller-Herman Boarding House was unusual in having two big projecting bays symmetrically aligned on either side of the front door. The house at 2010 Church, by comparison, exemplifies the two-story-high, three-bay-wide, side-hall, Southern town house prefaced with a double-level veranda, one of the most characteristic house types of 19th-century Galveston.

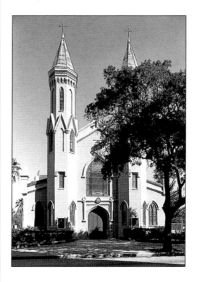

2011 Church Street   **A–96**
St. Mary's Cathedral (now St. Mary's Cathedral Basilica)
1848, T. E. Giraud
1878, 1890, N. J. Clayton
Rectory, 1929, R. R. Rapp

Church Street takes its name from St. Mary's Cathedral, built by the first Bishop of Galveston, the Most Rev. John M. Odin, to serve as cathedral of the diocese, which then encompassed almost the entire state of Texas. In 1845 the bishop was given one-half million Belgian bricks, which were shipped from Antwerp to Galveston. Construction of St. Mary's commenced in 1847, as the inscribed marble plaque above the pointed arch window facing 21st Street indicates. When completed in 1848, St. Mary's Cathedral was the first monumental work of civil architecture to be built in Texas since the Franciscan mission churches of the mid-18th century.

St. Mary's is representative of American Gothic Revival churches of the 1840s. The taut, smoothly planed shapes and blocky molding profiles of St. Mary's identify it as Early Victorian, in contrast to the High Victorian sense of depth, plasticity, and movement visible in the façades of the First Presbyterian Church. Interior detail at St. Mary's is attenuated in profile, so that a lightweight feeling prevails inside as well as out.

The architectural historian Willard B. Robinson established the identity of the cathedral's architect, Theodore E. Giraud, the Charleston-born, Paris-educated, younger brother—and sometime collaborator—of San Antonio architect François Giraud. Unlike his elder brother,

T. E. Giraud was peripatetic. In Galveston, he met and married the Scottish-born Margaret Sturrock. They moved to New Orleans, where Giraud designed a number of Catholic churches. After the fall of New Orleans early in the Civil War, Giraud and his family went to Monterrey, Nuevo León, where he was city engineer at the time of his death in 1863.

Between the 1870s and 1890s, N. J. Clayton was involved in several episodes of alterations. From 1874 to 1878 the interior was remodeled and improved, and the tower carrying a votive statue of the Blessed Virgin Mary was erected. In 1890, Clayton raised and recapped the twin towers flanking the 21st Street entrance as part of another program of extensive exterior and interior improvements. The sanctuary was refinished with mosaic tile paving, marble wainscoting, and a new marble altar in 1907, when the present pews were installed in the nave and the exterior of the cathedral was surfaced in stucco. Further marble additions were made to the sanctuary in 1922. However, the interior of the cathedral essentially retained the appearance it achieved with Clayton's remodeling of 1890. This was altered drastically in 1976 when the interior was repainted a glaring white, effacing the darker, more subtle coloration that had prevailed there.

The cathedral's original rectory was demolished and replaced by a new, but sympathetically scaled and detailed rectory by R. R. Rapp in 1929. Between the rectory and the back of the cathedral, on axis with Clayton's tower and facing Church Street, is a tensely bifurcated, two-story gabled bay, a small but forceful reminder of Clayton's presence.

St. Mary's was designated co-cathedral of the diocese when the see was transferred to Houston in 1959. In recognition of its antiquity, the cathedral was raised to the status of a minor basilica in 1979.

2105 Church Street   **A–97**
Jean Lafitte Hotel
1927, Andrew Fraser
The 10-story Jean Lafitte is representative of the type of urban "skyscraper" hotel built to serve business travelers in (and advertise the progressiveness of) Texas towns and small cities during the 1920s. Its L-shaped plan, planar street façades, stone base, light brown tapestry brick walls, and cast

stone historical ornamental detail (in this case, 18th-century English neoclassical in style) are all characteristic features. These features are also visible in the 5-story **Illies Building/Justine Apartments** a half-block away at 503 21st Street (1929, Donald N. McKenzie), built by C. J. H. Illies and his half-brother, architect McKenzie, as a memorial to their mother. Together with the **Martini Theater** at 524 21st Street and Church (1937, W. Scott Dunne), these buildings form a small outpost of "modern" commercial architecture that Galveston real-estate investors hoped would imbue downtown with a more up-to-date, post-Victorian image.

2116 Church Street   **A–98**
Electric Service Company Building
1927, R. R. Rapp
Contributing to this outpost was Raymond R. Rapp's major downtown building, a three-story, tapestry brick–faced office and showroom building.

2128 Church Street   **A–99**
Scottish Rite Cathedral
1929, Alfred C. Finn
The Scottish Rite Cathedral is one of Galveston's major examples of the modernistic Art Deco style popular in the late 1920s and early 1930s. It was built to replace N. J. Clayton's extravagant Harmony Hall (acquired by the Scottish Rite Masons after being vacated by the Harmony Club, it burned in 1928). H. Jordan MacKenzie, designer for the Houston architect Alfred C. Finn, produced an appropriately hermetic-looking building, surfaced with brown tapestry brick and cast stone. As was characteristic of 1920s' architecture, MacKenzie used variations in window and door placements to suggest the internal spatial organization of the building, especially the presence of an auditorium on the second floor. The loggia facing Church

Street and the tall, thin, cast stone–framed apertures above the rear (22nd Street) entrance are notable elements, as are the cast stone relief sculpture and the ornamental copper doors and lanterns.

2202-2206 Church Street   A–100

Telephone Building

1896, Alfred Muller

After N. J. Clayton, Galveston's best-known Victorian architect was Alfred Muller, who had been born and trained in Prussia. Muller died in a typhoid epidemic in 1896, the year the Telephone Building, his only major downtown building, was completed. Built for the Southwestern Telegraph and Telephone Company, it has lost most of its ground-floor detail as well as Muller's exuberant brickwork, which has been stuccoed over. The Telephone Building retains its big-scaled, handsomely profiled third-floor arched windows and the curvilinear gable and cylindrical columns that mark the 22nd Street entrance bay. This is only the residue of what the Telephone Building was like in its heyday.

At the opposite end of the 2200 block of Church is another three-story building, the **Pearce and Wilder Building** at 514-528 Tremont (1915, C. D. Hill & Company). Designed by one of Dallas's most prolific architects, the Pearce and Wilder Building indicates how tame commercial architecture became in the early 20th century in comparison with the generous scale and confident assertiveness that the Telephone Building originally exhibited. Both the Telephone Building and the Pearce and Wilder Building play important urban roles by anchoring the corners of this block.

2401 Church Street   A–101

D. C. & M. Jordan Building

1880

The Galveston corner store type is visible here at its most architecturally refined. The characteristic Victorian Italianate details of bracketed eaves and low-pitched hipped roof economically decorate a two-story wood clapboard building with ranks of double-leaf doors at street level and a sidewalk canopy to shade them. From 24th Street, the rear L-wing of the Jordan brothers' grocery, crockery, and liquor store building, with its back porch signaling the presence of

the family residential quarters, is visible. The brothers David C. and Michael M. Jordan operated the business and lived upstairs with their mother, Mary Jordan. At the 24th Street–Church intersection, where such buildings anchor three of the four corners (the Frederick C. Schmidt carriage manufacturing shop occupied **2402 Church**), one experiences a fragment of the Galveston that was. Late-19th-century photographs indicate that block fronts in these neighborhoods south of the business district proper were tightly packed with two-story wood buildings. Dwelling houses were interspersed among commercial buildings.

2406 Church Street   A–102

c. 1869

This is a characteristic example of the Southern town house type. The octagonal columns and the paired brackets beneath the eaves of the roof represent a combination of details associated with the post–Civil War period, when the carpenter's Greek Revival that had been popular in Galveston was beginning its migration toward more assertive Victorian shapes. The house was built by James P. Nash, a school teacher, who seems to have used it as rental property.

513-525 Rosenberg Avenue   A–103

Model Laundry & Dye Works Building

1913, Green & Finger

Joseph Finger was an Austrian immigrant who, in the 1920s, would become one of Houston's leading commercial architects. During his brief partnership with Lewis Sterling Green, he had the opportunity to undertake his first major commissions, all in Galveston. Perhaps because it was built at a time when there was concern for endowing Rosenberg

Avenue with a dignified appearance, Finger faced the Model Laundry in white glazed brick and marked it off with wide structural bays of reinforced concrete that facilitated its use as one of the city's biggest commercial laundries. These bays are filled in with wooden window and door sash whose faded green color contrasts with the weathered white of the brick. At the time this building was constructed, the Model Laundry was the only steam laundry in Galveston and the city's most up-to-date commercial laundry.

601 Rosenberg Avenue   A–104
United States Post Office, Custom House, and Court House
1937, Alfred C. Finn with Andrew Fraser; Louis A. Simon,
Supervising Architect of the Treasury

By the early 1880s, the U.S. Custom House on Postoffice Street was inadequate to contain all the federal offices in Galveston. To supplement it, a new U.S. Courthouse, Post Office, and Custom House was built at the corner of Rosenberg and Church between 1886 and 1891. By the mid-1930s that ponderous Victorian building had also become inadequate, even though a separate Custom House had been built on Strand in 1933. Therefore, this six-story federal building, occupying the entire block front on Rosenberg, was authorized. Designed by Alfred C. Finn of Houston, it exemplifies the penchant of American architecture during the New Deal era for simultaneous assertions of modernity and tradition. The building is faced with Texas Cordova limestone, a fossilated limestone frequently used for public buildings in Texas during the 1930s and 1940s because of its regional connotation. A Texas granite plinth and red tile roof coping further regionalize the federal building's modernistic classicism. Finn's office streamlined classical detail to a bare minimum, as the vestigial "pilasters," represented by vertical fluting at each end of the building, and the line of ghost "guttae"

(small blocklike projections that hang beneath a classical frieze of the Doric order) between the second- and third-floor windows suggest. The ends are emphasized rather than the center of the symmetrically organized front façade. The architecture is neither imaginative nor especially endearing. Yet it succeeds as an expression of public dignity, one that has weathered the climatic extremes of Galveston with admirable durability.

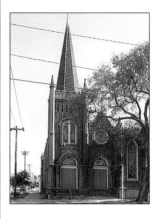

2401 Winnie Avenue   A–105
First Lutheran Church
1868
1916, W. S. Murdock

Although overshadowed by the newer limestone-faced, neo-Gothic **First Evangelical Lutheran Church** at Rosenberg and Winnie (1959, by San Antonio architects Henry Steinbomer and Jack L. Duffin with Thomas M. Price of Galveston), the original First Lutheran Church building survives on its original site, although raised, refaced, and expanded with the addition of a new corner tower and front façade by the Galveston architect W. S. Murdock in 1916. Like St. Joseph's, the German Catholic church at 2202 Avenue K, First Lutheran originally embodied the vernacular Southern church type. It was a gable-roofed, clapboard-faced wooden box with a short tower centered on the narrow front of the building, and its side walls were lined with tall, slender windows. Murdock's modernizing additions (which look more Victorian than the original church did) have not effaced First Lutheran's simplicity.

Across the street, at 2402 Winnie Avenue, is the **Ladies Aid Society House** (1905, Donald N. McKenzie), built, as the name suggests, by the women of First Lutheran. The square proportions, double-level verandas, transomed doors, and shuttered windows give it a slightly old-fashioned look that seems characteristic of much of McKenzie's residential architecture.

2310 Ball Avenue   **A–106**

c. 1853

This house, built by J. J. Thompson and subsequently operated as a boarding house by his widow Rhoda A. Thompson, is an example of another popular 19th-century Galveston house type, the I-house, so called because the plan of the house resembles the letter I. In Galveston, such houses were customarily prefaced with verandas, giving them a Southern accent. Mrs. Thompson bought this property in 1845. The tightly compressed proportions of her house were characteristic of Galveston houses of the 1840s and 1850s. Down the block, at 2328 Ball, is the ex-**Galveston Model Dairy Building** (1963, Ben J. Kotin & Tibor Beerman), a small, one-story office building that architecturally exhibits its precast concrete construction.

823 Tremont Street   **A–107**

Rosenberg Library

1904, Eames & Young

Henry Rosenberg charged the trustees of his estate with building and equipping what remains Galveston's foremost cultural institution, the public library dedicated to its benefactor's memory. Although their plans were delayed by the Storm of 1900, the Rosenberg trustees held an invited architectural competition in 1901, which led them to select the St. Louis architects Eames & Young to design the present building. The Rosenberg Library was one of the first generation of public libraries to be built in Texas, and it is one of the few buildings of that era that still remains in operation as a library.

Eames & Young produced a simply composed but boldly decorated two-story pavilion. It is the building's expansive scale and the exuberance of its terra-cotta classical decor that give it a strong figural presence. When the Rosenberg

opened, the speaker invited to dedicate its lecture hall was the Unitarian minister Jenkin Lloyd Jones, uncle of the architect Frank Lloyd Wright. Stationed before the Tremont entrance portal to the library is a seated bronze statue of **Henry Rosenberg** (1906, Louis Amateis, sculptor).

In 1971, the Rosenberg Library was more than doubled in size with the addition of the **Moody Memorial Wing,** through whose Sealy Avenue portal the public now enters the building. Designed by Galveston architect Thomas M. Price, it is a windowless, concrete-framed, travertine-faced box, designed to be as unobtrusive as possible. At the time the Moody Wing was added, the interiors of the original building (which now contains special collections and exhibition spaces) were remodeled, for the most part in inappropriate ways.

On the third floor of the Moody Wing is the **Galveston and Texas History Center,** one of the major research archives in Texas. It contains extensive collections relating to the history of Galveston, including a large archive of architectural drawings and office records of N. J. Clayton.

In the park north of the library building, facing Tremont Street, is one of J. Massey Rhind's **Rosenberg Fountains** (1898), installed in 1995. Among the most monumental of his fountains, it originally sat in the intersection of the Strand and Rosenberg Avenue.

Across from the front of the Rosenberg Library, at 822 Tremont Street, is the **First Baptist Church** (1958, Easterwood & Easterwood), designed by a firm of Waco architects especially identified with Baylor University, the largest Baptist educational institution in Texas. Its neo-Georgian look was the most popular architectural image for well-heeled Protestant congregations in Texas during the 1940s and 1950s. The First Baptist congregation has occupied this block since 1846. Previous churches faced 22nd Street, however, rather than Tremont. When the present building was constructed, the congregation demolished the John Sealy House of 1868, which occupied this site, so that they would not have to demolish their old church until the new one was built.

902-912 Tremont Street   **A–108**

1909

A curious survivor of the Sealy homestead is located across Sealy Avenue from the First Baptist Church. This is the two-story, brick and tile-roofed John H. Sealy Garage, built by the banker John Sealy's son across from the family home where he and his brother-in-law and sister, Mrs. and Mrs.

R. Waverly Smith, lived after their mother's death. Without doubt the grandest residential garage in Galveston, the Sealy Garage was so substantial that in 1940 one-story wings were added to each side of the building, and it was transformed into an auto showroom.

906 22nd Street   **A–109**
Medical Building (now El Cortez Apartments)
1924, R. R. Rapp
Although this stucco-faced building, crowned with scalloped Mission-style parapets, looks like it was meant to be an apartment building, it was built as a medical professional building by Dr. Frederick W. Aves. The Medical Building was an early indication of the spread of professional and business buildings beyond the downtown core to precincts where parking the car was easier.

816 22nd Street   **A–110**
Congregation B'nai Israel Temple (now Masonic Temple Building)
1871, Fred S. Steward
1887, N. J. Clayton
1890, N. J. Clayton & Company
Henry Cohen Community House, 1928, R. R. Rapp
Temple B'nai Israel stands out despite the defacement it suffered after Congregation B'nai Israel forsook its original house of worship for new quarters on Avenue O in 1955. Like other 19th-century religious monuments in the Central Park area, its architectural history was episodic. Thin-ribbed buttresses visible along the Sealy Avenue side of the temple mark the original building, a high-raised synagogue of vaguely Gothic Revival character by F. S.

Steward, an itinerant architect who practiced briefly in Galveston in the early 1870s.

N. J. Clayton was called on in 1887 to add a new entrance front to the synagogue, facing 22nd Street. His bravura frontispiece, containing the Tablets of the Law in the high peaked gable that frames a projecting arched opening, is flanked by chamfered-corner wings lit by horseshoe-arched windows. Historic photographs show that what remains today is the ghost of what once existed: corner tourelles, striped banding in the arched labels above window and door openings, and stained glass ornately framed in the now-blocked windows were bold, colorful components of the design. Like other High Victorian architects, Clayton sought to impress the synagogue with a Levantine aspect, a sort of Jewish analogue to the Gothic Revival. However, when Clayton expanded the temple to provide space for a Sabbath school (the congregation adopted Reform Judaism in 1890 under a new rabbi, Dr. Henry Cohen), he did so by discreetly adding extra bays to the rear end of Steward's original building.

In 1928, the congregation had R. R. Rapp design the adjoining Henry Cohen Community House in tribute to the congregation's longtime and best-known rabbi. As with Rapp's rectory at St. Mary's Cathedral, McKenzie's English Memorial Building at First Presbyterian, and the Stowes' parish house at Trinity, it displays the tactful deference of early-20th-century Galveston architects to the city's Victorian architectural monuments.

2117 Ball Avenue   **A–111**
1881
Built for the watchmaker and jeweler Julius Socha, this house stands among a row of substantial wooden houses that once marked the neighborhood south of Central Park as quite respectable. In 1969, the Socha House was used as an example of the conditions that authorization of an Urban Renewal program by Galveston voters would eradicate. The failure of this referendum lent momentum to preservationists' efforts to renew the city's historical fabric rather than destroy it wholesale. Next door, at **2113 Ball Avenue,** is the architecturally similar house that the paving and roofing contractor James W. Byrnes built in 1884.

721 22nd Street   **A–112**

Eaton Memorial Chapel

1879, Clayton & Lynch

Henry Rosenberg's first conspicuous act of philanthropy was to finance construction of a free-standing parish house and chapel dedicated to the memory of the Rev. Benjamin Eaton, the first rector of Galveston's oldest Episcopal parish, Trinity Church. Although the pyramidal ascent of pointed gable shapes is the most visible element on both street faces of the chapel, Clayton lent these shapes sculptural presence and depth by outlining them with stepped, molded bands, so that they figure boldly against the building's broad, planar, stucco-surfaced walls. Big scale is an essential Victorian effect. The interior contains classrooms on the first floor and a lofty auditorium on the second, which could also be used as a chapel. Eaton Chapel was eventually linked to Trinity Church by the arcaded **Parish House** (1930, Stowe & Stowe). Where it opens onto Ball Avenue, one can appreciate George and Elwood Stowe's efforts to replicate Clayton's vigorous scale and detail (very unfashionable in the 1920s and early 1930s) as a way to tie the new addition to Eaton Chapel. Projecting from the rear of the Parish House towards Tremont Street is **Moody Hall** (1968, Charles L. Zwiener).

Across Ball Avenue from the side of Eaton Chapel was the stupendous Herman Marwitz House (1894, Alfred Muller), a three-story-on-raised-basement brick pile that made up in height what it lacked in terms of site. It was demolished in 1969 by the First Baptist Church.

701 22nd Street   **A–113**

Trinity Church

1857, John de Young

Trinity Church, one of the oldest Episcopal church buildings in Texas, possesses the big scale of Eaton Chapel if not its sculptural assurance. The sturdy brown brick Gothic Revival–style church, with its low central tower, was the work of the Irish-born architect and master builder John de Young, who also designed and built St. Mary's University and the Ursuline Convent, Galveston's other two major institutional buildings of the 1850s, both now lost. De Young's approach to the revival of Gothic architecture was artisanal, as the curious buttresses that radiate from salient corners of the tower suggest. But the church has a weightiness and dignity that have served it well through subsequent cycles of stylistic change.

The interior of Trinity Church is simple and dimly lit. During the course of its history, it has undergone numerous minor alterations. The long south wall, facing Eaton Chapel, was blown down in the Storm of 1900. But the roof held and the church escaped destruction. During the grade-raising of Galveston, Trinity, like other old buildings of brick-bearing-wall construction, was laboriously elevated in height on hand-turned jacks, so that new foundations could be built. During 1905, N. J. Clayton remodeled the rear chancel wall to accommodate the Tiffany Studios' stained glass window donated by Mrs. George Sealy as a memorial to her husband.

Although the parish has been very respectful of its historic buildings, its parking lot at Tremont and Winnie consumed N. J. Clayton's Tartt Building of 1900.

621 21st Street   **A–114**

YWCA Building (now Jackson Square Building)

1924, William Ward Watkin with F. & A. B. Ware

George Ball's daughter, Mrs. J. C. League, built the graceful, stucco-faced, tile-roofed YWCA Building as a memorial to her daughter, Mrs. Waters S. Davis, Jr. William Ward Watkin of Houston, the first professor of architecture at the Rice Institute, designed the YWCA in the Italian Mediterranean style that he frequently employed in Houston. Raised on a high basement, it makes the most of a simple contrast between the arched windows of the first floor and the shuttered 12-pane-over-12-pane windows above these.

Watkin subtly emphasized the 21st-Winnie corner of the building, rather than either of its two street façades, by setting the building back from the sidewalk line and using the stepped parapet of the entrance stair to reinforce diagonal (rather than head-on) lines of sight. Houston developer J. R. McConnell rescued the YWCA Building from near dereliction in 1984. But to make it profitable as an office building, he had the Galveston architects Gaertner & Watson add a new top floor, which, although unobtrusive, competes visually with Watkin's building beneath.

When a gymnasium bay was added to the Winnie Avenue side of the YWCA, Watkin faced its entrance with a cast stone classical portico that continues to enliven this block. On the west end of the block, at 622 22nd and Winnie, is the modern **622 Building** (1963, Ben J. Kotin & Tibor Beerman).

Across the street from the YWCA at 2115 Winnie is the **American Indemnity Company Building** (1955, Charles L. Zwiener; 1968, Louis L. Oliver). Its bow-fronted, aluminum, glass, and concrete curtain-wall center section spans between an unlikely pair of three-story wings, the remnants of **Ball High School** (1924, William B. Ittner of St. Louis with DeWitt & Lemmon of Dallas). Ball High School, Galveston's first purpose-built public high school, was constructed on this block, facing Ball Avenue, in 1884 by Mrs. League's father, George Ball, in an act of civic philanthropy (Ball, his partner John Sealy, and Henry Rosenberg invested heavily in competitive philanthropy in the 1880s). Ball's widow, Sarah Catherine Perry Ball, retained N. J. Clayton to design a flamboyant, domed addition to the rear of the original building (1891). The extant pair of wings framed Clayton's florid Victorian classical façade. When the present Ball High School was completed on Avenue O in 1954, this block was sold to the Texas Prudential Insurance Company. All but the 1924 wings were demolished. These were converted to office space. On the site of the demolished building, Texas Prudential's successor, American Indemnity Group, expanded the complex with a stepped seven-story annex (1979, Rapp Fash Sundin).

722 21st Street   A–115
Galveston County Courthouse
1966, Raymond R. Rapp & Associates and Ben J. Kotin &
Tibor Beerman
Built astride the right-of-way of 20th Street and to one side

of (rather than centered on) its block, this administration building is representative of the bland county courthouses constructed in Texas since the 1950s. Its peculiar siting results from its being built around the preceding Victorian county courthouse and county jail buildings, which were demolished upon completion of the present building.

Galveston was never lucky when it came to county courthouse architecture. When Galveston County outgrew its 1857 courthouse (located on the Ball Avenue side of this block), the Commissioners Court elected to have Eugene T. Heiner of Houston expand and reface the 1857 building (completed 1882) rather than build a new one. That courthouse burned in 1896. To replace it, the Commissioners Court retained N. J. Clayton to design what would have been a magnificent Romanesque-style courthouse. But Clayton fell afoul of what he believed to be an intrigue between one of the county commissioners and the Fort Worth architect Marshall R. Sanguinet. The commissioner in question succeeded twice in having Clayton's commission revoked. The second time it was awarded to Sanguinet, whose firm, Messer, Sanguinet & Messer, was responsible for the imposing but graceless courthouse completed in 1899 and demolished in 1966. Clayton sued the Commissioners Court to recover fees for the full set of construction documents his office had prepared. He lost the case and subsequent appeals, which contributed to the precipitous decline of his career after 1902 and his bankruptcy in 1904.

The Courthouse faces **Central Park,** one of two public squares depicted on William H. Sandusky's 1845 Plan of the City of Galveston map. (Two additional public squares were dedicated by the Galveston City Company in accord with John D. Groesbeck's 1838 town plan, which called for public squares to be located at 10-block intervals between Avenues G [Winnie] and H [Ball].) Central Park was not improved and landscaped as a public park until 1873–74. It is unlike the archetypal Texas courthouse square in that the Courthouse faces the square, rather than being located in it. Central Park also lay in a near-town residential neighborhood, rather than in the business district, so that it has never figured as the city's symbolic spatial center, as do more typical Texas county courthouse squares. Instead, it is a pleasant midtown park. Central Park contains the one **Rosenberg Fountain** (1896, J. Massey Rhind, sculptor) that has remained in its original location, although it was moved from the center of the square when the bronze and granite Confederate memorial **Dignified Resignation** (1911) was installed there in 1912.

615 19th Street   A–116
(now Galveston County Parks and Recreation Building)
1886
Today, 19th Street marks a clear boundary between the Downtown–Central Park area and the residential East End neighborhood. But in the 19th century, this transition was much more gradual. The Victorian cottage at 615 19th Street was built by Dr. Cary H. Wilkinson to replace an earlier house destroyed in the great fire of 1885, which

burned its way around the First Presbyterian Church. Galveston County has rehabilitated the Wilkinson House to serve as headquarters for the Galveston County Parks and Recreation Department.

1923 Sealy Avenue   A–117
1896

The construction of a new Central Methodist Church in 1902 at 19th and Sealy emphasized the transition from the East End to the Central Park neighborhood. When the congregation moved to the Moody Memorial First United Methodist Church in 1964, the old church was demolished and its property sold to the State of Texas, which constructed office buildings on the north side of Sealy, even more sharply differentiating this block from those in the East End. Fortunately, the south side of the street is largely intact. This house, built by the tobacconist E. Samuels, appears to be the work of George B. Stowe. Stowe was responsible for the J. J. Davis House at **1915 Sealy** (1906) and the Dr. Seth M. Morris House at **1919 Sealy** (1906).

2017, 2019, 2021, & 2023 Sealy Avenue   A–118
(now called Rainbow Row)

1904, Robert Palliser, builder

The conservatism of Galveston house typologies is exemplified by these speculatively built two-story houses, two pairs of architectural twins. Built as investment property by the contractor Robert Palliser, they preserved the side-hall-plan Southern town-house type popular since

the founding of Galveston. The row was rehabilitated in the 1970s. In 1990 they were saved from imminent demolition when the Galveston Historical Foundation persuaded the Resolution Trust Corporation, which owned them, to donate them to the foundation. Rehabilitated under the direction of architect David Watson with substantial contributions of donated labor and materials, they were sold by the foundation as affordable housing to qualified low- and moderate-income families.

2102 Sealy Avenue   A–119
c. 1870

This unusual-looking house, built by Mrs. Emilia Gengler, exemplifies a phenomenon that was common in 19th- and early-20th-century Galveston: increasing the height of a house by adding a new floor beneath the existing house. The 1871 C. Drie bird's-eye view of Galveston depicts this as a two-story house with front verandas and a low hipped roof.

2020 Broadway   **A–120**
1906, George B. Stowe

This high-raised house, with its buoyant double veranda, is all that remains of a row of houses, most of them built after 1900, that stood at the west edge of Broadway's East End. Stowe designed this house for the moneylender and jeweler Sam Migel.

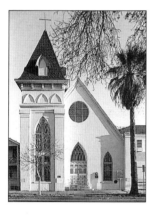

2013 Broadway   **A–121**
Reedy Chapel AME Church
1888, B. G. Chisolm

Reedy Chapel African Methodist Episcopal Church began as the slave congregation of the First Methodist Church. The congregation, one of the oldest African-American institutions in Texas, has occupied this site since 1848. Its church, built to replace a building destroyed in the Fire of 1885, is a simply profiled High Victorian structure of stucco-faced brick. An unusual feature is the pyramid-roofed tower, which rises out of the body of the church building rather than standing in front of, or alongside, it. This is the only Galveston building that can be attributed to Benjamin G. Chisolm, an itinerant architect who worked in Colorado and Alabama, in addition to Galveston. The church contains a very fine High Victorian Gothic organ case. The building was rehabilitated in 1995 by David Watson. Unfortunately, the blocks of Broadway west of 19th Street have lost the historic integrity that still prevails in the East End, as well as in the neighborhoods just south of Broadway. Thus, Reedy Chapel survives as an isolated fragment, stranded amidst parking lots and convenience shopping strips.

2217 Broadway   **A–122**
1884, N. Tobey, Jr.

Built for the sash, door, and blinds manufacturer John F. Smith, this simply configured but generously scaled Italianate-style town house is encrusted with such characteristic features as the paired brackets that support the cornice, elaborately scrolled and spindled shapes around the entrance canopy and front window bay, and the deep-set paneled entrance alcove. Coordinated coloring, applied when the house was rehabilitated, accentuates the multiple shapes and layers of trimwork with which Tobey animated its clapboard exteriors. The Smith House retains such typical Galveston elements as its tall iron fence and dark, tile-paved sidewalk.

2328 Broadway   **A–123**
Ashton Villa
1859

As Howard Barnstone wrote in *The Galveston That Was,* Ashton Villa was the first of the "Broadway palaces," the string of grand houses that represented the wealth and achievement of Galveston's self-made men in the last decades of the 19th century. Built by the wholesale hardware merchant, railroad corporation president, and banker J. M. Brown, it was the grandest, most stylistically current house in Texas at the time it was completed. Constructed of brick and decorated with cast iron, Ashton Villa is an example of the Italianate villa house type popular in the United States in the 1840s and 1850s. Its architecture and plan seem to be based on a design published by the Philadelphia architect Samuel Sloan. The cast-iron fence, with its famous cornstalk gateposts, was fabricated by Wood & Perot of Philadelphia, and it is assumed that the two-story cast-iron porch and the cast-iron sills and scrolled lintels (restored in 1996 by Galveston blacksmith Doug McLean) were also ordered from Wood & Perot. None of Brown's papers survive, so it has never been possible to identify the architect of Ashton Villa.

Kenneth Hafertepe, in his book *A History of Ashton Villa,* documents the alterations that the Brown family made to the house during their long tenure there. The chamfered wing that projects from the east side of the house, and also the stepped, double-height space that connects the back of the house to its still extant rear service buildings, are later additions. The rear service wing was itself a symbol of Ashton Villa's grandeur. Not only were its several components built of brick, but their design was coordinated architecturally with that of the main house.

From 1927 until 1970 Ashton Villa was owned and occupied by El Mina Shrine Temple (which added the back building). When the Shriners decided to sell the property, the house faced imminent demolition. A group of preservationists led by Patti Steph and Sally Wallace persuaded the City of Galveston to take the then-unprecedented step of buying the property with funds from the Department of Housing and Urban Development and the Moody Foundation to prevent demolition. The Galveston Historical Foundation took charge of restoring the house, under the direction of the dean of Texas restoration architects, Raiford Stripling of San Augustine. Houston decorative arts historian David B. Warren prepared a furnishings plan that was implemented by a corps of volunteers directed by co-chairpersons Mrs. A. D. Lasell and Edward R. Thompson, Jr. Since 1974, Ashton Villa has been open to the public as a historic house museum. Although it retains only a few pieces of the Brown family's original furniture, much of the architectural detail remains intact, as well as the decorative paintings executed by Brown's eldest daughter, Rebecca Ashton Brown.

Ashton Villa was an exceptional house by Texas standards. Its survival and preservation are no less exceptional.

2424 Broadway   A–124

The Open Gates
1891, McKim, Mead & White
Stable 1892, N. J. Clayton & Co.
In 1886, the banker and railroad corporation president George Sealy successfully negotiated the sale of the Gulf, Colorado & Santa Fe Railway to the Atcheson, Topeka & Santa Fe line. This produced windfall profits for the Galveston businessmen who had invested in the GC & SF railway when it was chartered in 1873 and fueled the competitive mansion-building along Broadway that began in the mid-1870s. Built by Sealy and his wife Magnolia Willis, the Open Gates stood at the symbolic crossroads of

Galveston, where its two boulevards, Broadway and Rosenberg, intersected. It also stood in the midst of a Willis-Sealy enclave. Sealy's elder brother, John, lived at Tremont and Avenue I, where the First Baptist Church now stands. Mrs. Sealy's uncle, R. S. Willis, her brother, and two of her sisters and their families lived nearby.

In terms of architectural sophistication, no Broadway house surpassed the Open Gates. Mrs. Sealy commissioned one of the most famous American architectural firms of the period, McKim, Mead & White of New York, to design the house. This was an unusual act of patronage in 19th-century Texas, when it was much rarer to hire well-known out-of-state architects than would be true in the 20th century. McKim, Mead & White produced a freestanding villa, raised a full story above grade in the Galveston manner. Its composition was more picturesque than that of the firm's imposing classical public and commercial buildings in Manhattan. But the house's exquisitely detailed brick and stone surfaces and terra-cotta classical ornament represented a rejection of the overstated shapes, colors, and textures of American High Victorian architecture. The Sealy House introduced the concept of architectural subtlety to Galveston's grand avenue, and it became the model that other aspiring Galveston houses emulated.

McKim, Mead & White designed the interiors of the Sealy House, as well as the limestone gate piers at the four corners of the property. N. J. Clayton's firm, which supervised construction of the house, designed the adjoining stable and carriage house, which was as ample and expensive to build as a substantial house. Mrs. Sealy retained an English horticulturist to supervise the planting and maintenance of the half-block site. Her children would be prominently identified with civic landscaping projects and plant propagation in Galveston during the first half of the 20th century.

As with Ashton Villa, the survival of the Open Gates (with both its interior appointments and much of its McKim, Mead & White furniture) is remarkable. After Mrs. Sealy's death in 1933, the house was occupied by one of her sons, Commodore Robert Sealy, until shortly before his death in 1979. Commodore Sealy and his siblings presented the house to the University of Texas Medical Branch as a memorial to their parents. The university converted the Sealy House into a teleconference center (Barry Moore and the Mathes Group, 1996). This has entailed extensive interior alterations, an addition to the back of the house, demolition of portions of the rear garden wall, and the clearing of the block behind the house for use as a surface parking lot.

Broadway and Rosenberg Avenue   A–125
Texas Heroes Monument

1900, Louis Amateis, sculptor

The City Beautiful movement of the turn of the 20th century sought to re-create rough, raw American cities in the image of 19th-century Paris and other great European capitals. One component of this movement was the installation of monumental works of civic art. The Texas Heroes Monument, one of the bequests of Henry Rosenberg (for whom 25th Street was renamed in 1897), was the first example erected in a Texas city. In terms of grandeur, it was never surpassed. The trustees of Rosenberg's estate commissioned the Italian-born and -trained sculptor, Louis Amateis, of Washington, D.C., to produce this 72-foot-high bronze and granite monument commemorating those who fought in the Texas Revolution of 1835–36.

The bronze statue of Victory atop the columned shaft extends her crown of laurels in the direction of the San Jacinto battlefield, fifty miles north of Galveston, along Buffalo Bayou, where the army of Anglo-Texians under General Sam Houston surprised and captured the forces of Mexican president Antonio López de Santa Anna on 21 April 1836, forcing Santa Anna to concede the independence of Texas from Mexico. Military victory resulted not only in Anglo-American ethnic and political supremacy, but in the liberation of capitalism, the founding of trading centers such as Galveston in territory where Mexico had previously forbidden settlement, and the formation of an entrepreneurial economy in which European immigrants of humble background, such as Henry Rosenberg, could achieve positions of wealth, influence, and respectability that would have been far more difficult to attain in Europe.

At the base of the shaft are a pair of seated bronze figures, Defiance (facing east) and Peace (facing west). Smaller figural ensembles facing north and south along Rosenberg frame portraits of Sam Houston and Stephen F. Austin. A bronze band at the base of the shaft contains relief portraits of the military heroes of the revolution. Set into the four faces of the stepped plinth upon which the shaft rises are bronze relief plaques depicting the Mexican victories at Goliad and the Alamo and two episodes of the battle of San Jacinto. The Washington, D.C. architect J. F. Manning & Company

collaborated with Amateis on the design of the plinth and shaft. The bronzes were all cast in Rome. The monument was dedicated on San Jacinto Day, 21 April 1900, by Governor Joseph D. Sayers.

The Texas Heroes Monument set the stage for the rather listless effort to redevelop Rosenberg Avenue as a civic center in the early 20th century. It set a standard of monumental civic grandeur that Galveston never duplicated.

In 1990, the Texas Heroes Monument was partially disassembled so that the figure of Victory could be restored, thanks to a campaign led by Mr. and Mrs. Ballinger Mills, Jr. The monument was rededicated in 1991.

823 Rosenberg Avenue   A–126
Galveston City Hall

1916 , C. D. Hill & Co.

Fire station, 1965, Raymond R. Rapp & Associates

Galveston's City Hall was built at the end of the City Beautiful period, when U.S. cities sought to endow their downtowns with monumentally scaled, classically designed civic centers. Deserting the old market site at 20th and Market Streets, Galveston's City Commission moved the offices of municipal government to the spacious, boulevarded precincts of Rosenberg Avenue. The Dallas architects C. D. Hill & Company (who had designed Dallas's imposing classical City Hall in 1914) produced a symmetrical, four-story building, based on the type of the Italian Renaissance palazzo, a favorite model for office buildings since the 19th century. The thick proportions, light brown brick, and tile roof of City Hall express its affinity with the Rosenberg Library. The Tuscan-order portico facing Rosenberg Avenue, with its crowning sculptured cartouche, punctuates what is, in other respects, a slightly bland building. A public auditorium originally projected from the rear of City Hall. During Hurricane Carla in 1961, the auditorium was badly damaged. It was demolished and replaced by a new central fire station, which led to the demolition of the old fire station, housed in the remnants of Alfred Muller's 1888 City Hall and Market House downtown.

Although the U.S. Post Office, Custom House, and Court House two blocks away reinforced the civic aspirations of City Hall in the 1930s, Rosenberg Avenue has never quite cohered as a civic center. The gracefully proportioned Southern Union Gas Company Building at 910 Rosenberg (1940, R. R. Rapp) sympathetically echoed the tawny brick and cast-stone surfaces and symmetrical composition of City Hall before its demolition in 1996 by the University of Texas Medical Branch to clear the site for a parking lot. Lack of an urban design and landscaping plan, and acquiescence to the insertion of massive parking lots facing the street, mean that these separate buildings never pull together to shape civic space.

2618 Broadway   **A–127**

(now the Moody Mansion and Museum)

1895, W. H. Tyndall

Although the stretch of Broadway between 27th Street and 22nd Street decisively lost its prestigious residential character in the 1930s and 1940s, some members of Galveston's conservative elite refused to retreat before the onslaught of commercialization and traffic. Just as Commodore Sealy held out at the Open Gates, so Galveston's foremost late-20th-century philanthropist, Mary Moody Northen, stayed on in this huge, late Victorian brick and stone showplace, which her father, William L. Moody, Jr., bought just after the Storm of 1900 from the estate of its builder, Narcissa Worsham Willis.

Mrs. Willis, the widow of Mrs. George Sealy's uncle, R. S. Willis, built the house just after her husband's death in 1892. Three stories high atop a raised basement, it is the work of William H. Tyndall, an obscure Galveston architect born and trained in England. Like other Galveston architects of the time, Tyndall seems to have tried to design a house with the subtlety and restraint of the Open Gates, while fighting his picturesque Victorian inclination to make the most of contrasts of shapes, colors, and textures. The glory of Mrs. Willis's house, however, was its interiors, designed and furnished by Pottier & Stymus of New York, one of the most fashionable decorating firms of the day. It is tempting to suspect that this represented Mrs. Willis's response to the decorating challenge posed by her niece, Mrs. Sealy.

Mrs. Willis died in 1899 and her house was sold (along with its Pottier & Stymus furniture, it is thought) to the cotton exporter and banker W. L. Moody and his wife, Libbie Shearn; thus its primary identification with the Moody family rather than Mrs. Willis. Moody lived in the house until his death in 1954, at which time his eldest daughter and heir, Mary Moody Northen, moved back into her childhood home. Mrs. Northen lived in the house

(without air conditioning, but with a year-round Christmas tree) until 1983. Water damage sustained during Hurricane Alicia that year prompted Mrs. Northen to begin a long-deferred rehabilitation of the house.

This evolved into a comprehensive restoration, completed in 1991, five years after Mrs. Northen's death, by Mary Moody Northen, Inc., a charitable foundation she established. A succession of preservation consultants and architects was responsible for the restoration work: Preservation Technology of Winston-Salem, North Carolina; W. Eugene George, Jr., of Austin; Graham B. Luhn of Houston; and Killis Almond & Associates of San Antonio. Particularly notable crafts restoration was performed by the Houston plaster contractors Tobin & Rooney and the San Antonio decorative artist Mary Canales Jary. Museum installations and the house's interpretation as it had been in 1911, when Mrs. Northen made her debut, were the work of the Moody Mansion & Museum's first curator, Patrick H. Butler III, and his successor, Bradley Brooks.

During the decades that they occupied the house, the Moody family bought up the rest of the block on which the house was built, demolishing all but one of the buildings that once stood there. Killis Almond & Associates designed the foundation's brick-faced Annex on the 26th Street side of the property (1990). This loss of neighborhood setting is to be regretted, since it leaves the house stranded in an institutional setting of security walls and surface parking lots. But preservation of the Willis-Moody House, and its opening as a museum, are a fitting tribute to Mrs. Northen, whose extraordinary generosity, through the Moody Foundation, which she chaired, was essential in realizing the preservation and restoration projects that made the rebirth of historic Galveston in the late 20th century possible.

2628 Broadway   **A–128**

1867, 1887

Surviving in the shadow of the Willis-Moody House is this raised cotttage, built by the paint and varnish dealer and painting contractor Joseph W. Rice but primarily identified with the family of his partner Victor J. Baulard, whose descendants occupied the property until the 1960s. In 1987 it was rehabilitated by W. Eugene George, Jr., to serve as offices for Mary Moody Northen, Inc.

aying that you live "in the East End" in Galveston means that you live east of 19th Street in the neighborhood with Galveston's richest collection of 19th-century houses. ∩ ∩ ∩ The East End has always been predominantly residential in character. After the Civil War, the bigger houses—the grand houses—tended to be built along Broadway (Avenue J), Sealy (Avenue I), and Ball (Avenue H) for very practical, as well as social and economic, reasons. It was the most valuable real estate in town not only because it fronted on the city's major east-west thoroughfare but also because it was on some of the highest ground that Galveston Island had to offer. ∩ ∩ ∩ Not unexpectedly, many of the names identified with buildings and businesses on the Strand are also associated with houses built in the East End during the last quarter of the 19th century. This was the neighborhood where Galvestonians most unabashedly displayed their wealth. ∩ ∩ ∩ Economic modesty and necessity edged north. A corner store, the standard fixture in most Galveston neighborhoods, did not appear until Winnie Street (Avenue G). Boarding houses and workshops were evident at Market Street (Avenue D), and such industries as ironworks and cotton warehouses were located on Mechanic Street (Avenue C). The closer you were to the bay, the more dense the population, the fewer the number of owner-occupied properties, and the heavier the industry—and attendant dangers. ∩ ∩ ∩ On

Broadway looking west from 17th Street, circa 1920s. The League House is in the foreground.

13 November 1885, sparks from an ironworks on the Strand (Avenue B) ignited a fire that swept through the East End, crossed Broadway, and destroyed over forty blocks and five hundred houses. As with other major disasters in Galveston's history, the fire altered the city architecturally.

Prior to the fire, buildings in "the fire district," as it was called at the time, represented forty years of development in the city. After the fire, many structures were replaced within a year, thereby giving the area a new uniformity.  The blocks east of 10th Street in the East End always consisted primarily of small workers' cottages

A view of the East End after the fire of 13 November 1885.

and rental property. The land was lower and prone to flooding. In fact, the daily distinction between land and Gulf on the eastern edge was defined by the rise and fall of the tide—as was true all along the Gulf side of the island. In 1971, 40 blocks in the East End became Galveston's first locally designated historic district, which meant that proposed rehabilitations, new construction, and demolition within the district boundaries were all subject to a public review process. The goal for the district was to encourage preservation and to stop an alarming trend toward demolition, the latter not always of derelict buildings. The district has been designated a National Historic Landmark District. In 1995, it was enlarged by 18 blocks—testimony to its success and to the constant vigilance of the East End Historical District Association.

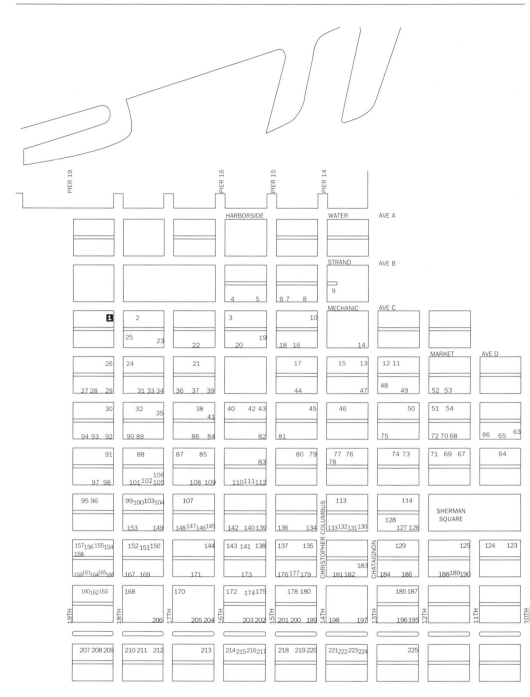

1. 1801–1803 Mechanic Street
2. 1719 Mechanic Street
3. 1527 Mechanic Street
4. 1524 Mechanic Street
5. 1508 Mechanic Street
6. 1428 Mechanic Street
7. 1424 Mechanic Street
8. 1412 Mechanic Street
9. 214 14th Street
10. 301 14th Street
11. 1217 Market Street
12. 1221 Market Street
13. 1301 Market Street

14. 1306 Market Street
15. 1317 Market Street
16. 1414 and 1412 Market Street
17. 1417 Market Street
18. 1426 Market Street
19. 1502 Market Street
20. 1520 Market Street
21. 1613 Market Street
22. 1614 Market Street
23. 1704 Market Street
24. 402 18th Street
25. 314 18th Street
26. 1801–1805 Market Street

27. 1818 Postoffice Street
28. 1816 Postoffice Street
29. 1808 and 1802 Postoffice Street
30. 1801–1803 Postoffice Street
31. 1720 Postoffice Street
32. 1717 Postoffice Street
33. 1710 Postoffice Street
34. 1702 Postoffice Street
35. 503 17th Street
36. 1628 Postoffice Street
37. 1614 Postoffice Street
38. 1609 and 1615 Postoffice Street
39. 1604 Postoffice Street

40. 1527 Postoffice Street
41. 509 16th Street
42. 1505 and 1509 Postoffice Street
43. 1501 Postoffice Street
44. 1414 Postoffice Street
45. 1401 Postoffice Street
46. 1319 Postoffice Street
47. 1302 Postoffice Street
48. 416 13th Street
49. 1212 Postoffice Street
50. 1207 Postoffice Street
51. 1127 Postoffice Street
52. 1128 Postoffice Street
53. 1122, 1118, and 1114 Postoffice Street
54. 1115 Postoffice Street
55. 810 and 806 Church Street
56. 809, 811, 813, and 815 Church Street
57. 818 Church Street
58. 824 Church Street
59. 828 Church Street
60. 903 Church Street
61. 923 Church Street
62. 926 Church Street
63. 523 10th Street
64. 1015 Church Street

65. 1016 Church Street
66. 526 11th Street
67. 1107 Church Street
68. 1116 Church Street
69. 1117 Church Street
70. 1124 Church Street
71. 1127 Church Street
72. 1128 Church Street
73. 1211 Church Street
74. 1217 Church Street
75. 1228 Church Street
76. 1311 Church Street
77. 1323 Church Street

78. 604, 606, and 608 14th Street
79. 1401 Church Street
80. 1409 Church Street
81. 1428 Church Street
82. 519 15th Street
83. Alley between 1500 block of Church and 1500 block of Winnie
84. 1602 Church Street
85. 1609 Church Street
86. 1618 Church Street
87. 1627 Church Street
88. 1717 Church Street
89. 1718 Church Street
90. 1722 Church Street
91. 1801 Church Street
92. 1804 Church Street
93. 1816 Church Street
94. 1824 Church Street
95. 1821 and 1823 Winnie Avenue
96. 1819 Winnie Avenue
97. 1816 Winnie Avenue
98. 1806 Winnie Avenue
99. 1727 Winnie Avenue
100. 1719 Winnie Avenue
101. 1724 and 1722 Winnie Avenue
102. 1712 Winnie Avenue
103. 1709 and 1711 Winnie Avenue
104. 1701 and 1707 Winnie Avenue
105. 1702 Winnie Avenue
106. 615 17th Street
107. 1617 Winnie Avenue
108. 1616 Winnie Avenue
109. 1602 Winnie Avenue
110. 1522 Winnie Avenue
111. 1520 and 1518 Winnie Avenue
112. 1512 and 1510 Winnie Avenue
113. 1317, 1319, and 1321 Winnie Avenue
114. 1209 Winnie Avenue
115. 712 10th Street
116. 926 Winnie Avenue
117. 905 Winnie Avenue
118. 728 Winnie Avenue
119. 724 and 722 Winnie Avenue
120. 819 Ball Avenue
121. 901 Ball Avenue
122. 902 Ball Avenue
123. 1007 Ball Avenue
124. 1025 Ball Avenue
125. 1103 Ball Avenue
126. 1202 Ball Avenue
127. 1208 Ball Avenue
128. 1212 Ball Avenue, rear
129. 1215 Ball Avenue
130. 1310 Ball Avenue
131. 1316 Ball Avenue
132. 1320 Ball Avenue
133. 1328 Ball Avenue
134. 1402 Ball Avenue
135. 1407 Ball Avenue
136. 1428 Ball Avenue
137. 1427 Ball Avenue
138. 1501 Ball Avenue
139. 1502 Ball Avenue
140. 1512 Ball Avenue
141. 1517 Ball Avenue
142. 1522 Ball Avenue
143. 802 16th Street
144. 1601 Ball Avenue
145. 1602 Ball Avenue
146. 1612 Ball Avenue
147. 1616 and 1614 Ball Avenue
148. 1622 Ball Avenue
149. 1702 Ball Avenue
150. 1709 and 1711 Ball Avenue

151. 1715 Ball Avenue
152. 1719 and 1721 Ball Avenue
153. 1724 Ball Avenue
154. 1801 Ball Avenue
155. 1819 Ball Avenue
156. 1821 and 1823 Ball Avenue
157. 1827 Ball Avenue
158. 812 19th Street
159. 1826 Sealy Avenue
160. 1819 Sealy Avenue
161. 1818 Sealy Avenue
162. 1817 Sealy Avenue
163. 1815 Sealy Avenue
164. 1814 Sealy Avenue
165. 1808 Sealy Avenue
166. 1802 Sealy Avenue
167. 1728 Sealy Avenue
168. 1727 Sealy Avenue
169. 1716 Sealy Avenue
170. 1627 Sealy Avenue
171. 1610 Sealy Avenue
172. 902 16th Street
173. 1514 Sealy Avenue
174. 1509 Sealy Avenue
175. 1503 Sealy Avenue
176. 1428 Sealy Avenue
177. 1416 Sealy Avenue
178. 1417 Sealy Avenue
179. 1412 Sealy Avenue
180. 1411 Sealy Avenue
181. 1318 Sealy Avenue
182. 1316 and 1314 Sealy Avenue
183. 815 13th Street
184. 1228 Sealy Avenue
185. 1213 Sealy Avenue
186. 1212 Sealy Avenue
187. 1205 Sealy Avenue
188. 1118 Sealy Avenue
189. 1110 Sealy Avenue
190. 1102 Sealy Avenue
191. 913 and 915 Sealy Avenue
192. 815 and 817 Sealy Avenue
193. 807 and 809 Sealy Avenue
194. 7th and Broadway
195. 1202 Broadway
196. 1210 Broadway
197. 1302 Broadway
198. 928 14th Street
199. 1402 Broadway
200. 1416 Broadway
201. 1428 Broadway
202. 1502 Broadway
203. 1516 Broadway
204. 1602 Broadway
205. 1616 Broadway
206. 1710 Broadway
207. 1819 Broadway
208. 1809 Broadway
209. 1805 Broadway
210. 1727 Broadway
211. 1721 Broadway
212. 1703 Broadway
213. 1607 Broadway
214. 1521 Broadway
215. 1515 Broadway
216. 1509 Broadway
217. 1501 Broadway
218. 1427 Broadway
219. 1407–1409 Broadway
220. 1403 Broadway
221. 1317 Broadway
222. 1313 Broadway
223. 1309 Broadway
224. 1301 Broadway
225. 1203 Broadway

1801-1803 Mechanic Street　　　　**B–1**
Island City Wood Working Company Building
1906
Although constructed in the 20th century, this quarter-block compound preserves the 19th-century identification of the area between 18th and 20th Streets with artisans' workshops. The Island City Wood Working Company was organized by the Galveston builder M. C. Bowden.

1719 Mechanic Street　　　　　　　**B–2**
1886
The narrow, "shotgun" cottage does not survive in large numbers in the East End. As was the case with this house, built by Mrs. William L. Sawyer, the widow of a ship's captain, it was a type frequently built as rental housing in Galveston.

1527 Mechanic Street　　　　　　　**B–3**
c. 1871
Although they now constitute the ragged northern edge of the East End, the 1700 through 1400 blocks of Mechanic Street retain a sense of the neighborhood as it must have looked in the 1860s and 1870s, before picturesque

Victorian house types became popular. This two-story, three-bay, side-hall-plan, Southern town house, visible in C. Drie's 1871 bird's-eye view of the city, is an example of one of the house types strongly associated with mid-19th-century Galveston neighborhoods. It was first occupied by William B. Hance, a ship's captain.

1524 Mechanic Street　　　　　　　**B–4**
1859
Another house type that recurs frequently in 19th-century Galveston neighborhoods is the two-story I-house, faced with a two-story veranda. This house was built by John H. Westerlage, who was City Marshall of Galveston.

1508 Mechanic Street　　　　　　　**B–5**
c. 1870
This is a Gulf Coast cottage, a side-gabled one-story house type, with its front veranda inset beneath the slope of the roof rather than attached to the front of the house. Here, the roof flattens out in profile over the veranda. Behind is a wing that probably began as a separate structure. By 1890, Robert C. Johnson owned the property and listed his residence and his commercial printing business at this address. His publishing ventures included *The Opera Glass,* which was described as a society and family paper.

1428 Mechanic Street　　　　　　　**B–6**
Date undetermined
One of the attractive features of Galveston's 19th-century wooden cottages was that, with only a little effort, they could be moved from one site to another. So pervasive was the practice that in 1884 the *Galveston Daily News*

complained about the "house moving nuisance." This one-story cottage seems to have been moved into what once was the side yard of the house next door.

1424 Mechanic Street   B–7

c. 1860

Wood construction, usually painted white, and the ever-present veranda gave Galveston houses of the Civil War era a strong sense of visual commonality. As is the case with this house, one of the larger in the neighborhood, such commonality tended to diminish differences in size that in the 1870s would begin to be asserted much more insistently. This house was owned by Hezekiah Wilson. Across the street at **1427 Mechanic Street** is a three-bay Southern town house that contributes to the pre-Victorian architectural character of Mechanic Street.

1412 Mechanic Street   B–8

1865

Victorian porch decoration (and asbestos siding) notwithstanding, this two-story-high, three-bay-wide, I-house, initially occupied by the family of the ice importer George H. Delesdernier, is another neighborhood veteran, as

its presence in the 1871 Drie's bird's-eye view attests. The transom above the front door and the sidelight windows that frame it are elements that frequently appeared on houses of this era in Galveston.

214 14th Street   B–9

c. 1860

Just how compact the three-bay cottage could become is evident in this tiny house, with its one-story rear extension. The property belonged to the stevedore James Waters, who lived in a house facing Mechanic.

301 14th Street   B–10

Ronald McDonald House

1989, Adams Architects

At 14th Street the University of Texas Medical Branch at Galveston (UTMB) manifests its presence with parking lots and warehouses, with which it expanded into the East End in the 1960s and 1970s. The Houston architects Gayle and Joe Adams designed this small hostel, providing housing for patients' families, to make the transition between institutional uses and the 19th-century scale and building typologies of the East End. The Adamses skillfully packed a small parking garage into the building's raised basement and maintained a domestic, rather than institutional, scale. Their efforts to devise a postmodern Victorian look met with less success.

1217 Market Street   B–11

c. 1871

This is a good example of another Galveston house type, the raised one-story cottage with a one-bay-wide attached porch, a feature more often seen on houses that faced north, as this one does. Also Galvestonian are the dormers that protrude

through the roof. These contain twin windows rather than single windows. The cottage was built by Frederick Martini, bookkeeper for Greenleve, Block & Company.

1221 Market Street   B–12
c. 1872

This is a classic example of a one-story clapboard cottage with a side-gabled roof and an attached veranda. The eaves of the side-gabled roof are clipped—that is, pressed tightly against the wall, rather than projecting out beyond it—a trait of Galveston houses built in the 1850s or earlier. Tax records indicate that this house was built by Robert Ohring, a locksmith, for use as a tenant house.

1301 Market Street   B–13
1916, Crow, Lewis & Wickenhoefer

Built by the prominent merchant Louis H. Runge, a second-generation Galveston German, this substantial raised house was constructed in what had long been an enclave of elite Germanic families. Runge's wife, Anita Focke, had grown up in a house at 13th and Market. The architect, Anton F. Korn, Jr., who represented the New York architects Crow, Lewis & Wickenhoefer in Galveston, adapted the Italian villa style popular for suburban country houses in the early 20th century to the confines of a city lot. He turned the façade of

the house toward the long dimension of the lot, facing 13th Street, rather than the narrower Market Street front. And instead of emphasizing the center of the symmetrically composed façade, Korn emphasized its edges, balancing the front door, set in a Tuscan portal at one end of the house, with an arched loggia at the other end. Korn's combination of stucco facing, shuttered sash windows, and a low-pitched roof with overhanging eaves struck a responsive chord in Galveston, as can be seen in the variations on this architectural theme built through the 1920s. In 1989, following the sale of the property by Miss Elisabeth D. Runge, Librarian of UTMB from 1922 to 1968, the house was rehabilitated by Houston architect Barry Moore to become the residence of the president of the University of Texas Medical Branch. Moore oversaw installation of the neo-Galvestonian tile sidewalk and designed the pedimented entry gate. John Kriegel, staff horticulturist at Moody Gardens, designed the lush garden district–style landscaping.

1306 Market Street   B–14
1859

Because of its prominent location on Broadway, Ashton Villa has claimed attention as Galveston's earliest picturesque Victorian house. It was, however, merely the largest of several such houses, another being this Italianate villa–type house, built by the German-Swiss immigrant merchant and philanthropist Henry Rosenberg. Rosenberg's house was constructed of brick and finished with stucco scored to simulate the appearance of stone blocks. Thus, not only in terms of its shape and stylistic details, but also in terms of its construction and surfaces, it stood out amid the wooden cottages of Civil War–era Galveston. As a type, the cubic villa house, freestanding in its fenced garden, with a one-story veranda, overhanging eaves with decorative brackets, and even a rooftop cupola, had become identified in prosperous Southern cities as the up-to-date house type by the middle 1850s, emblematic of domestic refinement and commercial success. Architectural drawings of the Rosenberg House survive in the Rosenberg Library, but they are unsigned.

After the death of Rosenberg's widow, Mollie Macgill Rosenberg, in 1917, their house became a fraternity house, then was divided into apartments, losing many of its original features over time. In 1990 the property was acquired by the Sealy & Smith Foundation for UTMB, which retained Benson Ford of Houston to restore the Rosenberg House and its dependencies to their original external appearance and rehabilitate them for use as a conference and guest house. John Kriegel was responsible for the landscape design, including the awesome palisade of ornamental date palms that now envelops the property.

1317 Market Street   B–15
c. 1868

Not as common as other cottage types, the small house with a gabled front is nonetheless a familiar Galveston house type, although the inset veranda and side-facing dormer windows visible here were less usual. This house, built by Gustavus Warner, a carpenter, has a side-hall plan and a front door framed by sidelights and a transom. From the street, a diminutive rear wing is visible. This was once a separate outbuilding which, as was often the case in Galveston, was eventually moved forward and attached to the rear of the primary house.

Next door at **1321 Market Street** is a narrow two-story house. The misalignment of its first- and second-floor openings, differences in the detailing of first- and second-story veranda supports, and a pronounced line along the east side at the second-floor level suggest that the two stories may once have been separate one-story cottages, stacked to form a two-story arrangement. As such expedient pairing implies, the Galveston wood cottage was infinitely flexible.

1414 Market Street   B–16
1876

1412 Market Street
1877, Clayton & Lynch

An intriguing feature of the East End is that one sees how persistent established 19th-century house types remained, despite changes in architectural style. N. J. Clayton's raised, two-story house at 1412 Market Street for the French-born insurance agent, financier, and public school board trustee Isadore Lovenberg is an example. Its rhythmic veranda, open-gabled upper porch, and vertical proportions

notwithstanding, the Lovenberg House is a three-bay-wide Southern town house. It even has a side-hall plan, although Clayton chose to emphasize symmetry and centrality in his treatment of the porches. The Lovenberg House was restored by Mr. and Mrs. Craig Lazzari in 1975, and it was one of the examples of Galveston "gingerbread" that Mary Clifford Lazzari illustrated in her delightful book *Mary Clifford Lazzari Paints Victorian Galveston.*

Next door at **1414 Market Street** is the Sam Levy House, which shares many of the architectural characteristics of 1412. However, a close examination of the decorative detail reveals that it lacks the sure sense of proportion and complexity that were Clayton hallmarks.

1417 Market Street   B–17
1893

John Hanna was a Galveston real estate agent and amateur photographer. His comfortable clapboard-and-shingle-faced house was the setting for a series of photographs of the Hanna family, now in the collection of the Rosenberg Library. These provide insight into the household of a middle-income Galveston family at the end of the 19th century. Next door, at **1409 Market Street** (1886), is a notable example of a customary East End landscape feature. Typically, the front yard was separated from the sidewalk by some sort of barrier, such as a fence. Here, the division is marked by a molded concrete curb studded with classical ball finials.

1426 Market Street   B–18
1885, N. J. Clayton

Clayton produced this center-hall-plan house for the grocer
Peter Gengler, whose family-owned store farther up Market
Street near the public market was also designed by Clayton.
The body of the Gengler House (now covered in asbestos
shingles) is restrained. But Clayton made the most of
articulated woodwork on the two-story front porch, which
is crowned by a center gablet with a divided middle, a
favorite Clayton theme. Such details as the wide front
sidewalk and the concrete parapet outlining the street fronts
of the property underscored the owner's substantiality. A
faceted window bay on the east side of the house overlooked
a deep side garden that, unfortunately, became the site of a
separate house in 1956.

1502 Market Street   B–19
1868

The Edward T. Austin House exemplifies a type of elite
house popular in Galveston between the 1840s and the
mid-1870s. This was a three-bay, side-hall type, pushed
back on its lot so that the front of the house faced the side
street and the long side opened up to a south-facing front
garden. Stimulating ventilation in the humid summer
months was an urgent priority in Galveston. This
arrangement gave the major rooms maximum accessibility
to the prevailing Gulf breeze, even though the front door
was relegated to the side street. Subsequent landscape
alterations to the Austin House have sought to "re-interpret"
its Market Street flank as though it were the principal
façade. Even so, it is redolent of the old East End. The rear
service wing (to the left of the verandas facing Market
Street) is screened with louvered blinds. Sidewalks are
unpaved. And the property is shaded by the dense canopy

of mature live oak trees. Austin, a cousin of the land
impresario Stephen F. Austin, was a lawyer who held a
number of public offices, including county judge of
Galveston County and acting mayor of Galveston.

1520 Market Street   B–20
1859

What sets this house, built for the wholesale and retail
grocer George W. Grover, apart is not its plan or appearance
(it is an example of the Southern town house type) but its
construction of brick rather than wood. The house has
characteristic Greek Revival architraves framing its front
doors and a vintage iron fence. It looks somewhat blank,
though, without its shutters.

Next door at **1526** and **1528 Market Street** are a pair of
rental houses built in 1913 by the jeweler M. W. Shaw.
They are so conservative in appearance that they resemble
the Grover House next door. Such conservatism was a trait
of the architect Donald N. McKenzie.

1613 Market Street   B–21
1904

This turreted house, built for Mr. and Mrs. John H.
Meyers, indicates how late-Victorian house types persisted
in Galveston into the new century. Meyers was a partner in
the household furniture firm of Kauffman, Meyers &
Company.

1614 Market Street   B—22

1886

Beyond its houses of individual note, the East End derives its significance as a National Historic Landmark District from the block fronts composed of houses such as this and its neighbors in the 1600 block of **Market Street.** All were built in 1886 to replace houses in this block destroyed in the fire of 13 November 1885.

1704 Market Street   B—23

Alterations 1888, N. J. Clayton

The great fire of 13 November 1885 began just north of here, near 16th and Strand. A strong north wind drove flames in a southerly direction, cutting a huge swath through this sector of the East End before jumping across Broadway and continuing south to Avenue O. As a result, the west side of the East End was rebuilt in the late 1880s. This house dates from that period of reconstruction. It seems to have been an existing house, moved onto this site in the "fire district," which N. J. Clayton altered and expanded for the Irish-American baking company owner Christopher Fox. Clayton's hand is visible in the woodwork detail of the wraparound galleries and the tall, faceted bay facing 17th Street, crowned with what Clayton referred to as a "pavilion" roof. A conservative feature of this house is its siting—like the Austin House at 15th and Market—with the front door facing the side street and the long side of the house opened to a deep-set south lawn. The cast-iron gallery rails were added in the 1920s.

Diagonally across the street, at **402, 406,** and **410 17th Street** are three architecturally coordinated tenant houses, built for Richard O'Rourke in 1905.

402 18th Street   B—24

Zion Lutheran Church (now Iglesia Metodista Unida Zion)

1926

Although built in the 1920s, this stucco-faced brick church, by virtue of its strong shape and simple detail, sits securely amid its older neighbors. It was home to a Swedish congregation.

314 18th Street   B—25

Martingano Building

1914

Michael Martingano, an immigrant Italian shoemaker, built this gabled-front, two-story brick building, decorated with brick and cast stone banding, as his shop and family home. In a neighborhood of raised wooden houses with ebulliently detailed porches, the Martingano Building stands out as very much the exception. It was rehabilitated in 1988 by architects Michael Gaertner and David Watson.

1801-1805 Market Street   B—26

Bohn and Neuwiller Buildings

1898

This pair of identical buildings represented a spillover from the workshop district to the north and east. The corner building contained George Bohn's sheet iron, tinware, crockery, and hardware business. The building at 1805, its stucco-faced exterior now weathered to a soft Galveston gray, contained Charles F. Neuwiller's cabinetmaking shop. Both had residential quarters above. The pair perpetuated the standard downtown loft building type, with an arcade of

tall, double-leaf doors set beneath arched transoms opening to the sidewalk.

1818 Postoffice Street   B–27
1886

The faceted center bay of this house, built in the 1885 fire district by Abraham Cohen, manager of the dry goods department of Leon & H. Blum, projects well forward of two recessed wings, one of which contains the front door. Each bay gets its own two-story porch. The centermost porch is chamfered to reflect the geometry of the bay behind it. Not only does this spatial configuration give rooms increased exposure to the prevailing breeze, but it lends the house a sculptural buoyancy that is quintessentially Galvestonian.

1816 Postoffice Street   B–28
1886

The Theodore Ohmstede House is an example of a popular American Victorian house type, the L-front villa with inset two-story porch. It is interesting to observe here how the type was "Galvestonized" with characteristic porch trim

detail, full-bodied but not thick and heavy, so that it could be richly modeled by changing conditions of sun and shade. Sonya's Beauty Shop at **1814 Postoffice Street** (c. 1950), a one-story, flat-roofed commercial building now used for professional offices, protrudes into the front yard of the Ohmstede House. It calls attention to itself with jaunty green-framed black tile facing.

1808 and 1802 Postoffice Street   B–29
1887, Alfred Muller

These substantial rental houses, built as an investment by the grocer Albert Rakel, are identical in plan and spatial organization, but vary in the configuration of their verandas. In contrast to the Ohmstede House next door, they illustrate the perpetuation in Galveston of earlier 19th-century house types—in this case the three-bay-wide, side-hall-plan, Southern town house—Victorianized with more assertive shapes and details. The front verandas of the Rakel houses show the arcuated lintel to have been as characteristic of Alfred Muller as of Clayton. But Muller's treatment was always a little heavier. If one may resort to ethnic stereotypes, it represented the difference between German oompah music and an Irish jig. The 18th Street side of 1802 illustrates how Muller vigorously telescoped rooms along an implied diagonal line, imparting not only a dynamic sense of movement to the exterior but multiplying exposures to the prevailing breeze. Facing the basements with rusticated stucco detailing seems to have been a trademark of Muller's. Shortly before his premature death, Muller advertised himself as having designed over 100 frame houses. Very few of these can be securely attributed. Therefore, the combination of stylistic elements visible in such documented designs as these houses provides clues for the tentative identification of other possible Muller-designed houses.

1801-1803 Postoffice Street   B–30
Jackson Building (now First Latin Assembly of God Church)
1887

Like the Bohn and Neuwiller Buildings a block away at 18th and Market, this two-story, stucco-surfaced, brick building stands out typologically in the residential East End, where the relative scarcity of corner stores was testimony to the neighborhood's high social status. Homogeneity was preserved, even if this meant a lessening of convenience shopping. However, from its inception this building was

used as a boarding house rather than for commercial purposes. It was built by an out-of-town investor, James Jackson, to replace a building destroyed in the Fire of 1885. From the 1920s through the 1950s, the Jackson Building was the playhouse of the Little Theater of Galveston.

bracketing of the porch's vertical posts, and the decorative timber stripping in the gable above the porch.

1720 Postoffice Street   B-31

1889, N. J. Clayton

Recent research by the Galveston Historical Foundation has revealed that this two-story house, built by Dr. Arthur F. Sampson in the 1885 fire district, was designed by Clayton. The curved-corner double galleries and the arcuated gablet that signals the location of the front door are indicative of Clayton. Here one observes how Clayton (like Muller at 1802 and 1808 Postoffice) adapted and Victorianized the Southern town house type. A Galvestonian feature of the house is the way that its double front doors are recessed into a shallow alcove that is capable of being closed off by shutters or sliding pocket doors.

1717 Postoffice Street   B-32

1890

Whether a house was built on the north side of one of Galveston's alphabetical avenues or the south side seems to have had an effect on how it was designed. The tall, planar-fronted house with porches (rather than verandas or galleries), represented by this house for Mrs. Elise C. Michael, is one that appears with far greater frequency on south-side lots than on north-side lots. It is a Victorianized version of the older I-house type. Here, the clapboard-faced body of the house is very plain, in contrast to the exuberant pierced-plate wooden porch ornament, the articulated

1710 Postoffice Street   B-33

1889

The real estate and investment broker William Reppen built this two-story Victorian house, with inset double porches that accentuate the corner with a cylindrical bay. The "fish-scale" shingle pattern on the walls of the Reppen House supplements the standard Galveston facing of wood clapboards. This pattern of overlapping shingles enabled Victorian architects and builders to give wood houses some of the textural variation and contrast that enlivened the wall surfaces of brick buildings. Note the wide sidewalk and the continuous stucco-faced parapet with piers, into which metal fencing is inserted, that run along this side of the block. These were landscape details that bespoke the gentility of the East End.

1702 Postoffice Street   B-34

1905, George B. Stowe

The East End's standing as a prestigious neighborhood remained unchallenged into the 1910s, as this house, built for the insurance company executive John D. Hodson, indicates. Stowe's design was in the late Victorian Colonial Revival mode. The house still adhered to characteristic Victorian shapes, but its surfaces were broad and smooth. An especially imposing feature of the design is its east-side terrace, facing 17th Street, which was added when Stowe's

original porches were replaced by stucco-faced piers and spandrels in the 1930s. These depress the house's external aspect and cramp its proportions.

503 17th Street　　　　　　　　　　　B-35
1900, C. W. Bulger

Galveston seems to have impelled its 19th-century architects to vie with each other for eccentric exuberance. Charles Bulger certainly put up a good show in this house for the pipe and concrete contractor Isaac Heffron, built to face 17th Street rather than Postoffice, so that its façade opens into the prevailing breeze. The first-floor porch posts, detailed like 16th-century Mannerist-style pedestals with exaggerated reverse tapers, and the bulbous turned colonnettes on the second floor are unequaled locally. The broad, double-decked gallery, carried on open arches, takes up a curvilinear theme as it rounds one corner of the house to embrace a south-facing side garden. Flattened attic dormers also exhibit Mannerist exaggeration. Note the opportunities for improved ventilation that Bulger created with his notched second-story window bays. The Heffron House is quite unusual in being so horizontally elongated, displaying none of the Victorian preference for verticality evident in Stowe's Hodson House across the street. Perhaps reflecting its owner's construction expertise, the house was a very early example of the use of brick simply as a facing veneer, rather than as a structural bearing wall. The concrete parapets outlining the property and the wide sidewalks are further indications of the owner's business interests. Two years after the Heffron House was built, Bulger virtually duplicated its design in the William R. Miller House in the central Texas town of Belton.

1628 Postoffice Street　　　　　　　　　B-36
1889, N. J. Clayton

Built for the restaurateur Rudolph E. Kruger, this three-bay-wide, side-hall-plan, Southern town house evinces Clayton's authorship principally in the detailing of its double-level front veranda. On the 17th Street side of the house, a secondary entrance is visible, as is a rear service porch, screened with louvered blinds in the Galveston manner. At the back of the property is one of the most engaging back buildings in Galveston, a freestanding two-story dependency that is only one-half bay wide.

1614 Postoffice Street　　　　　　　　　B-37
1886

The arcuated lintels spanning between the veranda posts and the simple bands of diagonals in the veranda rails enliven this Victorianized Southern town house, built for the lumber dealer Walter F. Stewart.

1609 and 1615 Postoffice Street　　　　　B-38
1898

In this pair of houses built by the carpenter and contractor Frederick Kreuzberger, the Southern town house type is modified by projecting the front-wall plane forward as a chamfered bay and slightly reshaping the front verandas to accommodate this geometry. The gable-capped veranda

"façade" becomes the virtual front-wall plane of the house, where decorative flourishes are concentrated.

1604 Postoffice Street   B–39

1887, Dickey & Helmich

The wholesale grocer, importer, and cotton factor Henry A. Landes was one of the many East End residents who lost homes in the Fire of 1885. He replaced his house with an imposing brick castle designed by D. A. Helmich, who practiced briefly in Galveston as partner to the Houston architect George E. Dickey. Helmich's design was singular. The theatrical composition of the 16th-Postoffice corner of the house, with its flat-topped gable, folded back to parallel each street face, plays to the street corner. Angled and cylindrical tower bays reinforce this spatial drama, as does the exceptional ornamental detail. Helmich deployed bands and sunk panels of terra-cotta ornament to underscore the major lines and points of the façade. Sunbursts of colored tile above windows and in the gable, as well as terra-cotta sunflowers, are exuberant decorative flourishes in the English Queen Anne style. The cast-iron porch panels visible in Ezra Stoller's and Henri Cartier-Bresson's photographs of the house in *The Galveston That Was* were sold by the Dominican sisters, who owned the house from 1954 to 1968.

Behind the house, off 16th at the alley, is a companion two-story brick stable and servant's house. This **alley** contains an array of some of the most characteristic

Galveston back buildings in the East End.

Across 16th Street from the Landes House at 1526 Postoffice was N. J. Clayton's large brick house for the banker Bertrand Adoue (1882). It marked this corner as one of the social-geographic high points of the East End. The Adoue House was demolished in 1953 to build the **Dominican Convent** (R. R. Rapp), next to the ex-**Dominican High School** (1940, R. R. Rapp). The Dominican nuns established what was originally Sacred Heart Academy on this block in 1882 and maintained their motherhouse here until it was moved to Houston in 1926.

1527 Postoffice Street   B–40

1913

This two-story wooden house, built for the wholesale grocer Ernest Stavenhagen, impresses with its stolid front portico. Its weightiness and symmetry contrast with the high-raised Victorian buoyancy of surrounding houses. Behind, at **512 16th Street,** is a two-story alley house, stationed like a sentinel at the alley.

509 16th Street   B–41

c. 1906

Throughout the East End, the numbered side streets often contain houses built in the back yards of corner houses facing the alphabetical avenues. These side-street houses tended to be smaller than those along the alphabetical avenues, suggesting both the city's 19th- and early-20th-century population density and the way in which even Galveston's most concentrated upper-income neighborhood accommodated more economic diversity than came to be characteristic of 20th-century suburban neighborhoods. This house, built by Thomas E. Bollinger behind his house at 1601 Postoffice and restored in 1995, is a good example of a side-street house.

1505 and 1509 Postoffice Street   B–42
1890

These adjoining houses—1505 rebuilt in 1890 for Mrs. Mary J. Batterson, and 1509 built for Isaac Heffron—represent the architectural fabric against which larger or more unusual East End houses figured. Heffron's house at 1509 displays, as does his later, more famous house at 17th and Postoffice, evidence of his specialty as a concrete contractor in the ceremonious concrete balustrade along the front sidewalk line.

1501 Postoffice Street   B–43
Date undetermined

Moved from 620 Market Street (a site to which it had probably been moved about 1895 by Victor Gustafson) and installed here in 1979, this raised cottage exemplifies a vernacular Galveston house type. Rather than having a front veranda inserted beneath the side-gabled roof as in the Gulf Coast cottage type, the Gustafson House has an attached front porch, which tended to be preferred for north-facing houses. The small scale and size of this cottage imbue it with an elemental dignity.

1414 Postoffice Street   B–44
1871; additions 1882

This one-and-one-half-story, side-gabled house, with its

twin-window dormers, floor-to-ceiling nine-over-nine-paned windows, and transom-and-sidelight-framed door, is a fine example of the Gulf Coast cottage type. It was built by the stevedore John Nelson.

1401 Postoffice Street   B–45
1876, 1889

Research by the Galveston Historical Foundation indicates that this classic, five-bay-wide, side-gabled cottage with twin-window dormers and a gabled front porch was built as an investment property but sold in 1888 to the Danish-born harbor pilot Lawson Luth. Luth had the house raised on the arched, stucco-faced brick basement in 1889. The detailing of the basement, the new front porch, and the interior, probably dating from 1889, suggest that Alfred Muller may have been Luth's architect. The Luth House was restored in 1991.

1319 Postoffice Street   B–46
c. 1873

This house, an example of the Gulf Coast cottage type (although its raised basement has been altered), was built by a widow, Mrs. Katharine Burke. Her sons, John, Edward, and Mike, were partners in J. Burke & Brothers grocery, which occupied the corner lot next door at 14th and Postoffice.

1302 Postoffice Street   B–47
1887

Backing up to the Runge House at 13th and Market, the imposing house of the Austrian-born grain and general commission merchant Gustav Reymershoffer (built alongside the now-demolished house of his brother and

business partner John Reymershoffer) was part of the enclave of elite Galveston Germanic families in this neighborhood. Raised on an arched, stucco-surfaced basement, the house is big in scale but simple in design. The exceptions are the veranda and the giant front gable, which, with their thin appliqué of wooden shapes, animate the otherwise plain surfaces of the house. In addition to its low iron fence, the Reymershoffer House retains a fine black-and-red tile sidewalk. Occupied by Reymershoffer's family until 1985, the house was restored in 1991.

(rather than a single door framed by sidelights) was an innovative feature that suggests the Blaylock House's 1870s date.

1207 Postoffice Street   B–50
c. 1875

A hipped roof, rather than a side-gabled roof, differentiates this five-bay-wide cottage from other East End cottages of its type. Sam M. Penland, a partner in the auction and commission house of Park, Lynch & Company, built this house.

416 13th Street   B–48
1880

The commission merchant and cotton factor Gustav Heye contributed to the formation of the German enclave with a towered villa–type house whose Victorian decorative accents belie its conservative spatial organization. The Heye House turns its narrow front toward 13th Street in order to open the long, veranda-lined side of the house toward Postoffice Street and the prevailing southeast breeze. The rear service wing is a subsidiary house built by Heye at the same time as the main house.

1212 Postoffice Street   B–49
c. 1873

Another example of the raised, side-gabled, five-bay-wide cottage with twin-window dormers and floor-length shuttered windows, this house was built by the printer Louis Blaylock. The presence of double doors

1127 Postoffice Street   B–51
Great A & P Tea Company Building
1931

The standard type of the Galveston corner grocery store, particularly those built in residential neighborhoods, was a boxlike, two-story wooden building with a low-pitched roof, sometimes ornamented with brackets beneath the eaves of the roof. The A&P corner store departed considerably from the type. It is a very late example of Craftsman-influenced design, adapted to its hybrid function and locale with the seeming insertion of a corner grocery into the raised basement of a wood bungalow. The second-story front porch, the banks of casement windows, and especially the marvelous outdoor stair, whose upward raking parapet discreetly separates the approach to the store from the approach to the family's residence above are distinguishing features of this corner store.

1115 Postoffice Street   B–54
1932
This 1932 bungalow was modified with a new screened front and a freestanding modern garage (1962, Louis L. Oliver). The rear garden, not visible from the street, is one of the most enchanting in the East End.

1128 Postoffice Street   B–52
c. 1860
The plainness of the gable-fronted veranda on this Southern town house, its tight proportions, clipped eaves, and the random-width wood clapboards suggest its relative antiquity. The house was built by the doctor, chemist, and apothecary H. C. L. Aschoff.

810 and 806 Church Street   B–55
c. 1882

1122, 1118, and 1114 Postoffice Street B–53
c. 1888
Mrs. H. C. L. Aschoff built this trio of similarly organized raised houses, all two stories high with side-hall plans, for three of her daughters. Here one appreciates the urban residential character of the East End, composed of a limited number of house types that give the neighborhood its underlying sense of order, but varied with ebullient applied decoration.

809 Church Street   B–56
1892

811 Church Street
1892

813 Church Street
1892

815 Church Street
1892 and later alterations

818 Church Street   **B–57**

c. 1885

824 Church Street   **B–58**

c. 1882

828 Church Street   **B–59**

c. 1883

In the East End, as in Galveston's other 19th-century neighborhoods, there is a correlation between tree cover and social prestige. The more trees there are, the higher the status of the neighborhood. On the eastern edge of the East End (which lies largely outside the East End National Historic Landmark District), the trees thin out. This was a much more modest neighborhood, socioeconomically, than the East End proper and it was filled with small wooden houses. Because of its proximity to the Gulf in the 19th century, it was devastated during the Storm of 1900.

Therefore, many of the older houses that survive here were either built after 1900 or moved into the area from other parts of town.

The 800 block of Church Street lay just outside what, in the aftermath of the 1900 Storm, was designated the "area of total destruction." Therefore, it contains houses that survived the impact of the hurricane. These, and post-1900 additions, constitute a spatial catalogue of more modest house types common in Galveston from the middle of the 19th century through the first decade of the 20th.

The houses at **806** and **810** are typical, small one-story Victorian cottages with modestly ornamented porches. They seem to have been built in the early 1880s after the real estate investor Henry M. Trueheart bought the three lots they occupy. Prior to Trueheart's purchase, the lots were rented to African-American tenants, Alfred Brown, Cato Fields, and Mary James, all of whom, however, owned their own houses. When the property was redeveloped, the tenants moved their houses to other rented sites, a not unusual practice for low- and moderate-income households in 19th-century Galveston.

At **809** is an unusually long example of a shotgun cottage, so long in fact that it has a secondary entrance on its east side with its own small porch. It was originally one of four identical houses built by the brick contractor Benjamin F. Barnes in 1892. The shotgun cottages at **811** and **813** were part of this group. Such houses were often built in series as "tenant houses," as rental properties were routinely described in late-19th- and early-20th-century Galveston.

So narrow is the two-story tenant house at **815** that it looks more like a two-story shotgun than a side-hall Southern town house. It was originally identical to 809, 811, and 813, but was expanded with the addition of a second story during the 1890s.

Although the Victorian veranda detail and paneled double doors suggest a date of the mid-1880s, the low-set, five-bay-wide Gulf Coast cottage at **818** possesses a romantic aura of typological purity, perhaps because it has not been remodeled or restored. It was a tenant house built by Benjamin Barnes.

At **824** is another low-set, five-bay-wide Gulf Coast cottage, which seems to have been built shortly after Benjamin Barnes bought this lot in 1882. Its scale is diminutive and it is set much farther back on its lot than other houses on this side of the street. It is unusual in having such a low-pitched roof. Note that it possesses a rear wing that is even smaller in scale than the body of the house.

Concluding this lineup of vernacular types is the five-bay-wide, center-hall-plan cottage at **828,** which is raised and has a hipped roof rather than a side-gabled roof. This was Barnes's own house. He lived on the property as early as 1872, but county tax records suggest he built this house about 1883.

903 Church Street   B–60
Date undetermined

Insurance records indicate that this Victorianized version of
a Gulf Coast cottage was moved here in 1931. As in other
examples of this vernacular house type, floor-length, six-
over-nine-pane windows imbue the house front with a very
graceful aspect.

As one proceeds up Church Street, it can be seen that the
socioeconomic status of the neighborhood (as indicated by
house size and tree cover) began to ascend.

At **907 Church Street** is a five-bay cottage with a
separately roofed porch (1867). It was the home of the
marble contractor John Quick.

923 Church Street   B–61
1901

It is intriguing to note how consistently house types and
their characteristics were adhered to, and how individual
variations seem to have been confined to added elements,
such as decorative detail. Therefore, such exceptions as this
four-bay tenant cottage, with its uncentered front door,
stand out. According to insurance records, it was built of
"old material" for Miss Kate Rogers.

926 Church Street   B–62
1883

This substantial raised house has so much personality that it
has withstood the filling-in of two of its five veranda bays. The
triple-pitched gambrel roof, the arched veranda bays, and the
extensive use of embricated (literally: bricklike) shingles as wall
covering suggest the 1890s. Yet, remarkably, this house was
radically remodeled in 1883 for Alice Patch and Arthur B.

Homer. Homer was a cotton buyer and the youngest brother
of Winslow Homer, one of America's most famous late-19th-
century painters. As comparison demonstrates, the texturally
enriched surfaces of the Homer House were a rarity among
Galveston wood houses of the 1880s.

523 10th Street   B–63
1874

This Italianate villa–type house, built for the insurance agent
Robert J. Hughes, faces 10th Street in order to open up to
the prevailing breeze. It differs from other examples of this
siting configuration by not having galleries or verandas along
its long, Church Street side. Although the front verandas
have been crudely altered, the rest of the exterior is well
maintained, especially the Italianate bracketed cornices,
bracketed window architraves, and the delightful paneled
window bay on the Church Street side of the house.

1015 Church Street   B–64
1902

After the turn of the 20th century, Galveston house builders,
designers, and clients began to abandon the vernacular house
types characteristic of the city since its founding. This
handsomely maintained raised cottage, built by Gaston H.

Wilder, co-owner of the Star Drug Store, exemplifies this subtle departure from tradition. It is not quite symmetrical, but its asymmetry is not pronounced. And it has paired front windows rather than single windows.

1016 Church Street   B–65
1926

It was rare for large houses to be built in the East End after World War I. Yet the stevedore company president Richard P. Williamson bypassed newer neighborhoods of fashion to construct this imposing brick veneer house with a multitude of timbered and stuccoed gables. Like other large 20th-century houses built in the district, it has a solemnity not characteristic of 19th-century dwellings. Though it has no verandas, the Williamson House retained such Galvestonian attributes as a high-raised basement and hinged, louvered blinds. It also has an expansive side yard to ensure exposure to the prevailing breeze.

626 11th Street   B–66
1876

While not as elaborately detailed as the Hughes House at 10th and Church, this house, built for the dentist Dr. William S. Carruthers, adopted the same siting configuration, facing 11th Street and opening its main rooms, behind a double-level veranda, to Church Street and the prevailing Gulf breeze. The house was rehabilitated by Eubanks/Bohnn Associates in 1993.

1107 Church Street   B–67
1873, T. Cordray, builder

The Galveston Historical Foundation's research disclosed that this house was built to sell by Thomas Cordray, a Galveston carpenter. It is an example of the gable-fronted cottage with front porch, a type that tended to be built on the south side of Galveston's alphabetical avenues. The concrete parapet and wide sidewalk give the front of the property a hospitable aspect.

1116 Church Street   B–68
1893; additions, 1899

James S. Waters, who built this house, was an officer of several loan and investment companies as well as treasurer of Galveston County. He was also the lord of the manor in this block of Church Street. Around the turn of the 20th century, he owned many of the houses on the south side of the street. His own house stands out by virtue of its size and its spatial buoyancy. Yet as so often is the case in Galveston, its insets, projections, angles, and curves belie the plain surface of the white-painted clapboard house. The "swag" pattern achieved by inserting wooden balls between the spindles of the second-floor porch rail shows up on other Galveston houses of the period. The Waters House sits in an unusually expansive garden, ornamented with palm trees, oleanders, and a tile sidewalk. Such expansiveness became possible when Waters bought this lot, which had been part of the now-demolished Fordtran homestead at 1102 Church, in 1897. It allowed him to add the east bay, with its gabled roof and curved balcony, to the side of his house.

1117 Church Street   B–69

1902

James S. Waters built this raised cottage, which, with its ornamented front porch and narrow, paired front windows, resembles the cottage at 1015 Church Street.

1124 Church Street   B–70

1892

Waters had to share suzerainty of the 1100 block of Church Street with the family of Mrs. Mary Cameron. Mrs. Cameron owned this one-and-one-half-story house, notable for the decorated vergeboards facing the raking line of the front gable.

1127 Church Street   B–71

1877

This raised cottage, built for the lawyer Charles L. Cleveland, is noteworthy for its extensive galleries, especially since it lies

on the south side of the street. It is also unusual in having Gothic-style pointed arches in the decorative gallery trim.

1128 Church Street   B–72

1891, B. N. Cooke

Framed by palm trees, this house, built by the merchandise broker Allen E. Cameron next to the house his mother owned at 1124 Church, enlivens the corner with its red roof and faded green blinds. The two-story gallery is screened with closely spaced turned posts and a second-story rail of alternating vertical and cross bars. The gallery's shadowed voids play off the solidity of the house's gable-roofed corner bay. The "kick-line" of the roof, as it flares out in pitch just above the eaves, was an unusual feature in Galveston.

1211 Church Street   B–73

1873, 1880, 1888

The blacksmith Alexander B. Everett built this house, then expanded it on several occasions, researchers for the Galveston Historical Foundation have concluded. This perhaps accounts for its stepped plan and the slenderness of the front-facing entrance bay, where a gableted balcony is played against the projecting window bay. The Everett House is distinctive for its Victorian Rococo–style architectural trim, which, with the rest of the house, was handsomely restored in 1984 by Houston designer John T. Robinson, who was also responsible for a new, compatibly designed back building. A delicate iron fence and the curbside carriage step, inscribed "Everett," are supporting landscape features.

1217 Church Street   B–74

1879

The "Dealey" inscribed on the curbside carriage step identifies the builder of this house, the English-born Thomas W. Dealey, an officer of A. H. Belo & Company, publishers of the *Galveston Daily News.* It is a conservative version of the Gulf Coast cottage type, with two pairs of six-over-six-paned shuttered windows flanking a transom-and-sidelight-framed central door. The turned spindles in the veranda rails, the gingerbread brackets framing the square veranda posts, and the twin-window dormers were later additions. Note the stepping out of service buildings on the west rear side of the house.

1228 Church Street   B–75

1857

What this five-bay-wide, side-gabled, Gulf Coast cottage reveals along its 13th Street side is the eccentric roofline achieved through incremental additions to the body of the house. It was not uncommon, especially on more modest houses, for outbuildings to be moved up and attached to the main house, especially as attached kitchens and indoor plumbing became common in the last quarter of the 19th century. One result was the picturesque stepping of wings, both in plan and roof line, that give prim street façades their often eccentric rear tails. The cottage was built by Joseph Ricke and owned by his descendants until 1976.

1311 Church Street   B–76

c. 1870

This house, a trim, one-story, side-gabled Gulf Coast cottage, was moved onto this site in the 1980s. It ushers one into what at first appears to be an urban anomaly in the 1300, 1400, and 1500 blocks of Church Street (and in the parallel blocks of Winnie Street to the south): a visible dip in the socioeconomic geography of the East End, right in the

center of the district. Yet as is apparent in other Galveston neighborhoods, the spatial boundaries separating working-class, middle-income, and elite households tended to be more intricately intertwined in 19th-century American cities than they were to become in the 20th century. What made the East End so distinctive in late-19th-century Galveston was the unusual consistency of its middle-to-upper-income demography. This district within a district calls attention to that phenomenon by virtue of its working-class status.

1323 Church Street   B–77

1885, N. J. Clayton

Mrs. Barbara L. Jacobs, a midwife, built this Victorianized Southern town house. The decorative semicircular brackets at the top of the veranda piers provide the only hint of Clayton's authorship.

604, 606, and 608 14th Street   B–78

1907

Perhaps as a result of their side-street location, these three tenant houses are unusual in their spatial organization. The houses are L-shaped in plan and incorporate enclosed garages in their raised basements. Unprepossessing individually, they make a strong impact on the streetscape with their repeating hip-roofed porches, straight-run exterior stairs, and inset yards. The houses were built by the real estate investor A. J. Henck.

1401 Church Street   B-79
William Werner Grocery Building
1859, 1886

This unassuming two-story building is one of the oldest surviving corner stores in the city. It appears in its present configuration in the 1871 C. Drie bird's-eye view of Galveston. The Werner Grocery Building has an L plan, so that the rear opens toward 14th Street and the prevailing Gulf breeze with double galleries. The twin projecting bay windows may have been part of the 1886 alterations recorded in Galveston insurance records.

1409 Church Street   B-80
c. 1869

This side-gabled cottage (actually double-gabled) is notable for its tiny scale. It was built by the carpenter Henry Gardner and appears in the 1871 bird's-eye view.

1428 Church Street   B-81
1882

Restored in 1995 by the Galveston Historical Foundation, this graceful, three-bay-wide Southern town house, built by the harbor pilot Captain Rufus Jameson, features a central gablet that appears to split the cornice above its front, two-story veranda. This was a decorative device popular during the 1880s and can be seen on other Galveston houses.

The Galveston Historical Foundation restored the

Jameson House through its Residential Preservation Program, with assistance from the Meadows Foundation of Dallas, as part of a broader initiative of neighborhood stabilization, **Operation Church Street.** Focusing on the 1400 and 1500 blocks of Church Street, this led to the rehabilitation of **1408 Church Street** in 1993 and **1420 Church Street** in 1994, and their sale as part of the foundation's Affordable Housing Initiative to moderate-income homebuyers. In 1995, the foundation completed rehabilitation, with assistance from the Favrot Fund of Houston and Community Development Block Grant funds from the City of Galveston, of the five-bay cottage at **1402 Church Street** (c. 1880), moved to this site from 906 30th Street in the West End, where it had been slated for demolition. David Mullican was rehabilitation architect. Through Operation Church Street, the foundation has reinforced what was perceived as a vulnerable spot in the East End Historic District without altering the character of what was historically a working-class enclave in the genteel East End.

519 15th Street   B-82
Darragh Fence
1889, Alfred Muller

The magnificent cast-iron Darragh Fence, featured in Ezra Stoller's dust-jacket photograph for *The Galveston That Was,* was installed in 1889 when Alfred Muller altered and expanded an existing house on this corner for the prominent Irish-American businessman John L. Darragh, who served as president of both the Galveston City Company and the Galveston Wharf Company, and his third wife, Laura Leonard Darragh. The Galveston Historical Foundation bought the Darragh House in 1986, following a misguided attempt at restoration that left the interior of the house gutted. In 1990, arsonists burned the Darragh House, leaving only the fragments of Muller's fence and the remarkable tile sidewalks along 15th and Church Streets. In 1992 the foundation moved the house now at **1510 Church Street** from its original location at 1823 Postoffice Street. Research revealed that it had been built by Judge Darragh in 1886 as one of three tenant houses. In 1995, the Darragh Fence and the remaining lots were bought by the East End Historical District Association from the Galveston Historical Foundation for conversion into a neighborhood park.

The Cherry House is also notable for being one of only two houses in the neighborhood to escape destruction during the great fire of 1885.

1609 Church Street   B–85
1903

This raised cottage, built by F. H. Sage, manager of the Galveston office of the Texas Transport and Terminal Company, calls attention to itself with its double spindle porch rails and the "swag" pattern achieved by stationing wooden spheres between the spindles.

Alley between 1500 block of Church and 1500 block of Winnie   B–83
Late 19th and 20th centuries

In addition to Galveston's front-street population, the city's residential neighborhoods always had a sizeable alley population who lived in one of two building types: secondary or service buildings that were oriented to a front house and included slave or servant quarters; and alley houses that were oriented to the alley and usually built as rental property. Both building types were built well into the 20th century. A series of typical alley houses can be seen on the north, or Church Street, side of this alley. On the south, or Winnie Street, side of the alley is the only surviving example of several service buildings that existed on that side—the alley buildings reflecting the socioeconomic status of residents on the front street.

1602 Church Street   B–84
1854

At 16th Street, Church Street historically returned to middle-class respectability. Marking this corner is one of the oldest houses in the district, built for the founding publisher of the *Galveston News,* Wilbur Cherry. It is a two-story I-house with a double-level veranda and an offset rear wing. The clipped eaves and tightly compacted proportions of the Cherry House were characteristic of Galveston's wooden houses from the 1830s through the mid-1850s.

1618 Church Street   B–86
1886; additions 1889

Mrs. Rosa McD. Peete replaced her house, burnt in the Fire of 1885, with a noncombustible successor of brick and slate. It is distinctive not only for its materials but also for its mansard roof. Through inappropriate alterations, the house has lost its front veranda and its original stucco surfacing. The parapet wall along the sidewalk is also an incompatible addition.

1627 Church Street   B-87
1908, N. J. Clayton

This house, and the smaller house behind it at **612 17th Street,** were built as tenant houses by Edward A. Colleraine, proprietor of the Brick Wharf Saloon. They are among the few known works in Galveston by N. J. Clayton after Clayton's declaration of bankruptcy in 1904. What the house at 1627 demonstrates is that Clayton, although he adhered to old-fashioned typologies and decoration, was still capable of producing spatially buoyant designs. The chamfered-ended verandas and the angled offsets on the 17th Street side of the house display Clayton's lyricism, as does the veranda rail detailing of both houses.

Across the intersection, at **1702 Church Street, 1706 Church Street,** and **513 17th Street,** are three substantial tenant houses built by Mrs. Jens Möller in 1896.

1717 Church Street   B-88
1887

Built quite close to the sidewalk, this house for Mrs. Emma Meyer is a Victorian recasting of the five-bay-wide, center-hall-plan, raised cottage type with a one-bay-wide front porch. Rather than a side-gabled roof, it has a low-pitched hipped roof.

1718 Church Street   B-89
1886

Like the Waters House at 1116 Church Street, this house, built by the dry goods merchant Nephtali Grumbach in the 1885 fire district, stands out by virtue of its sprawling, picturesque composition. It is an amalgamation of big-scaled shapes and boldly articulated detail, concentrated, after the accepted Galveston manner, on its porches. Facing Church Street is an extremely tall, open-gabled porch. This continues, at the first-floor level, as an open terrace to connect with another double-level porch facing a deep, east-side garden. C. W. Bulger was responsible for a remodeling in 1906.

1722 Church Street   B-90
1896, George B. Stowe

An early independent work by Stowe, built for the commission merchant and wine salesman William Meininger, this house displays the emphasis on elaboration of wall surfaces that became pronounced in Galveston in the 1890s. In this respect, it contrasts with Victorian houses of the 1870s and 1880s, in which the screen of veranda supports was decoratively elaborated, but the wall surfaces of the house remained a uniform surface of wood clapboards. By energizing the walls and piling up roof shapes, Stowe spatialized picturesqueness, so to speak, although the head-height clearance is so low where the roof dips down over the second-story porch that one suspects he needed a little more practice. The Meininger House was restored to its original condition as a single-family house in 1981.

1801 Church Street   B–91

1904

Like Clayton's Colleraine House at 1627 Church, this house, built for Aaron Levy, a clerk at the Blum Hardware Company, is an example of 20th-century Victorian survival. It also perpetuated into the 20th century the type of the three-bay, side-hall, Southern town house.

1804 Church Street   B–92

1886, N. J. Clayton

Thomas Goggan's sheet music and musical instrument sales company had outlets in most of Texas's largest cities and towns by the end of the 19th century. The house that Clayton designed for him, although not as grand as some of the Broadway mansions, is big in scale and generously dimensioned. It is a center-hall-plan house. The plasticity of detail of its front veranda is characteristic of Clayton, as is the vaulted gablet crowning the outthrust center bay. The Goggan House retains its fine cast-iron fence.

1816 Church Street   B–93

1916, L. S. Green

Pushed back on its site, this stucco-faced, concrete-block house, designed by the Houston architect Lewis Sterling Green, is very unassuming. Its screened porch was a 20th-century development. Note that the street-facing gable of the chalet-type house is marked with the initials H. T. for Henry Tinterow, the clothing merchant who built the house.

1824 Church Street   B–94

1891

In a variation of the standard Southern town house type, the veranda of this house, built for Mrs. John D. Sawyer and her son, William, is divided into two bays, rather than three, and the side entrance bay is spatially accentuated with a vaulted gablet. The paired posts and the X-bracing pattern of the rails constitute a virtual façade that accentuates the spatiality of the veranda. It was through this emphasis on spatiality and minor variations in decoration that Galveston builders and architects filled the blocks of the East End with a limited number of house types yet avoided the sense of monotonous repetition.

1821 and 1823 Winnie Avenue B–95
1893

The real estate investor H. M. Trueheart seems to have built this pair of high-raised, side-hall-plan houses as tenant houses. Despite their narrowness, they are sheathed with shingles, including a flared skirt of shingles beneath the second-floor windows, to advertise their middle-class respectability. The picturesquely detailed porches, and especially the way that the west-side walls are inset to allow access to light and air (visible on the exposed side of 1823), suggest the hand of C. W. Bulger.

1819 Winnie Avenue B–96
1886

Built for Dr. W. D. Kelley in the 1885 fire district, this house has a porch rail of repeating, double-flexed, cutout panels and a decorative grid set in relief within the front-facing gable of the roof. It also possesses a Galveston sidewalk of diagonally rotated tiles.

1816 Winnie Avenue B–97
1903

The classical columns of the inset first-floor gallery suggest the late date of this tall, white house, raised on a basement of red brick. With its angled front-window bay balanced by the bowed corner bay of the porch, and its high-peaked gable decorated with swags, it possesses the buoyant shapeliness one associates with Galveston. The house was built for Miss Sarah P. Root and her sister, Mrs. Charles F. W. Felt.

1806 Winnie Avenue B–98
1912

Just how long Victorian elements persisted in Galveston houses is demonstrated by the high-raised house built for Theodore Bauss, who worked for Hutchings, Sealy & Co. Contributing to its look of solidity and spaciousness are the concrete parapet bordering the extremely wide front sidewalk and the stout concrete piers with pyramidal caps.

1727 Winnie Avenue B–99
1893

Built as a tenant house by the real estate agent Asbury H. Casteel, this house possesses a distinctively profiled roof above its projecting, first-floor veranda. The roof has an S-curved shape that is visible on other Galveston houses of the period. There is a slight variation in the setback of house fronts from the street on this block of Winnie Street.

It creates a subtle spatial play that makes one aware of how the porch-fronted house type consistently shapes urban space in the East End. Indeed, both sides of the 1700 block present an especially good catalogue of East End house types.

1712 Winnie Avenue   **B–102**
1886

This house, built for Yetta Heidenheimer and Abraham Davis, is a fine example of the Victorianization of the Southern town house type so characteristic of Galveston. The split gablet with its central medallion, and the arcuated brackets of the veranda posts penetrated by diagonals tipped with pendants are decorative features that imbue the house front with its distinctive personality.

1719 Winnie Avenue   **B–100**
1886

This Victorian version of a side-hall-plan Southern town house was built by Louis Zimmermann, a stevedore, to replace a house destroyed in the Fire of 1885.

1709 and 1711 Winnie Avenue   **B–103**
1888

1724 and 1722 Winnie Avenue   **B–101**
1886

Why Charles A. Harris chose to build this pair of shotgun tenant cottages in the 1885 fire district is curious, inasmuch as a more substantial house might have yielded a higher rental income here in the East End. With their very narrow street faces and delicate attached porches, they are classic examples of the shotgun house type.

1701 and 1707 Winnie Avenue   **B–104**
1895

Built by the hardware merchant J. P. Davie as tenant houses, the two narrow, raised houses at **1711** and **1709 Winnie** have frontal gables and verandas capped, like 1727 Winnie, with an S-curved roof. Underscoring the conservatism of Galveston is the L-fronted raised Victorian cottage at **1707 Winnie,** built by the veteran Galveston builder R. B. Garnett for the lumber company executive A. Wilkins

Miller. This is a representative late-19th-century American house type. While such houses were built in numbers throughout Galveston's 19th-century neighborhoods, they nonetheless did not challenge the popularity of more established house types, such as the Southern town house. The house at **1701 Winnie,** built for H. J. Hagelman, is also an L-front Victorian cottage. Despite the picturesque asymmetry of this type, it is easy to see that it is simply a more shapely version of the old five-bay-wide cottage type.

1702 Winnie Avenue　　　　　　　B–105
1886

The Hungarian-born insurance executive Charles Vidor and his wife, Anna Walter, built this substantial, L-plan house in the middle of a three-lot site. In 1911 Mrs. Vidor moved it to the corner lot so that the property could be more intensively developed. This was the childhood home of their son, the film director King Vidor.

615 17th Street　　　　　　　　　B–106
1911

Built behind the Vidor House, this side-street house is distinctive for the way that its partial second story is played off against the inclined surface of the steep, side-gabled roof. Note the ascending windows, following the inclination of the stair, on the alley side of the house.

1617 Winnie Avenue　　　　　　　B–107
1886

Throughout Galveston's late-19th-century neighborhoods one finds small houses that attained more impressive aspects by being capped with "French" roofs. This carefully proportioned (albeit extensively altered), low-set, five-bay-wide cottage—built for the clothing store owner Charles I. Kory—is an example of this phenomenon. It demonstrates that it was often through the addition of an exceptional feature, such as a mansard roof, to a standard house type that an unusual appearance was achieved in Galveston.

1616 Winnie Avenue　　　　　　　B–108
1886

This is a conservative Italianate house with a hipped roof and a one-story front porch supported on boldly scaled Ionic colonnettes. The house was built by Miss Mathilda Wehmeyer, a teacher who eventually operated a school here, to replace a house she lost in the Fire of 1885.

1602 Winnie Avenue　　　　　　　B–109
L. W. Senechal Grocery Building
1901

Now encrusted with several layers of artificial stone covering, this cube-shaped corner store building forecasts a change in the social geography of Winnie Street, although one that is not quite as drastic as occurs on Church Street. This change seems to happen at what had been the east line of the 1885 fire district, suggesting that before the fire the

East End was more socially varied than would be true of those portions rebuilt after the fire.

1522 Winnie Avenue   B–110
c. 1876

This expansive Gulf Coast cottage, with its six-over-six-pane shuttered windows and twin-window dormers, was built by the Galveston police officer George W. Morris.

1520 and 1518 Winnie Avenue   B–111
1915

A pair of tenant houses, built by Dr. Cooper P. Bevil, these are unusual in being mirror images of each other rather than being serially repeated. Serial repetition was preferred in Galveston because it made it possible to organize interior spaces so that the side hall was consistently located on the side of the house that did not receive the prevailing Gulf breeze.

1512 and 1510 Winnie Avenue   B–112
1879

Another pair of tenant houses, built by the real estate investor Christian J. Henck. Indicative perhaps of their aspiring status, these houses differ in external appearance, although both are organized with side-hall plans, curiously located on the climatically "good"—east—side of each house, rather than the west.

1317, 1319, and 1321 Winnie Avenue   B–113
1893, 1893, c. 1897

Communal space, the space of the street, is what one experiences strongly not only in the East End, but in other 19th-century Galveston neighborhoods as well. This row of houses—the raised house at **1321 Winnie Street,** the pair of gable-fronted, chamfered-bay, raised Victorian cottages built by William Stephenson at **1319** and **1317 Winnie Street,** and the two similar raised side-gabled cottages with attached porches at **1315** and **1311 Winnie Street** (1899), built by Henry Schulte—demonstrates how such spatial sensations were achieved. By mirroring each other's basic shapes and dimensions, as **1316 Winnie Street** (1891, built by Henry D. Schutte) does, they contribute to an uninsistent sense of commonality. The repetition of porches and upward inclined flights of steps reinforce this space while varying in individual detail. Being raised and set very, very close together, the houses contain and channel the space of the street more effectively than they would if set lower to the ground or farther apart. Thus, even with compact wooden houses, it was possible to shape urban community space in 19th-century Galveston.

1209 Winnie Avenue   B–114
1882

The two-over-two-pane windows and the transom-topped
front door without sidelights date this conservative, side-
gabled, five-bay-front cottage as much as does the Victorian
detail of the front veranda. It was built by Medard Ménard,
a retired cotton weigher and the cousin (and brother-in-law)
of Galveston's founder, Michael B. Ménard, for himself and
his daughter, Mrs. Augustine Lancton.

continuously from the brick basement to the top of the wall.

Nearby, at **912 Winnie Avenue** (1885), is a slightly
Victorianized version of the Southern town house type, built
for Mrs. Louisa B. Danelly, a teacher at Ball High School.

712 10th Street   B–115
1902

Note how the multiple rear additions, with their different
profiles, contrast with the body of this house. While such
profiles usually represent additions, some Galveston houses
seem to have been built with such picturesque profiles to
begin with. This house and its neighbors at the intersection
of 10th and Winnie were built by Mrs. Stanka Agin, who
ran a grocery, feed, and dry goods store a block away at 9th
and Winnie.

905 Winnie Avenue   B–117
1869

Although modest in size, this five-bay-wide, side-gabled
cottage, built by the blacksmith Frederick C. Schmidt, has
simplified Greek Revival architraves framing its shuttered
front windows and the transom-and-sidelight-encased front
door. Such detail suggests that the present porch posts may
be later alterations.

926 Winnie Avenue   B–116
1888

The house built by the importer and wholesale grocer
Liberty S. McKinney is notable for its big scale and the vivid
decorative detail of its two-story porch, where a curvilinear
theme is played out with such wit and invention that it
distracts attention from the house's plain clapboard wall
surfaces. Energetic decorative woodwork and a high, stucco-
surfaced brick basement were attributes of Alfred Muller's
architecture, although there is no evidence to link him to the
design of this house. Restored in 1975, the house was badly
damaged by fire in 1993. This revealed the underlying
structure of the McKinney House: thick, vertical, wood
studs, spaced about 18 inches on center, that run

728 Winnie Avenue   B–118
1915

This two-story house, like several others in the East End
located on corner lots, architecturally addresses the corner
with a chamfered entry porch. It was built by the
dockworker Herbert L. Parsons.

724 and 722 Winnie Avenue   B–119
1914 and 1901

The tiny house at 722 Winnie is a classic example of the shotgun cottage. The house next door, a wider version of the two-bay shotgun cottage type with a front veranda, was built in 1914 but moved to this site in 1915.

902 Ball Avenue   B–122
1906

Built as a tenant house by the investor J. A. Boddeker, this cottage also testifies to the conservatism of Galveston house builders. One does find in the 900 block several examples of L-fronted picturesque Victorian cottages. However, since the block lay in the area of total destruction in 1900, these too seem to be of 20th-century origin.

819 Ball Avenue   B–120
1901

Built in the aftermath of the Storm of 1900 by the stationery company salesman Fred F. Hunter, this two-story I-house is enlivened with shingled surfaces. As was often the case for houses facing north, it has only a one-story veranda. The front entrance has been remodeled.

1007 Ball Avenue   B–123
1880

Built for the druggist Calvin W. Preston, this two-bay-wide house, decorated with Néo-Grec wooden ornament, belongs to a typological variation on the three-bay, side-hall house type popular in the 1870s. The two window bays were compressed into one (at the Everett House at 1211 Church and the Smith House at 2217 Broadway, they were compressed into a projecting bay window), and elaborate porches were dispensed with. Preston's house, as it survives today, is the result of a 1906 remodeling. The house originally faced 10th Street. It was rotated to face Ball, and a substantial rear wing was subtracted in the process.

901 Ball Avenue   B–121
1903

Insurance records indicate that this house was built by Joseph P. Fine, a watchman at Fort San Jacinto, after the 1900 storm. This was a very late date for a mansard roof.

1025 Ball Avenue   **B–124**
1884

This three-bay Southern town house was built by the lawyer Marcellus E. Kleberg. It was remodeled in 1897 and again in 1915, then—like C. W. Preston's house—moved onto one lot of what had been a two-lot corner site in 1929. What makes the Kleberg House unusual is its diagonally rotated rear tower, visible up the driveway on the west side of the house.

1202 Ball Avenue   **B–126**
1882

Built for Dr. Hamilton A. West, who became the first professor of clinical medicine and of the principles and practices of medicine at UTMB, this house typologically resembles N. J. Clayton's Lovenberg House at 1412 Market. Its porch detail is identical to that of Mrs. Yetta Davis's house at 1712 Winnie.

1103 Ball Avenue   **B–125**
1889

This five-bay-wide raised cottage is notable for its elaborate, three-bay-wide front porch. It was built for Henry Locke, a ship's captain, at the same time that the monumental Rosenberg Free School (1889, N. Tobey, Jr.) was built across the street, facing Sherman Square. In 1888 Henry Rosenberg gave the Free School Board of Trustees $40,000 to build the school, emulating the philanthropy of George Ball. Tobey's Rosenberg School was demolished following completion of the present **Rosenberg Elementary School** (1964, Thomas M. Price, Ben J. Kotin & Tibor Beerman, Raymond R. Rapp & Associates, and Charles L. Zwiener), which was constructed in Sherman Square. The site of the older civic building then became the new Sherman Square–Louis Adoue Playground. It contains, near the corner of 12th and Ball, one of the **Rosenberg Fountains** (1898, J. Massey Rhind, sculptor), installed in 1965.

1208 Ball Avenue   **B–127**
1875, N. J. Clayton

This is one of the earliest houses that can be securely attributed to Clayton. Built for the cotton factor and commission and grain merchant Henry A. Seeligson, it is an exceedingly restrained version of the Southern town house type, with little to betray Clayton's hand except its assured proportions. Here, as in other Galveston houses, the two-story, south-facing front veranda is wrapped around the east side of the house as a one-story gallery. As the Augustus Koch 1885 bird's-eye view of Galveston shows, the Seeligson House was built at the corner of 13th and Ball, where 1228 Ball now sits. It was picked up and moved to the east side of the five-lot site in order to permit construction of Clayton's much grander house for Seeligson's brother, George Seeligson, about 1887. The Henry Seeligson House retains a black-and-red tile sidewalk and a low iron fence.

212 Ball Avenue rear   **B–128**

1888, N. J. Clayton

Behind the nondescript late-1950s' house at 1212 Ball is Clayton's substantial stable and carriage house for the wholesale grocer and importer George Seeligson. It is detailed as a picturesque High Victorian version of a Swiss chalet. The George Seeligson House was demolished in 1934 by Seeligson's daughter, Lillian Seeligson Winterbotham. All that remains are the grandiose, diagonally rotated pedestals that framed the front steps to the Seeligson House (they virtually dwarf the house at 1224 Ball, whose front yard they occupy) and, at the alley line on 13th, behind 1228 Ball, portions of a stucco-faced brick wall.

215 Ball Avenue   **B–129**

1881

This raised cottage displays projecting bay windows and a one-bay-wide front porch as its distinguishing features. It was built by the merchandise broker Gracey W. Bell.

310 Ball Avenue   **B–130**

1885

William H. Griffin, an adjuster for Kauffman & Runge,

built this house. It has been very tactfully converted into a double house. Next door, at **1302 Ball Avenue,** is the sober stucco-faced house built in 1913 by the coal dealer George D. Flood.

1316 Ball Avenue   **B–131**

1895

Built nine years after the Cohen House at 1818 Postoffice, this house, constructed for Axel I. Roempke, who worked for a watchmaker, jeweler, and optician, adopted a similar spatial organization. The front wall of the house was projected forward as a chamfered bay with its own two-story porch, while the front door was recessed to one side and given a separate porch.

1320 Ball Avenue   **B–132**

1894

This substantial L-front Victorian cottage was raised high enough to justify a stair with an intermediate landing, heightening the drama of entrance. It was built by the bank cashier William J. Frederich.

1328 Ball Avenue   **B–133**

1868

Double-height fluted Doric columns transform this three-bay, side-hall, Southern town house, built for the shipping and commission merchant Charles W. Hurley, who also served as mayor of Galveston, into quite a grand house. The arched fanlights surmounting the front door probably represent an early-20th-century remodeling. Note the

telescoping of rear wings along the 14th Street side of the house. The back house, at **714 14th Street,** is quite old, dating to 1854, although remodeled in 1910. The Hurley House was rehabilitated in 1996.

1402 Ball Avenue   **B–134**
1908
Built for Mrs. George Fox, whose husband had been a partner of his brother Chris in the Model Steam Bakery, this house demonstrates the attraction of the Colonial Revival and the impulse toward simple dignity it seemed to represent, and Galvestonians' conservative attachment to established house types, in this case the Victorian towered villa.

1407 Ball Avenue   **B–135**
1895
Built close to the street, with a lateral entrance stair and a raised one-story porch capped with an S-curved roof, this house, first occupied by the noted horticulturist Henry M. Stringfellow, is an I-house, Victorianized with a projecting chamfered bay. Its planarity and one-story porch mark it as a north-facing house. Note that the rear water cistern remains in place on the west side of the house. Before

Galveston obtained a waterworks plant in 1889, householders collected rainwater in back-yard cisterns for domestic use.

1428 Ball Avenue   **B–136**
1900
Although it hardly looks revolutionary, this sober brick house was the first post-Victorian house in Galveston. Its symmetry, lack of picturesque protrusions, and the abandonment of lacy wood or iron porch supports for a portico carried on paired Tuscan columns indicate its attempt to replicate, with some degree of academic correctness, the sort of house that might have been built by Yankee master builders for a Southern planter in the 1820s. The raised basement and the handsome cement stucco-faced parapet framing the property lines are, of course, pure Galveston. Completed just before the Storm of 1900, this house was built for one of Galveston's pioneer jewelers, Michael W. Shaw, a Prussian Jew who came to Galveston in 1845. Its architect has yet to be identified.

1427 Ball Avenue   **B–137**
c. 1874
This simple, five-bay raised cottage with side-gabled roof, built by the carpenter Christopher Homrighaus, takes on greater formal complexity as one views it from 15th Street. There, the composite nature of the house is revealed, with roof shapes suggesting that the rear wing may once have been a freestanding building. Behind the main house are two tenant cottages. The house at **808 15th Street** is a type often seen south of Broadway, in which a veranda is inset beneath one edge of the front-facing gable to become an

ꝍpen-air side hall, producing a sideways variation on the Ɠulf Coast cottage.

501 Ball Avenue   **B–138**

Ɛast End Historical District Association Park

ꝑosenberg Fountain

1898, J. Massey Rhind, sculptor

The East End Historic District is Galveston's oldest historic district. It was created in 1971 by the Galveston City Ꞓouncil, listed in the National Register of Historic Places in 1975, and designated a National Historic Landmark in 1976. The neighborhood association maintains this park, to ᴡhich one of the Rosenberg Fountains was moved. The ᴀssociation publishes a walking tour brochure, the *East End Historic District Riding and Walking Tour.*

502 Ball Avenue   **B–139**

ᴄ. 1889, 1905

Ɓuilt for the admiralty lawyer and Galveston County judge ᴡ. B. Lockhart and his wife Esther Gresham, daughter of Ꞓolonel Walter Gresham, this house was constructed in two stages, in a manner not uncommon in Galveston. In 1905, the raised cottage that constitutes the second floor of the ꝑresent house was raised higher still and a new raised first ꝭoor was constructed beneath it. The picturesque ɡeometries of Victorian planning are played off against cool, ꝑrim Colonial Revival detail.

1512 Ball Avenue   **B–140**

1891

This large, raised wooden house, with its variations in veranda screening detail, was built for the commission merchant Walter F. Ayres. The treatment of the veranda and the roof gablet look like the work of Alfred Muller, although there is no documentation to support attribution to him.

The elaborately gabled house at **1514 Ball Avenue** (1897, C. W. Bulger), built by the marine insurance executive William F. Beers but first occupied by the dry goods merchant Edward S. Levy, has suffered inappropriate alterations.

1517 Ball Avenue   **B–141**

1882

The Cottage, as the house built for the cotton buyer Bernard Roensch is familiarly known, is a charming curiosity. It is a center-hall-plan cottage, decorated with a fantastic array of arcuated door and window surrounds, planes of wooden ornament layered onto its gabled front porch, and a chamfered "tower" that is sculpturally shaped and capped. The decorative exuberance of this modest house is quintessentially Galvestonian, which is perhaps why it has become an East End landmark.

1522 Ball Avenue   **B–142**

1890

The brick piers supporting the veranda are a later alteration
to what otherwise remains a good example of a
Victorianized three-bay Southern town house, built for
James Findlay, an employee of Ball, Hutchings & Company.

802 16th Street   **B–143**

1884

Remodeling, 1892, N. J. Clayton & Company

N. J. Clayton's office records indicate that in 1892 he
remodeled this house (built in 1884) and a no-longer-extant
stable building next door at 808 16th for the owner of the
property, Mrs. George Ball. Mrs. Ball seems to have rented
802 to tenants. Clayton's distinctive touch is hardly visible
on the exterior of the house, except in the decorative
vergeboard framing the roof gable facing 16th Street.

1601 Ball Avenue   **B–144**

1888

Built for H. S. Mather, this two-story house was,
architecturally, one of the most singular in the East End. If
one can disregard the suburban privacy fence, the powder
blue-and-cream paint job, and a subsequent raising of the
house on high piers, its original identity as a High Victorian
chalet becomes evident. The clapboard walls were initially

painted a dark tone. Only the stucco panels in the timbered
bays were light in color. Thus the Mather House exhibited a
much stronger affinity with the Henry Beissner House at
2818 Ball than its present appearance suggests.

1602 Ball Avenue   **B–145**

1886

It is tempting to ascribe this house to the architect William
H. Roystone because the decorative floral panels in its
second-floor balustrade are similar to those on the F. W.
Beissner House at 1702 Ball, which Roystone designed. The
decorative woodwork was unusual for Galveston in its
emphasis on closely spaced verticals and the big-scaled,
painted floral panels. It is interesting to note that the porch
posts do not line up with windows, although they do frame
the front double doors. Joel B. Wolfe, who built this house,
was a heavy-machinery wholesale and commission
merchant. He constructed it to replace one destroyed in the
Fire of 1885.

1612 Ball Avenue   **B–146**

1890

Built by the First Presbyterian Church as the pastor's
"manse," this three-bay Southern town house features
arcuated lintels between the first-floor veranda posts and
ogee arches between the second-floor posts. The association

of the ogival profile with Gothic religious architecture may
have been intended to signal humorously the clerical
association of this house.

1616 and 1614 Ball Avenue   B–147
1886

Their raised stature and street-facing gables bestow an
appearance of similarity on these adjoining houses, built for
the tailor John F. Michels in the reconstruction of the 1885
fire district. As one sees time and again in the East End and
other Galveston neighborhoods, such similarity allows them
to reinforce urbanistically the communal space of the street,
even though they are freestanding, single-family houses.

1622 Ball Avenue   B–148
1886

The German-born bookkeeper George Trapp built this house
to replace one destroyed in the Fire of 1885. It is a
straightforward rendition of the Southern town house type,
with minimal Victorian ornamentation. Despite its relatively
modest size, the Trapp House occupies what now seems to be

a large site, since it possesses spacious east and west side yards.
As 19th-century fire insurance maps of Galveston show, such
spaciousness was once more typical of the East End than is
now the case. Subdividing multilot sites to accommodate new
construction in the late 19th and early 20th centuries
considerably increased the density of buildings in the East
End and other Galveston neighborhoods.

1702 Ball Avenue   B–149
1886, William H. Roystone

As Dickey & Helmich did at the Landes House at 1604
Postoffice, Roystone designed this house for the cotton clerk
Frederick W. Beissner to address its street-corner site with
bravura. Its spatial overture to the intersection was reiterated
across the street at **1628 Ball** (1899). Roystone was an
itinerant architect who worked in Galveston between 1886
and 1890, spending a short time in N. J. Clayton's office.
This is one of only two buildings that can be securely
attributed to him. It is distinctive for the variety of
decorative surfaces Roystone compacted into one building,
and for his evident dedication to the sunflower as a
decorative device. The sunflower was identified with the
English Aesthetic movement of the late 1870s and early
1880s (promoted locally by no less an exponent than Oscar
Wilde, who spoke on "The Decorative Art" in Galveston in
June 1882, during his American tour). Its prominence at
the Beissner House was highlighted by a sumptuous
polychrome painting scheme in 1995. An echo can be seen
in the high gables at **1701 Ball** (1887).

1709 and 1711 Ball Avenue   B–150
1892, William Pautsch, builder

This pair of gable-fronted tenant cottages, built for Mrs.
Dorothea Juneman, widow of the carpenter and builder
George Juneman, are faced with three-bay verandas. Their

decoration-filled arches, turned posts, and X-paneled rails, as well as the shingle-surfaces of the gable fronts, give the cottages the architectural presence their high-end setting required.

1715 Ball Avenue   B–151
1886

This five-bay-wide raised cottage with an attached, gable-fronted porch displays a High Victorian interpretation of the door and window surrounds most often seen on Galveston houses of the late 1850s through mid-1870s. It was built as a tenant house by Mrs. Juneman.

1719 and 1721 Ball Avenue   B–152
1893, 1894

Like the cottage next door at 1715 Ball, the three-bay Southern town house at 1719 Ball exhibits decorative detail that seems old-fashioned for the year it was supposedly built for the saloon owner Richard S. Coon.

  Mrs. Juneman built the raised, three-bay tenant cottage at 1721 Ball. It is quite similar to the pair she built at 1709 and 1711 Ball. Note on the exposed west side of the house the rear service porch, screened with layers of louvered blinds.

1724 Ball Avenue   B–153
1901

This high-raised three-bay house looks more like a north-facing house than a south-facing house, in large part because it has only a one-story veranda rather than a double veranda. It is the extraordinary woodwork detail of the

veranda that gives this house its special distinction, reflecting the fact that it was built by the carpenter and builder James H. Kissinger.

1801 Ball Avenue   B–154
1896

The meat supplier Alfred S. Newson built this house, which, like so many north-facing houses in Galveston, appears very different in character from more expansive and relaxed south-facing houses. Its height, its nervous proportions, its tight planar fronts, and its constricted porch are all attributes of north-facing houses, despite efforts to imbue the Newson House's chamfered porch with some corner-facing brio. (It saluted N. J. Clayton's splendid Louis Block House of 1887 across the street at 1804 Ball, knocked down in the late 1960s to build the apartments now at that corner.) The Newson House was handsomely rehabilitated in 1989. It marks the beginning of one of the best lineups of porch fronts in the East End.

1819 Ball Avenue   B–155
1891

Built for the clothier Jacob Wenk, this substantial, raised, two-story, L-front house is encrusted with horizontal bands of decorative shingle work, X-panels, and Victorian Mannerist classical decor framing the three-part first-floor window facing

the street. Like other houses on this side of the block, the
Wenk House is pressed close to the sidewalk line.

821 and 1823 Ball Avenue   B–156
1893

Reinforcing the coherence of the block front are these two
Victorian versions of the Southern town house type, built
for Mrs. Augusta Peters.

827 Ball Avenue   B–157
1895

This substantial, high-raised house was one of two built as
tenant houses by Maud Wilson Möller. Because the
architect George B. Stowe designed a tenant house for Mrs.
Möller's husband, Jens Möller, two years after these tenant
houses were built, they have been attributed to him. Formal
evidence makes the attribution quite plausible. This house is
especially notable for its conically roofed porch turret,

poised at the 19th-Ball corner of the house, around which
the porch steps curve sinuously down.

812 19th Street   B–158
1895

As Mrs. Möller did with another group of tenant houses she
built at 17th and Church in 1895, she had both the house
at 1827 Ball and this house built on one lot. Thus it shares
the high-set, slightly cramped feel of 1827. In place of
1827's corner porch turret, this house has a tight, but
spatially orchestrated, entry sequence leading up to its front
porch. The elaborate porch detail that both houses share is
echoed in the decoration of the roof dormers at 812. In
1995, the street front of this house was brilliantly repainted.

1826 Sealy Avenue   B–159
1887

One of the most spectacular houses in the East End, this
two-story, wood frame L-front house was built by the
businessman and insurance agent Jacob W. Sonnentheil.
Although some architectural drawings of the house survive,
they are not signed. Attributions have been made to various
architects of the time, but none is credible.

The Sonnentheil House is notable for its richly decorated
surfaces. These were achieved, as was customary in

Galveston, with framing and paneling overlaid on the house's otherwise ordinary clapboard surfaces. The west side of the house, facing 19th Street, is an almost symphonic presentation of the possibilities of decorative framing, especially as such elements as the stucco-surfaced brick chimney, the projecting bay window at the landing level of the main stair, and the inset side-entrance porch spatialized the surface patterning. These themes are reiterated in a two-story stable and carriage house at 19th and the **alley,** one of the most architecturally imposing alleys in the East End.

It is, however, the double galleries on the front of the house, and especially their frieze screens of one-way diagonal lattice work, that spatialize the play of light and shade, ultimately the most powerful decorative effect in Galveston. There is nothing comparable to this sophisticated use of screening on surviving Galveston houses, which is one reason that attributions of the house to Clayton or Muller are not convincing. The *Galveston Daily News* reported that in the aftermath of the Fire of 1885, there was an influx of "foreign" (i.e. out-of-state) builders coming into Galveston, many of whom had left by the fall of 1886. Alfred Muller and W. H. Roystone both came to Galveston in the wake of the fire. Therefore, it is possible that the Sonnentheil House was built by an itinerant contractor or designer who did not remain in town long enough to claim due credit.

The Sonnentheil House was rehabilitated in 1977.

their geometries in the alternation of wide-span arcs and narrow arches between the double sets of turned posts.

1817 Sealy Avenue B–162
1907, Donald N. McKenzie

Although sedate in shape, this house, built for the dry goods merchant Morris Wansker, adhered to traditional Galveston typologies, in this case the side-hall-plan house. In 1977 the house was restored by Carlotta Morris and David V. Barker. Barker, an architect, designed a new front gallery to replace the original, demolished in the 1930s. Carlotta Barker is an artist who frequently uses historic Galveston architecture as her subject.

1819 Sealy Avenue B–160
1904

According to insurance records, this house was built of materials salvaged from an 1890-era house destroyed in the Storm of 1900.

1818 Sealy Avenue B–161
1897, George B. Stowe

Stowe could be a very restrained architect, especially when compared with Alfred Muller or his former employer C. W. Bulger. But in this house, built as a rental property for the Danish-born shipping agent Jens Möller (husband of Maud Wilson Möller), he relaxed his inhibitions and combined a corner turret on the west side of the house with a chamfered window bay on the east side, and in the recess that they compose, he inserted the entrance doors. Stowe's double-level gallery encompasses the turret, bay, and recess, reiterating

1815 Sealy Avenue B–163
1898, George B. Stowe

Built for the boot-and-shoe-store owner Joseph Goldstein and

is sisters, the Misses Henrietta and Minnie Goldstein, this
ubstantial raised house is unusual in being four bays wide,
rather than three. With its arcuated veranda lintels, turned
porch posts, and stucco-faced basement arches, it corresponds
architecturally to the row of houses across the street.

814 Sealy Avenue   B-164
1886

This house, which was rehabilitated in 1966 by the
Houston architect Robert H. Wilson, Jr., is an expansive,
three-bay-wide Southern town house, surrounded on two
sides by a handsome, double-level gallery supported on
paired posts (which are detailed to contrast with, rather
than repeat, each other). Built for the dry goods merchant
Jacob S. Bernheim, it exhibits such features as scrolled
architraves above first- and second-floor windows that
appear in houses by Alfred Muller. Because the house was
owned in the 1890s by Mr. and Mrs. Jens Möller, it has
been attributed to George B. Stowe, confusing it with the
house next door, which Möller owned but did not occupy.

808 Sealy Avenue   B-165
1890

This spacious, two-story, L-front house, built for Mrs.
Abraham Levy, contributes to the collective ambiance of the
800 block of Sealy Avenue by virtue of its panels of
decorative shingles, the conical roof that projects out where
the double gallery turns the corner, and the handsome
railings, posts, and lintels of the gallery. The ornamental
woodwork resembles that of Alfred Muller.

1802 Sealy Avenue   B-166
1886

It is interesting to see on this block of Sealy, built up with
large, commodious houses following the Fire of 1885, this
very conservative Southern town house, which gives little
indication that it was not built fifteen years earlier than it
was. Constructed by Max Maas, a partner in the wholesale
grocery firm of Moore, McKinney & Co., it was
rehabilitated in 1972 and again in 1996. Note that its back
building at 18th Street and the alley is three stories high.

1728 Sealy Avenue   B-167
1900, George B. Stowe

During the 1890s, many of the largest houses built in
Galveston displayed the influence of McKim, Mead &
White's Sealy House, the Open Gates, at 2424 Broadway.
Stowe's grandest pre-Storm house, built for the marine
construction and salvage company president Charles Clarke,
pays homage to the Sealy House in its rounded bays and
porches, carefully integrated within the unifying geometry
of the roof. Stowe turned the corner-porch bay, carried on a
high-raised, arched basement, toward the street, which it
addresses with spatial generosity. It is this sense of
generosity, and the solidity of the stucco-faced brick arches
and walls of the Clarke House, that give it an air of
grandeur. Visible up the east-side driveway, behind the
house, is an architectural companion, a two-story stable and
carriage house.

1727 Sealy Avenue   B-168
1886

The unusual appearance of this house may result in part from an extensive remodeling it underwent in 1891. The front façade of the house suggests that the porch was reconstructed to give the house a more balanced look than the roofline above indicates it deserves. This house was built by Nathan S. Redlich, a partner in the wholesale clothing firm of S. Jacobs, Bernheim & Co., diagonally across the corner from the house of his wife's brother Max Maas. Mrs. Redlich's mother, who owned this lot at various times, also lived in this house. She was Isabella Offenbach Maas, sister of the Parisian composer Jacques Offenbach. Mrs. Maas and her two sisters immigrated to Texas from Germany in the 1840s. From 1994 until 1996 the Redlich House was occupied by the painter Joe Glasco.

1716 Sealy Avenue   B-169
1896

Overshadowed by the Clarke House on the corner, this high-raised house, built for the harbor pilot Joseph B. Woolford, is easily overlooked. Yet it is imposing, both because of its stature and its five-bay-wide expanse.

1627 Sealy Avenue   B-170
1890, Alfred Muller

Alfred Muller's grandest surviving Galveston house was built for a retired Danish-born merchant, J. C. Trube. It is a very unusual house. Muller ignored conservative social conventions on how houses should be planned in order to orient the major rooms of the Trube House to the back of the lot, so that they had unrestricted access to the prevailing southeast breeze. It was this conflict between propriety (which dictated that major rooms face the street) and climate (which made it advisable to face rooms toward the south or east) that caused lots on the north side of

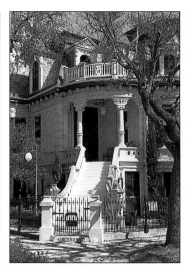

Galveston's alphabetical avenues to be so much more desirable than those on the south side. That is the principal reason why almost all of the most ambitious 19th-century houses in Galveston were built on south-facing (and, therefore, north-side) lots. What is so extraordinary about the Sealy Avenue "front" of the Trube House is that behind it are minor rooms and a lateral hall, containing the main stair, rather than double parlors.

As if to compensate for this breach of propriety, Muller lavishly ornamented the street faces of the Trube House with Victorian classical decor, rendered in stuccoed brick. Whereas George Stowe, ten years later, sought to smooth out the surfaces of the Clarke House at 1728 Sealy as much as possible, Muller maximized the decorative potential of this shadow-catching exterior surface with gusto. A mock tower facing Sealy and a protruding chimney bay on the 17th Street side of the house frame the corner of the house. This is vividly spatialized by the splendid ramped stair with which Muller provided access to the diagonally rotated corner entrance porch. It leads down to black-and-white tile sidewalks along both street faces of the house. As a demonstration of High Victorian sculptural plasticity, the Trube House scarcely has an equal in Galveston.

The house was occupied until 1985 by descendants of the Trube family.

Across the street, at **1620 Sealy Avenue,** is the high-raised L-front house built for the commission broker Louis Marx (1898).

1610 Sealy Avenue   B-171
1916

This Craftsman-style house demonstrates a propensity for horizontal extension, both in the wide spans of its wraparound first-floor gallery and in the detailing of its second-story parapet wall. Yet it retains, in part for climatic reasons, a side-hall plan and a stepping of internal spaces to grant access to the prevailing breeze. As can be seen from the street, the interior of the house is quite open. The house was built for the cotton merchant Henry W. Hackbarth. It was rehabilitated in 1984 and again in 1994.

Next door to the Hackbarth House at 1602 Sealy stood the magnificent Sydnor-Heidenheimer House (built in 1857, extensively remodeled in 1887, and added to again in 1890), which was demolished in 1974 after having been damaged by fire. Like Muller's Trube House, it exhibited pretensions to castlehood, but on an even grander scale. Eventually built on the site was a series of rental housing units originally designed by Taft Architects of Houston (1978), but constructed without architectural supervision. The Galveston Historical Foundation brought Taft Architects in to produce the abstracted Victorian shapes of the apartment buildings in an effort to prevent a much less compatible design from being constructed.

Across the street at **1609 Sealy Avenue** (1886) is a three-bay, raised cottage with veranda and twin-window dormer. It was one of two adjoining houses, built by the real estate investor Henry M. Trueheart, that backed up to his imposing N. J. Clayton-designed house at 16th and Broadway.

02 16th Street   B–172
1908

The house built for the wholesale grocer Morris Stern was a full-blown example of the so-called Colonial Revival. If modern examples of the style did not bear much resemblance to actual American colonial houses, they nonetheless met with the approbation of wealthy Texans in the years around 1910. Such houses retained the big scale and some of the picturesqueness of Victorian house types, but sought a new architectural image of respectability and success in colossal columned porticos. The paired Corinthian columns upholding the pedimented portico of the Stern House were especially popular. It is indicative of Galveston's uncertain status in the decade following the Storm of 1900 that relatively few such houses were built here.

1514 Sealy Avenue   B–173
1877, Duhamel & Lawler

Despite the intrusion of a freestanding garage in the front yard, this house, built for Judge George E. Mann, retains the essential elements of its Victorian chalet–type decor, or, as the *Galveston Daily News* described it at the time of its construction, "New England Gothic." The low-pitched roof with its wide overhangs, paired brackets, and pierced screens, the vertical lathe stripping on the upper part of the wall, and the pointed arched opening at one side of the one-story gallery mark the Mann House's departure from the accepted conventions of Galveston domestic architecture of the period. In contrast to much of E. J. Duhamel's other known work, it is a relatively simple design.

1509 Sealy Avenue   B–174
c. 1866

This five-bay-front raised cottage with a one-bay-wide front porch, built by Henry W. Bentinck, has rear wings projecting from each side. The east rear-wing is crowned with a pavilion roof. The lack of a paved sidewalk along this part of the block is very old-Galvestonian.

1503 Sealy Avenue   B–175
c. 1873

This graceful Southern town house, which has a projecting west-side wing, is evocative of the Garden District in New Orleans or Government Street in Mobile. It is perhaps the overlay of Victorian ornamentation on its classical three-bay format (especially the cast-iron rails, which were rare in Galveston) that suggests the fancifully decorated yet conservative houses associated with the Reconstruction-era building boom in all three cities. This house also displays, on its 15th Street side, a rear wing faced with double porches and screens of louvered blinds. The house was built

1859, John de Young

The Irish-born master builder John de Young built this
house, apparently for the cotton factor J. Carroll Smith. It i
very plain. Interestingly, it is neither a Gulf Coast cottage
nor a three-bay Southern town house, but a center-hall-plan
house with double-level verandas supported on widely
spaced square posts. The only external ornamental touches
are the heavy Grecian architraves framing the front windows
and door.

for Joseph Brockelman, a coppersmith and gas fitter. It is
also identified with a subsequent owner, the wholesale
druggist T. C. Thompson.

1428 Sealy Avenue   **B–176**

1875, T. J. Overmire

Julius H. Rühl, an official of Kauffman, Runge &
Company, retained the obscure Chicago architect T. J.
Overmire to design this big-scaled, two-story, center-hall-
plan house. Like the house at 1503 Sealy diagonally across
the street, it is a conservative house type ornamented with
Victorian Néo-Grec classical decoration. Overmire
apparently came to Galveston to design Sampson
Heidenheimer's ill-fated Grand Southern Hotel. This is the
only extant building known to have been built to his design.

    Next door, at **1418 Sealy Avenue,** is the Robert M.
Gunther House (1929), a raised brick bungalow typical of
the early work of R. R. Rapp.

1412 Sealy Avenue   **B–179**

1897

This raised Victorian cottage, built by the real estate broker
and builder August J. Henck, exemplifies the ultimate
Victorianization of the five-bay-wide cottage. Two of the
bays were advanced forward as a chamfered bay, creating the
sort of L-front plan configuration popular for large houses
since the 1870s. This bay was crowned by a gabled roof.
Decorative brackets at the cornice level and panels of
shingles enriched the surfaces of the bay and the gable.
Decorative screening marked off the inset porch. In the
Henck House the whole was raised on arched brick piers.
The house was rehabilitated in 1978.

1411 Sealy Avenue   **B–180**

Diocese of Galveston Chancery Office Building
1924

After Bishop Byrne bought the Gresham House at 14th and
Broadway in 1923, the Diocese of Galveston discreetly
inserted this little Mission-style office building onto the
block behind it to contain the administrative offices of the
diocese. With its brick-lined scalloped gable and clay-tile-
capped porch hood, it is a delightful building. Note

1416 Sealy Avenue   **B–177**

c. 1873

This is a good example of the Gulf Coast cottage type,
notable for its shuttered floor-length front windows.

how the walls to either side of the building flare out to
screen the approaches to the narrow side yards.

1318 Sealy Avenue   B–181
1896, C. W. Bulger

The effusive Bulger let himself go with this multi-gabled
house for the banker William C. Skinner. Bulger seems to
have aligned the windows facing the street with an elusive
axis that shifts position from one floor level to the next.
And the action doesn't stop on the street front, as the
stepped stair window on the curved roof bay on the east
side of the house demonstrates.

1316 and 1314 Sealy Avenue   B–182
c. 1876

There is something almost New England–like about this
pair of three-bay Southern town houses, built by Marcia
Allen Aiken on two lots given to her by her father, the
marble contractor Alexander A. Allen. Perhaps it is the

combination of thick, bracket-capped octagonal pillars and
the gable-fronts that they support. When the houses are
seen from the side, it is clear that they were originally very
compact. The house at 1314 was extensively reconstructed
following a serious fire in the 1980s.

815 13th Street   B–183
1979, Jack W. Morris

Galveston architect Jack Morris built this stucco-surfaced
infill house of concrete block as his own residence.

1228 Sealy Avenue   B–184
1876

This elegantly proportioned and detailed Southern town
house, built for Lemuel Burr, an employee of Leon & H.
Blum Company, has been attributed to N. J. Clayton.
There is no documentation to support such an attribution,
but the lyrical profiling of the double-level veranda, with its
central gablet, and the assured proportions of the huge,
two-pane-over-two-pane shuttered windows, capped by
Néo-Grec architraves, make such an attribution quite
persuasive. The Burr House has both an offset secondary
entrance on 13th Street and an architecturally treated east
side, overlooking a deep east garden. It retains its iron fence
and a carriage block at the curb.

1213 Sealy Avenue   **B–185**
1875
This gabled, raised cottage has a picturesque front window bay and side-facing dormers.

1212 Sealy Avenue   **B–186**
1894
Twin gables imbue the front of this high-set house, built for the cotton factor and commission merchant Joseph A. Robertson, with a symmetrical aspect, although it has an L-front plan configuration. Its verticality and planarity make it seem like a north-facing house that has somehow ended up on the opposite side of the street. Cement stucco piers and a parapet wall reinforce its air of substantiality.

Next door at **1204 Sealy Avenue** is the childhood home of the Galveston-born modern architect Donald Barthelme.

1205 Sealy Avenue   **B–187**
c. 1881, 1893
A famous panoramic photograph taken of the 1200 block of Sealy just after the Storm of 1900 shows the wrecked condition of all the houses on the south side of the street. What is remarkable is that in 1996, this five-bay-wide cottage with a gable-fronted porch, occupied by Mrs. M. W. Thomas at the time of the storm, has reverted to its wracked 1900 condition, as it lists alarmingly, but picturesquely, to the west.

1118 Sealy Avenue   **B–188**
1875
This is a very handsome five-bay-wide, center-hall-plan house with double-level verandas inserted beneath a side-gabled roof. It was built by the marble contractor and monument maker Alexander A. Allen. Only the two-pane-over-two-pane windows (and the gable windows, obviously later additions) hint at its post–Civil War construction date. Otherwise, it looks like a modest planter's house that somehow made it to town. The house at **1114 Sealy Avenue** was originally a wing added to the Allen House in 1886.

1110 Sealy Avenue   **B–189**
1889, 1915
This is an engaging little house, built as part of the Allen homestead, then remodeled in 1915 by a subsequent owner, W. L. Garbade. Across the street at **1109 Sealy Avenue,** brick veneer surfaces and academically correct Colonial Revival detail identify the cubic house of the dry goods merchant Henry C. Eiband (1927, R. R. Rapp) as a 20th-century insertion. This was where the area of total destruction resulting from the 1900 storm began. A similarly shaped and detailed wood house, built for Nathan V. Morgan, an official of the American National Insurance Company, sits around the corner at **901 11th Street** (1926).

102 Sealy Avenue   B–190

. 1879, 1896

Despite extremely adverse modifications, this house, built
by the sand and coal distributor Frank A. Park, then
expanded in the mid-1890s by the shipping agent J. Henry
Langbehn, is quite imposing. The house survived the Storm
of 1900 but required extensive reconstruction. It was raised
high on a new arched basement and surrounded with
double-level galleries, which are now partially infilled. From
the 11th Street side, it appears that a back building was
connected to the rear of the house by a network of porches,
as was not uncommon in Galveston.

13 and 915 Sealy Avenue   B–191

1901

The blocks east of the East End between 10th and 7th
Streets developed as a lower-income neighborhood after
the Civil War because the area was low-lying and prone to
flooding, and therefore not desirable real estate. Along
Ball, Sealy, and Broadway, these were blocks where lower-
income African-American and Caucasian families lived and
where such African-American institutions as St. Paul's
Methodist Church and East District School were located.
This low-lying neighborhood (6th Street was where the
tidal flats began) was devastated by the Storm of 1900,
resulting not only in the destruction of most of its modest
buildings but also in substantial loss of life. After the
storm, the area was initially rebuilt as a low-income
neighborhood, as this pair of shotgun cottages, each one
just 12 feet wide, indicate. These were constructed by the
family of Horace Scull, an African-American cabinetmaker
and carpenter who had organized some of the first schools
for African-American children in Galveston after the Civil

War. Members of Scull's family including his widow Emily
lived at 915 Sealy Avenue.

815 and 817 Sealy Avenue   B–192

1906

807 and 809 Sealy Avenue   B–193

1908 and 1906

Shotgun cottages acquired the name "commissary houses" in
early-20th-century Galveston because they were built to
provide temporary housing for families left homeless after
the Storm of 1900. The two at **809** and **807 Sealy Avenue**
are indicative of the type, with their small size, front
verandas inserted beneath hipped roofs, shuttered windows,
and modest Victorian decorative detail. The cottages at **813,
815,** and **817 Sealy** were built by the house painter Charles
Edwards on the site of his house, destroyed in the Storm of
1900. George Edwards built 807 and 809 Sealy on the site
of his destroyed house.

The Seawall originally turned inland from the beach and
ran along the line of 6th Street, the easternmost street in
19th-century Galveston. That is why Sealy Avenue begins to
incline upward in the 700 block, heading for what had been
the top of the Seawall. Construction of the Seawall made
the neighborhood more desirable socially, as the
Mediterranean-style, stucco-surfaced house of Lyda
Kempner and Arthur W. Quinn (1936, extensively altered)
at **701 Sealy Avenue** indicates.

7th and Broadway   B–194

Sidney Sherman Monument
1936, Gaetano Cecere with Pierre Bourdelle, sculptors;
Donald Nelson, architect

This standing bronze figure of General Sidney Sherman,
who played an important role in the Battle of San Jacinto in

1836 and moved to Galveston in the 1850s, was produced and installed as part of a statewide program to commemorate the centennial of the Texas Revolution of 1836. The sculptors Cecere and Bourdelle were Europeans who came to Texas from the Century of Progress Exposition in Chicago of 1933 to work on the sculptural program for the Texas Centennial Exposition, held in Dallas in 1936. The Sherman Monument is easily overlooked amidst the rush of traffic as Broadway intersects Seawall Boulevard. It lacks the urbanistic impact of the Texas Heroes Monument at 25th Street and Broadway.

On Broadway, flood protection resulted in a shift in social geography, registered in the construction of substantial brick veneer houses in the 1920s. R. R. Rapp designed the Joseph Varnell House at **704 Broadway** (1924) and, next to it, the Varnell Apartments at **708 Broadway** (1925).

1202 Broadway
B–195
1903

This sober, post-1900 house, built for Willoughby J. Chapman, manager of the Gulf Fisheries Company, marks the beginning of the Broadway grand avenue. From the mid-1870s until the early 1900s, Broadway was Galveston's show street of New South fortunes, which were displayed in a series of high-raised, picturesque villa-type houses that lined the north side of the street as far west as 20th Street.

1210 Broadway
B–196
1906

It is not so much the size of this house as its buoyant double-level galleries and rhythmic roof shapes that strike a Galvestonian note. Built for the druggist F. George Leinbach, the house features widely spaced classical colonnettes and a simple rail of alternating verticals and Xs. The cement-stuccoed parapet bordering the front sidewalk features ball finials. This parapet also encompassed the now-vacant site next door at 1228 Broadway, formerly occupied by the house designed in 1884 for Mrs. Elise Michael by N. J. Clayton.

1302 Broadway
B–197
Rectory, Sacred Heart Catholic Church
1925, R. R. Rapp

At 13th and Broadway is R. R. Rapp's white, stucco-surfaced rectory for Sacred Heart Catholic Church. As conservative as his 19th-century Galveston predecessors, Rapp designed new houses in conformance with a limited number of types. The rectory represents his expansive type: a symmetrically organized, hipped-roof block with offset wings. Indicative of the Rapp firm's domination of Catholic architectural commissions in 20th-century Galveston is **Sacred Heart School** at 901 13th Street, behind the rectory. It was built in two stages (1954, 1959), replacing buildings constructed for St. Mary's University, which the Diocese of Galveston opened on this block in 1855.

028 14th Street   **B–198**

Sacred Heart Catholic Church
1904, Br. Peter Jiménez, SJ
Dome, 1912, N. J. Clayton

Sacred Heart Church is startlingly white. It is of cast-in-place reinforced concrete construction, surfaced with white stucco. The church was designed to replace one of N. J. Clayton's masterpieces, the great High Victorian Romanesque-style Sacred Heart Church, completed in 1892 and destroyed totally in the Storm of 1900. Ironically, the destruction of Sacred Heart, Galveston, in September 1900, corresponded with the dedication of Sacred Heart Catholic Church in Augusta, Georgia. Brother Cornelius Otten, SJ, a Jesuit lay brother who worked with Clayton at Sacred Heart, Galveston, built the Augusta church with Clayton's plans for the Galveston church (apparently without Clayton's permission). Today, the scale and splendor of Clayton's original design are preserved in Augusta.

Clayton's church had stood where the rectory now is, facing Broadway. A team of Jesuit lay brothers, including Otten, was called in to build the second Sacred Heart. Brother Peter Jiménez, a Spanish-born carpenter and architect, designed the new church. Its slightly awkward, but nonetheless compelling, Moorish style paid tribute to the order's church in New Orleans, Immaculate Conception (1857, designed by T. E. Giraud, who had designed St. Mary's Cathedral in Galveston), and, according to the *Galveston Daily News* at the time of the church's dedication, the "Puerta Santa María" in Toledo, Spain, which was, in actuality, the early-13th-century Grand Synagogue of Toledo.

What Jiménez produced at Sacred Heart were corrugated surfaces that richly absorb sun and shade. It is the sculptural animation of the church's intensely white surfaces and fanciful roofline, rather than the correctness of its decoration, that makes it a stunning presence. Inside, the church is high, open, and white. The firmly profiled onion dome that rises above the crossing was an alteration made to the church in 1910–12 by N. J. Clayton, who replaced Jiménez's squatter, less spatially buoyant dome.

Clayton's failure to obtain the commission to rebuild Sacred Heart in 1902 forecast his professional decline. Jiménez's church does not measure up to Clayton's architectural standards. Yet, Sacred Heart is a landmark in its own right, for it spatializes the eccentricity and exuberance that are so characteristic of Galveston architecture.

1402 Broadway   **B–199**

(now the Bishop's Palace)
1892, N. J. Clayton & Company

The Bishop's Palace is Galveston's best-known building. Built by the lawyer, politician, and railroad investor and lobbyist Walter Gresham, it was an urbanistic companion to N. J. Clayton's original Sacred Heart Church. Like the first Sacred Heart, the Gresham House is richly colored and textured; sculpturally activated with gables, towers, and fantastic chimney stacks; and awesomely big. In the competitive mansion building that ensued along Broadway in the 1870s, 1880s, and 1890s, the Gresham House outsized and outshone all contenders. In 1923, it was bought by the Roman Catholic Diocese of Galveston to serve as official residence of the bishop. The Most Rev. Christopher Byrne was the only bishop to live in the house. In 1963, thirteen years after Bishop Byrne's death, the diocese opened the house to the public as the first historic house museum on Broadway.

The Gresham House was built during the years 1887 to 1892. It cost a reported $125,000 to construct, an enormous sum at a time when two-story houses for middle-income families often cost $2,000. It is built of Texas limestone laid up in random ashlar patterns and decorated with bands of gray and pink granites, red sandstone, and detail executed by the Galveston decorative sculptor John O'Brien. The Gresham House is an expanded version of Clayton's other large-house designs: an L-front towered villa with a central hall plan. Its three-story (plus raised basement) height, its steel-framed, cast-iron rimmed gallery, and its architecturally incorporated conservatory—built to contain Mrs. Gresham's collection of specimen ferns—advertised its status as foremost among what the journalist Julian Ralph, writing about "Joyous Galveston" in the nationally circulated magazine *Harper's Weekly* in 1895, called the "bird cage palaces . . . of the new generation of successful men in trade." Clayton, in a description he wrote of the house during its construction, asserted that it "recalls to the traveled of our community the stately mansions of England and the chateaux of France." Clayton's High Victorian bravura has won for the Gresham House architectural immortality. In 1957 Frederick Gutheim illustrated it in his survey of representative American buildings, *One Hundred Years of Architecture in America*, published to mark the centenary of the founding of the American Institute of Architects.

The main rooms of the house are as richly finished as the exterior. The rear service wing, however, as one can see from the 14th Street side of the house, is quite plain, although surfaced in stone. Clayton carried decorative stonework down the grand flight of ramped steps, which descends from the first-floor gallery, and around the sidewalks on both street fronts of the site in the form of raised curbing. Howard Barnstone in *The Galveston That Was* remarked on the relatively small size of the Gresham House site. Yet it was not uncommon along the late-19th-century grand avenues of U.S. cities for imposing towered villas to be built on city lots. Exhibition, not domestic reticence or a quest for privacy, motivated the construction of such houses.

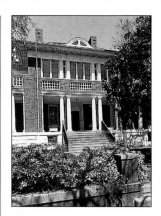

1416 Broadway   **B–200**
1916, Crow, Lewis & Wickenhoefer

This house, and the house next door at 1428, were designed by Anton F. Korn, Jr., for the families of two business partners, members of the younger generation of Galveston German families. They were built on the site of N. J. Clayton's house for Sylvain Blum of 1885, which in size and scale had reinforced the East End of Broadway's claim to be, as the *Galveston Daily News* once described it, the "Castle District" of 19th-century Galveston. Korn's houses represent the reaction that occurred in American architecture around the turn of the 20th century against the "excesses" of Victorian design. They are symmetrically composed, relatively low in height, and discreet rather than demonstrative. Carl C. Biehl, of the shipping firm of Wilkens & Biehl, built this house. Note Korn's academic reinterpretation of the traditional Galveston front porch as a glass-faced loggia. The house is still owned by Biehl's descendants.

1428 Broadway   **B–201**
1916, Crow, Lewis & Wickenhoefer

Korn's companion house for Biehl's business partner, Richard M. Wilkens, also treats the raised front veranda as a classical loggia. Advancing the end bays slightly forward of the central bay was a spatial arrangement associated with the New York architect Charles A. Platt, whose influence is visible in other houses by Korn. Platt was one of the inventors of the "country house," a new elite house type

that, even when built in cities, sought to make connections between the inside of the house and its garden. Korn's Wilkens and Biehl houses architecturally aspire to be country houses. Yet Galvestonian conservatism is evident, especially when the rears of these two properties, still used as service yards, are compared with their street fronts, which resolutely face the public view rather than retreat from it.

The Wilkens House was subsequently owned by Dr. Titus H. Harris, professor of neurology and psychiatry at the University of Texas Medical Branch, and his wife, Laura Hutchings. From 1966 until 1994 its raised basement was occupied by Louis L. Oliver's architectural office.

1502 Broadway   **B–202**
1906, C. W. Bulger

In Southern cities, the intermediate step between the Victorian villa and the early-20th-century "country house" was the Colonial Revival showplace. The cotton exporter and sugar refiner I. H. Kempner, a leading figure in Galveston's business community from the 1890s through the 1960s, built just such a house, one of the few erected in the Castle District in the decade following the Storm of 1900. The classical symmetry of the street front of the Kempner House was anti-Victorian. But its big scale and insistent frontality were attributes of the late 19th century that the architects of elite houses were not quite ready to abandon. One of the most unusual features of the Kempner House is its pebble-dashed finish, which gives the exterior wall surfaces a denser, more intricate texture than it was possible to achieve with wood clapboards. In 1924, the house was expanded to the west with the addition of a substantial, but very understated, two-story wing. This was one of the earliest independent works of Houston's outstanding country house architect, John F. Staub. The black-marble-floored "loggia" room on the ground floor of this wing is one of the great interior spaces of Galveston.

I. H. Kempner and his wife, Hennie Blum, lived here until their deaths in 1967 and 1970. The house was rehabilitated by Mr. and Mrs. H. Lee Trentham in 1979. Mary Moody Northen lived in the house during the last three years of her life, despite the fact that her father and I. H. Kempner were bitter rivals.

516 Broadway   B–203
940, Robert M. Coltrin

n 1934 Mr. and Mrs. Kempner's daughter married Dr. Edward Randall Thompson, then a resident at John Sealy Hospital. Although both bride and groom were from established Galveston families, their resources were slender, nd to economize they moved into the servant's apartment bove the Kempner garage. In 1940, they retained Coltrin, n engineer, to transform the garage-apartment building into his modernistic house, set deep in its garden. Subsequent dditions in the 1940s and 1950s by Charles L. Zwiener xpanded the original without compromising its intimacy.

602 Broadway   B–204
931, Cameron Fairchild

low obscured by a tall privacy wall, this two-story house, ced with double verandas, is in the Monterey regional yle popular in the 1930s. Its red tile roof and turquoise-lored blinds give the house, built by Dr. Albert O.

Singleton, professor of surgery at UTMB, a certain presence, despite its unassuming demeanor. Cameron Fairchild was Galveston society's favorite Houston architect during the late 1920s and 1930s. The black-and-red tile sidewalk along the Broadway frontage of the property provides a clue to the history of the site. From 1886 until 1929, this was the site of another one of Clayton's major houses, built for the real estate investor Henry M. Trueheart. The Trueheart property encompassed the site of the Singleton House and also the house site next door.

1616 Broadway   B–205
1929, Cameron Fairchild

Sally Trueheart Williams tore down her childhood home after building this compact Mediterranean-style villa in what had been its side yard. (The old carriage house survives at the rear of the site.) Pink stucco walls, turquoise blinds, and a red tile roof are engaging features. This was Fairchild's first Galveston commission and it led to subsequent residential work from the allied Trueheart-Adriance-Menard-McCullough families. Mrs. Trueheart Williams's house was, despite its modest size and Broadway location, a "country house" in one important respect: it abandoned a frontal relationship with the street. The front door is underneath the porte-cochère on the back corner of the house. In place of a front porch, there is a screened loggia, but it is treated as a private extension of the interior rather than as a space of entry. Twice during its history, this house has stood abandoned for long periods of time. During one such period, its romantically shabby aspect especially captivated the architect Aldo Rossi. It was rehabilitated in 1992.

1710 Broadway   B–206
1893, N. J. Clayton & Company

The last great house that Clayton designed in the Broadway Castle District is almost lost in a dense woodland garden. Built for the real estate investor John Charles League and his wife, the daughter of George Ball, it displays the influence of McKim, Mead & White's Sealy House in its relative restraint and Colonial Revival detail. Although the League House is big in scale and picturesque in profile, it lacks the exhibitionistic drive of the Gresham House. The porte-cochère, at the east side of the house, was a high-status accessory. The League property is unusual in running the depth of the block to Sealy Avenue. Even so, Clayton

1809 Broadway   B-208

1889

The 1800 block of Broadway fell victim to the fire of November 1885. The raised cottage that the druggist J. J. Schott built (but did not live in) represents the Galveston tendency to dress familiar house types in up-to-date decoration. It is the five-bay-wide cottage with side gables, twin-window dormers, and a three-bay attached front porch perked up with Victorian porch detail and a center gablet atop the porch roof.

respected long-standing conventions of domestic accommodation and oriented the League House toward its street front rather than its rear garden.

From 1919 until 1947, the house was occupied by Eliza Seinsheimer Kempner, widow of H. Kempner and matriarch of the Kempner family. For her and several of her children who lived with her, the Houston architect Birdsall P. Briscoe added a garden room to the back of the house and enclosed what had been an open porch in the curved bay on the second floor in 1920.

Sharing the block front with the League House was N. J. Clayton's sumptuous house for the banker Morris Lasker at 1718 Broadway (1892). Surfaced with pink stucco, it was visually stunning. The Lasker House survived long enough to be photographed by Stoller and Cartier-Bresson for *The Galveston That Was*. Its demolition in 1967 occasioned one of the earliest preservation crises in Galveston.

1805 Broadway   B-209

1893, H. C. Cooke & Company

Built for Thomas E. Bailey, general manager of the Galveston Wharf Company, this shapely house is intriguing because instead of having porches, verandas, or galleries affixed to the front of the house, the first-floor entrance porch is inset beneath an elliptically curved arch. The wide span of the arch is played against the adjoining angled front window bay, capped by a shingle-surfaced compound gable. Belting the walls with a horizontal band of shingles, slightly flared in profile, gave the Bailey House a sense of surface density and tactility not usually found on Galveston houses of this period. The architect was Henry C. Cooke, who practiced briefly in Galveston in the early 1890s before moving his practice to Houston.

1819 Broadway   B-207

1887

Despite numerous alterations, this house, built for Mrs. M. F. Talfor, retains its spatial buoyancy. The layered gallery trim (note that each horizontal band displays a different pattern) and the placement of a roof gablet on the chamfered east corner bay (an unusual detail for a Galveston house not located on a street corner) contribute to its effervescence. The house next door at **1815 Broadway** (1887), built for the lawyer Henry J. Labatt, is a simplified version of Mrs. Michael's house at 1717 Postoffice Street.

Next door to the Bailey House is the **1801 Broadway Building,** architect Thomas M. Price's refacing of a one-story ex-C. P. Evans grocery store (1937) to serve as a medical professional building (1956). Price's original exterior colors—white, with trim and the vertical panel joints picked out in red—emphasized the building's proportions and made it appear far less obtrusive than its present all-gray coloration. Note the modern entrance canopy on the 18th Street side of the building.

727 Broadway   B–210

1911

When new residential construction resumed on Broadway in the decade following the Storm of 1900, there was a marked preference for more modestly sized and proportioned house types than had been common before 1900. This house, built for the electrical and mechanical engineer Max Levy, is an adaptation of the twin-gabled early-17th-century English Jacobean type to the 20th-century country house type.

721 Broadway   B–211

1886, N. J. Clayton
1904, C. W. Bulger

Another example of the five-bay-wide, side-gabled house faced with an attached, three-bay front porch, this modest house is believed to have been moved from the site of the Gresham House at 14th and Broadway to this lot in 1886 to replace a house destroyed in the Fire of 1885. The new owner, Galveston lawyer and judge John Z. H. Scott, was instrumental in drafting the city charter that established the Galveston commission form of government after the 1900 storm. N. J. Clayton rehabilitated the house for Scott, apparently adding both the west-side wing and the rear east-wing and remodeling the interior. In 1904, Scott had C. W. Bulger make further alterations to the house.

1703 Broadway   B–212

1914, L. S. Green

Joining the I. H. Kempner House at 1502 as one of the few new Colonial Revival houses built on Broadway was this high-raised house designed by the Houston architect Lewis Sterling Green for the real estate investor John Adriance and his wife, Caroline Trueheart.

1607 Broadway   B–213

1940, Ben Milam

Despite the inroads made by automobile traffic after Broadway was paved in 1913, parts of the boulevard remained an attractive locale for elite houses into the 1940s. The adoption of a zoning code by the City of Galveston in 1937 gave the East End of Broadway greater legal protection and security than the central and western segments of the boulevard, which had already experienced commercialization. This house, built by Mr. and Mrs. Louis Haberman for their son-in-law and daughter Mr. and Mrs. Robert E. Oldfield, was a suburban country house, like those across the boulevard, in the neo-Regency style popular in the 1930s. In contrast to its high-raised neighbors, Ben Milam designed the Oldfield House with the first slab-on-grade foundation in Galveston. Next door, at **1605-1601 Broadway,** is the one-story apartment complex (1965, Joseph F. Cooley) that replaced the Skinner-Girardeau House of 1873, a graceful example of the Southern town house type.

1521 Broadway   B–214
1925, R. R. Rapp

R. R. Rapp was responsible for this brick-veneer bungalow, built for the grocery company executive Peter M. Gengler and his wife Theresa Schulte, as well as the adjoining raised, stucco-surfaced bungalow at **1527 Broadway** (1921), which was the first building that Rapp designed after beginning independent practice.

1515 Broadway   B–215
c. 1871, 1883, 1888

The house built for the lawyer Archibald R. Campbell, and occupied for nearly a century by his family, seems to owe its present appearance to the 1888 remodeling. The arcuated porch lintels, the circular porch railings, the Victorian classical architraves framing door and window openings, the curved corner bay on the east, and the stucco-faced arched basement all suggest Alfred Muller.

1509 Broadway   B–216
1865

This is an expansive version of the front-gabled, five-bay cottage with a veranda inserted beneath the gable and side-facing dormer windows. It was built as an investment by

John S. Rhea and occupied originally by the family of the banker John Hertford. The house was rehabilitated by architect Greg Hackett for Steve Malkin.

1501 Broadway   B–217
Doctors Clinic Building
1957, R. R. Rapp

Nearly three and one-half decades after starting out at the west end of the 1500 block of Broadway, R. R. Rapp's firm designed this medical professional building for doctors Garber, Sarwold, Stubbs, and Bromberg at its east end. The building's thin, flat roof plate, its low profile, and shallowly curved wall planes of thin Roman brick framing the entrance pavilion were characteristics of the 1950s' Contemporary-style look. Although it differs from neighboring houses in scale, materials, and land use, the Doctors Clinic holds the street line along Broadway and 15th Street and does not suburbanize Broadway with surface parking lots.

1427 Broadway   B–218
St. Paul's Methodist Church
1902, C. W. Bulger

St. Paul's Methodist Church is one of the oldest African-American congregations in Galveston. Its present church was built to replace a building near the corner of 8th and Ball destroyed in the Storm of 1900. Bulger's wood-frame church is a variation on the mid-19th-century church type: a gable-fronted rectangularly planned building, which Bulger Victorianized with a corner tower and spire, multiple side entrances rather than a centered front door, and a complex roof shape.

1407-1409 Broadway B–219
Lucas Terrace
1907, 1908, Thomas Lucas, designer and builder

This curious building, now containing apartments, was built as a pair of row houses. It was successor to the Lucas English Terrace Row, a row of six attached houses built by the English-born Galveston brick mason Thomas Lucas in 1894. The Lucas Row was located at 6th and Broadway, facing the beach, and was totally destroyed in the Storm of 1900. Lucas salvaged brick from the row and on the site of his own house built the Lucas Terrace. According to the *Galveston Daily News* in 1908, Lucas built the east side of the building in his spare time between 1901 and 1907, then expeditiously completed the west wing by 1908. Vertically attenuated proportions, the repetition of narrow arched openings (some of which are windows, others open-air staircases), and the projecting, shell-form cast-concrete planter boxes give the Lucas Terrace its delightfully eccentric aspect. Beneath the exterior stair (a later addition), one can see, through a passage under the building, into a rear courtyard, one of the most charming spaces in Galveston. Sadly, this quintessentially Galvestonian building has structural problems that urgently require sympathetic intervention.

1317 Broadway B–221
1946, 1954

This flat-roofed modernistic-style house was built by the engineer Edwin P. Aronsen. Like instances of Victorian porch decor in Galveston, its porthole windows are faced with radiating muntins, suggesting a ship's-wheel.

1313 Broadway B–222
1869

Built by the Scottish-born harbor pilot Captain James McDonald, this is a version of the five-bay-wide, side-gabled cottage with an attached, gable-fronted, three-bay front porch, subsequently modernized with Victorian porch trim and a shingling of the gable face. The house was rehabilitated in 1982.

1403 Broadway B–220
1885

This variation on the five-bay-wide, side-gabled cottage features a porch arrangement that can also be seen at 3123 Avenue N (and in modified forms at 1601 Avenue M and 3202 Avenue P 1/2). The front porch rises upward to become the balcony of the central second-story dormer. The house was built for the real estate agent and title company owner Powhatan S. Wren.

1309 Broadway B–223
c. 1867

This house, built by Captain Thomas S. Dignan, is a classic example of the Gulf Coast cottage. Big in scale, the Dignan House suggests its age by virtue of the fact that it is not high-raised. It is also closer to the street than was customary of subsequent houses. Note the preservation here of the unpaved, shell-surfaced sidewalk.

1301 Broadway   **B–224**

1878

As with other examples in Galveston, this three-bay-wide
house, also built by Captain Dignan, stands out by virtue of
its "French roof." The projecting center bay originally rose
into a third-story tower. The thick-membered woodwork of
the offset front porch shares similarities with the porch at
1819 Winnie Street.

1203 Broadway   **B–225**

1923

The cotton exporter Herman Nussbaum built this large,
stucco-faced, tile-roofed house, with its Spanish
Mission–style gabled porch. The Nussbaum House is typical
of houses built by Galveston's elite in the 1920s. It
adopts the model of the "country house" without, however,

sacrificing such Galvestonian attributes as the front porch.
The windows of the Nussbaum House are covered with
applied aluminum jalousies known in Galveston as Aramco
blinds, after the corporation that markets them. The bane of
local preservationists, Aramco blinds were a 20th-century
successor to the (admittedly) more picturesque hinged,
louvered shutters.

Farther east on Broadway are two adjoining brick-veneer
apartment buildings, the Riviera Apartments at **725
Broadway** (1929, Andrew Fraser) and the Sonia Apartments
at **719 Broadway** (1928, R. R. Rapp). Although suffering
from unsympathetic alterations, Anton F. Korn, Jr.'s house for
the cotton exporter Earl R. Milroy at **701 Broadway** (1915,
Crow, Lewis & Wickenhoefer) remains quite recognizable as
one of his Charles Platt–influenced country houses.

In 1845, the Galveston City Hospital was tucked in the northeast corner of the city at 9th Street and Strand. Placement of the hospital as far as possible from the center of town typified 19th-century health standards—and fears. ∩ ∩ ∩ After Galveston was chosen in a statewide referendum in 1881 as the location for the Medical Department of the University of Texas, this pocket of Galveston Island began its ever-shifting physical and economic development. Once on the fringes, the medical complex is, today, a focus of the community. ∩ ∩ ∩ When the University of Texas Medical Department opened in 1891, developed blocks ended at 8th Street. Beyond this point were the East End Flats, a marshy, lowland area that many still remember as "a great place to fish and hunt," especially for snakes. ∩ ∩ ∩ The Flats began to be systematically filled in the 1940s, creating made land for the city's eastward expansion. From Market Street south to Ball Avenue, the Groesbeck grid (the original town plan) was extended east to what had been, in Groesbeck's day, an imaginary 1st Street. Thus, these blocks, although built-out with post–World War II buildings, retain the spatial rhythm of the rest of the townsite. Other sections of the East End Flats, however, have been laid out according to 20th-century suburban standards.

The University of Texas Medical Department complex, circa 1902. The buildings left to right are: City Hospital, which, after 1891, became the Negro Hospital and then the Nurses' Home; annex to John Sealy Hospital; John Sealy Hospital; and the University of Texas Medical Building, now Ashbel Smith Hall, more popularly known as "Old Red." N.J. Clayton designed all but the annex.

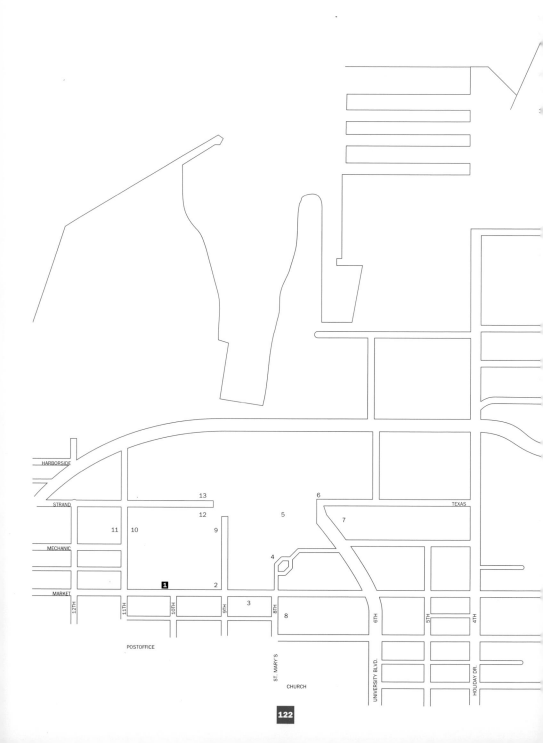

1. 1002–1028 Market Street
2. 900 Market Street
3. 815 Market Street
4. 8th Street and Mechanic Street
   John Sealy Hospital Tower
5. John Sealy Hospital and R. Waverly Smith Memorial Pavilion
   Clinical Sciences Building
   John Sealy Children's Hospital
   University Hospital Clinics Building
   Texas Department of Corrections Hospital
   John Sealy Hospital Trauma Center
6. 7th Street and University Boulevard: Jenny Sealy Hospital
7. 200 University Boulevard
8. 404 8th Street
9. 9th Street and Mechanic Street
10. 1018–1028 Mechanic Street
11. 1102–1128 Mechanic Street
12. 901–927 Strand
13. 902–928 Strand
14. 127 and 128 Bonita Drive
15. 1009 Harbor View Drive
16. 1301 Harbor View Drive
17. 1306 Harbor View Drive
18. 1310 Harbor View Drive
19. 1515 Harbor View Drive
20. 1113 Marine Drive
21. 168 San Marino Drive

1002-1028 Market Street   **C–1**

William C. Levin Hall

1983, Kenneth Bentsen Associates

Taut planes of light brown brick, angled to reflect interior spatial use, contrast with expanses of solar glass in this high-set classroom and auditorium building by the Houston architect Kenneth Bentsen. Across the street at 1001-1027 Market is the university's **Pharmacology Building** (1980, Louis L. Oliver & Tibor Beerman).

900 Market Street   **C–2**

Moody Medical Library Building

1972, Ford, Powell & Carson

Ford, Powell & Carson's library, for which Boone Powell was responsible, is the one campus building constructed since 1965 that has a strong urban presence. Typologically, it relates to a series of college libraries that the San Antonio–based architects designed, beginning with Powell's Scribner Library at Skidmore College in Saratoga Springs, New York. These are all brick-walled buildings with overhanging pitched roofs and projecting glass window bays. Powell Galvestonized the Moody Library by elevating it a full story above grade, as called for in the Brooks & Barr Master Development Plan of 1965 for UTMB. Although an effort was made to bring a sense of spatial measure to its open-air ground floor with brick vaulting, this space feels bleak, in contrast to the assured treatment of the exterior faces of the library.

815 Market Street   **C–3**

Shriners Hospital for Crippled Children Galveston Burns Institute

1992, Henningson, Durham & Richardson

The Burns Institute is a flamboyant example of postmodernism in American architecture. The Dallas

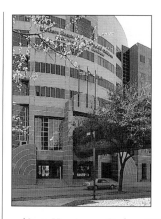

architects Henningson, Durham & Richardson designed the Burns Institute with an emphatic center, which relates it to the position the building occupies astride the center of a city block. Centrality is reiterated architecturally in the symmetrical composition of the exterior of the hospital. By being keyed to its urban site, the Burns Institute becomes part of Galveston. It opts for imageability rather than anonymity, and architecturally fulfills such traditional urban responsibilities as letting one know where the front door is.

8th Street and Mechanic Street   **C–4**

John Sealy Hospital Tower

1978, Pierce Goodwin Alexander

Clinical Sciences Building

1973, Brooks Barr Graeber & White

John Sealy Children's Hospital

1978, Golemon & Rolfe

University Hospital Clinics Building

1983, Page Southerland Page

Texas Department of Corrections Hospital

1983, Bernard Johnson and Jessen Associates

John Sealy Hospital Trauma Center

1991, Pierce Goodwin Alexander

ohn Sealy Hospital and R. Waverly　　　**C–5**
mith Memorial Pavilion
953, C. H. Page & Son with Eggers & Higgins

ne might be tempted to describe this building complex as a
le of two architectures if the 1978 hospital tower and its
any annexes had not totally subsumed the 1953 original.
his in itself can be read as a spatial commentary on how
merican modern architecture, as applied to large public
stitutions during the last half of the 20th century, tried to
ask its institutional nature. The paradoxical result is that
placing figuration, symmetry, and hierarchical composition
he architectural properties that signified "public building")
ith sculptural massing, engineering scale, and unarticulated
rfaces has led to the production of an environment that is
apeless and confusing.

The 1953 John Sealy Hospital, designed by the Austin
chitects C. H. Page & Son in consultation with Eggers &
iggins of New York, was a pyramidal brick pile that stepped
, in symmetrically arrayed wings, to a 10-story, hipped-roof
mmit, terminating the vista down 8th Street. The 1,000-bed
 spital was ponderous and ungainly, but there was no doubt
out where the front door was located. Although it straddled
o city blocks and incorporated as its outlying west wings the
w-demolished Crippled Children's Hospital (1937, Robert
on White) and John Sealy Outpatient Clinic (1930, C. G.
rnell with Robert Leon White; subsumed within the
inical Sciences Building of 1973), the 1953 hospital was
signed to be part of the city.

The John Sealy Hospital Tower of 1978 and its annexes have
en glommed onto the 1953 hospital, which they completely
velop. Today, the 1953 hospital is almost invisible, except for
e R. Waverly Smith Memorial Pavilion facing University
oulevard. Given its huge bulk, this was no mean achievement.
he design of the 1978 hospital tower and its annexes
sponded to considerations of modernist functional planning.
though the earlier hospital was also functionally planned, it
as within the context of an architectural typology that
rivileged symmetry and sought to relate the building
ternally to the city because it was a public building. Modern
chitects tended to deride such considerations as mere
rmalism. Modernism considered function a more honest basis
r design than urbanism, and delighted in the dramatic, and
resumably more performance-oriented, shapes that
nctionalist design analysis might arrive at.

Responding to these imperatives are the series of building
eces that stretch from Market Street three blocks north to
/ater Street. From a distance, their smooth, 13-story-high

vertical planes, stacks of splayed window bays, and chamfered
ends are sculpturally powerful. But these buildings have no
beginning and no end. Even the basic ordering system of the
street grid is gone. The triangular porte-cochère at 8th and
Mechanic that marks the present main entrance to John Sealy
Hospital needed to depart radically from the repetitive shapes
of the hospital building and be big in scale because its
relationship to the city, as grounded in the street grid, had
become so ambiguous that finding the front door was a
problem.

At 301 University Boulevard is the **University of Texas
Medical Branch Administration Building** (1972, Rapp
Tackett Fash).

7th Street and University Boulevard　　　**C–6**
Jenny Sealy Hospital
1968, Pierce Goodwin Flanagan
Built by the Sealy & Smith Foundation, this five-story,
175-bed hospital demonstrates that modern architecture is
not inconsistent with public-building design. Pierce
Goodwin Flanagan's Edwin J. Goodwin, Jr., used the
building's reinforced concrete construction system to achieve
variations in scale and depth. Tall, wide openings at the base
of the building contrast with smaller, offset window
openings on the upper floors. These are recessed deeply
within precast concrete panels, creating variations not only
in scale but in depth, which are measured in the classic
Galveston way with sun and shadow.

200 University Boulevard　　　**C–7**
Sealy & Smith Professional Building
1964, Thomas M. Price
The 10-story Sealy & Smith Professional Building is Tom
Price's tallest Galveston building. It was erected by the Sealy
& Smith Foundation, established by John H. Sealy and his
sister Jennie Sealy Smith in 1922 specifically to support

John Sealy Hospital. Price integrated parking and offices around a central elevator core. The much bigger floor plates of the garage are wrapped in an aluminum solar screen, while the office floors are sheathed with solar glass, deeply recessed beneath parasol-like extended floor trays. The Sealy & Smith Building successfully combines the attributes of dignity and unpretentiousness.

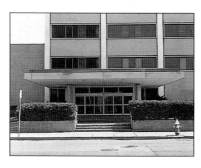

404 8th Street   **C–8**
St. Mary's Hospital
1965, Golemon & Rolfe
South wing, 1948, I. E. Loveless
St. Mary's Hospital, founded by the Sisters of Charity of the Incarnate Word in 1867, was the oldest continually operating hospital in Galveston and Texas at the time it sold its property and assets to the University of Texas Medical Branch in 1995. N. J. Clayton designed the first purpose-built building for what was originally called St. Mary's Infirmary (1876) and expanded the hospital complex on this block in the first years of the 20th century. The completion of Golemon & Rolfe's eight-story, 246-bed building was followed by the immediate demolition of Clayton's original. In 1948, the Sisters of Charity had the Beverly Hills, California, architect I. E. Loveless design the four-story south wing. He was also the architect of **Ave Maria Hall** (1954) at 728 Market, now the UTMB Administration Annex. Both are restrained versions of the modernistic style that Loveless essayed with much more enthusiasm at the sisters' St. Joseph's Hospital in Houston.

9th Street and Mechanic Street   **C–9**
Gail Borden Building
1951, Kenneth Franzheim; Mark Lemmon, consulting architect

The four-story, block-long Gail Borden Building was the first UTMB building to venture, if hesitantly, a modern architectural expression. This did not preclude spatially reinforcing the building's Mechanic Street frontage in an urbane way, which architects of Franzheim's and Lemmon's generation seemed to do almost out of habit. As part of the 1965 master plan, Mechanic Street was closed to traffic and turned into a pedestrian park.

1018-1028 Mechanic Street   **C–1**
Medical Research Building
1991, 3D/International
The 11-story slab of the Medical Research Building, designed by the Houston architects 3D/International, attempts to recover some of the ornamental repertoire associated with N. J. Clayton in its rows of *opus spicatum,* the Latin name for the spiky effect achieved by laying brick so that their corners project diagonally out from the wall plane. These ornamental bands are integrated into a building that otherwise relies on its articulated concrete frame construction and its exposed rooftop ventilating paraphernalia for architectural effect.

To the east of the Medical Research Building, on 10th Street between Mechanic and the Strand, is the stolid **Libbie Moody Thompson Basic Sciences Building** (1971, Brooks Barr Graeber & White of Austin). Across the street at 10th and Strand is the mildly modernistic ex-**Galveston State Psychopathic Hospital** (1931, Wyatt C. Hedrick of Fort Worth) with its east-side **Annex** (1937, R. R. Rapp) and the curvilinear **Mary Moody Northen Pavilion** on the west (1983, Koetter Tharp Cowell & Bartlett of Houston).

1102-1128 Mechanic Street   **C–11**
School of Allied Health Science and Nursing
1986, Kenneth Bentsen Associates
Like Bentsen's Levin Hall, this building is tensely configured with smooth planes of brick and glass. A block away, at 1302-1324 Mechanic Street, is the university's **Materials Management Warehouse** (1973, Louis Lloyd Oliver). As with many of Oliver's buildings, it is an articulate essay in reinforced concrete construction. Porthole-shaped grilles

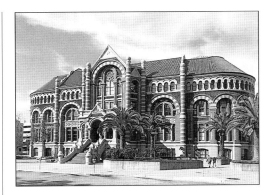

ive the windowless warehouse a sense of rhythmic measure
nd a jaunty nautical touch.

01-927 Strand   C–12

Medical Laboratory Building (now Keiller Building)

1924, Herbert M. Greene Co.

1932, Greene, LaRoche & Dahl

Designed by the Dallas architect Herbert M. Greene and his
eventual partner George L. Dahl, the Medical Laboratory
Building corresponded to the buildings they were also
producing on the university's main campus in Austin during
the 1920s. It is a three- and four-story rectangular block,
capped with an overhanging tile roof, and surfaced with a
mixed blend of light brown brick, limestone, and yellow
Renaissance-style terra-cotta ornament. Greene and Dahl's
model was Sutton Hall (1918), which the distinguished
New York architect Cass Gilbert had designed on the Austin
campus. Although Dr. Edward Randall, retired professor of
therapeutics at UTMB, chaired the UT Board of Regents'
building committee when the great Philadelphia architect
Paul P. Cret was commissioned to prepare a master plan and
design new buildings for the Austin campus in 1930, new
buildings at UTMB during the 1930s were mostly the work
of Robert Leon White, the university's Austin-based
consulting architect. White's buildings adhered to the
pattern established with the Laboratory Building. UTMB's
building campaign of the 1970s and 1980s resulted in the
demolition of almost all of White's buildings, leaving the
Laboratory Building the most conspicuous survivor of
UTMB's Mediterranean era.

902-928 Strand   C–13

University of Texas Medical Department Building (now
Ashbel Smith Hall)

1891, N. J. Clayton & Company

The great work of architecture at UTMB remains the
building with which the medical department began,
popularly known since the 1970s as Old Red. Here Clayton
masterfully explored the affective potential of architecture.
His orchestration of contour and shape is particularly
evident. Beginning with the marvelous ramped front stair,
the curve is projected into the monumental arcade that
embraces second-story windows as a large-scale organizing
device. The curve is brilliantly spatialized in the building's
rounded end bays. Clayton animated the wall surface of Old
Red by dissolving the wall plane above the major arcade into
a lush field of *opus spicatum.* His extraordinary ability to
evoke visceral response from architecture derives from the
rigor, consistency, and exuberance with which he integrated
contour, shape, and texture. Spraying deteriorating sandstone
components with concrete plaster tinted a purple-pink when
the building was rehabilitated in 1985 lessened the
sensational quality of Old Red.

Because it was built on what, in the 19th century, was
the edge of the island, the Medical Department Building
was vulnerable to the full force of the wind during the
Storm of 1900. The tall, tiered pavilion roof with which
Clayton originally topped the central section of the building
was destroyed, and it was not rebuilt when Clayton repaired
the building in 1901. Consequently, Old Red has a more
horizontal appearance today than it did in its original
configuration. Until 1923, when the Medical Laboratory
Building was built across the street, Old Red served as the
university's only permanent academic building.

The 1965 Master Development Plan called for its
demolition. Thereafter, Old Red was closed down, section
by section. No maintenance was performed. The great
anatomy amphitheater in the rounded east wing became
home to hundreds of pigeons (and hundreds of
decomposing pigeon bodies). The university's elevated
service network was built up against the back of Old Red,
and incompatible new construction closed in on it.

University alumni, faculty, and the Galveston Historical
Foundation pressed for Old Red's rehabilitation. Finally, in
1983, the University of Texas System authorized
rehabilitation of the Medical Department Building.

Crain/Anderson Architects of Houston were responsible for the rehabilitation, which ensured Old Red's preservation.

Clayton designed the Medical Department Building as a civic monument. The wisdom of this approach is demonstrated by the loyalty that has accrued to it. It is now the oldest building still in operation in the entire University of Texas System.

Clayton was also the architect of Old Red's companion, the original John Sealy Hospital (1889, demolished 1962), located just to the east in the 800 block of Strand. This was extensively remodeled in 1916 by the New York–based hospital architects Crow, Lewis & Wickenhoeffer and their representative, Anton F. Korn, Jr.

a

b

127 (a) and 128 (b) Bonita Drive   C–14
Alterations and additions, 1992, David Watson
David Watson cleverly recast this pair of opposing 1950s' ranch-type houses in postmodern style for the builder Ed Rismiller. By adding second stories to both houses, he made them into the architectural gateway to the Lindale Park subdivision, which all Galvestonians know—on account of its street names—as Fish Village.

1009 Harbor View Drive   C–15
1964, Raymond R. Rapp & Associates
Harbor View was Galveston's swank 1950s neighborhood. It was developed on reclaimed land, beginning in 1954, and was laid out for the Harbor View Development Company by the Houston landscape architect Herbert Skogland. Spectacular views of the harbor, the downtown skyline, and the Bob Smith Yacht Club marina are available to houses on the west side of Harbor View Drive. Because of its proximity to the medical center, Harbor View has been a favorite locale for doctors and their families. This flat-roofed modern house was the home of the architect

Raymond Rapp, Jr. It is one of the architect-designed modern houses that give Harbor View its distinction. Note the boldly colored panel of orange glazed brick.

1301 Harbor View Drive   C–16
1969, Howard Barnstone & Eugene Aubry
Although the street front of this flat-roofed house, faced with panels of pink St. Joe brick and solar glass, is unassuming, it cloaks what is one of the great houses of Galveston. The house is tailored in plan to its parallelogram-shaped lot in order to orient major rooms to the harbor view. This results in internal eccentricities, which Barnstone & Aubry cleverly resolve in the house's lofty, proportioned, glass-walled spaces.

1306 Harbor View Drive   C–17
1958, Thomas M. Price
Built for the marine repair company executive John A. Mehos, Price's Contemporary-style house features not only a glazed gable, but projecting window bays on its long north side that bring light into the house while minimizing exposure to the house next door.

1310 Harbor View Drive   C–18

1960, Thomas E. Greacen II

This curious-looking modern house was a student work of
the Houston architect W. Irving Phillips, Jr., produced
while he worked for the architect Tom Greacen. Phillips
designed the house with its principal rooms on the second
floor, so that the owners, Mr. and Mrs. Louis Pauls, Jr.,
could look over the one-story house on the water side of
Harbor View Drive for a vista of the ship channel. To
compensate for the house's west exposure and to ensure
privacy, Phillips (who had studied under Bernard Hoesli
and Colin Rowe at the University of Texas in the 1950s,
and would resume his study under Rowe at Cornell in the
early 1960s) incorporated a *brise-soleil* (sunscreen) that
stands boldly in front of the house. In contrast to the low-
key modernism that tended to prevail in Galveston in the
1950s and 1960s, the Pauls House calls attention to itself
with its dramatic sunscreen, a tribute to the Parisian
modern architect Le Corbusier. The avocado color and
internal window treatment are later alterations.

1515 Harbor View Drive   C–19

1964, Herbert W. Hudler, Jr.

Tucked into a cul-de-sac, this trim house is in the
mainstream Galveston tradition of discreet modernism.

1113 Marine Drive   C–20

1959, Thomas M. Price

Along with his Stirling House at 28 South Shore Drive, this
house, built for Dr. and Mrs. Moore Yen, is one of Price's
outstanding works. The economy and sense of proportion
with which he organized its street front imbue it with
architectural character, even though it is a compact,
modestly scaled house.

168 San Marino Drive   C–21

1953, Milton Foy Martin with Ford & Rogers

Shortly after having the Houston architect Milton Foy
Martin design a new house for their family in Houston,
Cynthia and George Mitchell had him design a second
house in the San Marino subdivision, which backs up to the
dike separating the east edge of Galveston from the East
End Flats and began to be developed in 1951 by Omero
Del Papa and T. D. Affleck. During military service in
World War II, Mitchell had become acquainted with the
San Antonio architect Jerry Rogers, and the Mitchells
retained Rogers, along with his partner, O'Neil Ford, as
consulting architects for this modest, Contemporary-style
house (which in 1995 had its open carport enclosed). It was
the medium for bringing the Mitchells together with Ford,
with whom they would join forces 25 years later to
participate in rehabilitating the Strand.

Next door at **170 San Marino Drive** is a handsome,
flat-roofed modern house (1957) that has been
exceptionally well maintained. It was built by the Loomis
Construction Company, which was responsible for many of
the Contemporary-style houses in San Marino.

evelopment south of Broadway differed from that north of Broadway for several reasons. First of all, the land was not prime real estate. The topography was lower as the island sloped towards the Gulf. Lower land values invited ownership by the laboring class, a demographic pattern that remained intact, as related by one Galvestonian who described his 1930s' childhood neighborhood as "the southeast end . . . the working man's part of town. We used to get up at five o'clock. People in the west end got up at nine o'clock." ♠ ♠ ♠ Speculative investors were attracted to what is now called the San Jacinto area (after San Jacinto Elementary School) not only because of the lower land values but also because much of the area—specifically, all of that south of Avenue M—was laid out in "outlots," each of which comprised four undivided blocks. For obvious reasons, the larger tracts of land appealed to investors,

A view looking north from the canal bridge at Tremont (23rd) on the south end of the San Jacinto area during the grade-raising project, circa 1907. The canal was filled in after the island was raised.

who developed them for both resale and rental income. ∩ ∩ ∩ The buildings in the San Jacinto area reflect these social and economic influences. It contains the city's largest concentration of workers' cottages, with many variations of all the small- to medium-sized typologies. The groupings of duplicate buildings that you see along the streets (and there are many) are an indication of just how many houses were built as speculative investments. Present-day Americans might be surprised by how much housing in a city like Galveston was built as rental property in the 19th and early 20th centuries. ∩ ∩ ∩ As the outlots were developed, most were divided in the same way as blocks in the original historic city, although there were irregularities. One of the most noticeable of these is on 24th Street between Avenues M and N, in what is now the Silk Stocking Historic District. It is a neighborhood that developed as an enclave for professionals; the residences are larger, and more of them are individually designed than is typical of the San Jacinto area. ∩ ∩ ∩ Like all of Galveston, the San Jacinto area has suffered its share of disasters. The Fire of 1885, which began in the East End, destroyed 20 blocks between 17th and 21st Streets south of Broadway. Almost all the properties were rebuilt within a year, giving the neighborhood an architectural consistency both in date and appearance. In fact, it is the "fire district" that forms the core of the Lost Bayou Historic District, the city's most recently designated historic district (1996) and the second after the Silk Stocking Historic District (1975) in the San Jacinto area.

16. 1508 Tremont Street
17. 2408 Avenue N
18. 1422 Rosenberg Avenue
19. 1416 Rosenberg Avenue
20. 1414 Rosenberg Avenue
21. 1412 Rosenberg Avenue
22. 1408 Rosenberg Avenue
23. 1322 Rosenberg Avenue
24. 1301 Rosenberg Avenue
25. 1208 Rosenberg Avenue
26. 1124 Rosenberg Avenue
27. 2419 Avenue L
28. 2411 and 2415 Avenue L
29. 2410 Avenue L
30. 2402 Avenue L
31. 1124 24th Street
32. 2327 Avenue K
33. 2223 Avenue K
34. 2202 Avenue K

1. 1103 Tremont Street
2. 2314 Avenue M
3. 2326, 2322, and 2318 Avenue M
4. 1303 24th Street
5. 1305 24th Street
6. 1317 24th Street
7. 1319 24th Street
8. 1322 and 1326 24th Street
9. 1325 24th Street
10. 1329 24th Street
11. 1405 24th Street
12. 1410 24th Street
13. 1417 24th Street
14. 1419 24th Street
15. 2328, 2324, and 2320 Avenue N

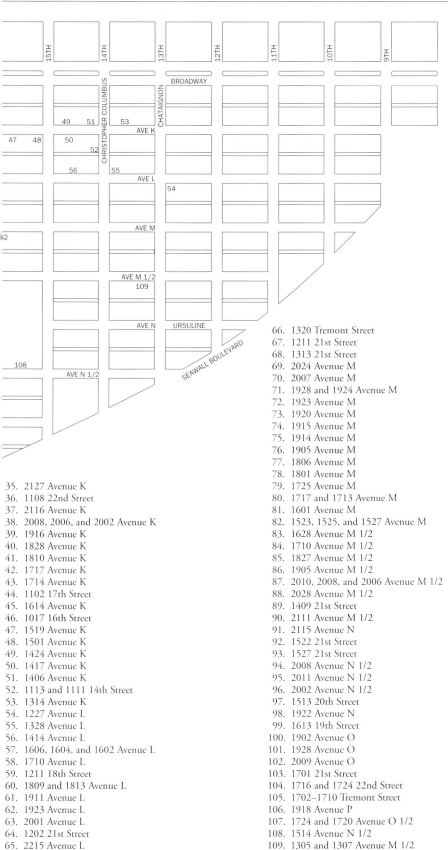

66. 1320 Tremont Street
67. 1211 21st Street
68. 1313 21st Street
69. 2024 Avenue M
70. 2007 Avenue M
71. 1928 and 1924 Avenue M
72. 1923 Avenue M
73. 1920 Avenue M
74. 1915 Avenue M
75. 1914 Avenue M
76. 1905 Avenue M
77. 1806 Avenue M
78. 1801 Avenue M
79. 1725 Avenue M
80. 1717 and 1713 Avenue M
81. 1601 Avenue M
82. 1523, 1525, and 1527 Avenue M
83. 1628 Avenue M 1/2
84. 1710 Avenue M 1/2
85. 1827 Avenue M 1/2
86. 1905 Avenue M 1/2
87. 2010, 2008, and 2006 Avenue M 1/2
88. 2028 Avenue M 1/2
89. 1409 21st Street
90. 2111 Avenue M 1/2
91. 2115 Avenue N
92. 1522 21st Street
93. 1527 21st Street
94. 2008 Avenue N 1/2
95. 2011 Avenue N 1/2
96. 2002 Avenue N 1/2
97. 1513 20th Street
98. 1922 Avenue N
99. 1613 19th Street
100. 1902 Avenue O
101. 1928 Avenue O
102. 2009 Avenue O
103. 1701 21st Street
104. 1716 and 1724 22nd Street
105. 1702–1710 Tremont Street
106. 1918 Avenue P
107. 1724 and 1720 Avenue O 1/2
108. 1514 Avenue N 1/2
109. 1305 and 1307 Avenue M 1/2

35. 2127 Avenue K
36. 1108 22nd Street
37. 2116 Avenue K
38. 2008, 2006, and 2002 Avenue K
39. 1916 Avenue K
40. 1828 Avenue K
41. 1810 Avenue K
42. 1717 Avenue K
43. 1714 Avenue K
44. 1102 17th Street
45. 1614 Avenue K
46. 1017 16th Street
47. 1519 Avenue K
48. 1501 Avenue K
49. 1424 Avenue K
50. 1417 Avenue K
51. 1406 Avenue K
52. 1113 and 1111 14th Street
53. 1314 Avenue K
54. 1227 Avenue L
55. 1328 Avenue L
56. 1414 Avenue L
57. 1606, 1604, and 1602 Avenue L
58. 1710 Avenue L
59. 1211 18th Street
60. 1809 and 1813 Avenue L
61. 1911 Avenue L
62. 1923 Avenue L
63. 2001 Avenue L
64. 1202 21st Street
65. 2215 Avenue L

1103 Tremont Street   **D–1**

1913, Mrs. George C. Smith, designer

George C. Smith, a telegraph operator for the Postal
Telegraph-Cable Company, and his wife built this 25-room
boarding house. According to the *Galveston Daily News,*
Mrs. Smith designed the three-story building, which was
equipped with ice-water dispensers on each floor, speaking
tubes, and electrical call bells. This was one of the
apartment buildings constructed in the early 1910s that
took advantage of the prestige of Tremont Street. After
years of standing vacant, the Smith Apartments were
rehabilitated in 1996.

2314 Avenue M   **D–2**

1866

This house originally faced Tremont Street on a large parcel
of land. It was moved and rotated to face Avenue M in
1921 in order to permit commercial redevelopment of the
Tremont front of the site. This turn of events landed the
house in a far less prestigious location, without diminishing
its simple stateliness. Its big scale, center-hall plan, and
modest details make it look more like a rural planter's house
than a town house. Property records suggest that the house
was built by the T. M. League estate. Its first owner-
occupant seems to have been Mrs. Nancy A. Gaines.

2326, 2322, and 2318 Avenue M   **D–3**

Mid-1860s to mid-1870s

This row of houses illustrates the ability of vernacular house
typologies to shape strongly formed urban space through
the repetition of characteristic profiles and spaces. Each is
an example of the Gulf Coast cottage—the five-bay-wide
house at 2318, the three-bay-wide version at 2322, and the
five-bay-wide version at 2326, which has been raised to

permit construction of a full-height ground floor beneath
the original first floor.

Tax records document that meat market proprietor Anton
Heiman acquired two of the three lots on which these houses
are situated as early as 1858 and the third lot by 1861. By
1865, there were structures on the lots to which additions
were made in the early 1870s. Insurance records dated 1888
note that all three structures were already considered "old." At
some point, the houses were pressed even closer together to
make room for a fourth house—the house now on the corner.

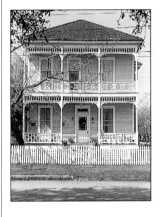

1303 24th Street   **D–4**

1898

Built for the Misses Frances, Rosella, and Bertha Harris, this is
one of the earliest houses in the long block of 24th Street that
constitutes the heart of what has been, since 1975, Galveston's
Silk Stocking Historic District. This neighborhood is
distinctive in several respects. It represents the residential
development of an outlot which was never bisected by one of
the alphabetical "half" avenues that strike visitors to Galveston
as so curious. Thus it has a much more self-contained feeling
than was characteristic of contemporary Galveston
neighborhoods. Houses are aligned along the east and west
sides of the street, rather than the north and south sides. There
is also much more consistency in house size than was
characteristic of other Galveston neighborhoods, although it is
interesting to note that the customary north-south divide was
here played out as an east-west divide, with the larger houses

built on the west side of the street, so that their major rooms faced the prevailing breeze. There is a continuous paved sidewalk on the west side of 24th, whereas the sidewalk is intermittent, and not always paved, on the east side.

Until the 1890s, 24th Street ended at Avenue M. Its right-of-way from M to N 1/2 was occupied by the walled compound of the Texas Cotton Press, built in 1871 and extending west all the way to Rosenberg Avenue. After the Texas Press went bankrupt, it was demolished in 1893. Its three-block site was subdivided into residential lots and sold at auction in 1898. By that time, this comparatively large tract was surrounded by desirable residential real estate. It therefore developed into a very respectable neighborhood, even though its lots were, at 31 feet in width, comparatively narrow.

The 1300 and 1400 blocks of 24th Street and of Rosenberg Avenue exhibit a high degree of architectural consistency. This has made the neighborhood very attractive for preservation and rehabilitation.

1305 24th Street   D–5

1908

The house originally owned by Mrs. Annie Chapman is representative of the west-side houses. It is a variation of the Southern town house type, with a side-hall plan. Since the houses on 24th Street were so close together, one can observe in this house how middle-class proprieties were preserved. Windows on the north side of the house were shuttered or glazed with frosted glass. Windows on the south side were clear-glazed. Thus, one could open south-side windows to the prevailing breeze without being observed—at least in an obvious way—by one's next-door neighbor. The Chapman House was rehabilitated in 1995.

1317 24th Street   D–6

1899, C. W. Bulger

No architect did more to impress the 1300 and 1400 blocks of 24th and Rosenberg with their distinctive architectural character than C. W. Bulger. Designing houses for individual clients—as here, for entrepreneur Harry S. Spangler—or in multiples for speculative builders, he produced some designs that were austere and others that were extremely flamboyant. Many adhered to the basic design visible in the Spangler House, in which a shallow offset breaks the street front into two planes, and a one-story

attached veranda is decorated with the showy wooden ornament that Bulger excelled in designing.

1319 24th Street   D–7

1899, George B. Stowe

Built for E. R. Cheesborough, secretary-treasurer for both a land company and the Texas Portland Cement & Lime Company, this house has a ground-floor gallery that steps up to a second-story porch on the south side of the house. This was Stowe's Victorian-Galvestonian approximation of the side-veranda "single" houses of Charleston.

Stowe's client for this house is one of Galveston's unsung heroes. As secretary of the Grade Raising Board, Cheesborough patiently shepherded city officials, contractors, and literally thousands of property owners and residents through what has to be one of the most complicated projects ever undertaken by a community anywhere.

1322 and 1326 24th Street   D–8

1895

This pair of high-raised tenant dwellings, like other houses on the east side of the street, are more cottagelike in size than their west-side counterparts. Yet the degree of spatial shaping that these houses display, their enriched wall surfaces, and their decoration—notably the wooden spheres stationed between spindles in the porch rails to produce a swag profile—indicate that they were aimed at a middle-income market.

1325 24th Street　　　　　　　　　　D–9
1906, Charles F. Schelewa, builder

Here, prim Colonial Revival decor has replaced the exuberance of late Victorian wooden ornamentation without radically changing the shape or spatial organization of the house, built for roofing contractor Fred Hartel.

1329 24th Street　　　　　　　　　　D–10
1899, Thomas B. Dinsdale, builder

The arched "thermal" window (so-called because such half-round windows were associated with the *thermae,* or public baths, of ancient Rome) considerably enlivens this house, built for the jeweler August F. Lange.

1405 24th Street　　　　　　　　　　D–11
c. 1854, 1902

Moved from its original site on Tremont Street to make way for construction of the Rosenberg Library, this house ended up on 24th Street in 1902. Yet it does not appear out of place, an indication of the typological continuity that underlies the stylistically varied architecture of older Galveston neighborhoods.

This Doric-columned Greek Revival side-hall town house was built for the wholesale merchant George Ball, although he did not live in it for many years. N. J. Clayton carried out extensive alterations to the house for Mr. and Mrs. Joseph G. Goldthwaite in 1882. It is thought that such decoration as the paneled double doors, the surrounding architrave with its Greek key frieze, the band of triglyphs and metopes in the frieze above the columns, and perhaps even the columns set on paneled bases, dates from 1882, since such elaborate detail was uncharacteristic of Galveston houses of the 1850s. When the wholesale grocer, importer, and commission merchant John Focke bought the Ball House in 1902 and moved it to this site, he detached its rear wing and converted it into a separate house, situated next door at **1401 24th.**

The persistence of the Ball House through remodelings, moving, and reconstitution testifies to its will-to-survive, exemplifying the Galveston penchant for preserving and rehabilitating, rather than discarding and destroying.

1410 24th Street　　　　　　　　　　D–12
1895

This raised Victorian cottage, with its unusual shingled frieze skirt above the veranda columns, is the backdrop for one of the most exuberant displays of yard art in Galveston.

2328, 2324, and 2320 Avenue N   D–15
1905, C. W. Bulger

It is intriguing to witness here how Bulger reconciled the issues of urban unity and architectural individuality in this row of three houses, two of which were built as rental property, while the third (2324) was to be owner-occupied. Bulger took what was basically the same house shape and used street-facing roof gablets to establish a center-and-bookends urban composition. But he varied the handling of ornamental details to suggest that each design was singular. As was repeatedly the case in Galveston's older neighborhoods, the result was an underlying architectural order that avoided monotonous duplication.

1417 24th Street   D–13
1899, W. H. Tyndall

This house, built for the real estate agent William S. Conness but occupied for most of the 20th century by the family of the Alsatian immigrant Isadore Arnold, embodies to an exceptional degree the elation that Galveston domestic architecture frequently achieves. Research by the Galveston Historical Foundation established that it was the work of W. H. Tyndall, who practiced in Galveston for more than 25 years, but whose career is not well documented. His combination of the rounded double galleries, rimmed with arcuated lintels infilled with radiating ball-spindles, and the marvelous first-floor thermal window endows the Conness-Arnold House with its buoyant aspect.

1508 Tremont Street   D–16
1897

During the last quarter of the 19th century, Tremont Street contended with Broadway as Galveston's most fashionable residential avenue. One of the few houses to survive in good condition is this two-story wood house built for Martin P. Morrissey, manager of a company that imported building materials and served as steamship agents. The Morrissey House exhibits composition, proportions, and details that were characteristic of N. J. Clayton's domestic architecture at this period, although there is no documentary evidence that he was its architect.

Next door at 1518 Tremont, the **Elks Club Building** dates from Tremont's redevelopment as a commercial strip. It is the work of Galveston architect Clarence E. Stevens (1950). At 1424 Tremont, a storefront added in 1957 obscures the Mission-style **Silberman Apartments** (1913, Green & Finger).

1419 24th Street   D–14
1908

This restrained Colonial Revival house, built as rental property for the real estate agent Tim Sullivan, was constructed in what had been the side yard of the Conness House next door. Its sobriety is typical of the architecture of Donald N. McKenzie. Sullivan's first tenant was the insurance company executive J. Fellman Seinsheimer.

2408 Avenue N   D–17
1902

When first built, the three houses at 2402, 2408, and 2412 Avenue N were identical in their appearance and three-room plan, although 2402 was built, according to insurance records, one year later (1903) than the other two. All three were the investment of real estate agent Tim Sullivan, who owned other property in the area, including his own residence at 1423 25th Street. Worth noting at 2408 Avenue N is the manner in which the garage and driveway have been accommodated in a small and older house.

1422 Rosenberg Avenue   D–18
1910

Curiously, this very conservative house terminates what is one of the most effusively ornamented rows of houses in Galveston. Painted in an array of pastel colors and facing the palm-*allée* of Rosenberg Avenue, they represent Galveston at its most theatrically Southern-Victorian (on the order of something that might have been imagined by Tennessee Williams, who never wrote about Galveston, but should have). Many of these houses resemble the work of C. W. Bulger, although the only one that can be securely attributed to him, the Luther Murff House at **1320 Rosenberg** (1899), is comparatively restrained. These houses share a quirkiness of proportion, often involving the composition of their front porches, which is where ornamentation was indulged to the utmost.

1416 Rosenberg Avenue   D–19
1899

The arcuated gable, at almost disproportionate scale, establishes the Victorian chalet theme of the high-set,

tensely proportioned house on the right [above], built by the developer Gustav Kahn. The gabled off-center porch appears slightly squeezed when contrasted with the voluminous amplitude of the master gable above.

1414 Rosenberg Avenue   D–20
1899

Although the house on the left [above] is smaller than its neighbor at 1416, it shares a similar porch structure (minus 1416's big gable). Here again, one sees the way in which, in the midst of apparent decorative excess, there is an underlying layer of typological continuity that makes this long block front read as a coherent urban composition rather than as a riot among competing exhibitionists.

Documentary sources suggest that the core of the house was built in 1899 for Mrs. Marie Buechner, perhaps as rental property, because the Buechners were never listed at the address. In 1904, Lawrence P. Dignan, coal elevator superintendent at Fowler & McVitie, coal dealers and importers, acquired the property to which he made substantial improvements in 1907, as suggested by an increase in his tax assessment.

1412 Rosenberg Avenue   D–21
1899

The gabled off-center porch is reduced to its essential condition in this gable-fronted house, built as a tenant house by George H. Nicholls and subsequently owned by the banker Fred W. Catterall.

1408 Rosenberg Avenue D–22

1899

Built for William R. White, manager of the Southern Coffee Co., this house offers yet another variation of the porch with its covered first-floor gallery defined by the open deck with balustrade on the second story.

1322 Rosenberg Avenue D–23

1903

As in other Galveston neighborhoods, the advent of the 20th century did not dim some Galvestonians' attachment to the house types and decorative flourishes of the late 19th century. This house, built for the businessman Isadore Predecki, with its L-plan, shingled wall panels, and wraparound galleries with corner oriel, is indicative of the strength of conservative preferences.

1301 Rosenberg Avenue D–24

1904

The west side of the long 1300-1400 block of Rosenberg Avenue was developed just after the turn of the 20th century by Stephen Eaton, following the pattern established on the east side of the boulevard. The house in the foreground (above) was built for Eugene H. Compton, proprietor of the Island City Turf Exchange and saloon, and later owner of the Compton Plumbing Company. David Mullican was architect for the rehabilitation of the property in 1995, which included undoing extensive disfiguring alterations and additions, and reconstructing the front façade.

1208 Rosenberg Avenue D–25

c. 1850s; rebuilt 1885

The origins of this exquisite small house are obscure, leading to the conclusion that it may have been moved to this site from another location or repositioned from another spot on the same property. Early tax records suggest that this was a lot where the land and the building(s) were separately owned—with the owner of a building paying ground rent. This was not uncommon in Galveston throughout the 19th century.

According to insurance records, the house was rebuilt in 1885, a date that coincides with purchase of the property in 1884 by widow Eliza Moser. Within a short time, her son, marble cutter John H. Moser, was not only living at the 1208 Rosenberg address but had also moved his workshop to what is now the side garden at Rosenberg and Avenue L. The house is a raised, three-bay-wide cottage, with a veranda inserted beneath its hipped roof. From the south, one can see the process of its growth, where a side-gabled rear addition, surfaced with vertical boards-and-batten rather than horizontal clapboards, tails down to a rear lean-to, an object lesson in vernacular building geometries.

Purchased for rental property in 1982 by Weez and Mike Doherty, the house reflects the continued attention and care of both owners and renters. The small formal garden, which is hardly what the property would have looked like when Moser's work yard was here, complemented the intentionally precious restoration of the house by renters Mr. and Mrs. John Hutchings Spencer in the 1980s. The design of the vertical rail fence is based on a remnant discovered in an East End back yard by Mike Doherty and John Spencer. The sidewalks around the property are surfaced with oyster shells, which emit a musty, coastal odor.

1124 Rosenberg Avenue — D–26

A. Vaiani & Company Building

1912

The Vaiani Building, which is very faithful to the Galveston corner-store building type, replaced an earlier one-story store and residence. Note the chamfered corner entrance and the extremely wide canopy shading the sidewalks on both Rosenberg Avenue and Avenue L. In the 1913 city directory, Albert Vaiani was listed as a grocer at this location and as proprietor of the Silver Spray Bar in downtown Galveston. Vaiani's wife and other family members, in all probability, ran the grocery store.

Next door at **2424 Avenue L** is one of three identical speculative houses built in 1883 by the Galveston Real Estate and Loan Association. This one was purchased in 1884 by Adolph Frenkel, a Bavarian immigrant who worked as a cashier for a real estate and livestock firm. Within a year after buying the house, the Frenkel family added two rooms and installed electricity, which had recently become available in Galveston.

2419 Avenue L — D–27

1896

The south side of the 2400 block of Avenue L was dominated architecturally by the houses of the children of German immigrant Peter Moser and his wife, Eliza. Their son John, the marble cutter, established his home and business on the corner lot facing Rosenberg. Miss Paula Moser was owner of this raised, L-front Victorian cottage.

2411 and 2415 Avenue L — D–28

1888 and 1889, John Hourigan, builder (2415)

This pair of five-bay-wide, gable-fronted houses were built for members of the Moser family. In the case of 2415, Agnes Moser Roemer and her husband, saloonkeeper John, signed, on 8 May 1888, a contract with John Hourigan in which the latter agreed to build their house for $1350. Like other Galveston examples of this north-facing house type, both houses have one-bay front porches. The Moser houses are generously dimensioned and are decorated with Victorian woodwork detail. Hourigan also built Mrs. Roemer's mother's house at 509 19th Street in 1888.

2410 Avenue L — D–29

1927

The insurance company executive Clinton G. Wells, Jr., built this anomalous neo-Georgian-style, brick-faced country house in the midst of Victorian neighbors. The arched wooden surround framing the front door seems to have been inspired by the work of the Houston architect John F. Staub. Note how the faded green louvered blinds of the Wells House manage to impart a Galveston aura, its aspirations to suburban fashionableness notwithstanding. During the 1950s, this was the home of Dr. Truman G. Blocker, Jr., professor of surgery and president of UTMB, and his wife and professional collaborator, Dr. Virginia Blocker.

2402 Avenue L — D–30

1884, 1890

According to tradition, this house was built by James M. Brown as a wedding present for his daughter Matilda, upon her marriage to Thomas H. Sweeney. It is one of the most ornately appointed "cottages" in Galveston, and old photographs show that with a polychome (literally: multi-

colored) slate roof and circular cutout lattice screens that once infilled the bays between the veranda posts, it was originally even more elaborately outfitted. Note that a tower roof, visible from 24th Street, preserves its red-white-and-gray slate tiles. Apparently the one surviving polychrome roof in Galveston, it makes one understand just how aesthetically uninhibited the Victorian middle class could be.

Insurance board records indicate that the Sweeney House was "rebuilt" and added to in 1890. Although the house has often been attributed to N. J. Clayton, formal evidence makes an attribution to Alfred Muller more likely, since the slightly heavy decor, the round wooden cutout panels in the veranda rail, and the stucco-faced arched basement were characteristic of other Muller-designed houses.

1124 24th Street   D–31

c. 1870, 1895

Built for Waters S. Davis, a commission merchant and prominent businessman, this was a gable-fronted house facing 24th Street that opened on its south side to a garden along Avenue L. Alterations in 1895 resulted in the addition of a pavilion-roofed octagonal tower on the 24th Street side of the house (which contained the new, side-facing front door) and a more fancifully decorated gallery that wrapped around the Avenue L side of the house. The scale of the Davis House can be appreciated from the size of its big, shuttered first-floor windows. The grounds are outlined with an iron fence set into stucco-faced brick curbing between stucco-surfaced brick piers. Davis was a vestryman of Trinity Church, his mother was buried from St. Mary's Cathedral, and his wife, Sarah Huckins, was the daughter of the founding pastor of the First Baptist Church. He fought

for the Confederacy, but his brother, Edmund J. Davis, was Texas's Reconstruction governor. As a new city and a center of dynamic entrepreneurism, 19th-century Galveston routinely absorbed contradictory circumstances that in more settled communities would have entailed strict social divisions among citizens.

2327 Avenue K   D–32

1907, E. W. Smith, builder

1923

Enshrouded by live oak trees, this raised two-story house, built for Sarah Davis and Harry Hawley next to Mrs. Hawley's parents' house, is one of the most evocative in Galveston. Its slightly old-fashioned air, the poignant contrast of its red louvered blinds with its weathered gray stucco walls, and its arched basement and screened-porch openings give the house a romantic, timeless look that makes it hard to date. This inscrutability is not accidental, as the Hawleys extensively rebuilt their original house in 1923, when it acquired its present appearance.

Across 24th Street from the Hawley House is **Congregation Beth Jacob Synagogue,** Galveston's oldest Conservative Jewish congregation. The original synagogue, on the corner, was the work of R. R. Rapp (1931). It was remodeled as an educational building when the present synagogue and the adjoining Bessie and Ben Clark Hall were built next door, facing Avenue K (1963, Ben J. Kotin & Tibor Beerman).

2223 Avenue K   D–33

1898, N. J. Clayton & Company

This is one of a pair of houses that Clayton designed for the Rev Antony M. Truchard, a French-born priest whose nephew married the daughter of Mrs. George Craycroft.

Mrs. Craycroft and her family lived next door at Tremont and K, in a house that no longer exists. Father Truchard seems to have represented the Craycroft family's business interests after his nephew's early death. Although modest (the house was used as a tenant house), the two-story, L-plan house displays evidence of its architectural authorship in its assured proportions, expansive composition, and lilting yet simple ornamentation.

The Hitchcock House at **2209 Avenue K** was moved to this location in 1996. Construction details and archival research suggest a pre-1860 date for sections of the house, which was originally located at 21st Street and Avenue K and belonged to L. M. Hitchcock, Jr., who owned property in Galveston as early as 1839.

2202 Avenue K   **D–34**
St. Joseph's Catholic Church
1859, Joseph Bleicke, builder
1901, N. J. Clayton
The nucleus of this neighborhood was the unassuming wood church that served Galveston's German parish, St. Joseph's. St. Joseph's is the oldest wooden church building in Galveston. It adheres faithfully to the mid-19th-century Texas vernacular church type. It is a boxlike building, three bays wide, with a gable front. The main entrance is centered beneath a steeple-topped tower. The long side walls contain five windows. St. Joseph's was virtually destroyed in the Storm of 1900, but was rebuilt, under Clayton's direction. Clayton added a new sanctuary and the flanking sacristies to the back of the church. Today, the green, louvered blinds with which the windows are faced, the louvered top stage of the tower, the palm trees that frame the street faces of the church, and even the shell-surfaced sidewalk along 22nd Street evocatively Galvestonize the vernacular church type.

The interior of the church is surprisingly ornate, with painted wood walls and a coffered ceiling decorated with quatrefoils and other Gothic symbols. Still in place are the original grained cedar pews, hand-carved altars, and plaster stations of the cross with German inscriptions.

In 1968, after the parish was declared redundant, the Galveston Historical Foundation leased the building from the Diocese of Galveston-Houston and rehabilitated it. St. Joseph's is maintained as a historical museum and is opened by special arrangement.

2127 Avenue K   **D–35**
1887
Many corner stores were built as rental property, as was true for this structure, which follows the typical form with commercial space on the first floor and a living unit on the second. Frequently, small rear additions provided an extra living space, often a dining room, which allowed the storekeeper's family to eat their meals while still tending to the store.

1108 22nd Street   **D–36**
c. 1875
This is an appealing little tenant cottage, already considered old (as the clipped eaves of the roof and its tight proportions imply) when it was added to in 1893. The house appears to be composed of two shotgun cottages, pushed together to form a double-wide house and united with a common front porch. Next door at **1112 22nd Street** is a companion cottage, also added to in 1893.

2116 Avenue K   **D–37**
1887, Alfred Muller
The lyre in the porch gable iconographically identifies this raised cottage as the home of Professor Emil Lindenberg, Galveston's foremost band leader of the 1880s and 1890s.

008, 2006, and 2002 Avenue K D-38
1907 and 1886

Although they have the same house typology and the same investment motivation—rental income—these three houses were built by two different owners and twenty years apart. The corner house at 2002 and its backyard companion on 20th Street were among the residences built immediately after the November 1885 fire that laid waste to this sector of the neighborhood. The adjacent property remained undeveloped (except for one small one-story dwelling) until 1907, when the twin houses were built.

916 Avenue K D-39
1886

Physician McKenzie Johnston and his wife Mary replaced their burned house with one of the larger houses built in the aftermath of the 1885 fire. Although the arcuated central gablet crowning the double-level veranda emphasizes the symmetrical organization of the five-bay-wide house, a bay window bows out to one side of the front door, inside the veranda. Note the coved tin soffit beneath the eaves of the roof, decorated with pierced patterns. Framed by deep-set side yards—a setting now unusual for Galveston—the house retains its iron fence and concrete curb.

The Johnston House is located in the Lost Bayou Historic District, an 18-block area established in 1996 as Galveston's fourth locally designated historic district. The 1900 block of Avenue K is one of the most consistent blocks in the district. Its integrity is compromised, however, by **San Jacinto Elementary School** across the street at 1100 21st Street (1964, Thomas M. Price, Ben J. Kotin & Tibor Beerman, Raymond R. Rapp & Associates, and Charles L. Zwiener), which replaced N. J. Clayton's 1886

San Jacinto School. The school building deflates the delicately constructed neighborhood scale not because of its modern design, but because of its suburbanity. Monotonous in scale, unengaged with the spaces around it, and bereft of architectural clues that would allow one to distinguish the front from the sides and back, it demonstrates the liberties that mid-20th-century Americans took with their cities by failing to respect the character, scale, and texture of existing neighborhoods.

1828 Avenue K D-40
1900

In this house, built as rental property by Mrs. Clara G. Batts, convention was violated by putting the front door on the 19th Street side of the house so that the front gallery, facing Avenue K, is accessible only from inside the house, rather than from the front sidewalk. Having bought the lot in 1884, Mrs. Batts lived in the house that she built on the alley line at **1014 19th Street** (1885). In 1995, rehabilitation of 1828 Avenue K was a project of the Galveston Historical Foundation's Residential Preservation Program.

1810 Avenue K D-41
1882

This two-story, five-bay-wide I-house has an archetypal look, with only a few details that hint at its actual date of construction. It is also an example of a house that started out much smaller than it is now, the insurance records noting additions in 1894 and 1897. This is where the architect R. R. Rapp and his wife, Edith Reybaud, lived from the 1920s through 1959, the year Rapp died.

1717 Avenue K　　　　　　　　　　　　**D–42**

1900, George B. Stowe

Pilot Rucker T. Carroll's timing for building his two-story
side-hall house was not good. According to insurance
records, it was built on seven-and-a-half-foot brick piers in
August 1900, only to be "blown off foundation Sept 1900."
All buildings in Galveston sustained some damage in the
hurricane, but many survived relatively intact, Carroll's
house perhaps being one of the latter.

1714 Avenue K　　　　　　　　　　　　**D–43**

1923

An anomalous presence in the Lost Bayou neighborhood,
this diminutive bungalow-type house is so narrow that it
almost qualifies as a shotgun bungalow. Erected by the
contractor J. K. Deats for the real estate investor John
Adriance, it was apparently built as a rental property.

1102 17th Street　　　　　　　　　　　**D–44**

c. 1875

There are several features that give this small dormered
cottage at the corner of 17th Street and Avenue K such a

stately presence: its placement on the sidewalk line on both
street sides, its orientation to the numbered street, and the
height to which it is raised.

There were always multiple small residential buildings on
this lot, some of which may have been repositioned at
different times. According to the city directories, Max Best,
a molder, was living here in 1875, and this house, located
on the lot owned by Max and his brother Charles, is clearly
visible on the 1885 bird's-eye view of Galveston at its
present corner site.

1614 Avenue K　　　　　　　　　　　　**D–45**

Engine House #5

1891, W. H. Tyndall

It is interesting to observe that 19th-century architects and
their clients were not compelled to adapt institutional or
commercial buildings to their surroundings in residential
neighborhoods. Therefore, this two-story, stucco-faced brick
fire station—one of several Tyndall designed and the only
one still standing—was built all the way to the sidewalk
line, as though it were located downtown. But, it should be
noted, the structure respects its surroundings in scale and
detailing.

1017 16th Street　　　　　　　　　　　**D–46**

Lasker Home for Homeless Children (now Heritage Christian
Academy)

c. 1869–70

1912, Donald N. McKenzie

This imposing galleried house was the family home of Marcus
C. McLemore, a prominent Galveston lawyer, who purchased
two lots in 1868. In 1901 the property was acquired by the
Society for the Help of Homeless Children and converted into
an orphanage. With funds donated by the wholesale
merchant, banker, and real estate investor Morris Lasker, the
house was raised on brick piers and expanded in size by

McKenzie in 1912. Despite its conversion from domestic to institutional use and the additions of 1912, the house retains its characteristic "Galveston Greek" (to use Howard Barnstone's term) architectural attributes.

519 Avenue K   D–47
. 1870

Monumentally scaled, fluted Doric columns are the distinguishing feature of this Southern town house, which is shown on the C. Drie bird's-eye view of 1871. Insurance records indicate that the house underwent extensive repairs n 1901 when it was owned and occupied by John Goggan, musical instruments merchant. It has been converted into partments.

501 Avenue K   D–48
867

This five-bay-wide, side-gable-roofed cottage, along with its neighbor at **1505 Avenue K,** represents one of the house ypes most identified with the southeast section of the city, o judge from Drie's 1871 bird's-eye view. Drie's perspective hows both houses without porches, which were probably dded after the Storm of 1900, since this block stood on the ine of the zone of total destruction. Although porches are onsidered an almost essential Galvestonian attribute today, ate-19th-century photographs indicate that it was not ncommon for cottages such as these to be without them.

424 Avenue K   D–49
895

This three-bay-wide, two-story, Victorian Southern town house right) joins with its neighbors at 1426 and 1428 to form one

of those rows of similar house types that give Galveston its distinctive character. The decorative panels of shingles beneath windows on the side of this house recall the work of Alfred Muller, as do the arcuated lintels of the front veranda.

1417 Avenue K   D–50
1882

What is unusual about this three-bay Victorian cottage is the diminutive tower on its east side that was an addition in the late 1890s, when the house was owned by Herman Riedel, a bookkeeper at the American National Bank. Riedel also added the bay window.

1406 Avenue K   D–51
1891

Like the cottages at 1501 and 1505 Avenue K, this is a modest, wood-clapboard-faced cottage, notable for its small scale. Originally, the house stood on six-foot brick posts, not an uncommon characteristic for both large and small houses.

1113 and 1111 14th Street   **D–52**
c. 1875
Like sentinels, these two small houses guard the entrance to
the alley from 14th Street. The two-bay house at 1113
exhibits a picturesque roofline as a result of successive rear
additions.

1314 Avenue K   **D–53**
1875
This Southern town house, with its big scale, stands out
among its modest neighbors.

1227 Avenue L   **D–54**
Graugnard's Bakery Building
1940
Graugnard's streamlined modernistic baking plant turns the
street corner with due ceremony. Projecting concrete hoods
above the second-story windows are repeated above first-

floor openings. They demonstrated the modern way to war
off excessive sunlight. Across the street, at 1301 Avenue L,
St. Luke's Missionary Baptist Church (1911), another
neighborhood landmark.

1328 Avenue L   **D–5**
1895
Set closer to the street than was usual along this stretch of
Avenue L, this raised, five-bay-wide, side-gable-roofed
cottage features distinctive finials decorating the peaks of
the attic dormers and the gabled front porch.

1414 Avenue L   **D–5**
c. 1865–70
A high ceiling gives this three-bay-wide Gulf Coast cottage a
unusual proportion. The porch columns and railings may
date from 1892, when additions were made to the cottage,
which was described in the insurance records as "old."

1606, 1604, and 1602 Avenue L   **D–5**
1897
The three houses on Avenue L exhibit decorative wood
screens framing bow fronts set within the verandas. As a
result of their lilting repetition of shape and shadow, these
little houses make quite an impression. Originally, they wer
one-story structures with raised basements, the latter
eventually being finished to create living units on the lower
levels, an alteration that became more practical throughout
the city after the Seawall was built and the island was raise

The house at **1113-15 16th Street,** on the alley side of 1602 Avenue L, was built at the same time but was always a two-story structure.

1710 Avenue L   **D–58**
1888
A raised tenant cottage built by Mrs. Charlotte Krohn, this gabled house with its pair of front twin-windows was built in a discontinuous series along Avenue L, as can be seen in the next block.

1211 18th Street   **D–59**
1891
On its original site at the corner of 18th Street and Avenue L, this house, raised on seven-foot posts and having a rotated three-story tower and concave mansard roof, must have presented a formidable sight to those traveling toward the Gulf. The house was built for Conrad Lenz, who was

listed in the 1891–92 city directory as a butcher and, ten years later, as proprietor of the Enterprise meat market on Tremont Street. Eventually, Lenz's house was moved into what had been its back yard and lost its porch, original windows, and siding. Yet despite such indignities, a certain determined spirit persists.

1809 and 1813 Avenue L   **D–60**
1888 and 1887
Reprising the cottage at 1710 Avenue L, this pair keep up the rhythm along the street. In outline, they are typical cottages with their hipped roofs, boxlike shape, and small kitchen wing. Unusual features are the attached porch, which is more fanciful than most on smaller houses, and the double-wide front windows with peaked architraves. On the interior, a small triangular entrance hall with two angled doorways leads into the rooms on each side. Two widows, perhaps sisters, and one of whom also owned the house at 1710 Avenue L, built the houses as rental property.

Lying within the 1885 fire district, these houses and their neighbors on both sides of the block create not only one of the strongest streetscapes in the Lost Bayou Historic District but also one of the best collections of vernacular building types.

1911 Avenue L   **D–61**
1886
As the consistent late-1880s construction dates suggest, this block also lay in the 1885 fire district. The street-facing gable of this side-dormered cottage is the locus for its architectural decoration: the pierced vergeboard facing the eaves, and the decorative pendant tracery inset beneath the gable peak.

1923 Avenue L   **D–62**
1886, Dickey & Helmich

One of the most animated new houses in the 1885 fire district, this was designed by D. A. Helmich for George Schneider, who, at the time he rebuilt his house, had retired as a wine and liquor merchant. With its paneled exterior walls, shingled banding, and mariner's-wheel porch railing, the Schneider House is spatially buoyant, if not very gracefully proportioned.

2001 Avenue L   **D–63**
1886

This two-story house possesses lively porch detail and a pair of front doors ensconced within a "hurricane" alcove. The bulk of the house was built immediately after the 1885 fire. In the early 1890s, Bernard Levy, partner in a livery stable business, purchased the property, to which he made additions to accommodate his family of six children. One son, Adrian Felix Levy, served as mayor of Galveston from 1935 to 1939.

Farther down the block at **2209 Avenue L** is the A. H. Wainwright House (1899, George B. Stowe).

1202 21st Street   **D–64**
1888, N. J. Clayton

Although this raised cottage, built for the German-born real estate broker Gustave A. Meyer, has been extensively altered

(it originally faced Avenue L), it displays Clayton's skill in impressing an ordinary house type with graceful architectural detail and authoritative proportions.

2215 Avenue L   **D–6**
1882, 1906

This L-front cottage possesses porch brackets penetrated by diagonals and an unusual hanging balcony on the east side. Squeezed between commercial and institutional development, it is obviously a survivor. The house was buil for the attorney John C. Walker, who still owned the house when it was rebuilt, according to insurance records, in 1906. It bears a strong resemblance to the Fisher House at 3503 Avenue P.

1320 Tremont Street   **D–6**
Kirwin High School (now O'Connell Senior Campus)
1942, R. R. Rapp

A bowed limestone front marks the central entrance bay of Rapp's straightforward, brick-faced institutional building, giving Galveston's Catholic high school for boys a modest monumentality. Unfortunately, Kirwin's construction precipitated demolition of the huge Thomas M. League House (1860), which stood where the gym and cafeteria wing were eventually built (1962, Raymond R. Rapp & Associates). This was a three-story brick house that sought to compete architecturally with Ashton Villa. Subsequently the home of Colonel William L. Moody, the League House was acquired by the Diocese of Galveston in 1927. To the other side of Rapp's building was N. J. Clayton's handsome and substantial brick house for the lawyer John W. Harris (1890), which was also demolished to permit additions to Kirwin High School.

211 21st Street   **D–67**

Gulf Breeze Apartments

1969, Raymond R. Rapp & Associates

Built by the Housing Authority of the City of Galveston, this 11-story, 200-unit apartment complex for the elderly reflects the architectural influence of Victoria Plaza in San Antonio, a trend-setting public housing complex that rejected "project"-type organization for a mid-rise apartment configuration. By treating the two wings as a hinge, Rapp gave residents views across the rooftops of Galveston toward both the Gulf and the bay. At ground level, however, the building does not intersect its surroundings gracefully.

313 21st Street   **D–68**

Galveston Orphans Home

1902, George B. Stowe

The Orphans Home, a major beneficiary of Henry Rosenberg's philanthropy, shows Stowe at his most stolid. This ponderous, brown brick building was built by the trustees of the Rosenberg Estate to replace Alfred Muller's ebullient original of 1895, so severely damaged in the Storm of 1900 that it was demolished. Stowe treated the Orphans Home as a public institution, isolating it on its full-block site. Today, the high, cement-plaster-surfaced brick walls along M and M 1/2 and mature woodland vegetation, especially the great live oak trees, give these sides of the property an intensely Southern, garden district ambiance. From M 1/2, one can see the big, arched, second-story windows on the rear of the Orphans Home. These give the building a more impressive aspect than does its front façade. The building has been rehabilitated as a private residence.

Until 1873, the 21st-M corner of this site (and all of the block where the Gulf Breeze Apartments were built) lay in Hitchcock's Bayou, one of two draws filled with salt water that meandered across the southern half of the Galveston townsite before emptying into the Gulf. The damming,

draining, and filling of Hitchcock's Bayou by the City Engineer made the neighborhoods south of Avenue L much more attractive for settlement, especially along 21st Street, where the tracks of the horsecar system led from the center of the city to the beach.

2024 Avenue M   **D–69**

1907

This L-front raised cottage, a particularly good example of the type, was either built on this lot for Herman H. Gold, assistant chief clerk in the U.S. Engineer's Office, or moved, perhaps, from another location. The latter seems plausible because to the immediate east, at **2018 Avenue M,** is a similar house that was built in 1888, a more likely date for both houses.

The raised shotgun house across the street at **2019 Avenue M** (1892) was built as a tenant dwelling by James M. Burroughs, a real estate investor who presided over an empire of tenant cottages, to judge from the properties that late-19th-century county tax records show he owned. Insurance documents indicate that this cottage was "wrecked" in the 1900 hurricane and rebuilt in 1901.

2007 Avenue M   **D–70**

1886; rebuilt with additions 1901

Set in a dense grove of live oak trees, this substantial two-story house features an angled front veranda whose rhythmic geometry is repeated by the angled window bay alongside the front door bay. At the time it was built, the owner, George M. Prendergast, was an engineer on the lighter *Bessie.* By 1901–2, he had become master, according to the city directory, of the dredgeboat *C. B. Comstock,* and of a household of eight. The double veranda was part of Prendergast's additions and repairs after the 1900 storm.

1928 and 1924 Avenue M   D–71
1894

This pair of raised, Victorianized, Gulf Coast cottages feature angled window bays, with shingled panels above and below, inset within the front veranda, and big-scaled veranda balusters with impressive concrete piers at the bottom of the front steps. The elliptical fanlight with sidelights that frames the front door of each seems anachronistic, but since the feature appears in both houses, it is presumed to be original. The houses were built as rental property by Christian Wolfer, a builder.

1920 Avenue M   D–73
1886

Like the Flake House at 1923 M, this two-story, five-bay-wide I-house with a separately roofed two-story veranda prolongs a house type and architectural detail more characteristic of the 1870s than the 1880s. The two-pane-over-two-pane shuttered windows and double-leaf front door grouped beneath a transom give the house its impressive scale. It was built for attorney Robert M. Franklin.

1923 Avenue M   D–72
1886

This two-story, two-bay-wide house is one of the few houses in Galveston to have been built and occupied continuously by the same family. Built for real estate agent Adolph Flake, it resembles other Galveston houses constructed by the builder Robert B. Garnett. Its front-facing window bay, paired windows grouped beneath raked architraves, low-pitched hipped roof, and proliferating decorative brackets were features related to the Italianate style of the 1860s and 1870s, and were perpetuated here in this replacement for a larger, Southern town house type destroyed in the Fire of 1885. During the 1870s, the earlier house had been occupied by H. Kempner, whose son I. H. Kempner wrote in his memoirs that the Marx & Kempner firm stored its drays and livestock on the property, which then lay in the suburbs, near the edge of continuous town settlement.

1915 Avenue M   D–74
1886

The lawyer Walter Gresham built this raised, hipped-roof I-house as a tenant cottage. N. J. Clayton's architectural records indicate that he designed tenant houses for Gresham at various times. Although this symmetrically composed, five-bay-wide cottage is not one of those projects, it is tempting to attribute the design of the house to Clayton, so felicitous are its proportions and decorative veranda detail.

1914 Avenue M   D–75
1887, Alfred Muller

Built for Howard Carnes, cashier in the Galveston office of a regional steamship and railroad corporation, this two-story house was much more up-to-date architecturally than its neighbors at 1923 and 1920 Avenue M. Muller complicated the spatial organization of the Southern town house type by expanding it with an angled bay on the west corner of the house, which rises into an implied tower. This allowed him to shift the axis of centrality as it descends from the roof into the body of the house. His love of arched shapes is particularly visible in the slightly heavy decorative woodwork on the front of the house. The Carnes House is set unusually close to the ground for a Galveston house, the

...xplanation being that the ground level was filled during the grade-raising.

architectural change occurred as a process of evolution rather than one of abandonment and radical innovation.

905 Avenue M   D–76
1889

Two-story houses with verandas fill out this block, just as the building type fills out many blocks in Galveston. Notable at 1905 Avenue M are the flat cutout balustrade and the full-length windows opening onto the verandas of both stories. The two houses on the end lots across the street at **1906** and **1904 Avenue M** were built by contractor Robert Palliser but almost ten years apart—testimony to the popularity of the type. In 1886, Palliser built 1906 for John S. Rogers, who was affiliated with several insurance and loan companies, and a big investor in Galveston real estate. After buying both lots, Palliser, in 1895, built 1904 as his own residence.

806 Avenue M   D–77
1886

Built for the manufacturers' agent Benjamin F. Disbrow, this raised cottage exemplifies the Victorian L-front type that became popular in Galveston in the 1880s. Although it fractured the architectural regularity of traditional Galveston house types (as had occurred in the 1870s among high-style Galveston houses), it is easy to see the L-front as a modification of the symmetrical five-bay-wide cottage, implying that, amidst affordably priced houses,

1801 Avenue M   D–78
1888

This three-bay-wide, hip-roofed, one-story cottage, faced with a one-bay front porch, is notable for the inset and louvered porch on the rear wing, facing 18th Street. This was a feature found on many houses, but relatively few examples exist that have not been enclosed or had the shutters removed. The house was built for the Spalding family, one of whom, Albert T., Jr., manager of the fancy goods department of a Galveston store, was listed at the address in the 1890s.

1725 Avenue M   D–79
1878

Although not a large house, this five-bay-wide Gulf Coast cottage exerts a considerable presence on its open corner site. This presence derives in part from the thick piers upholding the veranda roof and the decorative bracket work on the house.

This is one of those houses whose construction date and early history remain a little murky. Research conducted in the early years of Galveston's preservation efforts credited jeweler John M. Jones with having built the house circa 1868 for his residence. The availability of additional sources and subsequent research suggest a different history. Carpenter Frederick Milde and his wife owned the two corner lots from 1867 to 1870, having bought the property for $1350 from three individuals who included John M. Jones, an early investor in this part of town. The 1871 bird's-eye view of Galveston shows a house on the corner, and indeed, the Mildes sold the property for $2000, indicating that they had made improvements. Insurance records dated 1896 are very precise in listing the construction date as 1878, when the property was owned by watchmaker D. H. Pallais. The 1878 date is supported by the $6000 that Pallais's widow received for the property when she and her second husband sold it in 1883.

a

b

1717 (a) and 1713 (b) Avenue M   D–80
1877 and 1887

This pair of raised cottages, built 10 years apart by the same owner, reveals the typological conservatism of Galveston houses in their virtually identical organization and composition. Both are three-bay-wide, side-gable-roofed houses faced with gable-fronted porches. Owner Adolph Mennike, first listed in the city directories as a carpenter, then as night inspector at the U.S. Custom House, occupied 1717 M. The larger of the two houses, it presented the more imposing, elaborate face to the street with its six-foot brick piers and its grander porch with steps originally running parallel to the house on both sides.

1601 Avenue M   D–81
1883

This five-bay-wide, side-gable-roofed cottage with a two-story, hip-roofed front porch represents a typological variation of the side-gabled cottage that appears in several Galveston houses of the 1880s, usually built on the south side of the street. The house was built for Charles Engelke, who, with a brother, owned a hardware, crockery, tinning, and cornice manufacturing business—the latter, obviously, the source for the pierced tin cornice on the house. Engelke's property joined that of another crockery merchant, A.C. Crawford, whose house occupied the rest of the block front, a suburban country house on the edge of town, one of the grand houses of the area when it was built in 1867. Enhancing the streetscape are the houses at **1604 Avenue M** (early 1900s), **1606** and **1608 Avenue M** (1909), and **1610 Avenue M** (1882).

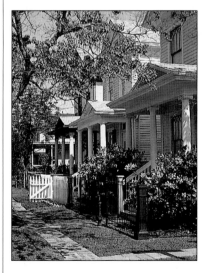

1523, 1525, and 1527 Avenue M   D–82
1910

These three late, late Victorians, decorated with Colonial Revival detail, were built as tenant houses by Dr. David H. Lawrence in a portion of the neighborhood completely destroyed during the Storm of 1900. In 1981, the house at

1527 served as the first demonstration house of the Galveston Historical Foundation's Residential Preservation Program. A series of open houses and workshops were held during rehabilitation, and once completed, the house was sold with protective covenants.

1628 Avenue M 1/2　　　　　　**D–83**
German Methodist Episcopal Church (now Galveston Seventh-day Adventist Church)
1909
Despite its early-20th-century date, this is a picturesque Victorian folk church type, an L-front building configured around its tower and steeple.

1710 Avenue M 1/2　　　　　　**D–84**
c. 1875–80
Tax records document that farmer Julius Loebenstein, in 1881, owned six of the seven lots on the north side of this block, all having some improvement of varying value. The 1889 Sanborn insurance map shows six rectangular houses, each with a gallery, lined up along the street, the only house out of step being a small L-shaped house at the corner of 18th. Five lots across the street on the south side of the block were yet unbuilt. Mr. Loebenstein was listed in city directories as living in the country from 1876 to 1881, after which he was listed in this block, although not retired until 1888.

1827 Avenue M 1/2　　　　　　**D–85**
1887
A high-raised, side-gable-roofed cottage takes distinguished command of its corner lot. The piers of the attached front porch

look as though they are later, 20th-century, bungalow-type alterations. The house was built for musician August Neumann.

1905 Avenue M 1/2　　　　　　**D–86**
1886
The almost cubic proportions of this raised cottage derive from the lack of prominence of its one-bay-wide front porch and the steep, mansard-like profile of its hipped roof. Sanborn insurance maps show that when it was originally built by carpenter and contractor William Pautsch, it was placed directly on the sidewalk line with no front yard, not a unique but also not a typical placement for Galveston houses on east-west streets.

2010, 2008, and 2006 Avenue M 1/2　　**D–87**
1892
As was true for numerous blocks in this part of Galveston, one person—in this case, developer and attorney James M. Burroughs—owned and developed most of the lots on the north side of the 2000 block of Avenue M 1/2, including these three gable-fronted structures with inset porches. Throughout the 1890s, Burroughs both roomed and had his office in downtown Galveston.

2028 Avenue M 1/2   D–88
Early 1900s

Because this two-story, five-bay-wide, side-gable-roofed house is set so close to the street, it exerts more spatial dominance than it might if set farther back. The house features a roll-profiled roof atop the attached double veranda. The 1889 and 1899 Sanborn insurance maps show three one-story square houses oriented to 21st Street on this lot, suggesting that 2028 M 1/2 was not just an enlargement of an earlier structure, as stated in insurance records, but a total replacement. Attorney W. Frank Kelly and his household of six had moved into this house by the time the 1908–9 city directory was published, having rented 2412 Avenue N prior to then.

1409 21st Street   D–89
c. 1870

When this one-story, five-bay-wide cottage with attached veranda was built, it occupied a little promontory looking out across Hitchcock's Bayou.

2111 Avenue M 1/2   D–90
1883

Although architect Alfred Muller did not build this house, which is in an exceptional row of small dwellings, this was

where he and his family resided at the time of his death from typhoid in 1896. His obituary in the *Galveston Daily News* noted that the house lay across the street from the original Galveston Orphans Home, which he had designed. The Mullers' rent house was built by Christian Walker, a house painter, who lived in the 2800 block of Avenue L. It was one of the house types built throughout the city by contractors and builders without the aid of an architect.

2115 Avenue N   D–91
1891

This raised, five-bay-wide, side-gable-roofed cottage with a three-bay attached porch was built by Mrs. Madeline Fivel, a widow who, along with other members of the Fivel family, owned property and lived on the block. Even though a one-story garage has been glommed onto the front of the house, it has not spoiled the house's exuberant decorative porch trim. The house at **2119 Avenue N** is similar in appearance, but, according to insurance records, was built circa 1879.

1522 21st Street   D–92
1885

This imposing suburban villa remains a neighborhood landmark. Built by Frederick William Muller (no relation to architect Alfred Muller), who worked for a ship chandler, it is an enlarged version of the familiar five-bay-wide, side-gable-roofed house, dignified with floor-length, arcuated, shuttered windows and a continuous terrace deck, once enclosed with X-paneled railings. Behind it, at **2018 Avenue N 1/2,** is what could almost be a companion house, a five-bay-wide cottage with floor-length window openings and paired Ionic columns, built in 1886 with additions from the early 1890s.

1527 21st Street   D–93
1896

Since Avenue N 1/2 was never cut through between 21st and Tremont (it was where a meander occurred in the course of Hitchcock's Bayou), this two-story, three-bay-wide house with an angled window bay inset in the double veranda acquires community significance by terminating the sightline up N 1/2. The lacy detailing of the veranda woodwork is up to this responsibility.

2008 Avenue N 1/2   D–94
1893

This is an especially exuberant raised cottage, built as a tenant cottage by Henry C. Henck, Jr. It is notable for its three-bay porch, inset beneath a front-facing gable, and the panache of its decorative woodwork. The cottage also features an open deck along its east side, the survivor of what was once a much more common spatial type in Galveston. A similar house previously stood in what is now the open side yard.

2011 Avenue N 1/2   D–95
c. 1875

A three-bay-wide, side-hall-plan, one-story cottage set beneath a street-facing gable, this modest house sits next to **2015 Avenue N 1/2** (1870), a classic example of the post–Civil War Southern town house type, with octagonal columns and bracketed eaves. The larger and older house,

which appears on the 1871 bird's-eye view, was the home of cotton buyer Charles Albertson.

2002 Avenue N 1/2   D–96
c. 1870

This three-bay-wide cottage was built at 3813 Broadway by Rudolph Bullacher, a German-born drayman. It was moved to this site in 1978 by the Galveston Historical Foundation to prevent its demolition. Rehabilitation by the Galveston contractor W. G. Mayo in 1979 revealed that the geometry of the house accurately documented its growth: from the original two-room front house, to a pair of houses butted together, to a third phase of expansion with a long rear dependency. The view from 20th Street presents this geometry lesson in the cottage's simple but compelling profile.

1513 20th Street   D–97
1867

This small and charming cottage, moved by the Galveston Historical Foundation from its original site in the 1500 block of Strand, is all that remains of a larger complex of buildings. Like the Bullacher House next door, it is the clarity of the single gabled front and the repeating rhythm of the board-and-batten wood construction that give what was originally a little outbuilding its strong architectural character.

1922 Avenue N   D–98
1895
What distinguishes this high-raised, five-bay-wide, side-gable-roofed cottage with twin-window dormers is the pierced bird and flower motifs in the inset arches of its three-bay attached porch and its generous site, studded with Washingtonia palms and a big live oak tree. The house was built for Simon J. Meenen, a porter at Wallis, Landes & Co., wholesale grocers, importers, and cotton factors.

1613 19th Street   D–99
1899
Built by bookkeeper Daniel W. Nettleton as a tenant house, this raised, L-front cottage frames the alley entrance with **1611 19th Street** (1898) to the north. Note how portions of 1613 are cantilevered over the alley to gain extra floor space. It has been carefully rehabilitated, but its alley neighbor, built as a tenant house by city tax collector Ira E. Collins, has not been so lucky.

1902 Avenue O   D–100
1888
Originally the site of Daniel W. Nettleton's house, this corner lot acquired its present house, a high-raised, five-bay-

wide, side-gable-roofed cottage with a one-bay gable-fronted porch, in 1983. The house was moved here from the 1400 block of Strand to save it from demolition, a move that also secured this highly visible corner with a structure compatible to the neighborhood.

1928 Avenue O   D–101
1906, Donald N. McKenzie
If anything betrays the late date of this Victorian house, it is its relative horizontality, achieved by suppressing gablets and dormers, and by widely spacing the paired gallery piers, which are turned rather than detailed as classical colonnettes, as was more often the case for late Victorian house types. McKenzie departed from strict typological adherence to expand the veranda into a gallery that shields a portion of the west side of the house. The house was built for Nathaniel A. Spence, a partner in the Texas Produce & Commission Co.

2009 Avenue O   D–102
1892
A spreading live oak tree shelters this L-front cottage. Its projecting angled bay contains decorative shingled panels beneath and above the windows. Note the pierced woodwork detail of the inset front porch. Although

insurance records state that the house was built as a tenant house by dressmaker Tenie Dobbert, city directories indicate that members of the Dobbert family, including Tenie, her mother, and a brother, were living at this address by 1893.

701 21st Street   D–103
1885
The prominence of 21st Street as a cross-town thoroughfare in the late 19th century is attested by the fact that houses were built to face it rather than the intersecting alphabetical avenues. This five-bay-wide, gable-fronted house was raised and added onto in 1892 by original owner Louis Schmidt, a stock raiser and butcher. Floor-length shuttered windows and a double-leaf front door give the house an expansive ambiance. The property also exhibits an impressive display of Galveston oleanders, an unwitting reference to Schmidt's Garden, a pleasure park that Schmidt's father developed in the early 1870s on the outlots between Avenues O and P and 20th and 21st Streets. The park, which had a saloon, refreshment stand, and an octagon-shaped dance hall, closed in 1887, after which the property was subdivided and sold for residential lots.

a

716 (a) and 1724 (b) 22nd Street   D–104
1874 and 1875
This pair of five-bay-wide cottages must have seemed out in the country when they were built. They lay very close to the edge of the zone of total destruction in the 1900 storm. The house at 1716 is one of the most intact examples of a

b

square hipped-roof house in Galveston. The jagged tooth detail on the porch at 1724 is to be noted.

1702-1710 Tremont Street   D–105
Dell'Osso Shopping Center
1962, 1965, Ben J. Kotin & Tibor Beerman
Built in two stages, this neighborhood convenience center makes architecture out of its roof slab of precast concrete Ts. The dominance of cars and parking area contrasts sharply with the earlier version of the neighborhood shopping center—the corner grocery store.

1918 Avenue P   D–106
The point of this house with its view of the Gulf is not dates and architecture, but rather color and self-confidence! The result is a traffic-stopping combination.

1724 and 1720 Avenue O 1/2   **D–107**

1898, 1923

This pair of substantial tenant houses were built at 19th and K in 1898, then moved to this location, almost within sight of the Gulf, in 1923. What makes them unusual locally is their steeply pitched pyramidal roofs. Exposure to the salt air and sand of the beach has given the pair a very Galvestonian character. With one's back turned to Seawall Boulevard, it is easy to imagine them isolated amid the sand dunes.

1514 Avenue N 1/2   **D–108**

Stephen F. Austin Junior High School

1939, Ben Milam

Despite its setback profile and modernistic horizontal banding, Austin Junior High is a bland institutional building. Yet in contrast to later Galveston public schools, it seeks to exert a public presence in the neighborhood through its frontality and symmetry. The building achieves its high point at the main entrance portal, decorated with a relief panel depicting, in good Public Works Administration iconographic style, bales of cotton being loaded onto ships in the harbor, oil derricks, and smokestacks, all embraced by the rays of the sun.

1305 and 1307 Avenue M 1/2   **D–109**

1905 and 1901

These are examples of post-Storm "commissary houses," precut shotgun cottages shipped to Galveston and quickly erected to house storm survivors whose own dwellings had been destroyed. Property insurance records indicate that both structures were eventually moved to their present sites to serve as rent houses—a not infrequent occurrence.

Architecturally, the West End is not as uniform as other older residential areas in Galveston. But its larger size is only part of the explanation. Whereas other areas were well established by the mid-19th century, the period of initial development in many sections of the West End did not occur until the beginning of the 20th century. Consequently, the buildings represent a broader mix in age and architectural style. ∩ ∩ ∩ Much of the West End was laid out in outlots, which encouraged a looser pattern of development. The two oldest houses in the city—the Ménard and the Williams houses, dating 1838 and 1839 respectively—are examples of outlying estates built on larger tracts of land than was customary for Galveston. Other properties, developed in the 20th century, followed the same pattern. ∩ ∩ ∩ The town blocks in the West End—those that extended

West District School, successor to Barnes Institute, south side of Avenue M between 28th and 29th streets, photograph early 20th century.

to the north side of Avenue M and were closest to the city center— developed an urban density typical of 19th-century Galveston. After the Civil War, an African-American neighborhood evolved in the area with which the black community had had strong associations even during slavery. The African Baptist Church, founded in the 1840s, began meeting in 1855 at the present site of the Avenue L Baptist Church. Following the Civil War, other churches as well as the Barnes Institute, the first educational institution for African-American Galvestonians, were concentrated here. ∩ ∩ ∩ Many Galvestonians were buried (and some still are) in the West End—in the City Cemeteries bordered by Broadway, Avenue L, 40th, and 43rd Streets. The funerary monuments display almost as much variety as the buildings in the city. ∩ ∩ ∩ Historically, two other sizeable tracts of land within the area have been dominated by nonresidential uses and extraordinary structures. The site of the

Garten-Verein park with Ursuline Academy, designed by Nicholas J. Clayton, in the background, circa 1895.

Ursuline Convent and Ursuline Academy, the latter once accommodated in a spectacular Clayton building, is now the Galveston Catholic School. The Garten-Verein, originally a residential site that was adapted for use as the German social club, is a city park. Commercial development has always been minimal in the West End except for neighborhood stores and markets and, in the 19th century, such ventures as cattle yards and slaughterhouses, which, along with squatters, defined the always-fluctuating western boundaries of the city limits. With the building of the Seawall and the raising of the island, the city's western edge began to assume a tidier definition. The West End became an area for more deliberate development, some of which took the form of bungalows and other small frame houses, especially in the blocks nearest the Gulf. The names of Galveston's major 19th century architects can be attached to a scattering of buildings in the West End. Equally prominent, however, are such names as Raymond R. Rapp, John F. Staub, and Cameron Fairchild, who are identified with the 1920s and the 1930s—the years during which much of the West End acquired its prevailing architectural characteristics.

A street near 36th Street and Avenue M, photograph circa 1930. Many streets cut through outlots looked more like alleys than like main streets.

1. 2517 and 2519 Avenue L
2. 2612 Avenue L
3. 2621 Avenue K rear
4. 2627 Avenue M
5. 2812 and 2810 Avenue L
6. 2928 Avenue K
7. 3105, 3109, and 3111 Avenue K
8. 3114 and 3110 Avenue K
9. 1020 32nd Street
10. 1223 32nd Street
11. 1326 31st Street
12. 3003 Avenue M
13. 2920 Avenue M 1/2
14. 2802 Avenue M 1/2
15. 2814 Avenue N
16. 1500 block J. H. Clouser Lane
17. 1504 31st Street
18. 3123 Avenue N
19. 3210 Avenue N
20. 3301 Avenue N
21. 1220 34th Street
22. 3517 Avenue M
23. 3518 Avenue M
24. 3528 Avenue M
25. 3625 and 3627 Avenue M
26. 3702 Avenue M
27. 1124 37th Street
28. 3607 Avenue L
29. 3612 Avenue L
30. 1115 36th Street
31. 1116 36th Street
32. 3501 Broadway
33. 1015 35th Street
34. 1019-21 35th Street
35. 1115 35th Street
36. 1121 35th Street
37. 3426 Avenue L
38. 3419 Avenue L
39. 3410 Avenue L
40. 3327 Avenue L
41. 3301 Avenue L
42. 1121 33rd Street
43. 1103 33rd Street
44. 1019-21 33rd Street
45. 3314 Avenue K
46. 1013-1027 34th Street

47. 3112 Broadway
48. Old City Cemetery: J. P. Davie Vault
49. Old City Cemetery:
    J. Reymershoffer Monument
50. Old City Cemetery: Justine
    Illies-McKenzie Monument
51. City Cemetery:
    Athen V. Pichard Monument
52. City Cemetery: John Sealy
    Monument and B. R. Davis
    Monument
53. Hebrew Benevolent Society Cemetery:
    Henrietta Blum Monument
54. Hebrew Benevolent Society Cemetery:
    Moritz Kopperl Monument
55. Hebrew Benevolent Society Cemetery:
    Agnes Lord and Robert I. Cohen
    Monument

56. Hebrew Benevolent Society Cemetery:
    David Freeman Monument
57. Episcopal Cemetery:
    Short A. Willis Vault
58. Episcopal Cemetery: P. J. Willis Vault
59. Episcopal Cemetery:
    Mrs. F. A. Wilson Vault
60. Episcopal Cemetery:
    George Sealy Monument
61. 3920 Avenue L
62. 3812 and 3810 Avenue M
63. 3918 Avenue M 1/2
64. 1410 41st Street
65. 2601 Avenue N
66. 2328 Avenue O
67. 2419 Avenue O
68. 2428 Avenue O
69. 1602 Rosenberg Avenue

104. 3523 Avenue P
105. 3503 Avenue P
106. 3502 Avenue P
107. 3421 Avenue P
108. 1903 34th Street
109. 3201 Avenue P
110. 3101 Avenue P
111. 3011 Avenue P
112. 2927 Avenue P
113. 2702 Avenue O 1/2
114. 2600 Avenue O 1/2
115. 1723 Rosenberg Avenue
116. 1804 Rosenberg Avenue
117. 2408 and 2406 Avenue P
118. 2018–2024 Rosenberg Avenue
119. 2002 Rosenberg Avenue
120. 1917 Rosenberg Avenue
121. 2012 29th Street
122. 3102 Avenue P 1/2
123. 3127 Avenue P 1/2
124. 3202 Avenue P 1/2
125. 3428 Avenue Q
126. 2127 37th Street

2504 Avenue O
2528 Avenue O
2529 Avenue O
2602 Avenue O
2603 Avenue O
2701 Avenue O
2705 and 2709 Avenue O
2704 Avenue O
2816 Avenue O
2805 Avenue O
2901 Avenue O
2908 Avenue O
3001 Avenue O
3011 Avenue O
3017 Avenue O
1704 31st Street
3028 Avenue O

87. 3102 Avenue O
88. 1605 33rd Street
89. 3328 Avenue O
90. 3401 Avenue O
91. 3427 Avenue O
92. 1705 35th Street
93. 1718 35th Street
94. 1804 35th Street
95. 3518 Avenue O
96. 3527 Avenue O
97. 3701 Avenue O
98. 3827 Avenue O
99. 3815 Avenue P
100. 1919 37th Street
101. 3823 Avenue P 1/2
102. 3601 Avenue P
103. 3528 Avenue P

2517 and 2519 Avenue L   E-1
c. 1880

This is a classic pair of shotgun cottages. They bespeak the historical identification of the blocks west of Rosenberg Avenue with African-American occupation in the period of post–Civil War Reconstruction and thereafter. Like many of the modest houses in the area, these cottages were built as tenant houses, in this instance by the ship's carpenter Henry Stühmer. Yet here, as elsewhere in Galveston, social geography was intricately configured. The 2500 and 2600 blocks of Avenue K, to the north, were identified with houses for white, middle-class families, among them the lifelong home (now demolished) of the architect George B. Stowe.

Across the street, at **2518** and **2520 Avenue L,** is another pair of shotgun cottages. They were built by Bartholomew M. Fleming and seem to predate 1880.

2612 Avenue L   E-2
Avenue L Missionary Baptist Church
1917, Tanner Brothers

The Avenue L Baptist Church is one of the oldest African-American institutions in Texas. It is an outgrowth of the African Baptist Church, formed in the 1840s as the slave congregation of the First Baptist Church and which began meeting on this site in 1855. The property was acquired by the congregation in 1867. Between 1881 and 1887, a brick church was built here, but it was destroyed in the Storm of 1900. The present church was designed and built by the African-American architect-builders Tanner Brothers of Columbus, Texas. It is a tall, vertically proportioned building framed by twin towers, a church type distinctively identified with African-American Protestant congregations in the South from the 1910s through the 1950s. Window openings are capped with round, depressed, and pointed arches.

Visible on the west side, behind the brick church, is the congregation's wooden church of 1905, a picturesque Victorian structure that, in the Galveston tradition, was moved to the back of the property and incorporated into the successor church rather than demolished.

2621 Avenue K rear   E-3
Date undetermined

Many alley dwellings are an amalgamation of two houses that have been joined, as is the case here. The main, or alley, entrance is placed in what was a one-room square house with hip roof. A two-room house was attached to the back, or yard, side, and the ell (on the west side) was enclosed. In Galveston, alley addresses are denoted by "rear."

2627 Avenue M   E-4
Central High School (now Old Central Cultural Center)
1924, William B. Ittner and DeWitt & Lemmon
Rosenberg Colored Library, 1905, George B. Stowe

This area was the foremost African-American neighborhood of late-19th-century Galveston, in part because the Barnes Institute (which began as the Colored Free School) was opened at 28th Street and Avenue M during Reconstruction. In 1893, N. J. Clayton's Central High School, the public high school in Galveston for black students, was built at 27th and Avenue M. The trustees of Henry Rosenberg's estate had Stowe add the African-American branch of the public library to the back of Clayton's building in 1905. This is now the oldest surviving part of the complex, inasmuch as the Clayton school was demolished and replaced with what is now the Old Central Cultural Center, one of several Galveston public schools designed in the early 1920s by the St. Louis architect William B. Ittner and his Dallas collaborators, Roscoe DeWitt and Mark Lemmon.

812 and 2810 Avenue L — E-5

. 1910

These tenant cottages, built by David Rossi, an agent of the Houston Ice & Brewing Company, incorporate deep galleries on their east sides. These provided sheltered outdoor space that expanded the tiny area available inside.

928 Avenue K — E-6

889, Joseph Treaccar, carpenter

The Galveston-German carpenter Joseph Treaccar built this southern town-house–type dwelling for his family. It was owned, and intermittently occupied, by his descendants until 1983, when the Galveston Historical Foundation bought the vacant, fire-damaged house, carried out repairs, and sold it with protective restrictions. The Treaccar House was rehabilitated in 1989.

105, 3109, and 3111 Avenue K — E-7

ates undetermined

3114 and 3110 Avenue K — E-8

Dates undetermined

This compelling group of wood cottages could date to the 1860s or 1870s. They strongly evoke the landscape of working-class Galveston neighborhoods of the late 19th century in their small size and purity of shape. According to insurance records, **3105** and **3109 Avenue K** were moved onto this site in 1924. The Gulf Coast cottage at 3105 K and the larger, five-bay-wide Gulf Coast cottage at **3111 Avenue K** spatially bracket the gable-fronted cottage at 3109 K. Across the street at **3110** and **3114 Avenue K** are a pair of trim, side-gabled, story-and-a-half cottages with attached front porches, built by John Bullacher, whose grocery store stood at the corner of 31st and K. The house at 3114 K has picturesque rear attachments, as can be seen by looking down the alley along the west side of the house.

Photographs from the 1890s indicate that much of the West End, both south and north of Broadway, was populated by dense clusters of modest vernacular house types such as these. Many of them seem to have been built in the immediate post–Civil War period, when the neighborhood lay at the southwest edge of continuous town settlement.

Note that the town blocks between 29th Street and 33rd Street are bisected by alleys running north-south rather than east-west, as is the case with all of the Galveston City Company's other town blocks.

1020 32nd Street — E-9

Live Oak Missionary Baptist Church
1975, 1989, Haywood Jordan McCowan

As in many of their buildings, the Houston architects Haywood Jordan McCowan display here the influence of Norcell Haywood's mentor, San Antonio architect O'Neil Ford. The tawny brick surfaces, the combination of steel pipe columns and corrugated green plastic sheeting in the porte-cochère canopy facing Avenue K, and the decorative detailing of the church's entrance doors and ornamental light diffusers pay homage to the modern-regionalism espoused by Ford and carried on in the work of several generations of Texas architects.

1223 32nd Street   **E–10**

Trinity Baptist Church

1885

Remodeled and added to several times during the 20th century, Trinity Baptist Church demonstrates the presence and authority that vernacular buildings can have despite small size and simple construction.

1326 31st Street   **E–11**

Rex Steam Laundry Company Building

1930, Andrew Fraser

Trained as an engineer, Andrew Fraser produced building designs that often were rather mechanical in appearance. It is therefore ironic that this concrete-framed, brick-faced light-industrial loft building with no-nonsense steel-sash windows and Art Déco ornamental detail should be one of his most persuasive works of architecture. The Rex Steam Laundry Company was an enterprise of W. L. Moody, Jr., and his son Shearn.

3003 Avenue M   **E–12**

West Point Missionary Baptist Church

1921, Fred Hadcock, builder

In its neighborhood setting, West Point Baptist Church appears quite monumental, thanks to its brick construction, its pedimented portico and front doors, and its octagonal cupola. Perhaps because of the importance of religious

institutions in Southern African-American communities during the long era of racial segregation, the church's architectural assertion of classical dignity imbues it with a resonance that it might lack if set in a more affluent, white neighborhood.

2920 Avenue M 1/2   **E–13**

Macedonia Baptist Church

1901, 1946

When alphabet-and-a-half avenues were cut through outlots in an east-west direction, the City of Galveston did not require that they adhere to uniform widths. Therefore, the avenues sometime narrow down to alleylike dimensions, as they do here, giving blocks a sense of spatial intimacy not found elsewhere in the city. Macedonia Baptist Church takes advantage of this situation. It is a picturesque Victorian structure that is given a churchly appearance with pointed windows and a corner steeple. Across the street at 2915 Avenue M 1/2 is the imposing, twin-towered **Spiritual True Church** of 1927.

2802 Avenue M 1/2   **E–14**

c. 1884

This five-bay cottage with a three-bay front porch features an unusual single dormer, set flush with the front wall of the house and centered above the front door. The vertical

roportions of the window openings and their decorative
rim give this cottage, built for the boilermaker Dell N.
chmalm, special distinction.

814 Avenue N   **E–15**

.885

This one-and-one-half-story cottage is a vernacular classic,
with its attic-level vent windows just below the eaves of the
ide-gabled roof and its diminutive rear ell wing. It was
uilt for the laborer Charles Johnson.

500 block J. H. Clouser Lane   **E–16**

Kelly Avenue Tenant Cottages

:. 1908

n a city notable for the extraordinary consistency of its ruling
grid of streets and blocks, this "lane" is one of the most
rchitecturally rewarding instances of spatial non-conformity.
Renamed several times—Kelly Avenue seems to have been the
arliest name of the street, followed by Ballinger Lane, now
Clouser Lane after the public school teacher and civic leader
ohn Henry Clouser—the half-block street represents the
ubdivision of two lots for a cluster of tenant houses historically
ccupied by African-American families. In 1908, the tract was
ought by the real estate investor L. W. Pautsch, who seems to
ave assembled the houses here, probably by moving them

from other locations in the city. The Kelly Avenue tenant
cottages represent one of the best collections of exceptionally
small 19th-century vernacular cottages in Galveston.

Pautsch bought the tract from the estate of Mrs. William P.
Ballinger. It is part of Outlot 39, which had been identified with
the prominent lawyer William P. Ballinger since the 1850s. He,
various family members, and other elite Galveston families built
their houses on the south side of the outlot facing Avenue O
and the west side facing 31st Street between the mid-19th and
mid-20th centuries. Indicative of the variations in prestige that
occurred within short spatial dimensions in Galveston was the
identification of the Kelly Avenue–Clouser Lane portion of the
outlot with the African-American neighborhood to the north.

1504 31st Street   **E–17**

1899, George B. Stowe

Backing up to the Kelly Avenue tenant cottages is this late
Victorian house, designed for the railroad executive Lucius J.
Polk. It is one of Stowe's more restrained houses, as its flattened
angular geometries and one-story veranda demonstrate. Although
the Polk House has been resurfaced in asbestos shingles, its
features are intact, and it retains a rear cistern, visible from Avenue
N. Prior to the extension of mains from the city waterworks,
cisterns were used to catch and store rainwater for domestic use.

3123 Avenue N   **E–18**

1883

This expansive, raised five-bay-wide cottage with twin-
window dormers protruding through a side-gabled roof is

particularly notable for its delicately detailed wooden front porch. This rises above the eaves to provide a full-height second-story porch crowned by a decorated gable. Vertical assertion and delicate Victorian decoration imbue this house, which is set far back on its lot behind a screen of mature live oak trees, with definite spatial presence. The house was built by Henry Cortes, who manufactured soda, sarsaparilla, and ginger ale.

3210 Avenue N   E–19
c. 1885

This is a delightful, small-scaled, three-bay-wide cottage with a side-gabled roof and tightly clipped eaves. On the east side, the single-room depth of the front block of the house is apparent. On the west side, the cottage expands into a rear ell-wing picturesquely roofed with multiple gables. Many Galveston houses, both large and small, have a double-gable profile. This is the only house to have a triple-gable profile. The house first appeared on this lot about 1885, when it was purchased by Henry Bütterowe.

Across the street at **3219 Avenue N** is the substantial brick veneer bungalow built by Dr. Mack J. Moseley in 1919 and remodeled in 1924, when it probably achieved its present appearance. Dr. Moseley was an African-American gynecologist. Galveston did not provide African-American professionals with much opportunity or social mobility in the early 20th century. Consequently it was rare for African-American Galvestonians to be able to afford to build a middle-class house type such as Dr. Moseley's.

3301 Avenue N   E–20
1893

Holding the street corner is this raised five-bay-wide house, Victorianized by projecting an angled window bay forward of the western half of the house front. Note the back of the house with its dormers and narrow L-plan, matching the

trim on the front. Note also the small hipped-roof appendage. This raised cottage was built by Charles F. Marschner, president of the Texas Bottling Work.

1220 34th Street   E–21
1886

Insurance records date this three-bay-wide Gulf Coast cottage with shuttered windows and a transom-topped door to 1886, indicating just how long this quintessential Southern cottage type continued to be built in Galveston. The great live oak tree in front reinforces the Southern identity of this particular example.

3517 Avenue M   E–22
c. 1857

This five-bay-wide, hipped-roof house derives considerable dignity from its gabled front porch, its high-raised stature, and the three live oak trees that screen it from the street. Built by Edward T. Austin (who subsequently built the house at 1502 Market Street), this house stood in suburban isolation at the time of its construction, several blocks beyond the bounds of town settlement. The shouldered architrave that frames the sidelight-and-transom-surrounded front door is reiterated internally in fine examples of vernacular Grecian architectural detailing. The Austin House was raised in 1906.

3518 Avenue M   E–23
1877, Robert B. Garnett

This two-bay-wide Italianate-type house was built by Robert B. Garnett as his family home, and, according to research by the Galveston Historical Foundation, he lived here until 1899. Although not a large house, Garnett's

ouse exhibits the architectural paraphernalia associated with this type: extensive use of decorative scrolls and rackets, projecting hoods and angled window bays including a cantilevered second-story bay on the east side of he house), and round-headed, paneled double-leaf doors, nset in a paneled alcove. Such ornamental features contrast ith the narrow wood clapboards and the vertically roportioned window openings. Garnett's house resembles ther Galveston Italianate houses, including the Smith House t 2217 Broadway and the Flake House at 1923 Avenue M.

528 Avenue M   **E-24**

1874

his raised, five-bay-wide house exhibits an arcuated and ableted front porch. Built about 1874 by Amos B. Tuller, who was associated with a firm of shipping agents and rokers, the house was remodeled by Tuller's widow in 884, which is probably when the arcuated and gableted ront porch was added. This feature, together with the wide orch steps, gives the straightforward cottage type a Galvestonian lilt. The Tuller House is supported on tall, lender brick piers, like so many others of its type.

625 Avenue M   **E-25**

880

627 Avenue M

892

oth of these houses were owned, and occupied in uccession, by Henry Eimar, a house painter and aperhanger. The earlier of the two is an unusual example f a side-hall plan applied to a small, one-story cottage. lthough Galveston's climate would seem to have made

such an arrangement highly desirable, since it allowed major rooms to be lined up on the side of the house with the best orientation to the prevailing breeze, side-hall plans were far less common in one-story cottages than in two-story houses. As Eimar prospered, he built the larger, raised house next door with its ornamented porch and shuttered door and window openings. After moving into 3627, he retained 3625 as an income-producing tenant cottage.

3702 Avenue M   **E-26**

1871

Built by Walter C. Ansell, whose Texas Ice Company shipped ice from Maine and Massachusetts to Texas, this is a handsome, five-bay-wide Gulf Coast cottage with shuttered windows and twin-window dormers. The house is slightly raised, so that it is elevated above its fenced front garden.

1124 37th Street   **E-27**

c. 1867

This three-bay-wide Southern town house features an unusually low-pitched hipped roof. It was built for Dr. and Mrs. Lafayette Garrett.

3607 Avenue L E–28

c. 1876

Like the Garrett House at 1124 37th Street, this five-bay-wide cottage with an attached veranda and floor-length shuttered windows dates from the early settlement of the West End. It was built by James S. Montgomery, an official of the Galveston Bank & Trust Company.

3612 Avenue L E–29

Grace Episcopal Church (now Grace Episcopal Church Parish House)

1874

In the middle of the 3600 block of Avenue L is the parish house of Grace Church. The original parish church, it was moved and remodeled when its stone successor was built in 1895. The raised wooden building is recognizable as the vernacular Southern church type, architecturally updated with pointed arch openings and High Victorian gablets along its sides.

1115 36th Street E–30

Grace Episcopal Church

1895, N. J. Clayton & Company with Silas McBee

Henry Rosenberg, a parishioner of Grace Church, left the parish a $30,000 bequest to build the new church. This was the only Rosenberg bequest that resulted in a building by N. J. Clayton. Clayton's High Victorian Gothic design is restrained, as befit the 1890s, but full-bodied in its massing. The church's stepped, gabled shapes are sculptural in profile. They seem to step back as the building rises. Yet they possess a strong volumetric quality, as though it is interior space that informs external shape. Clayton's proportional skill is evident in the contrast between the thick, buttressed tower and the long folded planes of the nave and aisle roofs.

Rosenberg's widow gave additional funds for the design and decoration of the interior. Clayton worked with the parish's liturgical consultant, Silas McBee of the University of the South, on the interior. McBee seems to have been responsible for the decoration of the altar and reredos, which replicate those he designed at the same time for Christ Church in Houston.

1116 36th Street E–3

1890

A newcomer to the neighborhood, this unusual four-bay-wide house with double verandas was originally built across Broadwa at 31st and Postoffice. It was moved to this site in 1927.

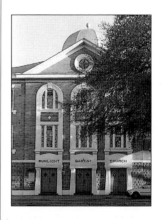

3501 Broadway E–3

Broadway Baptist Church (now Sunlight Baptist Church)

1914, C. W. Bulger & Son and Rudolf Mudrak

1916

The Broadway Baptist Church is perhaps more notable as

ban design than as a work of architectural distinction. Its
rm mass, civic scale, and low dome hold the corner at
5th and Broadway with authority. According to the
alveston Daily News, the church was originally designed by
. W. Bulger & Son, which, after moving its office from
alveston to Dallas, developed a specialty as an architect of
aptist churches. However, Bulger's design was modified by
udolf Mudrak, a Czech architect and engineer who came
 Galveston to administer construction of the Hotel Galvez
r the St. Louis architects Mauran & Russell, then
mained to begin his own practice.

015 35th Street   **E–33**
. 1873

his raised cottage, which is set so close to the back of the
roadway Baptist Church that it almost seems to lean on it,
as an episodic shape that suggests it may be composed of
/hat were originally two, or more, cottages. In 1871 the
roperty was acquired by Sydney Martin, who was
onnected with the wholesale and commission firm of P. J.
Villis & Brother. Martin sold this site, which was originally
art of his homestead next door, as a separate tract to his
usiness associate W. G. Belding in 1876.

019-21 35th Street   **E–34**
. 1873, 1876

As with several other houses in the neighborhood, this two-
tory I-house dates from the days when the area was the very
dge of Galveston. Built by Sydney Martin, it preserves a
ense of suburban amplitude in its spacious grounds, notable
or mature vegetation, including two live oak trees, and
umerous outbuildings. The Martin House appears to have

once been similar to the Cherry House at 1602 Church
Street in the East End. However, its thin, sharp edges and
tight proportions were relaxed when the house was raised,
bay windows were added to the front façade, and a much
more elaborately shaped and decorated veranda evidently
replaced the original. These changes were probably made in
1876, when insurance records indicate that additions were
made to the house by the next owners, P. J. Willis's daughter
Ella Willis and her husband, Joseph G. Goldthwaite.

1115 35th Street   **E–35**
1877, Robert B. Garnett, builder
Despite multiple incompatible alterations, this mansard-
roofed raised cottage with tower retains its architectural
identity. It was built by Joseph J. Hunter, a salesman for
P. J. Willis & Brother. Thanks to Sydney Martin, 35th
Street seems to have been staked out as an enclave of
P. J. Willis employees in the 1870s.

1121 35th Street   **E–36**
1924
Dr. Bernard A. Schmidt, a dentist, was the client for this
spacious raised bungalow, similar to those that R. R. Rapp
produced for other Galveston clients at this time. The
arched basement below the front porch, the side stair, the
light gray stucco surfacing of the house, and so old-
fashioned a touch as the concrete curbing outlining the
property give the Schmidt House as strong a Galvestonian
aspect as its 19th-century neighbors.

3426 Avenue L   **E–37**

1873

This three-bay-wide cottage, faced with a three-bay porch
with bracketed eaves, and capped by a low hipped roof, was
where Galveston architect Charles W. Bulger and his family
lived at the turn of the 20th century, before he moved his
practice to Dallas. N. J. Clayton and his family lived
diagonally across the street in a three-bay Southern town
house at 1205 35th Street from 1892 until Mrs. Clayton's
death in 1944. Clayton's house, built by General Thomas
N. Waul, no longer exists. Bulger's house had been built by
William C. Dibbrell.

3419 Avenue L   **E–38**

c. 1867

Another graceful example of the Gulf Coast cottage, with a
transom-topped, side-lit door framed by a Greek Revival
architrave, this house is thought to have been built by
William G. Boepple. It was restored in 1935 by longtime
owners, who bought the house at the urging of architect
Donald Barthelme. Barthelme had intended to buy the
house himself, but decided that professional opportunities
in Depression-era Galveston were so limited that he needed
to leave the island.

3410 Avenue L   **E–39**

1875

Anthony Brock, a Galveston businessman, built this
handsome cottage, faced with a three-bay-wide veranda.
Mrs. Annie L. King seems to have built the gable-fronted
cottages at **3406 Avenue L** and **3402 Avenue L** (1883),
which were rented as tenant houses. Together, these form a

characteristic Galvestonian row, punctuating the street
frontage with the rhythm of their column-lined porches.

3327 Avenue L   **E–4⬤**

1893

Built for Arthur A. Dietzel, an employee of the Galveston
Coffee & Spice Company, this is a late and simplified
version of the Italianate villa style. Behind the Dietzel
House, at **1212** and **1214 34th Street** is a pair of raised
tenant cottages built by Dietzel in 1892. They form a
complex typical of middle-class Galveston neighborhoods of
the late 19th century: the "big" houses faced the alphabetical
avenues, while behind, facing the side street or the alley, were
rental cottages for families of more modest means.

3301 Avenue L   **E–41**

1892

Like the Dietzel House at the west end of the block, this house
for the produce commission merchant John Hagemann was
built well after the peak in popularity of the Italianate
villa–style. Its conservatism allows it to pay respect to the
neighborhood context with planar walls, low-pitched hipped

oof with bracketed cornice, and a one-story gallery, all features ssociated with the Italianate style. The gallery of the Hagemann House is notable for both its delicate woodwork and its -curved roof profile. The house was rehabilitated in 1996.

121 33rd Street   E–42
.874

Built for Mrs. Sarah C. Hurtley, the sister of Mrs. John ealy, the two-bay-wide Italianate town house at 1121 33rd street conforms to the way this Victorian house type was often built in Galveston. In terms of siting, Mrs. Hurtley's house adhered to Galveston custom by facing the numbered ide street, so that the south frontage along the alphabetical venue could be treated as a deep garden. Here, the garden is planted with a grove of mature live oak trees, overlooked by front and back side porches. It is tempting to attribute Mrs. Hurtley's house to the builder Robert B. Garnett, who was responsible for a number of similarly detailed houses during he 1870s. This portion of the West End, developed in the 1870s, is notable for its collection of Italianate villa–style houses. Mrs. Hurtley's house was rehabilitated in 1996.

103 33rd Street   E–43
(now Bethel Church)
1866, 1889

The wholesale grocer Herman Marwitz bought this three-bay Southern town house and had it remodeled and expanded for his daughter Ida at the time of her marriage to John Charles Gross in 1889. The fluted Doric columns and shouldered architraves surrounding the first-floor openings probably date from 1866. The fanlight arch above the front door, the high-arched basement surfaced with rusticated cement plaster, and the corner tower probably date from 1889. So too the Gross House's architectural *pièce de*

résistance, the ornately swirled parapets bracketing the front steps, which culminate in a startling pair of wooden lions. Crude sculptural execution enhances their surreal aspect.

1019-21 33rd Street   E–44
1903

A relative latecomer to the West End, this raised, L-plan Victorian cottage, built for William J. Newcomb, an employee of the Galveston, Houston & Northern Railway, stands out by virtue of the paired posts and ornate wood frieze of its wraparound gallery. Visible along Avenue K is a picturesque series of one- and two-story additions to the Newcomb House.

3314 Avenue K   E–45
1868

This is a fine example of the Southern town house, monumentalized with double-height fluted Doric columns, its major openings framed with shouldered architraves. It was built by the prominent lawyer, land agent, and property title abstract company owner Joseph Franklin.

1013-1027 34th Street   E–46
St. Patrick's Catholic Church
1877, Clayton & Lynch
1902, N. J. Clayton

St. Patrick's was N. J. Clayton's parish church. As the peculiar texture of its sprayed-on concrete exterior finish demonstrates, the Clayton connection has not saved St.

Patrick's from ill-considered alterations. Construction of St. Patrick's, begun in 1872, predated Clayton's involvement. By 1874 he seems to have produced a design for the body of the church, which was dedicated in 1877. Clayton carried out the decoration of the interior in the mid-1880s, and in 1899 completed St. Patrick's crowning touch, the 225-foot-high Ménard Memorial Tower, the tallest tower in Galveston. The Ménard Tower proved to be St. Patrick's undoing. During the Storm of 1900 it was blown down onto the church, crushing the roof and the upper portions of the nave walls.

St. Patrick's was reconstructed, with minor modifications, to Clayton's design, although its present tower, only 120 feet high and built of reinforced concrete, was not constructed until 1922, six years after Clayton's death. Facing Broadway is the ex-**St. Patrick's School** (1925) by Donald N. McKenzie. Charles L. Zwiener designed the banded brick and limestone-faced **Rectory** at 3420 Avenue K (1950).

St. Patrick's was an important commission in Clayton's body of work. With it he established a church type that became the model for a number of the many Catholic churches he subsequently designed. The gabled bays flanking the central tower are the hallmark of this type. In them, one can see how Clayton adroitly used simple geometric figures—the triangle and the circle—to build up generously proportioned surface compositions framed by sharply defined profiles. The texture of the concrete finish (the church was first stuccoed in 1915) obscures the beautiful brickwork that originally gave Clayton's surface patterns tectonic resonance. The closing of 34th Street to through traffic and its absorption into the parish's parking lot further undermine the dignity of St. Patrick's by suburbanizing the space around it. St. Patrick's was rehabilitated in 1990 by Killis Almond & Associates of San Antonio.

3112 Broadway　　　　　　　　　　　　　E-47
1928, R. R. Rapp

It is interesting to see in this house, built for the dry-goods merchant Joe G. Eiband next to Eiband's parents' house at 3118, how Rapp conservatively maintained that old-Galveston standby, the front porch. By the 1920s, the front porch had been retired from style-conscious domestic architecture. Evidently, some of Rapp's clients were not ready to sacrifice custom to fashion, and so it survived here, on the West End of the Broadway grand avenue. With the opening of the new paved highway to Houston the year the Eiband House was completed, this end of Broadway became more profitable for commercial than residential real estate. Hence the prefabricated

metal building that is now in what was once the east side yard of the Eiband House. Rapp contributed to this transformation in a more architecturally dignified way with his **F. P. Malloy & Sons Funeral Home** at 3022 Broadway and 31st (1930), designed to appear like a classically porticoed mansion.

Old City Cemetery　　　　　　　　　　　E-48
J. P. Davie Vault
1878, Duhamel & Lawlor

In 1840 and 1841, the Galveston City Company set aside four city blocks far beyond the western edge of continuous settlement as a public burying ground. The City Company had John Groesbeck subdivide this real estate into a series of cemeteries. Some are religious in affiliation. Others are secular. All follow a similar pattern of site organization: paved sidewalks, laid out in orthogonal grids, are edged by high curbing. Ornamental vegetation is minimal. The feeling is urban rather than pastoral. As in New Orleans, Galveston's high water table encouraged burials near or above grade, further enhancing the urban, architectural aspect of Galveston's city cemeteries.

As in life, so in death, Galveston's Victorian elite architecturally aggrandized themselves with sculptural monuments and mausoleums.

E. J. Duhamel designed the Davie vault with a steeply pitched High Victorian gabled roof, column-framed Gothic portal, and marble door. The flanks, however, are subdivided by paneled pilasters, and the brick structure is thickly coated with weathered gray stucco.

Old City Cemetery　　　　　　　　　　　E-49
J. Reymershoffer Monument
c. 1900

The Reymershoffer Monument is a stepped cenotaph of gray granite, handsomely finished with low-relief classical ornament and capped by the figure of a kneeling woman.

Old City Cemetery   **E–50**

Justine Illies-McKenzie Monument

c. 1917, Donald N. McKenzie

McKenzie designed this gray granite monument, composed of shallow, overlapping planes and surfaced with minimal classical detail, for his mother's grave. He and his half-brother are also buried here.

City Cemetery   **E–51**

Stephen V. Pichard Monument

c. 1883

The Pichard Monument is a flamboyant High Victorian catafalque "permanent-ized" in polished red granite and weathered white marble.

City Cemetery   **E–52**

John Sealy Monument

1885, N. J. Clayton

City Cemetery

B. R. Davis Monument

c. 1882

One of the tallest monuments in the city cemeteries is Clayton's gray granite obelisk marking the grave of John Sealy. Note the shapely curbing surrounding the burial plot.

Mrs. John Sealy's brother, the merchant B. R. Davis, is memorialized in a quintessential Victorian funerary monument, combining the rather crude figure of a draped woman and the column-supported open aedicule atop which she is stationed.

Hebrew Benevolent Society Cemetery **E–53**

Henrietta Blum Monument

c. 1877

Leon H. Blum had this white marble High Victorian Gothic monument, bristling with gablets, pinnacles, and a compound crocketed spire, erected above the grave of his wife Henrietta. The Hebrew Benevolent Society Cemetery was platted in 1852 just west of the original group of cemeteries, then expanded in size in 1868.

Hebrew Benevolent Society Cemetery   E–54
Moritz Kopperl Monument
c. 1883
The Kopperl Monument combines figural statuary, relief portrait plaques, and winged angel heads in a sculpturally spirited marble monument. Like most of the other architecturally ambitious entombments in the Hebrew Benevolent Society Cemetery, the Kopperl Monument faces the cemetery's central broad way.

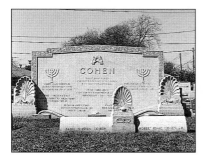

Hebrew Benevolent Society Cemetery   E–55
Agnes Lord and Robert I. Cohen Monument
1935, William Ward Watkin
Houston architect William Ward Watkin produced this dignified stripped classical granite tombstone for the parents of his client, the Galveston-born Houston department store magnate George S. Cohen.

Hebrew Benevolent Society Cemetery   E–56
David Freeman Monument
1900, N. J. Clayton

Clayton's treatment of classical funerary architecture was more sober and austere in the Freeman obelisk than it had been in the High Victorian John Sealy obelisk.

Episcopal Cemetery   E–57
Short A. Willis Vault
1878, N. Tobey, Jr.
Built of block, this tomb displays High Victorian exaggerated proportions and details, such as the giant pinnacles that rise from splayed buttresses at each corner of the tomb.

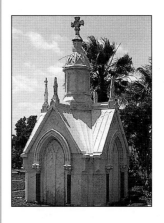

Episcopal Cemetery   E–58
P. J. Willis Vault
Date undetermined

A Greek cross in plan, the P. J. Willis Vault is yet another example of High Victorian–style funerary architecture, built of white marble with red granite flourishes.

piscopal Cemetery　　　　　**E–59**
Mrs. F. A. Wilson Vault
1880
The full-bodied detailing and assertive domical cap of the Wilson Vault lend themselves to rendering in white-finished stucco.

piscopal Cemetery　　　　　**E–60**
George Sealy Monument
1903, McKim, Mead & White
McKim, Mead & White repeated in Episcopal Cemetery their achievement on Broadway: they designed the funerary monument by which all subsequent Galveston monuments were measured. The tall, slender, polished pink granite stela, inlaid with a delicate metal wreath and crowned by barely detailed acroteria, is a work of enormous understatement. Magnolia Willis Sealy commissioned this work for her husband's grave. She and several of her children are also buried here.

The Sealy Monument was executed by the stone contractor Charles S. Ott, who was responsible for many of the Victorian monuments in the city cemeteries. Successive generations of his descendants have continued his craft at the Ott Monument Works.

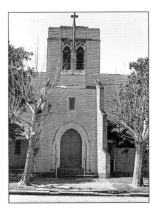

3920 Avenue L　　　　　**E–61**
St. John's Lutheran Church
1954, Hiram A. Salisbury & T. G. McHale
The Houston architects Salisbury & McHale produced one of their characteristic suburban neo-Gothic parish complexes for what began at this site in the mid-1890s as the West End Evangelical mission.

3812 and 3810 Avenue M　　　　　**E–62**
1896, N. J. Clayton & Company
Although the ground floors of both of these raised cottages have been altered, the pair retain their geometrically configured spatial presence, achieved by thrusting the chamfered front bay forward beneath a faceted hipped roof, centered with a shingle-surfaced gable. Clayton designed these tenant cottages for Adolf Kruger.

3918 Avenue M 1/2　　　　　**E–63**
1896, N. J. Clayton & Company
Clayton's gift for creating a sense of spatial buoyancy is

especially evident in some of the more modest houses he designed in the 1890s. This raised cottage, built for the meat market owner C. Leopold Biehler, is a good example. Clayton played solid against void (the carefully composed planes of the wall, outlined with wood stripping, versus the voids of the wraparound gallery), angled versus circular geometries, and picturesque projection versus the encompassing enclosure of the roof, with its wide, horizontally continuous eaves' line. The generous dimension of the ramped front stair complements the assured proportion of the simple porch rail. A subsidiary porch on the east overlooks the deep side garden. The property, which sat at the west edge of the townsite when it was built, contains marvelous ornamental date palm trees, oleanders, and bush-sized ferns. Note the metal fence set in concrete curbing and the presence of two architecturally subordinate rear buildings.

1410 41st Street   **E–64**
St. Augustine's Church
1902, 1940
St. Augustine's Church was built to replace a predecessor destroyed in the Storm of 1900. The church was originally located at 22nd and Broadway, where this building was constructed. In 1940, it was moved to this location. St. Augustine's was organized in 1884 to minister to black Anglicans from the British West Indies. It is the oldest historically African-American parish in the Episcopal Diocese of Texas. The gableted nave windows along both sides of the church reproduce a feature found several blocks away on what is now the parish hall of Grace Church in the 3600 block of Avenue L.

2601 Avenue N   **E–65**
Ursuline Academy (now Galveston Catholic School)
1964, Raymond R. Rapp & Associates
The V-shapes of a reinforced concrete folded roof plate are

the distinguishing architectural feature of Raymond Rapp, Jr.'s replacement of one of the masterworks of Victorian Galveston, N. J. Clayton's spectacular Ursuline Academy, a huge, three-story-on-raised-basement institutional building finished with alternating bands of red and white stripes. Built facing Ursuline Avenue (Avenue N), at the 27th Street corner of the property, it was completed in 1895 and demolished, amidst great controversy, in 1962, after suffering tornado damage during Hurricane Carla in 1961. Clayton described the school (of which his daughters were alumnae) as "Italian Gothic . . . of the Venetian school." The academy, which attracted students from throughout the state, seems to have represented Clayton's effort to define an Adriatic-Galvestonian style. He did so by turning to the most ornately encrusted medieval architectural tradition he could find, the Venetian.

Clayton's Ursuline Academy was attached to a building that was as substantial, if not nearly as architecturally showy, the Ursuline Convent, built in two stages between 1855 and 1861 by John de Young for the Ursuline sisters. This two-story-on-basement brick building faced Rosenberg Avenue. It was sober and dignified, but imposing because of its size. The Ursuline sisters established the first religious order for women in Texas at Galveston in 1847. Despite the antiquity of both the building and the institution with which it was identified, the trustees of O'Connell High School, who had acquired the property from the Ursuline sisters, demolished the Ursuline Convent in 1972.

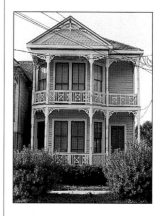

2328 Avenue O   **E–66**
c. 1896
A divided middle theme was pursued in the design of the projecting double veranda that faces this house, built for the plasterer John M. Rourke. It exhibits a similarity to the Kleinecke House at 1527 21st Street.

Nearby are the Henry Trueheart Adriance House at **2323 Avenue O** (1924) and the Rosario Maceo House at **2412 Avenue O** (1934, R. R. Rapp).

2419 Avenue O   **E–67**
1892
Although severely crowded on its west side, this raised cottage lends a note of Victorian exuberance to a neighborhood that reached its peak during what,

front windows, and the arched front porch enhance its fanciful aspect.

architecturally, were the more serious-minded years of the early 20th century. It was built for Frederick M. Gilbough, an employee of the Gulf, Colorado & Santa Fe Railway.

2428 Avenue O   E–68

1914, Stowe & Stowe

During the 1910s and 1920s, Avenue O surpassed Broadway to become the residential street of fashion in post-1900 Galveston. What is apparent in this transition is a change in elite attitudes about images of domestic style. Houses here are lower, smaller in proportion, and far less ostentatious than their Broadway predecessors. Moreover, echoing Avenue O's long history as an elite suburban outpost (suburban in the 19th-century sense of being on, or beyond, the line of continuous town settlement) is its spatial organization, with the largest houses set in wooded parks, sometimes behind high screen walls in the English fashion.

This expansive but austere stucco-faced house, built for the lawyer William T. Armstrong III and his wife, Josephine, the daughter of Walter Gresham, commences the Avenue O villa district. Its emphatic, thick-lidded horizontality contrasts with the branching live oak trees that encircle the house.

2602 Rosenberg Avenue   E–69

1925

A gable-fronted suburban chalet, this house, built for the cotton and bagging company owner Joseph Swiff, asserts its Galveston identity with its facing of white stucco. The slender brackets beneath the roof eaves, the triple arched

2504 Avenue O   E–70

1908, Mauran, Russell & Garden

Instrumental in establishing the prestige of the Avenue O villa district after the turn of the 20th century was this stucco-faced, tile-roofed house, designed for the cotton merchant, planter, and rancher Daniel W. Kempner by the St. Louis architects Mauran, Russell & Garden. In contrast to the Colonial Revival house that Kempner's brother, I. H. Kempner, had recently completed at 1502 Broadway, this is a Mission-style suburban country house. It eschews classical pretension for a more rustic and romantic architectural image. Rather than advancing toward the street, the Kempner House recedes deeply into its garden behind a high stucco-faced wall outlining the Avenue O frontage of the property, its gate piers ornamented with ball finials. A palisade of Washingtonia palm trees spatially reinforces the alignment of the street wall. The front of the house reflects alterations made to repair damage inflicted during Hurricane Carla in 1961. Therefore, the scalloped side gable facing Rosenberg presents a more imposing façade than does the front elevation. The house was rehabilitated in 1981 by Kempner's descendants, who still occupy the property.

Dan Kempner bought the south part of the outlot facing Avenue O between Rosenberg and 27th Street. Thus he was in a position to ensure that his new neighbors build at a scale commensurate with the example he set.

2528 Avenue O   E–71

1914, A. J. Bellis

The insurance company founder J. Fellman Seinsheimer built this stucco-faced house with a Spanish Mission–style scalloped gable next to the similarly detailed house of his cousin, D. W. Kempner. Following the model of the

Kempner House, the Seinsheimer House is set back in a luxuriantly planted garden, screened from Avenue O by a high, stucco-faced wall. The house is approached from the street by a circular drive—an attribute of the country-house type—rather than by a sidewalk from the curb.

2529 Avenue O   E-72
1915

As in Galveston's Victorian neighborhoods, a typological distinction was made along Avenue O between north-side and south-side houses. This compact, cubic house with a portico-faced side-hall entrance and a low-pitched hipped roof represents the south- side type. Less expansive than the north-side villas, it nonetheless asserts propriety through its somewhat flattened Anglo-Palladian decorative detail. The house was built for the Galveston dentist Dr. Alex A. Dyer.

East of the Dyer House is another example of this south-side house type at **2523 Avenue O** (1915), built for Edward P. Hanson, a signal supervisor for the Gulf, Colorado & Santa Fe Railway.

2602 Avenue O   E-73
1915

The clothing manufacturer Samuel I. Miller built this brown-brick and red-tile-roofed house, which reflects

progressive American architectural tendencies in its undiluted horizontality and its lack of historical ornament. The horizontality and the detailing of the wooden muntins in the second-story windows suggest, at a considerable remove, the radical experiments in modern residential design carried out by Frank Lloyd Wright and the architects of the midwestern Prairie School in the early years of the 20th century. The planted street wall and palm trees display allegiance to the Avenue O villa look.

In 1933, a subsequent owner, the cotton exporter Heinrich Renfert, had Houston architect John F. Staub remodel the house internally.

2603 Avenue O   E-74
1917, C. D. Hill & Company

Although not large, this house, built for the shipping agent and broker Charles Fowler, Jr., is a patrician addition to the villa district. It conforms to the south-side cubic house type. Its wide, bracketed eaves, gray stucco walls, and dark louvered blinds produce just the right degree of understatement, punctuated by a side-hall entrance portal framed by an elliptical fanlight. A thick street hedge, brick-paved sidewalks, and deep east and west side gardens complement the discreet charm of the Fowler House.

Next door, at **2611 Avenue O,** is R. R. Rapp's version of the south-side house type, built for Sol L. Levy in 1923.

No longer in the picture is the monumental First Church of Christ, Scientist (1920, W. S. Murdock) at 27th and Avenue O. It was built by Mrs. John H. Hutchings, who left Trinity Church to become an adherent of Christian Science. A decline in membership left the congregation unable to maintain its imposing church building, and it was demolished.

2701 Avenue O   E-75
c. 1870, c. 1891, c. 1906

Dr. Ferdinand Steffens built this house, which was eventually inherited by his daughter Sophie and her husband, the

lasterer and cement contractor Edward F. Drewa. In its
resent form, the house appears to reflect two episodes of
najor alterations and additions. One seems to have occurred
bout 1891 (the year of Sophie Drewa's marriage) when the
ody of the house acquired its present form as a five-bay-wide
Victorian cottage, with a bay window projecting forward of
he front porch. A second episode of improvement occurred
bout 1906, when the porch was apparently updated with
tubby Craftsman-like porch piers, giving the Steffens-Drewa
House an unexpected bungalow look.

705 and 2709 Avenue O   **E–76**

.895

This pair of raised cottages were built as tenant houses by
Edward F. Drewa, next door to his wife's childhood home.
Research by the Galveston Historical Foundation, indicating
hat Drewa was aided at the beginning of his career by the
rchitect Alfred Muller, suggests that Muller may have been
Drewa's architect. The elaborate surfaces of the cottages—the
unburst strips in the gables, the porch frieze screens, and the
lecorative shingle panels beneath the bay windows—imbue
hem with a Mulleresque sense of animation.

2704 Avenue O   **E–77**

Kempner Park

Garten-Verein Dancing Pavilion

.880

.911, Albert Kuhn Memorial Pergola, Donald N. McKenzie

Although the Dancing Pavilion of the Galveston Garten-
Verein survives in splendid condition in what is now
Kempner Park, a city park, its context has changed
lrastically. The east half of the outlot that the park occupies
vas the suburban homestead of Robert Mills, Texas's leading
linancier of the pre–Civil War period. Mills's bankruptcy in

the aftermath of the Panic of 1873 precipitated the sale of
his five-acre estate to Galveston's foremost German social
club, the Galveston Garten-Verein, in 1876. The Garten-
Verein adapted the Mills House as its clubhouse, erected a
bowling alley, and commissioned one of its members,
August Bader, to landscape the grounds with plants ordered
from New York, Philadelphia, St. Louis, and Europe,
according to reports in the *Galveston Daily News.*

When the popular travel writer Julian Ralph visited
Galveston in 1895 on assignment for *Harper's Weekly,* he
extolled the Garten-Verein in the most effusive terms: "The
place is laid out as a park, with lawns and walks and a clubhouse, a dancing pavilion, bowling-alleys, tennis courts, and
croquet-grounds. Where the trees have not been thinned
they all but touch one another, and not only roof the park,
but turn the night scenes into fairy views, showing the
brilliantly electric-lighted buildings through curtains of
greenery. . . . At night—and that is when the Garten-Verein
enjoys its play ground—every building is a brilliant lantern,
and the foliage is tipped with silvery light; the band sifts its
music through the leaves; the walks are gay with women
and girls in white, or in the soft, mild colors that
distinguish the costumes of all the women of the Gulf cities;
the great open dancing pavilion murmurs beneath the feet
of the dancers . . . and the roar and crash of the bowling
alleys is softened against the leafy cushions of the trees."

The octagonal plan and tiered massing of the pavilion are
architectural attributes of other social buildings erected by
Germans in Texas. Among these buildings, the Dancing
Pavilion stands out by virtue of its professional architectural
design and stylish paneled ornamentation. The construction
of the Dancing Pavilion in 1879–80 was noted in the
Galveston Daily News, which failed, however, to identify the
architect. The most likely candidate is John Moser, then the
leading German-born architect in Galveston. The Dancing
Pavilion, with other improvements at the Garten-Verein,
suffered severe damage in the Storm of 1900. It was
reconstructed. The pavilion was restored in 1981 by San
Antonio architect Joe Stubblefield with Michael Hilger,
following damage it sustained in a fire.

What stands out about the pavilion is its big scale and
extraordinary sense of spatial openness. Architectural ornament
(repainted in 1981 in contrasting tones, as old images show it
was in the 19th century) is simple but effective, because it is so
expertly calibrated with the scale of the building.

The Garten-Verein, as a social organization, was a
casualty of anti-German sentiment during World War I. In
June 1923 the insurance company executive Stanley E.
Kempner bought the property, then transferred it to the
City of Galveston as a public park dedicated to his parents,
Eliza Seinsheimer and H. Kempner. Today, the only
remnant of the park's association with the Garten-Verein,
other than the Dancing Pavilion, is Donald N. McKenzie's
Albert Kuhn Memorial Pergola, consisting of Tuscan
columns and paneled end piers of reinforced concrete
supporting a grid of widely spaced rafters with tailed ends.

From the Pergola one can glimpse the **carriage house
and stable** of the Hutchings House next door (1889, N. J.

Clayton & Company). Despite crude alterations when the building was converted into a garage, it is quite an interesting work of architecture in its own right, with its imposing scale, weathered stucco surfaces, Syrian-arched stable entrance, and side-facing thermal arched window.

2816 Avenue O   **E-78**
1859
1892, N. J. Clayton & Company
The John H. Hutchings House is to the Avenue O villa district what Ashton Villa, the Gresham House, and the Open Gates are to the Broadway grand avenue: it is the master villa in its fenced woodland park. Architecturally, the house combines the two eras of pretentious mansion building that gave 19th-century Broadway its showplace reputation. Atmospherically, it is unsurpassed, since the house retains the look of Miss Havisham-like abandon that the novelist Edna Ferber wrote all of Galveston possessed when she visited in the 1930s. It is a huge pile whose streaked stucco walls are only dimly visible through the dense vegetation that enshrouds it.

Minnie Knox Hutchings, wife of Ball, Hutchings & Company co-founder John H. Hutchings, was the niece of the banker Robert Mills. Upon her marriage to Hutchings, her uncle gave the couple the west half of the outlot next to his house. There, in 1859, they built a suburban Italianate villa–type house. What seemed cutting edge in the late 1850s must have appeared far too retiring by the late 1880s, as Hutchings's fellow investors in the Gulf, Colorado & Santa Fe Railway begin to build their imposing new castles. So Clayton was called in. First he added the freestanding carriage house and stable on the east edge of the property, visible from Kempner Park. This was followed by the total reconfiguration of the Hutchings House. Clayton added a full third floor to the house and redesigned its exterior walls.

The front of the house (facing 29th Street) is symmetrically composed. A projecting two-story portico is centered beneath the gabled roof parapet. Clayton violently rammed a subsidiary porte-cochère through this portico to mark the main entrance to the house. The south front (facing

Avenue O) is faced with an ebullient terraced "piazza," which projects into the garden in a series of graceful concave thrusts. From the street, Clayton's architectural detail appears to be classical. On closer inspection, the column capitals are seen to be Romanesque. This suggests that Clayton reshaped and recast the Hutchings House as a modern Romanesque villa, softening the stony surface treatment associated with the inventor of this trend, the Boston architect H. H. Richardson, in deference to its Southern lowlands setting. Distinctly Richardsonian is the great horizontal slot opening at the third-floor level, facing Avenue O.

Both Mr. and Mrs. Hutchings were very long-lived. After Mrs. Hutchings's death, the property was sold to J. Henry Langbehn. In 1946, Sealy Hutchings, Jr., and his wife bough and remodeled Hutchings's grandparents' house, and lived in it until Hutchings's death in 1995, when it was bequeathed to the University of Texas Medical Branch.

2805 Avenue O   **E-79**
1896, George B. Stowe
The suburban house that Mr. and Mrs. Hutchings's son, Sealy Hutchings, and his wife, Mary Moody, built across from Hutchings's parents' house is a big-scaled Victorian Colonial Revival. Stowe's "Palladian" detail—the classical colonnettes supporting the wraparound gallery and the modillion cornice beneath the deep roof overhang—contrasts with a late Victorian sense of spatial buoyancy, evident in the curved corner bays on both the east and west sides of the house.

In 1994, Sealy Hutchings's descendants had the Houston architect Robert Herolz rehabilitate the exterior of the house and tactfully reorganize its interiors into a series of apartments. The enclosure of the property with a chain-link fence topped by strands of barbed wire is not in keeping with the villa district–ambiance of Avenue O.

Next door to this second Hutchings House, at **2827 Avenue O,** is R. R. Rapp's picturesque Mediterranean version of the south-side Avenue O cubic house type, built for Dr. and Mrs. Wiley J. Jinkins (1925).

2901 Avenue O   **E-80**
1939, Cameron Fairchild
The Houston architect Cameron Fairchild designed his most graceful Galveston house for the lawyer Ballinger Mills, Jr., and his wife Margaret Leonard. The symmetrical, planar front, organized beneath a low-pitched hipped roof, is indebted architecturally to an influential house that the Houston architect John F. Staub designed early in his career

suburban rendition of the Spanish Creole architecture of
arly-19th-century New Orleans. The cast-iron balcony rail
nd shuttered front door (with its deep-set, Galvestonian
urricane alcove) pay explicit homage to what Staub called
he Latin Colonial style.

908 Avenue O   **E–81**

911, 1922

allinger Mills, Jr., built his house across from the house
vith which his parents, Evy Waters and Ballinger Mills,
eplaced The Oaks, the 1856 house of the senior Mills's
randfather, William P. Ballinger, destroyed in the Storm of
900. Both father and son's accumulation of resonant
Galveston surnames suggests the extent to which the Avenue
O villa district, like sectors of Broadway and the East End,
vas identified with a concatenation of elite families—Mills,
allinger, Jack, Bryan, Hutchings, Harris, and Randall—who
eft their architectural imprint on the district.

 Were it not upstaged by the John H. Hutchings House,
he Mills House would figure as one of Avenue O's grandest
ouses. Its raised front loggia, wide shuttered windows, tan
rick-veneer walls, and horizontally continuous, green-tile-
lad hipped roof seem, like Anton F. Korn's houses in the
ast End, to quietly but explicitly develop the villa theme,
uggesting the Italian, yet moderated with gentlemanly
Georgian restraint. The live oak trees outlining the Avenue
O front of the property pay homage to the ancestral
edication of the Ballinger homestead.

 At **2920 Avenue O** is the house that William P.
allinger's daughter-in-law, Carrie Mather Ballinger, built
ext to The Oaks (1900). It was remodeled in 1916 for A.
Qvistgaard Peterson, an agent of the New Orleans
xporting Company, and refaced with a front porch–loggia,
ery much like the one that Anton F. Korn, Jr., produced at
he Biehl House at 1416 Broadway.

3001 Avenue O   **E–82**

1894

A raised five-bay cottage, this house, originally occupied by
Elise Hildenbrand, widow of Christian F. Hildenbrand and
owner of one of the city's major sash, door, and blind
factories, exhibits the modernization of traditional
Galveston house types seen in other 19th-century
neighborhoods. The bays to the right of the front door step
out into the space of the porch, and an angled window bay,
decorated with shingled wall panels, is appended to the east
side of the house. Lending distinction to the house is the
dog-legged front stair.

 Contrasting with the Victorian typicality of Mrs.
Hildenbrand's cottage is the dark, brick-faced house at **2927
Avenue O** (1926), built for the contractor and building
materials supplier Walter A. Kelso. The Kelso House made
the leap in fashion from the north to the south side of the
street, theretofore dominated by more modest houses such
as Mrs. Hildenbrand's.

3011 Avenue O   **E–83**

1899

This is a rhythmic house, with its flared skirting beneath
the second-floor windows, its triple-arched porch, and the
circular west-side bay where the porch turns the corner to
become an open deck along the west side of the house. It
was built by the ship chandler, manufacturer's agent, and
commission merchant Thomas L. Cross.

 Across the street from the Cross House, at 3006 Avenue
O, is **Congregation B'nai Israel Temple** (1955, Ben J. Kotin

& Associates). This is where Galveston's oldest Jewish congregation moved when it left its original temple building on 22nd Street.

Kotin's complex is inspired by the late work of the Finnish-American Eliel Saarinen, who had a profound influence on modern religious architecture in Texas in the early and mid-1950s. Kotin's rendition is rather perfunctory and lacks the distinction of his later work. It possesses neither the urbanistic impact of the congregation's Victorian Saracenic temple nor its architectural bravura.

3017 Avenue O   E–84
1897, George B. Stowe
This high-raised house exhibits in its verticality, planarity, and in such details as a one-story veranda the characteristic attributes of south-side houses in the East End. Stowe designed the house for the lawyer and banker R. Waverly Smith as a rental property.

1704 31st Street   E–85
1896
This high-raised house, built by the clothing store owner Robert I. Cohen, resembles the Smith House next door in its sharply planed gabled bays. Despite their profusion, these bays give the Cohen House a disciplined, rather than picturesque, appearance. Its orientation toward 31st Street, rather than Avenue O, further draws attention to the house.

Alongside the Cohen House are smaller houses built in the 1890s at **1714 31st Street** and **1724 31st Street,** which

were owned by Cohen's sons and business associates George S. Cohen and Robert I. Cohen, Jr. George Cohen eventually moved to Houston where he and his father bought the city's major department store, Foley Brothers. A **1723 31st Street** is George B. Stowe's house for the lawyer Thomas W. Masterson (1906).

3028 Avenue O   E–86
1915, C. D. Hill & Company
Like the Miller House at 2602 Avenue O, this house, built for John E. Pearce, owner of a marine contracting and stevedoring company and mayor of Galveston in the 1920s and 1930s, displays progressive tendencies in its emphatic horizontality and suppression of historical ornamentation. I is intriguing to see how C. D. Hill's office composed the Avenue O front of the Pearce House with a series of shifted axes to subtly undermine the perception of a single, central point of focus. The wide span of the front porch underscores the fact that the house is of concrete construction (in the form of stucco-faced concrete blocks), not wood. During the 1880s and 1890s, the lots that run from the site of Congregation B'nai Israel to this property were filled with a number of houses designed by N. J. Clayton for Thomas McKinney Jack, Jr., and his brother-in-law and sister, Mr. and Mrs. R. V. Davidson. The Jacks were related on their father's side to the Ballinger and Bryan families and on their mother's side to the Mills and Hutchings families. Robert V. Davidson (who was Attorney General of Texas from 1904 to 1910) built his Clayton-designed house at this corner in 1887. Pearce replaced Davidson's house with his own.

3102 Avenue O   E–87
Galveston Artillery Club
1959, Thomas M. Price
Although the Artillery Club demolished the columned Greek Revival country house built about 1867 by William P. Ballinger's sister-in-law, Laura Jack, and her husband, Guy M. Bryan, a nephew of Stephen F. Austin, to construct its clubhouse, Tom Price compensated by producing a classic of 1950s contemporary design. The one-story clubhouse is dominated by a low-pitched gabled roof that spreads out across the building's long dimension. The street front is hidden from Avenue O by dense vegetation. The building is entered beneath a porte-cochère on the north (alley) side. Demolition of historic buildings, disregard for the convention

hat regulated a building's setting, and an approach to scale completely at variance with the surroundings were the means by which the spatial coherence of American urban neighborhoods was shattered by new buildings in the 1950s and 1960s. Here, though, Price produced a modern building that is so well detailed and that uses planting so effectively to maintain the space of Avenue O that the Artillery Club represents an architectural contribution to the villa district, not an assault on its integrity.

605 33rd Street   **E–88**

c. 1838

This house, built by Michael B. Ménard, the Québec native who organized the Galveston City Company to lay out and develop the Galveston townsite, is the oldest building in the city. It was also Galveston's first ambitious work of architecture. It is a Greek Revival-style, three-bay-wide, side-hall-plan Southern town house, faced with double verandas and fluted Ionic columns on bases. It faces east (toward 33rd Street) like other early suburban houses in the outlot district, where a number of Ménard's fellow investors in the Galveston City Company built their houses. Outside (and inside), floor-length, triple-hung windows are framed with shouldered Grecian architraves. Although the Ménard House is no larger than other Galveston houses of its type, its location on what remains of the original 10-acre outlot estate, and the scale of its parts, such as the big Ionic capitals, give the house a monumental presence. The live oak trees surrounding the house enhance the suburban, parklike aspect of the property.

During construction, the house was acquired by another investor in the Galveston City Company, A. C. Allen, one

of the founders of Houston. After Ménard regained ownership of the property, he added the wings flanking the rear of the house around 1845, according to research by the Galveston Historical Foundation. The south wing, only two bays wide, is a miniature temple. In 1994, a Grecian-type pavilion was built alongside the house, where a privy was located in the 19th century.

After Ménard's descendants sold the property in 1880, it became home to several generations of the Ketchum family, including Galveston historian and author Virginia Ketchum Eisenhour. Between the time it was sold by the Ketchum heirs in 1977 and bought by Pat and Fred Burns of Houston in 1994, the Ménard House was partially remodeled, then abandoned. The house suffered damage during Hurricane Alicia in 1983 that posed a long-term threat to its structural integrity. In 1992 the Galveston Historical Foundation, with assistance from the National Trust for Historic Preservation and the Moody National Bank, bought the house to save it from destruction. Between 1994 and 1995, Mr. and Mrs. Burns had Galveston architect David V. Barker carry out comprehensive restoration of the Ménard House. The Ménard House won First Place in the 1996 Great American Homes Awards, sponsored by the National Trust for Historic Preservation, for the high caliber of its exterior architectural restoration.

Like the Hutchings House, the Ménard House demonstrates the longevity of the suburban identity of the outlot sector along Avenue O. The range of houses present in the district today reflects the changing architectural interpretations of suburban domesticity from the 1830s through the 1950s.

3328 Avenue O   **E–89**

1908

A crenelated turret gives this house, built for Joseph P. Day, an employee of the Galveston, Houston & Henderson Railroad, its delightful mock-castelled appearance.

3401 Avenue O   **E–90**

1909

Built for Alfred C. Torbert, an officer of the Gulf, Colorado & Santa Fe Railway, and his wife, Amelia Labatt, this house appears to be an early version of the south-side Avenue O cubic house type.

3427 Avenue O   **E–91**

Powhatan House

1847

Alterations, 1896, W. H. Tyndall

Of the same vintage as the Ménard House, the Powhatan House was moved to this site in 1896 from its original location in the 2100 block of Avenue M in order to clear the way for construction of the Galveston Orphans Home. Magnolia Willis Sealy's sister, Caroline Willis Ladd, bought the Powhatan House and had architect W. H. Tyndall divide it into three separate houses, which were moved to separate sites. One of the three houses has been lost; the other survives five blocks to the south at **2222 35th Street.** This division accounts for the peculiar incongruity between the big scale of the Powhatan House and the two-bay width of its monumental Doric portico.

The flush siding on the front wall of the house, the robust size of the molded frames outlining the front doors and windows, and the depth of the entablature above the slender Doric columns indicate that the house must have been quite imposing before its division. The Powhatan House was built by the Galveston merchant John S. Sydnor. It functioned at various times as a hotel (called the Powhatan House), a school, and an orphanage, prior to its dismemberment. Since 1965, the Powhatan House has been operated as a historic house museum by the Galveston Garden Club. It was rehabilitated in 1985 by Killis Almond & Associates of San Antonio.

1705 35th Street   **E–92**

Windsor Court Apartments

1937, Cameron Fairchild

Mrs. Hans Guldman built the eight-unit Windsor Court Apartments in the side yard of her large brick house at **1715 35th Street** (1915, C. D. Hill & Company). Fairchild came up with a considerably more spirited design for its modernistic neighbor, the Windsor Court. The Windsor Court is stepped in plan and at the roof level. Fairchild took advantage of these corner conditions to install cantilevered hoods and balconies, the latter faced with curved tubular railings. The horizontal divisions of the window screens enhance the building's streamlined look. Interior stairs are marked with panels of glass block.

1718 35th Street   **E–93**

1934, Donald Barthelme

The only extant building in Galveston by native-born architect Donald Barthelme is this small stucco-surfaced house. It is a compact French manorial–style house, with a streamlined curved entrance pavilion offsetting the taut planes of the walls and the steeply pitched roof with flared eaves. Note the spur wall that comes off the north end of the house. Aramco blinds and high-contrast trim colors give the house a coarser texture than it would have had originally.

Barthelme became chief designer for the Texas Centennial Exposition in Dallas (1936), and after that one of Houston's first, and most important, modern architects. He practiced briefly in his hometown during the depths of the Great Depression. Barthelme designed this house for Robert K. Hutchings, an officer of the Hutchings-Sealy National Bank, and his wife, Drusilla Davis.

804 35th Street   E–94

.899, George B. Stowe

This high-raised house for the dry goods merchant Felix E.
Mistrot possesses the severe planarity that Stowe often
avored. He contrasted its rather subdued superstructure with
he rhythmic delicacy of the single-story veranda (which
rupts at its south end into a generous circular bay and then
urns the corner to face a deep-set side garden) and the
massiveness of the rusticated cement-plastered basement
rches. Facing Avenue O 1/2 is a high-roofed porte-cochère.
ubstantial curbing outlines the Mistrot property.

518 Avenue O   E–95

.897

West of 35th Street, the Avenue O villa district subsides into
respectable late Victorian middle-income area. This raised
house, built for Captain George Wilson, is characteristic of
he neighborhood. Note especially how the west-side bay is
antilevered on brackets over the side yard. This was the
ouse to which Miss Matilda Walters moved when she
etired as the Postoffice Street District madam Mollie Waters.

527 Avenue O   E–96

.909

The entrance bay of this raised cottage ascends into a short,
quat pyramid-roofed tower.

3701 Avenue O   E–97

Carmelo LaBarbera Store
1906

The LaBarbera corner store deviates from the cubic building
type associated in Galveston with such neighborhood
convenience shopping. It is a collection of roof shapes: from
the gable-roofed primary volume, to the two-story extension
of this triangular geometry, to the low-pitched hipped roof
of the lean-to canopy that surrounds the building on its
street sides. Facing it at 1702 37th Street is the **West End
Bakery** (1908), a classic example of the cubic, hipped-roof,
wooden corner-store building type.

3827 Avenue O   E–98

Magnolia Petroleum Company Filling Station 134
1926

Inasmuch as John H. Sealy organized the Magnolia
Petroleum Company (which he named in honor of his aunt,
Magnolia Willis Sealy, and which subsequently became part
of Mobil Oil Corporation) with his brother-in-law R.
Waverly Smith, it is appropriate that this hip-roofed brick
service station, which is diagonally rotated to face the 39th
Street-Avenue O intersection, should be one of the oldest
surviving gas stations in Galveston.

3815 Avenue P   E–99

1928, John F. Staub

By the standards of his Houston houses, John Staub's house
for the cotton exporter William C. Helmbrecht was modest.
Yet it is a very resolved design, into which Staub
incorporated the spatial amenities of a larger house. These
are concealed behind a restrained, beautifully proportioned
street façade finished with a subtle mixed blend of orange,
black, and yellow brick. The louvered blinds (originally
painted a dark green) give the house a Galveston flavor, as do
the iron fence along Avenue P and the screen of oleanders

planted along the sidewalk. Note the arched service door on the driveway side of the house. It is treated as an elegantly composed figure, indicative of the skill with which Staub addressed all aspects of house design. So satisfied were the clients that when they moved to Dallas, they had Staub design a second house for them there. The Houston landscape architect C. C. Pat Fleming planned the rear garden, toward which the house's major rooms are oriented.

Across the street at **3812 Avenue P** is a two-bay-wide, two-story wooden house (c. 1905) built by the German-born contractor John Egert. In 1985 the Galveston Historical Foundation bought this house to stop demolition, which was in progress. The foundation moved it from its original site at 2319 37th Street to this location, rehabilitated it in 1986, and sold it with protective restrictions.

1919 37th Street   E–100
1900, N. J. Clayton & Company

Like other houses that Clayton designed in the West End, this house impresses not by its size but by the consummate ability that he displayed in orchestrating its shapes, proportions, solids, voids, and the detailing of material. As is often the case with his buildings, it quietly radiates architectural authority. Evangeline Loessin Whorton's research revealed that the house was built for Miss Ida D. Baden, a woman who went to great lengths to keep her identity a secret, even to the extent of dealing with Clayton through an agent. The Baden House was rehabilitated in 1975.

3823 Avenue P 1/2   E–101
1924, R. R. Rapp

The outlot on which the Baden House and the houses on both sides of Avenue P 1/2 in the 3700-3800 block were built was originally owned by Thomas H. Borden, an investor, along with his illustrious brother, the inventor Gail Borden, in Ménard's Galveston City Company. The Sandusky "Plan of the City of Galveston" map, of 1845, illustrates the famous windmill that T. H. Borden built on this property. In the early 1920s, when 39th Street was still the west edge of civilization, the lots facing this block of P 1/2 were developed as the Nichols-Byrne Subdivision, the first residential addition in Galveston to have deed restrictions. Consequently, the first residents were members of Galveston's most respectable families. Almost all of the houses seem to have been designed by R. R. Rapp, including this delightful, stucco-surfaced bungalow cottage, with big-scaled brackets framing the front entrance. It was built for Dr. William F. Spiller. Rapp was also responsible for the Charles A. Holt House at **3806 Avenue P 1/2** (1924), the Edward Rudge Allen House at **3828 Avenue P 1/2** (1923), and the house of the general contractor Adolph G. Johnson, who constructed many of Rapp's buildings, at **1919 39th Street** (1926).

3601 Avenue P   E–102
Samuel May Williams House
1839

This raised planter's house was the home of S. M. Williams the Galvestonian who figured most prominently in the Mexican and Republic periods of Texas history. After the Ménard House, it is the oldest building in Galveston. An associate of Stephen F. Austin's during the 1820s, Williams was instrumental in securing financial assistance in the

United States to underwrite the successful Anglo-American rebellion against Mexico in 1835–36. After independence, he became one of the most successful commission merchants in Galveston and operated, on a quasi-legal basis, the only bank tolerated in Texas prior to the legalization of banking in the state after the Civil War. As an investor in the Galveston City Company, Williams built this house on the outlot that he owned. It is comparatively unpretentious.

Like the Ménard House, the Williams House faces east rather than toward the street. Its low-pitched hipped roof encompasses a gallery that runs along the east and south sides of the house. The front door is framed by a Grecian architrave. The windows to either side are floor-length, double-leaf casement windows, which were unusual in Galveston. As can be seen from Avenue P, the house stretches out to encompass rear outbuildings, including a brick kitchen house and a small shed. According to tradition, the Williams House was built with a timber frame precut and fitted in Maine before being shipped to Galveston. Margaret Swett Henson in her history *The Samuel May Williams Home*, discounts this story but states that some of the lumber with which it was framed may well have come from Maine.

In 1954 the Williams House was bought by the Galveston Historical Foundation from the family of Philip C. Tucker, who had purchased it from Mrs. Williams after Williams's death in 1858. Between 1978 and 1984, the Williams House was restored by Houston architect Graham B. Luhn. This included reconstruction of a rooftop cupola that had burned in the 1890s.

3528 Avenue P   **E–103**

1893

Thomas J. League, Jr., built this house on property inherited from his mother, a daughter of S. M. Williams. By Galveston standards it is a sober house. This impression was enhanced by replacement of the original veranda supports with brick piers in the early 20th century.

3523 Avenue P   **E–104**

1896, C. W. Bulger

Bulger concentrated much of the architectural brio of this cottage in its front-facing gable. Decorated vergeboards (now highlighted with polychromatic effusion), a shingled inset, and the decorative wood tie brace just beneath the apex of the gable give this little house, built for James W.

Foster, an employee of the Gulf, Colorado & Santa Fe Railway, a forceful presence.

3503 Avenue P   **E–105**

1888

This modest house, with a wraparound gallery, displays surface decoration that perhaps influenced Bulger's design of the neighboring Foster House. It was built for Dr. and Mrs. Frederick K. Fisher.

3502 Avenue P   **E–106**

1929, John F. Staub

Dr. and Mrs. Edward Randall, Jr., built this brick-faced, American Neoclassical-style house on the site of a Southern town house–type house erected in 1859 by Mary Williams and T. J. League. Dr. and Mrs. Randall originally commissioned John Staub to remodel the derelict League

House for them. No Galveston contractor was willing to submit a bid on the remodeling, so Dr. and Mrs. Randall had to ask Staub to design a new house instead. The Randall House is taut in proportion. All the details—notably the slender white wood pilasters—seem to have been stripped down to their most minimal. Staub added the east (1932) and west (1936) wings to the house. He set the house deeply back on its lot, treating the front lawn as a generous garden shielded from the street by live oak and magnolia trees, a hedge, and—a Galvestonian touch—an iron fence set in concrete curbing. This brought a bit of the Avenue O villa district to Avenue P, appropriate since Dr. Randall, professor of medicine at UTMB, was a grandson of William P. Ballinger.

3421 Avenue P   **E–107**
1898
This five-bay-wide, L-front Victorian cottage, built as a tenant cottage by Louis R. Koester, a wholesale grocer, features a delicate frieze screen along its front porch.

1903 34th Street   **E–108**
1953
This house, built for the engineer Bard O. Gage, is an unexpected sight in the neighborhood because it is a Contemporary-style house, designed around existing trees in a courtyard configuration.

3201 Avenue P   **E–109**
1892
The Swedish-born stevedore Charles T. Suderman built this cottage next to the house of his partner Ben Dolson, Jr.

3101 Avenue P   **E–110**
1923
Three prominent physicians staked out this block with a trio of houses that now seem at variance with the neighborhood because of their size and style. The most engaging is the raised, stucco-surfaced bungalow built for Dr. Cooper P. Bevil. Trimmed with dark red brick, it features a wide, high front porch whose openings are outlined with inset trellises. A brick-paved stair descends from the porch platform on the 31st Street side of the front. Just around the corner, facing 31st Street, is the Bevil House's discreetly concealed garage. Companions to the Bevil House are the more pretentious houses of Dr. Edward M. F. Stephens at **3115 Avenue P** (1922) and of Dr. Julius L. Jinkins at **3121 Avenue P** (1923).

011 Avenue P   **E–111**
898, C. W. Bulger

What stops traffic here is the energy with which bright
aint has been applied to this house, built for Walter H.
Laycock, chief clerk for the wholesale grocers, ship
handlers, and steamship agents H. Mosle & Company.

927 Avenue P   **E–112**
Reconstruction, 1905

As a careful look at this house suggests, it is an I-house
expanded with eccentric additions in the early 20th century
y its owner, the builder James K. Deats. Black-and-red-tile
sidewalks are a touch of the East End. The portico,
supported by paired Ionic columns, probably dates from
905, as does the strange bay window to the east. Live oak,
magnolia, and ornamental date palm trees give the Deats
House a luxuriant setting.

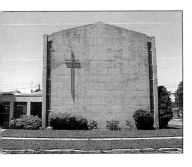

702 Avenue O 1/2   **E–113**
Central Christian Church
.969, Louis L. Oliver

The Central Christian Church is one of Louis Oliver's best

buildings. Its clarity and simplicity, and the
straightforwardness of its exposed reinforced concrete
construction, make it a potent presence amid the turn-of-
the-20th-century wooden houses of the neighborhood.

2600 Avenue O 1/2   **E–114**
1922

Backing up to the Avenue O villa district, this house,
constructed for the merchandise broker and local historian
William Manning Morgan and his wife Winifred Allen, is a
charming wooden version of the cubic villa type. Joining it
in the 2600 block are the Harry H. Levy House at **2610
Avenue O 1/2** (1923) and the John W. Focke House at
2628 Avenue O 1/2 (1925, R. R. Rapp). Like the Morgan
House, these represent an extraterritorial extension of the
Avenue O villa district.

1723 Rosenberg Avenue   **E–115**
1914

Built for Dr. and Mrs. Henry C. Haden, this austere stucco-
surfaced house has a peculiarly Galvestonian quality (which
was much stronger before its weathered gray stucco walls were
painted bright pink in 1995). The front loggia (originally
screened), topped by wooden rafters with curved tailings, sets
off the body of the house and spatializes the image of a
sheltered retreat open to the prevailing Gulf breeze.

1804 Rosenberg Avenue   **E–116**
Letitia Rosenberg Home for Aged Women
1896, Alfred Muller

Henry Rosenberg bequeathed $30,000 for the construction
of a home for aged women as a memorial to his first wife.
Alfred Muller won the limited competition that Rosenberg's
trustees held for the design. Muller's building, which was
simplified externally when it was repaired after the Storm of
1900, is big in scale and has an imposing presence. Yet on

examination, its surfaces are very plain. The walls (Muller's face brick was stuccoed early in the 20th century) are sparely detailed. It is the shaping of the molded bands framing openings and horizontally belting the walls that gives these plain surfaces a sense of richness and depth. From the sidewalk, the layering of vertical pilasters (which are smooth-surfaced, although the expanses of wall between them are scored) and the monumental feel of the ramped stairs leading up from Rosenberg Avenue to the entrance loggia energize the building. Muller contrasted the symmetrical dignity of the Rosenberg Avenue front with the picturesque disposition of shapes along Avenue O 1/2, where the main stair is housed in an octagonal tower that is the pivot point between the front block and a back wing. Surrounded by palm trees, and with its stucco surfaces streaked by weathering, the Womens Home possesses an aura of romantic decay endemic to Southern seaport cities.

The Womens Home ceased operation in 1970. The building suffered serious damage in 1983 during Hurricane Alicia and was not repaired until 1993. Faded dignity, however, becomes the Womens Home. It suggests strength of character and will to endure, cloaked beneath a veil of fragile Southern charm.

2408 and 2406 Avenue P   E–117
1910

This pair of simple raised tenant cottages were owned by the prominent Galveston building contractor J. W.

Zempter, who lived around the corner at 1813 24th Street. From the alley next to 2408 P, one has a sidelong prospect of the Letitia Rosenberg Womens Home.

2018-2024 Rosenberg Avenue   E–118
Waldorf Apartments
1939

The blocks of Rosenberg between the Womens Home and the Gulf lay in the zone of total destruction from the Storm of 1900. The reconstruction of Rosenberg Avenue in the early 20th century seems to have been weighted to multifamily and beach-oriented tourist housing. The Waldorf Apartments, built by Mrs. Eva Dorfman and Miss Sadell Dorfman, are the most architecturally notable example of this phenomenon. The flat-roofed, beige brick-faced modernistic block on Rosenberg is stepped in plan so that the apartments behind its west façade can gain maximum access to the sea breeze.

2002 Rosenberg Avenue   E–119
1913

This house and its two companions are the best maintained of a colony of nearly identical two-story houses that extend from Rosenberg along Avenue P 1/2 and around the corner onto 24th Street. They were built by Mrs. W. G. Tabb, who, with her husband, constructed this entire group of houses.

917 Rosenberg Avenue   **E–120**

925

Built for the loan company owner Max Baum, this stucco-faced Mediterranean style house features a bulbous, protruding circular entrance bay that is without precedent in Galveston. This element gives the Baum House an urbanistic distinction that the rest of the house could not have achieved otherwise.

012 29th Street   **E–121**

. 1950

This diminutive modernistic house, sited midblock next to an lley, was built for the engineer Paul W. Stanley. It is durably constructed of painted tile block, with steel pipe columns upporting the south-side terrace. A cantilevered canopy bove the front door and symmetrically stationed corner windows lend formal authority to its planar white front.

102 Avenue P 1/2   **E–122**

895

high-raised Gulf Coast cottage, this imposingly scaled ouse features a chamfered window bay inside the front eranda. The veranda continues around the east side of the ouse as an unroofed deck, a feature that was once more

common in Galveston than the number of surviving examples implies. The house was built for Charles W. Eisenfelder, a feed, hay, grain, and fertilizer dealer.

3127 Avenue P 1/2   **E–123**

1909

It is the roof of this house, built for Albert A. Fedder, that warrants attention. With major gabled façades on three sides, it constitutes an exercise in geometric faceting. Since Fedder was a manufacturer of sheet iron, metal cornice, and metal building components, he perhaps treated his house as an advertisement for his skills in flashing and waterproofing. Note on the east side of the house the presence of an elaborately cantilevered window bay, capped by a curved roof, that rises from the landing level of the main stair. The rock-faced plaster cement finish of the porch piers, fence posts, and curbing was very popular in Houston at this time, but relatively rare on Galveston houses. Complementing the Fedder House is a raised, L-plan back building at **2010 32nd Street,** where Fedder seems to have lived while the front house was under construction.

3202 Avenue P 1/2   **E–124**

1892

This high-raised, five-bay-wide, L-plan Victorian cottage exhibits a spindle-and-ball decorative pattern in its porch frieze screen seen on other Galveston houses of the period in the East End, 24th Street, and the West End. On the 32nd Street side of the house, the gabled roof dips down to encompass a rear, lean-to wing.

3428 Avenue Q   **E-125**

1901

A pyramidal hipped roof crowns this beautifully maintained
five-bay-wide cottage, outfitted with a two-bay-wide front
porch and two front doors. It was built by the carpenter
Charles Schiller to replace a house destroyed in the Storm of
1900 and is representative of the hundreds of unassuming
simple houses that, collectively, are so important to
Galveston neighborhoods.

2127 37th Street   **E-126**

Anne Trueheart Presbyterian Church (now Gethsemane
Missionary Baptist Church)
1925

Despite several changes in denomination during its history,
this twin-towered wooden church remains a Southern classic

I

t's hard to imagine that the Factory District, at one time, looked like other section of the historic city and not the wasteland that so much of it appears today.  ∩ ∩ ∩ The blocks bordered by Postoffice Street, Broadway, 25th, and 29th Streets were developed as residential streets and included some structures as grand as any built in the East End as late as the 1890s. This was especially true for Ball and Sealy Avenues and Broadway. ∩ ∩ ∩ Market and Mechanic Streets developed as a small-scale west-side extension of the business district, which was across 25th Street. Industrial and port activities dominated the area closest to the Bay as well as to the west of 29th. By the time of the Civil War, this area accommodated several full-block cotton compress complexes the city's gasworks, and the Galveston, Houston & Henderson Railroad depot. ∩ ∩ ∩ Whereas the Strand and adjacent streets east of 25th Street evolved into an architectural

Factory District looking northeast from the water works stand pipe in 1894. The cross-streets bordering the cotton compress are 29th Street (running left to right) and Winnie (Avenue G). The area was populated with small- to medium-sized vernacular houses. The Bay is in the background.

showcase that touted Galveston's port economy, the same streets west of 25th Street developed, following the Civil War, a very different identity—and reputation. It was here that Galveston squeezed its greatest concentration of poor immigrants, African-Americans, and transient workers, along with many of the smaller businesses, both respectable and not so respectable, associated with a port economy. ⋔ ⋔ ⋔ As the city expanded westward in the late 19th century, the Factory District, most particularly the streets closest to Broadway, became a popular location for housing owned and occupied by laboring-class families. At the same time, the area developed an even heavier industrial flavor, the blocks between 29th and 32nd Streets becoming an almost continuous strip of cotton compresses from the Bay to Sealy Avenue. Other large industrial complexes were built in the northwest section. ⋔ ⋔ ⋔ With its high density, poorly maintained properties—many, if not most, of them rental—and industrial activities, the Factory District was a prime target for demolition once the city pursued a serious code enforcement program in the 1960s. Large sections of the Factory District had already been replaced by public housing projects in the 1940s and 1950s. ⋔ ⋔ ⋔ Today, buildings that have been well maintained, often against all odds, are found scattered throughout the area in both isolated and group settings. Many of these are owner-occupied by minority families who are longtime residents of the neighborhood. There are some signs of individual rehabilitation efforts, as well as improvements to the public housing complexes, but the future of the Factory District remains uncertain.

1. Pier 28: Elevator B
2. Pier 33: Far-Mar-Co Export Grain Elevator
3. Pier 35: Imperial Sugar Company
   Galveston Raw Storage Warehouse and
   Bulk Sugar Handling Facility
4. 200 Seawolf Parkway: Kirkham Hall
5. 200 Seawolf Parkway: Physical Education Facility

6. 325 33rd Street
7. 3227 Market Street
8. 519 29th Street
9. 602 32nd Street
10. 3220 Ball Avenue
11. 3002 Ball Avenue
12. 2818 Ball Avenue

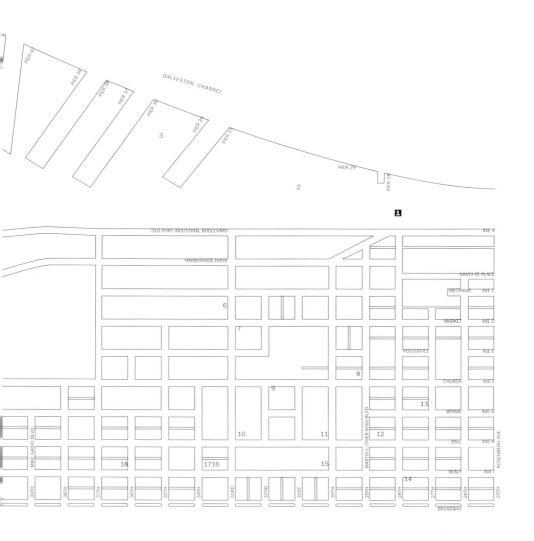

13. 613–629 27th Street   20. 718 41st Street

14. 902 28th Street   21. 4402–4628 Winnie Avenue

15. 3014 Sealy Avenue   22. 4702 Broadway

16. 3320 Sealy Avenue   23. 5005–5013 Broadway

17. 3322 Sealy Avenue   24. 5302 Broadway

18. 3602 Sealy Avenue   25. 5402–5628 Broadway

19. 905 44th Street

Pier 28   **F–1**

Elevator B

1931, Horner & Wyatt, consulting engineers

Elevator B incorporates an earlier grain elevator, built in 1897. It is imposing in size, with 427 hopper-bottomed concrete bins capable of storing nearly six million bushels of grain. The Kansas City engineers who designed Elevator B endowed it with minimal scalloped gables, a vestigial touch of civic architectural decor. From the 1880s through the 1960s, the Galveston waterfront was thickly populated with warehouses and other storage structures, several of which were as commanding in height as Elevator B.

Pier 33   **F–2**

Far-Mar-Co Export Grain Elevator

1976, R.S. Fling & Partners

1980, Homan & Lawrence Engineering Company

The Farmers Export Company high-speed, shipside grain elevator has its cylindrical storage bins aligned in a row, rather than bundled together like Elevator B. Together with the great diagonal conveyor houses, these give the structure a striking presence in the landscape, not only from Harborside Drive but from within the Factory District, especially the 3000 block of Market Street, where it terminates a panoramic vista. Built in 1976 by Cook Industries, the elevator's headhouse and office were destroyed by an explosion in 1977. The Farmers Export Co., which acquired the complex in 1977, expanded it during reconstruction.

Pier 35   **F–3**

Imperial Sugar Company Galveston Raw Storage Warehouse and Bulk Sugar Handling Facility

1963, Lockwood & Andrews, consulting engineers

This vast, 100-foot high, gable-roofed warehouse, designed

by the Houston engineers Lockwood & Andrews, is an awesome exception to the low skyline of the waterfront. It was built by the Imperial Sugar Company to receive offshore shipments of raw cane sugar for rail transport to the company's processing plant at Sugar Land, outside Houston. The warehouse has the capacity to store 60 million pounds. I. H. Kempner entered the sugar refining business in 1906 when he and W. T. Eldridge founded the Imperial Sugar Company. The corporation has remained a Kempner family enterprise since that time.

In 1974 the artist Michael Tracy used conveyor belts to pour sugar into a 40-foot-high pyramid inside the Raw Storage Warehouse, around which he organized a performance ritual, *Sacrifice I: The Sugar.* Tracy sacrificed what he regarded as his most important painting, *For H. B.* (dedicated to the architect Howard Barnstone), in a symbolic confrontation with the pyramid of sugar. This performance was seminal in Tracy's career, according to art critic Thomas McEvilley, because it introduced critical social themes that Tracy explored in his subsequent work.

200 Seawolf Parkway   **F–4**

Texas A&M University, Mitchell Campus

College of Geosciences and Maritime Studies

Emmett O. Kirkham Hall

1971, Rapp Tackett Fash

Kirkham Hall was one of the first buildings on the A&M campus, which is located on Pelican Island in Galveston Harbor. Gerald Tackett designed this two-story building to display the different surface finishes that can be achieved with reinforced concrete. The thick frame that establishes Kirkham Hall's spatial order has an exposed aggregate surface finish. Infill panels are of vertically striated board-formed concrete and are recessed. The loggia on the east end of the building frames views back to the harbor.

00 Seawolf Parkway   **F–5**

exas A&M University, Mitchell Campus
College of Geosciences and Maritime Studies
Physical Education Facility
1993, Melton Henry/Maurice Robison Architects

The development of the A&M campus has maintained
architectural consistency (with the exception of Dormitory A,
which, according to campus lore, was built from a set of plans
proffered by a motel chain). What the campus lacks is site-
planning coherence. Buildings seem to be grouped in small
clusters that belong to no larger order. Therefore the campus
has a suburban feeling. The Physical Education Facility
compensates for its happenstance site with a varied palette of
shapes, textures, materials, and colors. Yet it manages to
maintain allegiance to the campus's architectural theme.

25 33rd Street   **F–6**

GH&H, I&GN and MK&T Freight Office
1904

The Galveston, Houston & Henderson Railroad and two
other corporations built this freight depot after the Storm of
1900. It was the site of the first GH&H station, which
predated track extension to the downtown wharves in the
1870s. Upon bridging Galveston Bay in 1860, the GH&H
inaugurated railroad service between Houston and Galveston.

The Freight Office is built of handsome orange-red face
brick. Cast ornament and an inset limestone loggia give the
building a civic character. Note that the compact building
has three front doors, one for each of the railway lines that
occupied it. Stretching out behind the station is a long wing
containing canopied loading docks.

3227 Market Street   **F–7**

Galveston Gas Company complex (now Southern Union Gas
Company)
1860, S. R. Dickson, engineer
1901

Although rebuilt after partial destruction in the Storm of
1900, the gas company complex was one of the first gas
distribution plants in Texas and is now the oldest. The brick
Retort House, at the 33rd-Market corner, is backed up by
the Purifier, Scrubber, and Engine Houses. Along Market
Street, openings at various levels are contained in a 17-bay
rank. From inside the walled service yard, visible from 33rd
Street, the large arched windows are more regular in
disposition, and the roof is pulled out in an overhang to
shield them from the south sun. The high brick walls
outlining street frontages and enclosing center-block work
yards preserve a sense of the 19th-century spatiality of the
Factory District.

Visible from the intersection of 33rd and Market Streets
is the ex-**Galveston Brewery Association complex** at 33rd
and Church Streets. Between 1888 and 1895, this area,
which had been the cotton compress district, acquired its
identity as the Factory District with the construction of a
number of large enterprises backed by Galveston
businessmen seeking to diversify the city's economy and give
it a manufacturing base. One of the few enterprises that
endured was the Galveston Brewery (1895), with which the
St. Louis brewer Adolphus Busch was associated. As with
Busch's other Texas brewery projects, the original portions of
the Galveston Brewery were the work of the St. Louis
architects E. Jugenfeld & Company, who specialized in
brewery design. A major remodeling in 1965 covered the
exterior of the complex. Like Jugenfeld's Lone Star Brewing
Company in San Antonio (which now houses the San
Antonio Museum of Art), the Galveston brewery was in a
castellated Victorian Romanesque style.

519 29th Street   **F–8**

Galveston, Henderson & San Antonio Railway Company
Freight Depot

1918

Although it does not assert the civic character of the
GH&H Freight Office, the GH&SA's counterpart station
displays decorative horizontal ribbing above the arched
windows facing 29th Street. The two-story office building
and the wing of loading docks give Church Street a strong
architectural edge.

602 32nd Street   **F–9**

Waples Lumber Company Building (now Green's Funeral Home)

1948

Effacement of architectural features usually undermines the
design of a building. In the case of what was originally the
display room and office building of the Waples Lumber
Company yard, it emphasizes a cylindrical theme that
culminates in a modernistic corner tower. From the tall thin
bins of the grain elevators on the waterfront to the squat tanks
of the waterworks compound, the cylinder is a geometric
figure especially associated with the Factory District. Green's
Funeral Home raises it to the plane of architecture.

3220 Ball Avenue   **F–10**

Cedar Terrace

1954, R. R. Rapp, Fred T. Stafford, and Thomas M. Price;
Arne G. Engberg, consulting architect

During the early 1940s and again in the early 1950s, the
Housing Authority of the City of Galveston purposefully
concentrated almost all its low-income public housing
complexes in the Factory District. Cedar Terrace, produced
by a trio of Galveston architects in consultation with Arne
Engberg of Houston, is representative of the approach to
public-housing design in Texas during the period. It covers

eight discontinuous blocks. Its 48 two-story apartment
buildings are set at an angle to the street grid, to give them
optimum orientation. All outdoor space is communal. There
are no private spaces associated with individual apartments.

3002 Ball Avenue   **F–11**

Galveston Water & Electric Light Station

1904, C. W. Bulger

Still the distribution center for Galveston's public water
system, this is the oldest functioning municipal waterworks
plant in the United States. The plant building is a decorous
work of industrial classicism, reflecting Bulger's somewhat
heavy touch. Piers of dark red brick divide bays containing
tall, arched windows on either side of the pedimented entry
portico facing 30th Street. The rear wing and pavilion,
along Ball, are less ornamented. The fenced grounds of the
waterworks contain mature date palm, live oak, and
magnolia trees. To the north of the plant building, facing
30th Street, is the complex's oldest ground storage tank,
built when the system was put into operation in 1888–89.
Bulger's building replaced a predecessor destroyed in the
Storm of 1900.

2818 Ball Avenue   **F–12**

1891

The lumber merchant Henry Beissner built this house,
which is raised on high brick arches faced with scored
plaster. It is one of the most unusual houses of its period in
Galveston. It was out of the ordinary to build such a
substantial house in a neighborhood that was, in this block,
respectable but not fashionable. The character of the exterior
detail, especially the Japanese-like gridded band in the broad

ront gable, is not repeated on any surviving Galveston
.ouses. What also makes this band, and the rest of the
.laborate wooden detail on the exterior surface of the
.eissner House, unusual is that it was originally stained
ather than painted. The Mather House at 1601 Ball in the
.ast End seems to be the only other substantial house from
.he same period finished with dark-stained wood. The
.aceted roof planes of the projecting window bay on the
.ront of the Beissner House contribute to its broadly
.hythmic aspect, so different from the visual tempo of the
.abled center bays of the three-bay-front Southern town
.ouse. Note the extensive use of spindles in the gallery frieze
.nd hand rail. Typical of Galveston, however, the walls of the
.ouse, inside the decorative veranda screen, are finished with
.lain clapboards. Rehabilitation of the Beissner House was
.egun in 1996 (Mardi J. Mitchell), after decades of neglect
.nd abandonment. It will be used as a community center.
.he tall conical turret is a new addition, built on top of the
.ower, more subtly shaped roof cap.

First Presbyterian Church (a wooden building with Grecian
detail built in 1841) to this site in 1876. In 1881,
construction began on a new building, for which N. Wright
Cuney laid the cornerstone. This church was destroyed in
the Storm of 1900. Its replacement of 1901, designed and
built by John Tankersley, an African-American carpenter
who came to Galveston from Brazoria County after the
storm, was a handsome cottage-style church. It was raised,
enlarged, and faced with red brick by Stowe & Stowe to
make the present building. Rising a full story above grade,
Wesley Tabernacle Church stands out by virtue of its
bracketed corner tower cap and twin, bracketed porch
canopies facing 28th Street. These elements give the
building the slightly quirky bungalow look that is its
distinguishing feature.

13-629 27th Street   **F–13**

.ieman Building

.922

.he 1920s' version of the Galveston corner store: brick
.eneer and cast stone decorative detailing lend it an
.ppearance of substantiality and style.

02 28th Street   **F–14**

.Vesley Tabernacle Church (now Wesley Tabernacle United
.Aethodist Church)

.901, John Tankersley

.924, Stowe & Stowe

.)ne of the architectural landmarks of the Factory District is
.Vesley Tabernacle Church. Founded by African-Americans
.n 1869, the congregation acquired and moved the original

3014 Sealy Avenue   **F–15**

Central High School (now Central Middle School)

1954, Preston M. Geren and R. R. Rapp

Built at the same time as Ball High School on Avenue O,
Central replaced the earlier school of the same name at 27th
and Avenue M as the public high school for African-
American students. Geren, a Fort Worth architect, pursued
a design theme similar to that at Ball, with shaped masses
containing such space as the auditorium played against the
long blocks of classrooms. Bespeaking the early 1950s,
horizontal linearity is reiterated in the disposition of
classroom window bands, concrete sills and sunshades, even
the long, thin, dark red and brown Roman brick with which
the building is faced. Note how Central steps back from

Sealy Avenue the farther west one goes from the 30th Street intersection. The school's two-block site had been the site of the Gulf City Cotton Press in the late 19th century.

3320 Sealy Avenue   F–16
1888

During the late 19th century, this neighborhood seems to have been more closely associated with the West End than with the rest of the Factory District to the north. In blocks such as this that have not been cleared out, it retains a feeling similar to parts of the West End and San Jacinto areas. With its canopy of live oak trees, the 3300 block of Sealy is one of the most intact. This charming raised Victorian L-front cottage, built for the grocer Theodore Debner, displays panels of decorative shingle work and distinctive porch rail panels.

3322 Sealy Avenue   F–17
1904

Built as a tenant house by Debner, this is a particularly fine example of a raised shotgun-cottage type, notable for its generous size.

3602 Sealy Avenue   F–18
Mount Olive Missionary Baptist Church
1922, W. S. Murdock

Mount Olive Missionary Baptist Church is a simply organized but effectively composed gabled brick structure. The architect W. S. Murdock faced it with a mixed blend of dark brick set in dark mortar. Reverting to the High Victorian technique of the rising center, he thrust the central circular window through the entablature, rhythmically energizing the front façade of the church.

Note that the congregation has installed pictorial panels above the front doors depicting the church's architectural history. Next door is Mount Olive's successor church, dedicated in 1976. It is the work of the Houston architect John S. Chase.

905 44th Street   F–19
Palm Terrace
1942, Ben Milam, R. R. Rapp, and Fred T. Stafford

Palm Terrace, built by the Housing Authority of the City of Galveston under the auspices of the U.S. Housing Authority, is Galveston's most architecturally distinguished low-income public housing complex. It was originally the public housing complex for African-American families (**Oleander Homes** of the same date and by the same architects at 5228 Broadway was the counterpart complex for white families). The choice of dark red brick, the use of low-pitched hipped roofs to give the buildings a domestic aspect, the siting of the apartment blocks within the street grid rather than rotating them at an angle, and especially the provision of cantilevered exterior stairs of reinforced concrete make these two-story apartment blocks notable.

718 41st Street   F–20
USO Building (now Wright Cuney Park Recreation Building)
1941

This conservative modernistic building, like its twin in Ménard Park, continues to serve with architectural distinction. Across Winnie Avenue, the long three-block site now occupied by the Parkland Apartments was the power center of the Factory District. There, between 1888 and 1890, two massive brick manufacturing complexes were built: the grim four-story Galveston Cotton and Woolen Mills at 41st and Winnie (1890, C. R. Makepeace & Co.), and the towered compound of the Galveston Bagging &

Cordage Company in the 3800-3900 blocks (1889, W. H. Tyndall). Both complexes survived into the 1960s. At the time the Cotton & Woolen Mills was built, the city allowed the construction of densely clustered workers' cottages on the public park block subsequently dedicated as Wright Cuney Park.

4602-4628 Winnie Avenue   F–21

Cotton Concentration Company Warehouses
1948

Efforts at developing a manufacturing base notwithstanding, cotton trading remained the dominant business of the Factory District well into the 20th century. The spatial magnitude of cotton shipping by the middle of the century can be inferred from the fact that this two-block complex was merely a satellite of the Cotton Concentration Company's central storage and shipping compound on Broadway. As is often true of industrial architecture, these warehouses derive their visual power from the repetition of simple shapes, within which variations occur. Most of the bays are of Stran-steel-framed Quonset-type construction. Their curvature is fully evident along 44th Street. Within the repeating bays, sliding panel doors and squirming roof drainpipes animate the façades. The arches are interrupted by towers of board-finished concrete. In the 4600 block of Winnie, the construction systems (and shapes) change altogether. Occasionally, motorized cotton floats pass, evoking the kind of street traffic once characteristic of this area.

4702 Broadway   F–22

Island Community Center
1971; 1995, C. S. Gilbert

The Housing Authority of the City of Galveston had its staff architect C. S. Gilbert remodel and reface this ex-Globe Discount Center as a community services center. His canopied central entrance, square-sectioned windows, and implied dado give the formerly bland building a memorable countenance. New landscaping, installed along the Broadway frontage of the property, demonstrates how effective uniform planting can be in compensating for the indignities visited upon Broadway by massive parking lot construction in the 20th century. Adjoining the Island Community Center is the eight-block complex of the **Moody Compress and Warehouse Company** (1913, Green & Finger). The site which the center occupies was previously the Merchants and Planters Compress and Warehouse Company (1913), the Kempner brothers' cotton compress.

5005-5013 Broadway   F–23

Oehler Building
1940, Ben J. Kotin

After Galveston and Houston were connected by a paved highway in 1928, Broadway's far west end was developed as an urban highway, flanked with business buildings. One of the most architecturally assertive is this small, two-story modernistic office building constructed by the Galveston builder Charles H. Oehler. Its curved upper bay has a nautical flair that seems particularly appropriate to Galveston.

5302 Broadway   **F–24**

Coca Cola Bottling Company Building

1937

Stucco-surfaced walls, arched windows, and tile roof copings imply a Mediterranean look, sufficient to make the ex-Coca Cola plant a highway landmark.

5402-5628 Broadway   **F–25**

Cotton Concentration Company sheds

1928

This three-block-long palisade of exposed reinforced concrete walls, broken at intervals by gateways and screened by palm trees and bougainvillea, nobly monumentalizes the role of cotton in the economy of 19th- and 20th-century Galveston. George Sealy, Jr., organized the Cotton Concentration Company to integrate with the Galveston Wharf Company, of which he was president. The huge sheds are each four blocks deep, running all the way back to Church Street. Railroad spur lines feed in between the sheds from the north. Vacant since the early 1980s, the future of the Cotton Concentration Company sheds is in doubt. In 1995, the wooden Unit D at 57th and Broadway was demolished and replaced by a U.S. Post Office building. These are essential Galveston buildings. Just as the great Broadway houses east of 27th Street architecturally symbolize the consumption of wealth in Galveston's heyday, the Cotton Concentration Company sheds architecturally symbolize its production. Because they stand at the point where the Gulf Freeway merges into Galveston's historic street grid, they form an imposing urban wall that spatially anchors the west end of Broadway.

The Denver Resurvey encompasses the southwestern third of the Groesbeck town plan. It is the residential sector of Galveston that took shape between the Storm of 1900 and the early 1950s. The dominant impression is of repeating blocks of modest wood houses. Setting it apart from the older West End, which it adjoins, are the low profile of the houses and the general lack of tree canopies shading the long, straight alphabetical avenues and numbered cross-streets. ⋒ ⋒ ⋒ William H. Sandusky's 1845 map of Galveston shows that this district was cut through by McKinney's Bayou. Where the bayou branched into two draws, between Avenues O and P and the lines of 40th and 50th Streets, the Sandusky map indicates marshy conditions. ⋒ ⋒ ⋒ The Denver Resurvey takes its name from an ambitious suburban real estate development scheme launched in 1890. A number of Colorado investors joined the Galvestonians H. M. Trueheart and Julius Runge in the Galveston Land & Improvement Company to acquire 660 acres lying between Broadway

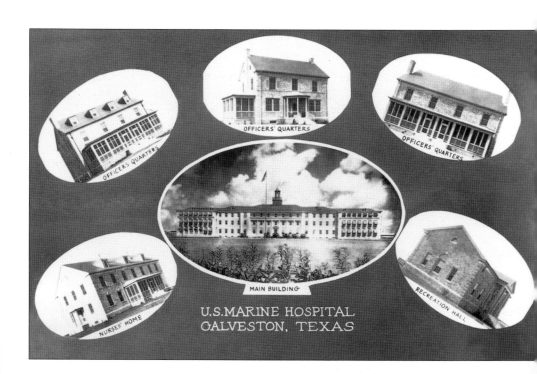

Postcard showing buildings in the U. S. Marine Hospital complex, built in 1931.

he Gulf, 45th, and 57th Streets. The outlots were replatted as city blocks bisected by alleys, ind the blocks were platted with 24 narrow lots per block (rather than the 14 lots of Groesbeck's blocks). Such narrow lots suggest that the Galveston Land & Improvement Company foresaw this section as providing housing for families of modest means. This "resurvey" and the chief investors' association with Denver, Colorado, gave the area its new 1ame. As was the case with similar, large-scale suburban developments in other Texas cities, he financial Panic of 1893 thwarted investors' hopes for a quick return. ⋔ ⋔ ⋔ Almost he entire district lay in the zone of total destruction occasioned by the Storm of 1900, principally because it was so low-lying. The grade–raising of the Denver Resurvey area in 1909, when McKinney's Bayou was filled, and the construction of permanent buildings at Fort Crockett between 1909 and 1911 set the stage for the area's development in the 1920s.

⋔ ⋔ ⋔ Two elite residential real estate developments of the mid-1920s, Cedar Lawn and Caduceus Place, raised the social status of the Denver Resurvey even as they radically inverted 19th-century approaches to urban residential place-making. Both subdivisions adopted street plans that interrupted the continuity of the Groesbeck grid in order to attain spatial insularity by turning their backs to the city. Their influence is reflected in the development of neighboring subdivisions, which clearly stand out as enclaves in a street map of the city.

⋔ ⋔ ⋔ Beyond 57th Street, the westernmost street in the Groesbeck town plan, the grid of streets and blocks dissolves into curving lanes as Galveston brushes up against the edges of Offatt's Bayou. The 20th-century suburbanization of Galveston is further reflected in the strip of businesses along the south end of 45th Street, the kind of typical auto-oriented, early 20th-century commercial corridor that replaced the corner stores of the 19th-century city. Yet Galveston's engagement with the 19th century is tenacious, as is apparent at Lakeview Cemetery, a landscape setting that evokes the treeless, scrubby aspect that Victorian photographs suggest was once typical of the city.

BROADWAY

McCULLOUGH

BORDEN

OFFATTS
BAYOU

BAYOU SHORE DRIVE

STEWART

FRAZIER

LAFITTE

15

16
SOUTH SHORE DRIVE

HEARD'S LANE

NEUMANN

Q

Q 1/2

R

R 1/2

61ST

58TH

57TH

56TH

55TH

54TH

53RD

52ND

51ST

50TH

49TH

MARY MOODY NORTHEN BOULEVARD

CROCKETT BOULEVARD

WOODROW AVENUE

AVE T

32

33

DENVER DRIVE

36

35

34

30

SIAS

SHERMAN BOULEVARD

AVE T 1/2

40

ADLER CIRCLE

37
38

39
MACO AVE.

1. 4400 Avenue N
2. 4415 Avenue L
3. 11 Cedar Lawn Circle
4. 58 Cedar Lawn Circle
5. 43 Cedar Lawn Circle
6. 16 Cedar Lawn Drive South
7. 15 Cedar Lawn Drive North
8. 11 Cedar Lawn Drive North
9. 84 Cedar Lawn Drive South
10. 15 Cedar Lawn Circle
11. 31 Cedar Lawn Circle
12. 40 Cedar Lawn Drive South
13. 4502 Avenue N 1/2
14. 4114 Avenue O
15. 5200 Avenue N 1/2
16. 28 South Shore Drive
17. 2100–2112 45th Street
18. 4804 Crockett Boulevard
19. 4313 Caduceus Place
20. 4321 Caduceus Place
21. 4402 Caduceus Place
22. 4420 Caduceus Place
23. 4505 Caduceus Place
24. 4510 Caduceus Place
25. 4525 Caduceus Place
26. 4530 Caduceus Place
27. 4615 Caduceus Place
28. 4602 Sherman Boulevard
29. 4603 Sherman Boulevard
30. 5012 Sherman Boulevard
31. 4810 Denver Drive
32. 5012 Denver Drive
33. 5115 Avenue T
34. 5127 Denver Drive
35. 5209 Denver Drive
36. 2803 53rd Street
37. 36 Adler Circle
38. 38 Adler Circle
39. 5816 Maco Avenue
40. Lakeview Cemetery:
    Woodmen of the World Galveston Tidal Wave Monument

4400 Avenue N   G–1

U.S. Marine Hospital (now the Park Apartments)
1931, James A. Wetmore,
Supervising Architect of the Treasury

Occupying an entire outlot, the ex-U.S. Marine Hospital
was an imposing complex of Anglo-Palladian-style
buildings before the Houston developer J. R. McConnell
acquired most of the property and had the Houston
architects Makover Levy alter and add to it as the Cedar
Lawn Apartments. The townhouse crescent in front of the
three-story hospital building is bad enough. What is
unforgivable is the damage McConnell inflicted on the
hospital building by gouging "garret"-level balconies into
the roof. The parts of the complex that are occupied by the
Galveston County Health Department preserve a sense of
the original. It is to be regretted that this fine group of
public buildings could not have been conserved and
adapted for new uses with the skill and sensitivity that the
University of Texas Medical Branch (UTMB) exhibited at
the ex-Custom House on the Strand.

4415 Avenue L   G–2

Our Lady of Guadalupe Catholic Church
1949

A spare version of the Spanish Mediterranean style was
applied to this church and parish group. Until it was closed
by the Diocese of Galveston-Houston in 1992, Our Lady of
Guadalupe was the traditional Spanish-language parish of
Galveston. The parish complex continues in use as a
diocesan social and educational services center.

11 Cedar Lawn Circle   G–3

1927, Andrew Fraser

Fraser's attempt to design a romantic Mediterranean
towered villa for the surgeon Dr. William E. Huddleston
betrays his unromantic engineering inclinations.

Nonetheless, it signaled the ambition of Cedar Lawn,
developed by W. L. Moody III and his brother-in-law, the
dry-goods merchant (and future congressman) Clark W.
Thompson, in 1926.

Cedar Lawn represents one of the most decisive attempts
to break free of the Groesbeck town plan and extract from
its grid a private-place enclave. The private-place ideal
reached Texas cities from St. Louis in the first decade of the
20th century. It involved the use of discontinuous street
layouts, restrictive covenants, and architectural symbols to
establish socioeconomically homogeneous pockets of visual
order and spatial control, isolating elite residential
neighborhoods from the unpredictability of urban real
estate. At Cedar Lawn this was accomplished by replatting
nine blocks and overlaying a somewhat awkward curvilinear
street network on the grid. All house sites face into the
enclave. The neighborhood turns its back on the rest of
Galveston. A peculiar feature of the streets in Cedar Lawn is
that they are graded to drain into central gutters, rather
than gutters at each edge of the street.

Although it defensively turned inward, Cedar Lawn was
very Galveston. It was the Moody enclave. Not only did three
of W. L. Moody, Jr.'s children live here, but many of the
other householders of the 1920s and 1930s were employees
of various Moody enterprises. In the late 1940s, Cedar Lawn
additionally became a Maceo enclave, as various business and
family connections of the Maceo brothers built houses here.

58 Cedar Lawn Circle   G–4

1950, Michael A. Loomis, designer

Woodrow J. Walker, who built this house, was manager of
the Palace Club, one of the Maceo enterprises. The Walker
House is a flamboyant example of what might be called

Mexican ranchero moderne. Like several other Cedar Lawn houses designed by the amateur architect Mike Loomis (and built by his brother, the prolific Galveston contractor Gus Loomis), it is based on a combination of angled and circular plan geometries and features a brash mixture of materials that give it a strong presence.

3 Cedar Lawn Circle   G–5
1950, Williams, Williams & Williams

Sam Maceo, a Sicilian-born barber, and his elder brother Rosario gave up their barber shop in the early 1920s to organize bootlegging, then gambling, in Galveston. By the end of the 1920s they had achieved wealth, a substantial network of businesses, and—in tolerant Galveston—a measure of recognition and respectability. The Maceo brothers were best known for the posh clubs and gambling casinos they operated—the Hollywood Dinner Club and the Balinese Room. They brought well-known entertainers to Galveston to perform at their clubs. That is how the Palm Springs, California, architects, Williams, Williams & Williams, came to be recommended to Sam Maceo for the design of this extremely large, but self-effacing California Contemporary house, which occupies a strategic peninsular site in the center of Cedar Lawn. Edna and Sam Maceo hired the New York decorator T. H. Robsjohn-Gibbings to design the interiors of the sprawling house. Note the bamboo fence on the Cedar Lawn South portion of the site and the undulating brick wall on the Cedar Lawn North edge. Unfortunately, Maceo died within a year of its completion. His house is still owned by family members.

6 Cedar Lawn Drive South   G–6
1929, Alfred C. Finn
Swimming pool, greenhouse, and gardener's cottage, 1930, Robert C. Smallwood

The grandest house in Cedar Lawn was built by W. L.

Moody III, the eldest son of W. L. Moody, Jr. Robert Smallwood, who was Alfred C. Finn's residential designer, was responsible for Moody's pedimented Georgian-style country house, detailed in the 18th-century neoclassical style of the Adam brothers. Shortly after the house's completion, Moody commissioned Smallwood to design an elaborate entertainment complex, consisting of a bath house, swimming pool, and tropical greenhouse on a series of lots backing up to Cedar Lawn Circle. When W. L. Moody III left Galveston in 1931, his house was acquired by his brother Shearn Moody, whose descendants still occupy it.

15 Cedar Lawn Drive North   G–7
1927, Donald N. McKenzie

W. L. Moody, Jr.'s daughter, Libbie, and her husband Clark W. Thompson built this big-scaled, simply detailed house. McKenzie designed the unpretentious house with an angled, Arts-and-Crafts "butterfly" plan, so that its major rooms open toward the sun and the prevailing breeze. The mellow mustard-green tone of the Thompson House's stucco walls complements lush woodland vegetation, which is shaded by tremendous live oak trees.

11 Cedar Lawn Drive North   G–8
1929

This house represents what might be called the Galveston Georgian house of the 1920s, a successor to the Italianate villas with Georgian undertones that Anton Korn essayed in the 1910s. Built for Dr. Charles T. Stone, professor of internal medicine at UTMB, it features a classical portico, an elliptical fanlight and sidelights framing the front door, hinged louvered blinds, and red brick wall surfaces that contrast with the cast stone lintels and sills.

84 Cedar Lawn Drive South   G–9
1950, R. R. Rapp

The dry-goods merchant Joe G. Eiband retreated to Cedar
Lawn from the house at 3118 Broadway that Rapp had
designed for him 22 years earlier. The asymmetrical
arrangement of window and door openings in its
symmetrically organized façade and the use of floor-length
shuttered windows were attributes of suburban house design
popular since the late 1930s. These give the Eiband House
its hospitable, easygoing character.

15 Cedar Lawn Circle   G–10
1949, Michael A. Loomis, designer

This was the first of Loomis's free-wheeling Contemporary-
style houses, built for—and still owned by—his own family.
The tan brick walls of the Loomis House step back in broad
curves and with jaunty bull-nosed corners to accommodate
the odd curvature of the lot. An entrance pylon tower of red
glazed brick is played against thick, protruding fascias,
whose horizontality emphasize the curvature of the house.
Glass block and curved, polished, red concrete front steps
enhance the modernistic theme. At **26 Cedar Lawn Circle**
is another Loomis-designed and -built house (1951),
occupied by Sam Maceo's lieutenant, Loranzy Grillette.

31 Cedar Lawn Circle   G–11
1927

Occupying a lot shaped much like that at 15 Cedar Lawn
Circle, this white brick house, built for Dr. William H.
Fletcher, is stepped in plan and somewhat hermetic in
appearance. Its austere Spanish Mediterranean style
possesses a harder edge than was customary in the 1920s.

40 Cedar Lawn Drive South   G–12
1948, Charles L. Zwiener

The composition and proportions of this trimly detailed
house seem to be indebted to the Cameron Fairchild-
designed house at 2901 Avenue O. Built for Alvin N. Kelso,
vice-president of the Texas Gulf Construction Company,
and his wife, Joan Harris, this is one of Zwiener's best
houses. Across the street at **24 Cedar Lawn South** is the
Edward R. Michaelis House (1931, Cameron Fairchild). At
4527 Avenue N 1/2 is the flat-roofed, white-walled, steel-
framed Warren F. Merritt House (1936, Fred T. Stafford),
an uncertain essay in modernistic design. Lawrence A.
Rehm, who with his wife Lillian was responsible for saving
and preserving N. J. Clayton's architectural drawings and
office records, designed the Walter L. Johnson House at
4517 Avenue N 1/2 (1940).

4502 Avenue N 1/2   G–13
1932, R. R. Rapp

This picturesque English manorial-style house marked a
departure from Rapp's typologically conservative boxlike
houses. Built for R. Wilbur Goodman, president of the
Model Laundry and Dry Cleaning Works, it is finished with
a veneer of face brick, the preferred surfacing material for
elite houses in Galveston after the late 1920s. Indeed, as

ne moves westward on Avenues N, N 1/2, and O, 43rd
treet marks the brick-veneer line, architecturally indicating
ocial arrival.

a

b

114 Avenue O   G–14

all High School
1954, Preston M. Geren and R. R. Rapp
1995, PBK Architects

When Ball High School left the Central Park area near the
ourthouse, it was moved out to what, in the early 1950s,
vas the center of white, middle-class Galveston. Preston
Geren's solidly constructed and detailed complex retains a
ertain civic character, especially the entrance pavilion at
1st and O, with its projecting stair tower with cutaway
vertical window sculpturally balancing the curved and coved
ront-door bay. Extensive additions to the complex, by PBK
f Houston, take up the spirit of the original with great
kill. PBK's Frank Kelly adroitly turned what could have
een a very damaging series of additions to the Avenue O
açade of Ball High School into an imaginative,
ympathetic, and witty reinterpretation of Geren's original.

West on Avenue O are **4404 Avenue O,** the Louis F.
Fox, Jr., House (1936, Harvin Moore & Hermon Lloyd),
another homage to the Latin Colonial–style house that
inspired 2901 Avenue O, and **4501 Avenue O,** the Joseph
Varnell House (1929, R. R. Rapp), which served as the
model for Rapp's later Maceo House at 2412 Avenue O.

5200 Avenue N 1/2   G–15

Alamo Elementary School
1935, R. R. Rapp

Alamo School is one of the few survivors from the
generation of public schools built in Galveston in the 1920s
and 1930s. Although none were exceptional architecturally,
they—like Rapp's Alamo School—occupied their sites with
a sense of civic decorum absent from later 20th-century
school architecture in Galveston.

28 South Shore Drive   G–16

1956, Thomas M. Price

Not until the post–World War II era did Galveston finally
exceed the westernmost bounds of John D. Groesbeck's
original town plan. Predictably, new "additions" to the city
of Galveston beyond the west and east edges of the original
townsite broke with Groesbeck's grid in favor of enclave-
type residential subdivisions with curving streets and limited
access points. Here, in the one-block-long South Shore
Addition, developed on the south edge of Offatt's Bayou in
1953 by John Gray, John J. Hill, and M. J. Gaido, is a
classic, post–World War II upper-middle-income street of
low, ranch-type houses, with those on the north side
overlooking the lakelike bayou.

This one-story, flat-roofed modern house, built for Dr.
and Mrs. E. Hopkins Stirling, is one of Price's finest
buildings. The proportional relationship of solid to void,
the integration of the garage door into the architectural

composition, and the glimpse of the bayou through the house are distinguishing features. It has been very well maintained. Subsequent owners included preservation pioneer Patti Steph and architect Ronald D. Fash.

2100-2112 45th Street G–17
Prets Lumber Company Building
1960, Charles L. Zwiener

As a favor to Frank W. Prets, president of the Prets Lumber Company, Zwiener dashed off a sketch for the façade of an extension to the company's retail store. His Contemporary-style storefront has stood the test of time.

4804 Crockett Boulevard G–18
1929, Cameron Fairchild

This French provincial–style house, built for the real estate agent John Adriance II, displays the translation of the 1920s' "country house" ideal to a small house on a suburban lot. In plan it is an H-shape, rather than the blocklike outline preferred for bungalows, the standard small-house type of 1920s' Galveston. This design allowed the Adriance House to be pavilion-like and one room deep throughout for maximum ventilation. Shuttered french doors set in arched openings bracket a central screened loggia, faced with ornamental trellis work, the stylish replacement for the old-fashioned front porch. Despite its modest demeanor, the Adriance House is one of the most important houses from the 1920s' decade in Galveston.

4313 Caduceus Place G–19
Methodist District Parsonage
1946, Harvin C. Moore

The Houston architect Harvin C. Moore designed this

house as the residence of the pastor of what is now the Moody Memorial First United Methodist Church. Faced with stone (very unusual for Galveston), it is based on the 19th-century Alsatian vernacular architecture of Castroville, Texas. The parsonage is located in Westmoor Addition, which vied with Cedar Lawn as an elite residential enclave in the 1920s.

4321 Caduceus Place G–20
1936

Galveston's foremost modernistic house was built for Robert I. Cohen III, an officer of his family's clothing business. It is a sculptural composition of interlocked, white stucco-surfaced cubes, with window openings incised into the corners of the cubes. Note that the front sidewalk participates in the interlocking theme. Despite its volumetric massing, the frontality of the Cohen House gives it an intensely planar quality.

4402 Caduceus Place G–21
1951, Bailey A. Swenson

The Houston architect Bailey Swenson was famous for his dramatic Contemporary-style houses. This house, built for Mr. and Mrs. Victor Reiswerg, is typical of a series of houses that Swenson designed in the Houston neighborhood of Riverside Terrace in the early 1950s. It even incorporates a defining feature of the Riverside Terrace Contemporary look: the second-story "mother-in-law room," which is popped up through the long, low roof line.

420 Caduceus Place   G–22

953, Thomas M. Price

The wide-swept low-pitched roof, cresting above a glass-lled gable and supported on exposed wood beams, was a wvorite architectural image for 1950s' Contemporary-style ouses. Price's house for Dr. and Mrs. Menelaus Caravageli is classic example of the type. Across the street at **4419 Caduceus Place** is the more conservatively designed, Monterey-style house of Mr. and Mrs. Miles K. Burton 1948, Charles L. Zwiener). Next door at **4428 Caduceus Place** is the Italian villa–style house (1930) that Miss Lillian chadt designed for her mother, Mrs. William Schadt.

505 Caduceus Place   G–23

932, Phelps & Dewees

The San Antonio architects Phelps & Dewees designed this uff brick–faced, picturesque manorial-style country house or the lawyer Bryan F. Williams. It sits at the entrance to Caduceus Place, the most prestigious, restricted, private-lace enclave in Galveston. Caduceus Place is two blocks ong. It is entered, in the classic St. Louis private-street ashion, between brick and cast stone gate piers at 45th treet. It was cooperatively developed in 1925 by Brantly Harris and Drs. Willard R. Cooke, George T. Lee, and oyd Reading (the doctors chose the name Caduceus in onor of their professional calling). To insulate themselves gainst the Groesbeck grid—within which Caduceus Place s set—the investors had the private street routed along the lley line, making these the grandest alley houses in alveston. As a sign of its special distinction, Caduceus lace is paved with rose-colored concrete.

4510 Caduceus Place   G–24

1926, Stowe & Stowe

The house that Stowe & Stowe designed for Dr. Willard R. Cooke, professor of obstetrics and gynecology at UTMB, signals his old-Galveston status in its homey front porch, unpretentious stucco-faced exterior, and lack of ornamentation. A many-windowed wing on the west side of the house (1962, Joseph Edwin Blanton) overlooks one of the social institutions of Caduceus Place, a tennis court, screened by luxuriant banks of oleanders, that spans the depth of the property. To compensate for the shallowness of house sites, most of the properties have expansive side yards. Next door is **4520 Caduceus Place,** a bungalow built by Mr. and Mrs. Brantly Harris (1926, R. R. Rapp, with additions from 1938 by Cameron Fairchild). Harris was a lawyer and mayor of Galveston during the 1930s.

4525 Caduceus Place   G–25

1930, Cameron Fairchild

Although no members of the Sealy family lived in Caduceus Place, it became the de-facto Sealy enclave because John W. McCullough, president of the Hutchings-Sealy National Bank and successor to George Sealy, Jr., as president of the Cotton Concentration Company and the Sealy & Smith Foundation, and his wife, a Ménard-Sherman-Trueheart descendant, built their Spanish Mediterranean–style country house here. Fairchild modeled the entrance front, which incorporates a porte-cochère, on a Houston house designed by the New York architect Harrie T. Lindeberg. It provided a suitably unpretentious, but elegant, image for this most patrician of Galveston streets. From 1962 until 1972, this was the home of the architect Thomas M. Price.

4530 Caduceus Place   G–26

1967, Charles L. Zwiener

The newest house in Caduceus Place, built for Dr. and Mrs.
William L. Glenn, Jr., is this modest courtyard house,
designed in a contemporary version of the California
Spanish style. Adding to its charm is the dense pile of
wisteria that, at the right time of the year, blankets the
pergola above the entrance patio.

4615 Caduceus Place   G–27

1941, Harvin Moore & Hermon Lloyd

This is one of the handsomest houses that the Houston
architects Moore & Lloyd designed. Faced with white
painted brick, it is long and low. Minimal brick detailing
and an elliptical entrance portico underscore the essential
austerity of the house, which was built for Leland S.
Dennis, vice president and general manager of the Cotton
Concentration Company. The contrast of its glistening
white surfaces with the intense, dark green of the low
vegetation that predominates in Caduceus Place establishes
the white-and-green color theme characteristic of the street.
Across the street, at **4600 Caduceus Place,** is Dr. George T.
Lee's house (1937). At the end of the street are **4625
Caduceus Place,** the Dr. George W. N. Eggers House
(1937, Ben Milam), and **4626 Caduceus Place,** the Louis
Pauls House (1938, Cameron Fairchild).

4602 Sherman Boulevard   G–28

1927, R. R. Rapp

So much interest was expressed by affluent Galveston
families in the development of Caduceus Place that in 1928
Brantly Harris and his brother Fletcher Harris subdivided
surrounding real estate as an enlarged version of the
original, which they called Denver Court. Like other early
houses in these neighborhoods by established Galveston
architects, Rapp's house for Joseph J. Kane, president of the

Kane Boiler Works, appears slightly old-fashioned because
of its typological conservatism, embodied in its strict
frontality and front porch. It is a very handsome house
nonetheless and, in its present state, reinforces the
neighborhood's white-and-green color scheme.

4603 Sherman Boulevard   G–29

1959, Thomas M. Price

Rupturing the somnolence of Denver Court is this one-
story, flat-roofed modern courtyard house, designed for the
restaurateur Nick M. Cokins. Solid brick planes, capped by
an uninterrupted fascia, face the street. These offset a wall
of glass, shielded by a solar screen that introduces a note of
decoration into Price's otherwise very spare exterior and
preserves visual privacy. The Cokins House plays off the
conventionality of its neighbors to emphasize its
nonconformist approach.

5012 Sherman Boulevard   G–30

1949, Charles L. Zwiener

Modernism came to Denver Court in this house, designed
by the architect Charles Zwiener for his own family. It is
composed of two intersecting bars: a one-story shed-roofed
wing perpendicular to the street, which slides beneath a
two-story bar, set parallel to the street. Zwiener was also

esponsible for the Contemporary-style house next door at **014 Sherman Boulevard** (1950) for Dr. and Mrs. Y. C. mith, Jr., and the more traditional McDonald House 1951) at **5017 Sherman Boulevard.**

810 Denver Drive   G–31
.940, Irving R. Klein

Designed by the Houston architect Irving Klein, this Regency-style villa is decorated with mannered classical detail. Although built for Marvin Kahn, manager of Nathan's, it was occupied from 1946 to 1991 by Ruth Levy and Harris L. Kempner, with whom it is especially dentified. Across the street, at **4813 Denver Drive,** is the W. Kendall Ménard House (1930, Cameron Fairchild), a compact picturesque manorial-style house.

012 Denver Drive   G–32
.947, R. R. Rapp

This is the grandest of the Galveston Georgian houses, built or Julian A. Levy, an officer of the E. S. Levy & Company clothing store, and subsequently occupied by Fanny Kempner Adoue. The portico of Adamesque columns rames a fanlit door flanked by windows with cast stone sills and lintels. Rapp had tested this combination at slightly reduced scale several years earlier in the Julian Ormond House at **4806 Denver Drive** (1941).

115 Avenue T   G–33
.938, John F. Staub

Up what appears to be a driveway (note, though, that it does have a street sign) is the largest of Staub's Galveston houses, a real country house set on a small estate, completely screened from surrounding streets by walls and dense vegetation. Built or W. L. Moody III and his wife, Mary Margaret Guinard,

this large brick house is simply composed with over-sized, floor-length, shuttered windows. From 52nd Street, one can see the service wing of the house, and the way that Staub telescoped the Moody House in plan and section so that it narrows down to a sliver at its west end. As Moody had done in Cedar Lawn in the 1920s, he succeeded in building the biggest house in the neighborhood, even if it is practically invisible. The great live oaks in front of the Moody House make one aware of how bare the rest of Denver Court, Caduceus Place, and Westmoor are by comparison.

Also visible from 52nd Street is the house at **5128 Avenue T** (1940). Moody built this house for his daughter Edna and her husband, David B. T. Myrick, an official of the American National Insurance Company. It virtually reproduces the front of John F. Staub's Helmbrecht House at 3815 Avenue P. The angled wing was added by the next owner, theater entrepreneur Giosue "Sonny" Martini, to contain a screening room.

5127 Denver Drive   G–34
1940, Ben Milam

This white-painted brick house, built for Ernest A. Rees, an official of the American National Insurance Company, is indicative of the penchant American architects of the 1930s had for picturesquely decomposing cubic Georgian and Regency house types. Milam cleverly incorporated the garage into the house front, using a curved screen wall (as he had at the Eggers House at 4625 Caduceus Place) to shield the driveway from Denver Drive.

5209 Denver Drive   G–35
1958, Ben J. Kotin & Associates

Kotin lived in this flat-roofed modern house. The solar screen enclosing the entrance court, the light-colored brick wall planes, and the emphatic fascia were architectural trademarks of Kotin and his associate Tibor Beerman.

2803 53rd Street   G–36
Moody Memorial First United Methodist Church
1964, Mark Lemmon

On axis with Denver Drive is the extraordinary Moody Memorial First United Methodist Church, a late work of the Dallas architect Mark Lemmon. This monumental building complex was constructed on a flat, featureless site, formerly a satellite of Fort Crockett. The Moody Memorial Church (W. L. Moody, Jr.'s wife, Libbie Rice Shearn, was from an old Houston family of English Methodists) is best characterized as a late modernistic version of a neo-Gothic-style church. Its dimensions are cathedral-like, its decoration hard-edged, and its surfaces detailed with granite and orange Kasota stone. The improbability of this combination gives the Moody Memorial Church a more substantive architectural character than was usually the case with Lemmon's neo-Georgian, suburban churches of the 1950s.

36 Adler Circle   G–37
1966, Ben J. Kotin & Tibor Beerman

Westwood, developed in the middle 1960s, was a prestigious address in Galveston. Its architectural distinction derives from this modern house—exhibiting Kotin and Beerman's architectural trademarks—briefly occupied by the family of Kotin's brother, Sol Kotin.

38 Adler Circle   G–3
1973, Joseph F. Cooley

Buttressing the claims to Westwood's architectural respectability made by Kotin & Beerman next door is this house, designed for the real estate broker Jack S. Evans by Joe Cooley. Cooley was an architect who spent his entire career in Galveston, much of it working for Tom Price. The Evans House is his foremost independent work. With its mellow wall planes of St. Joe brick, its carved wooden front doors, and low-pitched, intersecting roof planes with widel overhanging eaves, it is very much in the Texas modern-regional spirit of the San Antonio architect O'Neil Ford (as embodied in the Ford, Powell & Carson–designed house at 1504 Driftwood Lane).

5816 Maco Avenue   G–3
c. 1870

The Austin architect and historic preservationist Wayne Bel restored this gable-fronted Grecian cottage after his aunt, Mary Carol Harbruck, rescued it from potential demolition and moved it from the East End to this site in 1962.

akeview Cemetery   G–40

Voodmen of the World Galveston Tidal Wave Monument
1905, Pompeo Coppini, sculptor

Lakeview Cemetery has a kind of end-of-the-world feeling
o it. Because it is not well maintained, it preserves an
authentic sense of what Galveston's public landscape must
have been like before the era of paved streets, piped water,
and power lawn mowers. Adding to the mournful scene
(even on a sunny summer day, Lakeview feels remote and
isolated) is the distant rooftop flèche of the Moody
Memorial Church, visible above the fringe of palm trees
near the corner of 57th Street and Avenue T 1/2. It is rather
surprising that one can almost miss Lakeview's only
conspicuous architectural monument, which is, after the
Texas Heroes Monument, the grandest work of public art in
Galveston, Coppini's bombastic Galveston Tidal Wave
Monument. It was erected by the Woodmen of the World, a
fraternal organization and insurance company based in
Omaha, Nebraska. Atop a granite pedestal braced by a pair
of gnarled granite tree trunks rises the patinated bronze
figure of Joseph C. Root, the Iowa businessman who
founded the WOW (and who was still in office when this
supposed memorial to WOW members who died in the
Storm of 1900 was erected). Ornate bronze cartouches on
the front and back of the pedestal supply narrative
illustrations and credits. According to Coppini's
autobiography, the Woodmen of the World had him make a
copy of the statue, which was installed in Memphis.

T he beach, between 21st and Tremont Streets, became the nucleus of a seaside resort by the early 1880s. Its scale expanded during the 1890s as Galveston developed a resort economy attracting visitors from the rest of the state. In this respect Galveston was a rarity among Southern coastal cities: it was both a commercial port and a seaside resort. ⋔ ⋔ ⋔ The 1900 hurricane temporarily halted beach activity while the Seawall was built, and the island was raised. The two projects were designed to work together. The first step, construction of the Seawall, would buffer the island from storm surges in serious hurricanes and help control the not infrequent flooding caused by heavy rains. Once the Seawall was in place, then the land behind the Seawall could be filled in a gradual slope toward Galveston Bay. ⋔ ⋔ ⋔ Between 1902 and 1904, the 17-foot-high reinforced concrete wall, 16 to 20 feet wide at its base and

The completed Seawall on the far east end of the island, circa 1905. The land behind the Seawall has not, as yet, been filled. Even at this stage, the Seawall was a popular place to promenade for people of all ages.

3 to 5 feet wide at its summit, was built to the designs of retired military engineer Brigadier General Henry M. Robert (best known as the author of *Robert's Rules of Order*) and engineers Alfred Noble and H. C. Ripley for the city and the county of Galveston. It originally stretched along the line of 6th Street, on the east end of the city, then extended along the beach from 6th Street to 39th Street, three miles in all. In 1905, the U. S. Army underwrote construction of a one-mile extension between 39th Street and 53rd Street in front of Fort Crockett. Subsequent extensions (1921, 1925, 1953, and 1962) have carried the Seawall as far down the island as what would be 102nd Street. ∩

∩ ∩ The Seawall lifted Galveston above the Gulf, replacing the city's gentle slope down to the surf with a hard, structured edge. Galveston envisioned the Seawall and its boulevard in terms of Coney Island and Atlantic City: a popular urban beach resort. Great piers, first built in the 1890s and rebuilt after each hurricane, projected the city into the Gulf. These proclaimed the democratic character of Galveston's resort life. Although a succession of grand hotels, beginning with N. J. Clayton's Beach Hotel of 1883, were architectural symbols of the Galveston shoreline, it was to more modest hotels—and eventually tourist courts and motels—that most visitors went. Since the 1940s, urban space along the Seawall has been relentlessly, but indifferently, suburbanized. Today it requires more imagination to envision what the Seawall must have been like in the 1910s and 1920s than it does to imagine how Galveston's 19th-century neighborhoods appeared in their historic prime.

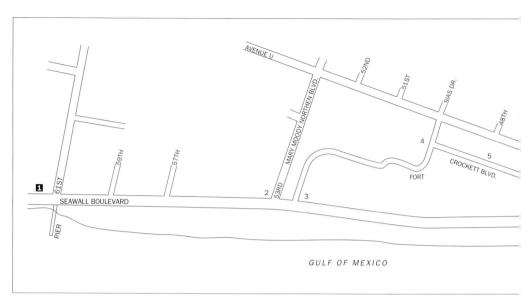

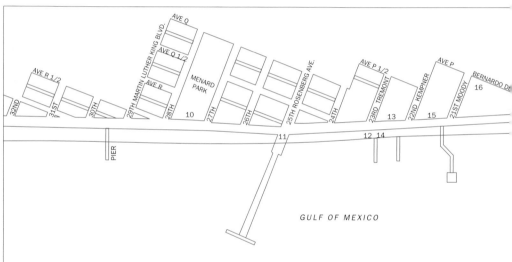

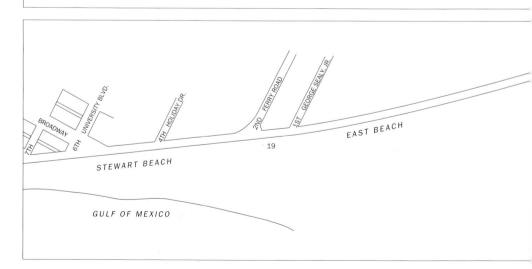

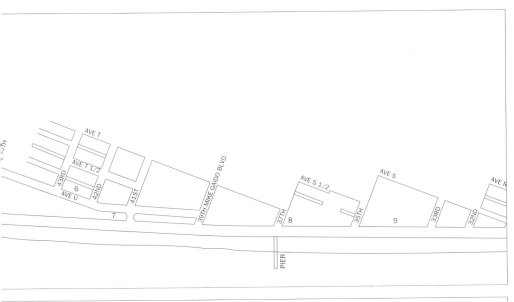

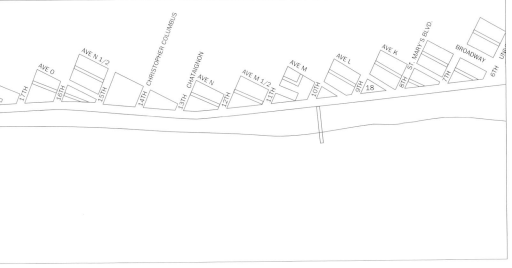

1. 6102 Seawall Boulevard
2. 5310 Seawall Boulevard
3. 5222 Seawall Boulevard
4. 5007 Avenue U
5. 4700 Fort Crockett Boulevard
6. 4214 Avenue U
7. 4100 block Seawall Boulevard
8. 3608 Seawall Boulevard
9. 3402 Seawall Boulevard
10. 2119 27th Street
11. 2501 Seawall Boulevard
12. Tremont Street and Seawall Boulevard
13. 2228 Seawall Boulevard
14. 2219 Seawall Boulevard
15. 2100 Seawall Boulevard
16. 2024 Seawall Boulevard
17. 1802 Seawall Boulevard
18. 802 Seawall Boulevard
19. 201 Seawall Boulevard
20. 1401 East Beach Drive

6102 Seawall Boulevard   **H–1**

Casa del Mar

1980, W. Irving Phillips, Jr.

Houston architect Irving Phillips designed the Casa del Mar for the U.S. Home Corporation, which prefabricated unit modules in its factory in the Panhandle town of Childress and trucked them 540 miles to Galveston, ready for occupancy once hoisted into place. The three floors of units sit atop a reinforced concrete substructure housing parked cars. Since there is a sharp drop in grade elevation between the top of the Seawall and abutting real estate, the concrete substructure lifts the balcony-fronted units above the top of the Seawall. Phillips organized units into a pair of Y-shaped blocks that frame a central space and give units at the back of the complex a vista of the water, a major design issue on the Seawall. It is amusing to note that the adjoining **Victorian Condo-Hotel** at 6300 Seawall (1983) repeats Phillips's basic design strategies, overlaid with "Victorian" styling.

5310 Seawall Boulevard   **H–2**

1931, Cameron Fairchild

Fairchild's largest Galveston house was this stucco-faced, tile-roofed Mediterranean villa for Eugenia Taylor and George Sealy, Jr. It is one of the few private residences built on Seawall Boulevard. Although the Seawall might have become a seaside version of Broadway—a grand residential avenue, like Ocean Drive in Corpus Christi—it developed instead as a commercial strip, a car-oriented "Boardwalk."

For much of its history, the Sealy House has stood unoccupied, isolated from the Seawall by what appeared to be an ocean of sand. In 1995 the house was rehabilitated by George Mitchell's Woodlands Development Corporation

and incorporated into **Landry's Seafood House at the San Luis,** 5310 Seawall Boulevard (1995, Morris Architects). The sand was replaced by a turf terrace and palm allée.

5222 Seawall Boulevard   **H–3**

San Luis Hotel and Condominium

1984, Morris★Aubry Architects

The biggest hotel on the Seawall is the 15-story San Luis, which contains 244 rooms and 100 condominium apartments. Built by the Woodlands Development Corporation of Houston, it sits on top of a pair of World War II gun batteries that were originally part of Fort Crockett. These have been effusively landscaped to create a subtropical, Acapulco-meets-*Hawaii Five-O* ambiance that encourages guests to linger in the thatched-roof *palapas* or swimming pool bars rather than venture down through the parking lot to the Gulf beach. Landscaping excess contrasts with the clean lines and serpentine sweep of the building, designed by the Galveston-born Houston architect Eugene Aubry. The building's S-curve plan (the vertical slit divides the hotel from the apartments) affords diagonal views of both the Gulf and Seawall Boulevard from inside.

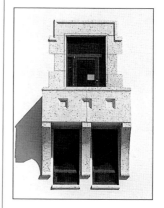

5007 Avenue U   **H–4**

Fort Crockett

Enlisted Men's Barracks (now Galveston County Community College District Building and Texas A&M University at Galveston)

1939, Construction Service, Office of the Quartermaster General, U.S. Army, designers

Fort Crockett, established by the U.S. Army in 1897, occupied a 125-acre reservation between 53rd Street and

st Street facing the Gulf. Garrisoned by the Coast
illery, the fort served principally for training and harbor
ense. U.S. involvement in the Spanish-American War led
he establishment of companion forts flanking the
rance to Galveston Harbor: Fort San Jacinto (at Fort
nt, at the east end of the island) and Fort Travis (on the
livar Peninsula). Fort Crockett was so severely damaged in
Storm of 1900 that no troops were garrisoned there
in until 1911. Fort Crockett was an active military
ervation through World War II. By the late 1940s, it was
d as a resort for military personnel. In 1953, the fort was
ctivated, and in 1957 portions of its site were sold by the
neral Services Administration. This accounts for the
fused array of strip shopping centers and garden-
artment complexes, interspersed with what are obviously
t buildings.

The pair of Enlisted Men's Barracks was constructed as
't of a major improvement program at the fort,
dertaken in 1938–39 and underwritten by the Works
gress Administration and the Public Works
ministration. The sources of funding perhaps explain the
ish exterior finish material: Texas Cordova fossilated
estone. Yet despite their size and finish, the Spanish
diterranean–style barracks have a bland character, to
ich the present lack of coherent open-space planning
tributes. The rear elevations of the barracks are lined
h access galleries.

00 Fort Crockett Boulevard   H–5

t Crockett
racks and Post Exchange and Gymnasium (now Texas
M University at Galveston)
11, Construction Service, Office of the Quartermaster
neral, U.S. Army, designers

is pair of barracks and the accompanying Post Exchange
d Gymnasium display a much stronger sense of
hitectural character than their 1930s' successors, although
y have not been treated as respectfully. This is because
barracks, with their scalloped Spanish Mission–style
ntispieces and arcaded galleries, give the sun greater
portunity to create the shadow play that is so important
animating, and lending a sense of depth to Gulf Coast
hitecture. The galleries spatially represent the need for
tected spaces open to the prevailing Gulf breeze. The
st Exchange and Gymnasium exhibits scalloped side
les that rise to frame its tile roof. This led to the

description of the building as "Dutch" in style, rather than
Spanish Mission style, at the time it was planned and built.
Behind the two barracks, adjoining Avenue U, are pairs of
subsidiary mess and lavatory outbuildings. At 4502 Fort
Crockett Boulevard is the ex-**Post Hospital,** still
recognizable despite extensive alterations.

4214 Avenue U   H–6

Crockett Courts
1937

Joseph A. Torregrossa built this complex of gable-roofed,
brick-faced tourist courts, facing the back of Fort Crockett.
An important survivor of the 1930s, when car-oriented
motels first appeared, they illustrate the type of tourist court
that was once visible throughout the United States. Note
that the Crockett Courts come in both two-bay and
stretched three-bay versions.

4100 block Seawall Boulevard   H–7

Non-Commissioned Officers Houses (now U.S. Coast Guard
Ensign Frank Sarna Family Housing)
Fort Crockett
1939, Construction Service, Office of the Quartermaster
General, U.S. Army, designers

These semidetached houses, built in two colonies—one off
53rd Street, the other here at the east point of the fort
grounds—are of board-finished, cast-in-place, reinforced
concrete construction. All are symmetrically organized, so
that each double house appears to be a single structure.
Despite inappropriate colors, inappropriate window
replacement, and the addition of fake shutters, they
maintain the architectural dignity of Fort Crockett along
Seawall Boulevard.

3608 Seawall Boulevard   H–8
Commodore Motel

1966, Louis L. Oliver

Louis Oliver adopted a tightly curved, whiplash floor plan for the Commodore in order to create the maximum number of guest rooms with a Gulf view. The exposed-concrete-frame structure contains infill panels of brick and of window-and-door assemblies typical of American modern architecture of the 1950s and 1960s. Oliver's spatial organization of the Commodore—guest rooms are sandwiched between private balconies on the Seawall side and a rear veranda-corridor—represents the developed motel type of the period as it was applied to Seawall Boulevard. The copper-faced fourth floor is a 1982 addition by Oliver & Beerman.

3402 Seawall Boulevard   H–9
Seahorse Motel

1956, Thomas M. Price with John T. Buckhart

With the Seahorse, built by Mrs. Shearn Moody and her sons Shearn, Jr., and Robert, Price introduced the curved floor plan to Seawall Boulevard as the optimal configuration for maximizing the number of rooms with a view of the water. In fact, the motel takes its name from the figural relationship of its crescent curve of 106 guest rooms to the two-story circular administration and restaurant building (a figure better appreciated from a seagull's-eye view than at street level). Typical of American modern architecture in the 1950s, Price's design stresses economy of means and direct expression of its reinforced concrete structural frame, its cross walls of concrete masonry blocks, and its infill of sliding glass doors. The Seahorse superseded the **Miramar Courts** (1928, Andrew C. Fraser), built by Mrs. Moody's father-in-law, W. L. Moody, Jr.

2119 27th Street   H–1
Ménard Park Bandstand

1950, R. R. Rapp

R. R. Rapp's modernistic reinforced concrete bandshell, which backs up to Seawall Boulevard, is located in Menard Park. Acquired by the City of Galveston in 1915, it is one of the few green parks in the city. Menard Park lies at the southern end of the corridor that stretches north beyond Broadway, identified since the Reconstruction period with African-American Galvestonians. This corridor is a curious urbanistic phenomenon, since it goes underground, so to speak, in order to circumvent the prestigious Avenue O-O 1/2 residential corridor, resurfacing at Avenue P and continuing south to the Seawall. From as early as the 1930 until the end of segregation, the stretch of beachfront facir Menard Park was, by custom, reserved for African-Americans. In addition to the bandstand, the park contain a World War II–era USO Building facing 27th Street.

2501 Seawall Boulevard   H–1
Flagship Hotel

1965, Neuhaus & Taylor with Thomas M. Price

It is difficult to visualize anything less imaginative architecturally than the boxlike, seven-story Flagship Hotel built by Houston developer James E. Lyon on top of what used to be Galveston Municipal Pleasure Pier (1943, R. R. Rapp). At 1,130 feet in length, the streamlined modernisti Pleasure Pier was to have been the Gulf Coast's ultimate amusement pier. It contained a dance hall, a 2,000-seat open-air arena, an open-air aquarium, restaurants and othe concessions, and a fishing pier. Built by the City of Galveston, it was under construction when the United States entered World War II. Pleasure Pier was requisitione by the U.S. Army and Navy for storage space. After belatedly opening in 1944, it proved far less popular than ad been anticipated because so little of its enclosed space was open to the prevailing breeze. In 1947, the city leased it o W. L. Moody, Jr., the Maceo interests, and Herbert S. Autrey, who air-conditioned it. In the late 1940s, Pleasure Pier enjoyed its autumn summer of popularity, before cars decisively replaced trains, motels replaced tourist courts, and television and rock 'n roll replaced live performances of big band music, driving Pleasure Pier into insolvency. Hurricane Carla in 1961 delivered the *coup de grâce*. What was left of Pleasure Pier's superstructure was scraped away, and the city leased the pier, with its closely spaced concrete columns, to Lyon for construction of the present building.

remont Street and Seawall Boulevard   H–12

Galveston Seawall and Grade Raising Monument
1904, General H. M. Robert, Alfred Noble, and H. C. Ripley, consulting engineers

This pair of Texas granite piers commemorates completion of the Galveston Seawall and the subsequent grade-raising of the island city. As the design of the commemorative piers implies, what the Seawall lacked was architectural imagination. Built at the height of the City Beautiful movement, it should have been a splendid *corniche*, a coastal boulevard with urban design, landscaping, and architectural embellishments commensurate with its status as the seafront promenade of what was then Texas's only coastal city. Instead, Seawall Boulevard became the setting for a southern version of Atlantic City and Coney Island.

Prior to construction of the Seawall, the city coasted directly down onto the beach. Thus, the great Victorian monument of the Galveston seafront was located on what subsequently became the Seawall. N. J. Clayton's extraordinary Beach Hotel (built 1883, burned 1898) backed up to the corner of Avenue Q 1/2 and 24th Street. Today, it would be in the middle of the boulevard between Tremont and 24th.

2228 Seawall Boulevard   H–13

Buccaneer Hotel (now Moody House, Edgewater Methodist Retirement Community)
1929, Andrew Fraser

The blocks of Seawall Boulevard between Tremont and 21st Streets tenuously preserve a spatial sense of the Seawall as an urban promenade. The Seawall was at its height during the Roaring '20s. The full-block-wide, three-story-high, Spanish Mission–style Crystal Palace entertainment establishment between Tremont and 24th (1916, Orlopp & Orlopp) was complemented by a huge, block-long roller coaster structure at Tremont and Avenue P 1/2, and at 22nd and Seawall lay the Tokio Roller Skating Rink. In the midst of this nexus of fun, W. L. Moody, Jr., built the 11-story, 400-room Buccaneer Hotel, its coffee shop featuring a novel "iced-air arrangement": a proto-air-conditioning system. During the expansive 1920s, Moody began the National Hotel Company, which provided management services for (and in some cases owned outright) major urban hotels in Texas and other Southern states. During the worst years of the Great Depression, National Hotels became the vehicle for Conrad N. Hilton to recover from the loss of his initial hotel chain, before going on to form the Hilton Hotels Corporation.

Fraser made the most of the Buccaneer's tight, awkward site, where the diagonal of Seawall Boulevard slices across the Groesbeck grid. In a way that was both expedient and urbane, he spatialized the overlap of street and shore. Anticipating Tom Price's curve at the Seahorse, Fraser organized guest rooms along double-loaded corridors that turn in response to the street plan outside, narrowing down to a dramatic knife's edge at the Avenue Q–Seawall intersection. At sidewalk level, Fraser faced the entire block front on Seawall with a tall brick arcade, above which special-function rooms and open and closed decks were located. Cast concrete ornament at the top of the building economically signals the Buccaneer's Spanish architectural theme, as does the cast concrete relief plaque atop the chamfered corner arcade bay at Tremont and Seawall of a galleon under sail.

In 1962, the Moody Foundation gave the Buccaneer to the Methodist Homes for Older People, which converted it into apartments for the elderly (1963, Cameron Fairchild).

Both Andrew Fraser and photographer Mary Clayton, N. J. Clayton's daughter, were residents of the Edgewater in their later years. In 1994 plans were announced to demolish the hotel tower, leaving only the base of the Buccaneer intact, because construction of a new apartment building would be more economical than bringing the Buccaneer into conformance with health and safety codes. Loss of the Buccaneer would inflict a grievous wound on Seawall Boulevard.

2219 Seawall Boulevard   H–14
Murdoch's Bathhouse
1962

Murdoch's is the grand old man among Galveston's beachfront piers. After being destroyed in the Storm of 1900, it was rebuilt in 1901 to the designs of the Chicago architects McAfee & Duncan. The Storms of 1909 and 1915 were so violent that reconstruction was required after each. Hurricane Carla in 1961 destroyed it again, which led Sam S. Serio, an associate of the Maceo brothers, to build the present replacement (repaired once again following Hurricane Alicia in 1983). Like the other post-Carla piers, Murdoch's is quite modest: an oblong wood shed, built several steps above the Seawall and carried out over the Gulf on wood pilings. Its modest size and lack of architectural pretension stand in contrast to Galveston's late-19th- and early-20th-century piers, which could accommodate diverse activities and very large crowds. Photographs from the 1920s, when the International Pageant of Pulchritude (a Miss Universe–like beauty contest held between 1920 and 1931) occurred, show the Seawall and its piers packed with merrymakers.

Next door to Murdoch's, at 2205 Seawall, is the **Mermaid Pier** (1962), which follows a similar architectural format. Farther down the Seawall, at 2107 Seawall, is the most famous of the 20th-century piers, the Maceo brothers' **Balinese Room** (1963). As its suburban, Trader Vic's–style decoration suggests, it too is post-Carla. Begun as Maceo's Grotto, then remodeled, first as the Sui Jen, then in 1948 as the Balinese Room, this was Galveston's premier nightclub and gambling casino of the post–World War II era. Because it was built on a pier, the Maceos could hide all evidence of gambling by the time law enforcement officials made it from the entrance on Seawall Boulevard to the gaming rooms at the far end of the structure. After gambling was suppressed in 1957, the Balinese Room lost its allure and its customers.

From a passing car, the piers look tacky. But from a pedestrian perspective, they break the monotony of the Seawall and make the beach and water accessible for those who are not dressed for swimming. They bring the beach up to the city and urbanize it. Therefore, as marginal as they are when compared with their elaborate predecessors, the piers make the experience of the sea front in the city an urban spatial event rather than merely a spectacle that is always seen from a distance.

2100 Seawall Boulevard   H–15
Moody Center
1957, George L. Dahl with Thomas M. Price

Although owned and operated by the City of Galveston since 1962, the Moody Center was built by the National Hotel Company as a corporate convention center. The Dallas architect George Dahl adjusted the building to its trapezoidal site much as Andrew Fraser did the Buccaneer. Dahl built the center up to the sidewalk, aligning the major interior spaces with Seawall Boulevard, so that as they project above the second-floor promenade level, they collide sculpturally with the Galveston grid. In this way, and through use of simple repetitive ornamental patterns, Dahl kept the largely windowless, boxlike center from having the urbanistic impact of an oppressive blob. The Moody Center was rehabilitated by Ford, Powell & Carson in 1979.

2024 Seawall Boulevard   H–16
Hotel Galvez
1911, Mauran & Russell

The *grande dame* of the Seawall is the six-story, 250-room Hotel Galvez. It was designed in the Spanish Mission style (which was especially associated with resort hotel and railroad station architecture in the southwestern United States in the 1900s and 1910s) to romantically evoke Galveston's nonexistent Spanish past. The Galvez was built by a syndicate of Galveston businessmen, headed by the Kempner brothers, to promote Galveston as a beach resort. It was designed by the St. Louis architects Mauran & Russell (who also designed the Rice Hotel in Houston and the Gunter Hotel in San Antonio, and were consulting architects for the Hotel Paso del Norte in El Paso) as a civic showplace.

The hotel was built at the corner of 21st and Avenue P, well back from Seawall Boulevard, so that a forecourt, originally planted with palm trees and oleanders, spreads out before it. This *tapis vert* (literally: green carpet) compensates for the lack of vegetation on the Seawall and spatially frames the massive, pyramidally composed hotel in an oasis-like setting. An arcade of oversized windows along the ground floor of the hotel, and the overhangs of the red tile roofs, spatially project an image of cool shade. As originally planned, guest rooms faced the water, while many of the north-facing rooms were reserved for hotel employees and services. The penthouse apartment, in the central tower, was where Sam Maceo lived in the 1930s and 1940s. Backing up to Avenue P is a monumentally scaled porte-cochère.

The Galvez was acquired by National Hotels in 1940, which added a motel wing to the east side of the building (1954, Andrew Fraser). During the 1970s the Galvez went into a decline before closing in 1978. In 1980 it was reopened and partially rehabilitated by John Kirksey Architects for a group of Houston investors.

The Galvez was bought by Mr. and Mrs. George Mitchell in 1993. For them, Ford, Powell & Carson have carried out a much-needed comprehensive rehabilitation, removing the most egregious additions of the 1950–1980s, restoring the main entrance to Seawall Boulevard, and recovering the cool simplicity of the hotel's spacious, ground-floor promenade. Mr. and Mrs. Mitchell even had Ford, Powell & Carson relocate a misplaced swimming pool, which is ingeniously tucked in beneath the original restaurant terrace, where it plays hide-and-seek with Seawall Boulevard.

No longer on the scene is the two-story, flat-roofed, modernistic building that the Galveston Artillery Club built at 19th and Avenue P (1934, Donald Barthelme), facing the Seawall. This was one of the first examples of modern architecture in Galveston.

1802 Seawall Boulevard   **H–17**

1913, Fred A. Langbehn, designer

Like the Sealy House at 53rd and Seawall, this much more modest house, designed and built by the shipping agent Fred A. Langbehn, is one of the rare private residences on the Seawall. It is a classic, early-20th-century Galveston house, with its weathered stucco surfaces and arched verandas. Photographs indicate that these architectural properties were once much more common along Seawall Boulevard than they are now. Note the piquant alley buildings that adjoin 18th Street, with their pair of peaked roofs. Langbehn's house attracted attention in Galveston because it rode out the Storm of 1915 with only minor damage. Langbehn attributed its durability to deep pile foundations and reinforced concrete construction.

Down the boulevard are the **Palms Motel** at 1628 Seawall (1969, Louis L. Oliver) and the **Treasure Isle Motel** at 1002 Seawall (1963, Ben J. Kotin & Tibor Beerman), both examples of modern motel design. Neither is in pristine condition. Ben Kotin and his brother Sol owned the Treasure Isle, and it is where Kotin maintained his architectural studio.

Note that in the **1200 block of Seawall,** where the boulevard curves, there is a change in the beach landscape. From this point east, the Gulf shore of Galveston Island is growing by accretion, thanks to the south jetty, which deflects wave-borne sand onto the shoreline. Not only is the level of the sand higher than farther down the beach, but beach vegetation is also in evidence.

802 Seawall Boulevard   **H–18**

S.S. Galveston Hotel Courts

1941, Ben Milam

The spirits of Pleasure Pier and Donald Barthelme's Artillery Club live on in Ben Milam's most vivacious Galveston building, the ship-shaped S.S. Galveston. Designed in the nautical modernistic style popular in the 1930s and early 1940s, the hotel, built for Hill Brothers, conforms to its oddly shaped site with a prowlike leading edge at 8th and L, from which Milam logically developed the rest of the building's streamlined design.

Here, near the point at which 6th Street and Broadway intersect Seawall Boulevard, a little colony of the old Seawall survives, displaying the type of modest tourist accommodations that preceded the arrival of the fully developed motel type. Note, at 1102 8th and Avenue K, the **Playground Courts** (1952, 1955), a sequence of hip-roofed, boxlike rooms-on-top-of-rooms.

These courts outlasted the Seawall's pioneer motel, formerly located at 528 Seawall and 6th, the modernistic Jack Tar Court (1940, John J. Croft, Jr., and H. S. Shannon; hotel addition, 1954, Thomas M. Price), built by E. C. Northen.

201 Seawall Boulevard   H–19

Sandpiper Motel

1963, Thomas M. Price

Here, where property was available next to Stewart Beach on the water side of the Seawall, Price designed this raised motel for Dr. Edmond A. Henderson. It is neatly constructed of back-to-back guest rooms, set atop a concrete substructure.

1401 East Beach Drive   H–20

The Galvestonian

1984, Lloyd Jones Brewer & Associates

The 13-story, 179-unit Galvestonian, a condominium apartment building designed by Houston architects Lloyd Jones Brewer & Associates for Jim Shindler Interests and Dr. Edmond A. Henderson, adapts the Seawall Boulevard S-curve plan to an open site facing the Gulf of Mexico, just behind the line of sand dunes on East Beach. The gently inflected slab shape of the Galvestonian figures strongly on its isolated site, amid beautiful wetlands, and gives what might have been an intrusive building a lyrical rhythm akin to the buildings of the Brazilian modern architect Oscar Niemeyer. Next door is an earlier venture by Dr. Henderson, the 14-story **Islander East** (1974, Swanson Hiester Wilson Boland).

From East Beach Drive, there are extraordinary vistas. To one side are immense oil supertankers, entering and exiting the Bolivar Roads, the channel between Galveston Island and the Bolivar Peninsula that leads to the Galveston and Houston ship channels. Out in the Gulf, one can see the spectral shapes of steel offshore oil and gas drilling platforms. These rise eerily in the tideland waters, imparting an implicit human presence to the open sea.

There are also vistas back to Galveston. The cluster of buildings at the University of Texas Medical Branch, the giant cranes of the container-loading docks, and Elevator B seem, in this perspective, to rise from a flat sea of tall, waving grass.

This landscape, all once part of Fort San Jacinto, was bought in 1984 by the Houston developer J. R. McConnell. McConnell retained architect Michael Graves to prepare a master plan for the 449-acre **Grand Reef** resort development, encompassing all the land between the beach and Apffel Park Road. Graves proposed a huge scheme, focused on an arc of 10 14-story apartment towers just east of the Galvestonian. Before construction commenced, McConnell's real estate empire collapsed in what became one of the epic events of the Texas real estate bust of the 1980s, the biggest title fraud scandal in U.S. real estate history. Consequently, the Mardi Gras Arch at Tremont and Strand remains Graves's only Galveston structure.

The Offatt's Bayou area is the one sector of Galveston penetrated by a freeway, which stops just short of 57th Street, where the Groesbeck town plan begins. It is the one sector that manages to look and feel like the 1960s-era suburban periphery of any small Texas city, palm trees and sand dunes notwithstanding. Missing is the spatial intimacy, particularity, and surprise that one encounters in Galveston's 19th-century neighborhoods. ⋔ ⋔ ⋔ The shores of Offatt's Bayou retain traces of their pre-suburban character in remaining "camp" shacks. It is interesting to observe how the seediness of Galveston's 19th-century neighborhoods has crept into some of the post-World War II neighborhoods ringing the bayou, imbuing them with a real Galveston feel. Moody Gardens, nearby, represents the paradox of late-20th century American urban planning. It seeks to avoid the confusion of suburban disorder through an internal regime of controlled design, maintenance, and access. But by cutting itself off from its surroundings, Moody Gardens forecloses any possibility of reforming and civilizing the larger suburban landscape. ⋔ ⋔ ⋔ Since the early 1980s, all of Galveston Island (with the exception of the separately incorporated resort community of Jamaica Beach) has been part of the City of Galveston. Yet once down island from Scholes Field, the municipal airport, and past the point where the Seawall ends, one leaves city and suburbs behind. Here, on West Beach, it is the larger shapes of land, water, and sky that prevail: the flat, green plain of the island; the constantly shifting formations of high, humid clouds; and glimpses of the Gulf of Mexico and West Bay along the low horizons. ⋔ ⋔ ⋔ Since the middle 1960s, the 20 miles between the end of the Seawall and San Luis Pass at the southwest tip of the island have become dotted with resort subdivisions. The Jamaica Resort Corporation and the Woodlands Corporation, both based in Houston, have been the primary developers of these subdivisions. They contain one- to three-story houses perched on high stilts to comply with hurricane-related code requirements. Houses face the Gulf in beachfront subdivisions, or they are aligned along finger canals accessible from West Bay that enable homeowners to dock boats at their back doors. ⋔ ⋔ ⋔ Jamaica Beach, one of the oldest resort communities, spans from the beach

The Interurban travels across the Galveston Causeway, 1934.

to the bay. Its cross-streets afford contrasting views of subdivision and wetland ecologies. Newer subdivisions, such as the Woodlands Corporations' Pirates Beach West and Laffite's Cove, combine environmentally mandated planning with an increasingly suburban ambiance. The protracted legal conflict that accompanied development of Laffite's Cove, following discovery there in 1975 of the most important Native American burial site along the Texas coast, indicates that in Galveston even "raw land" development has consequences for historic preservation. ♙ ♙ ♙ Along Termini Road, the continuation of Seawall Boulevard, the open landscape remains dominant. Resort subdivisions form discreet exceptions rather than a continuous blanket of sprawl. For the present, West Beach has escaped the fate of South Padre Island, farther down the Texas coast where shoulder-to-shoulder mid-rise condominiums wall off access to the Gulf. Here, you can still sense the immensity of Texas.

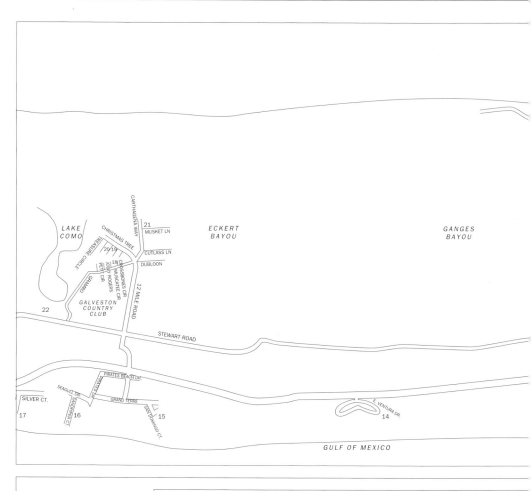

1. I–45 and Galveston Bay
2. 8522 Teichman Road
3. 7711 Broadway
4. 6801 Broadway
5. Calvary Cemetery: Mary A. Oppermann Vault and Goggan Vault
6. 1504 Driftwood Lane
7. 7202 Avenue N 1/2
8. 2100 block 69th Street
9. 65 Colony Park Circle
10. 63 Colony Park Circle
11. 2886 Dominique Drive
12. 81st Street and Hope Boulevard
13. 1700 Sydnor Lane
14. 12416 East Ventura Drive
15. 4228 San Domingo Court
16. 4246 Sandpiper Court
17. 4211 Rum Bay Circle
18. 3504 Cross Bones Circle
19. 3401 Muscatee Circle
20. 3425 Jolly Roger Circle
21. 13824 Musket Lane
22. 14520 Stewart Road
23. 18503 East DeVaca Lane
24. 18807 West DeVaca Lane
25. 19134 Kahala Drive
26. 22609 Kennedy Drive

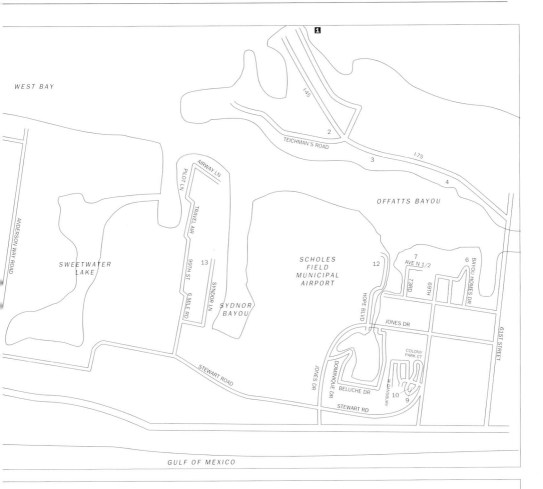

WEST BAY

TEICHMAN'S ROAD

I-45

I-75

OFFATTS BAYOU

AIRWAY LN

PILOT LN

TRAVEL AIR

ANDERSON WAY ROAD

SWEETWATER LAKE

99TH ST

6 MILE RD

SYNDOR LN

13

SCHOLES FIELD MUNICIPAL AIRPORT

SYDNOR BAYOU

12

7
AVE N 1/2

73RD

69TH

6
BAYOU HOMES DR

61ST STREET

HOPE BLVD

JONES DR

JONES DR

DOMINIQUE DR

COLONY PARK CT

LANSBURY

BELUCHE DR

10

9

STEWART ROAD

STEWART RD

GULF OF MEXICO

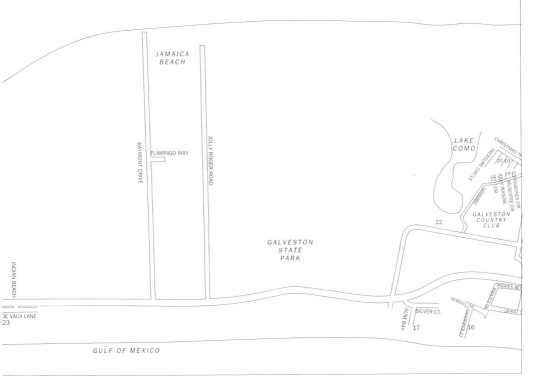

JAMAICA BEACH

BAYMONT DRIVE

FLAMINGO WAY

JOLLY ROGER ROAD

LAKE COMO

CHRISTMAS TR

TREASURE CIRCLE

20 19

CROSSBONES CIR

JOLLY ROGERS

MUSCATEE CIR

BELT CIR

HABARD

GALVESTON COUNTRY CLUB

22

GALVESTON STATE PARK

INDIAN BEACH

DE VACA LANE
23

RUM BAY

SILVER CT.

17

SEAGULL DR

SANDDOLLAR CT

16

PIRATES BEA

BRAZEN

GRAND T

GULF OF MEXICO

I-45 and Galveston Bay   I–1
Galveston Causeway
1911, Concrete and Steel Engineering Company
Galveston Bay was first bridged in 1860 by the Galveston,
Houston & Henderson Railroad, which constructed a
railroad trestle, nearly two miles long, from Virginia Point
on the mainland to the island, carried on piles driven into
the shallow depths of Galveston Bay. It was supplemented
by other railway trestles and, in 1893, by a wagon bridge
constructed by Galveston County. This incorporated a
drawbridge, to permit passage of shallow-draft bay vessels.
The Storm of 1900 destroyed all these bridges. Temporary
railroad bridges were built, but not until 1906 did planning
begin for a permanent replacement, the present Causeway.
Built by Galveston County, the major railroad corporations
serving Galveston, and the Stone & Webster Engineering
Corporation (which controlled the streetcar systems in both
Galveston and Houston and built the Galveston-Houston
Electric Railway's Interurban to provide high-speed, mass
transit between the two cities), the Causeway integrated rail,
streetcar, and motorcar transportation. A 100-foot-long steel
lift bridge facilitated the passage of bay vessels.

The Causeway is a two-mile long, reinforced concrete
viaduct, set 12 1/2 feet above mean high tide. Its succession
of elliptical arches, which seem to span just above the
water's surface, gives it an extremely elegant aspect. The
Storm of 1915 undermined the approaches at both ends of
the Causeway, but the viaduct rode out the storm, as it has
subsequently hurricanes.

Today, the 1911 Causeway functions as a railroad bridge
and a fishing pier. The Interurban ceased service in 1936, by
which time the volume of car and truck traffic competing
for use of the Causeway (the first paved highway between
Galveston and Houston opened in 1928) made a separate
vehicular bridge imperative. One of the best things about the
1939 causeway, and its 1961 supplement, is that they give
motorists a good view of the classic 1911 Causeway.

8522 Teichman Road   I–2
Galveston County Publishing Company Building
1965, Howard Barnstone & Eugene Aubry with William
Ginsberg & Associates
Shortly before Houston architect Howard Barnstone
published *The Galveston That Was,* he and his partner,
Eugene Aubry, completed this office and production
complex for the *Galveston Daily News.* Architecturally, the

suburban News Building economically expresses its board-
formed, cast-in-place, reinforced concrete construction.
Columns, beams, and concrete Ts, which form the roof
structure, constitute a frame that is infilled with spandrels of
painted concrete block on the first floor, painted concrete
on the second floor, and aluminum-framed window walls.
On the long east and west sidewalls of the building, precast
concrete-panels are suspended from the roof edge to shield
window glass. The triangular haunches, where the columns
tie into the roof structure, were designed to portray
expressively the necessity of resisting hurricane-force winds.
The whole complex sits on top of an artificial mound to
protect it from hurricane floods.

There is something tense and uneasy about the
architecture of the News Building. Its gestural elements are
overstated and underdetailed. Consequently, the building
lacks the assurance characteristic of Barnstone & Aubry's
work. Even so, it is important as a work of corporate
patronage produced by the architect who was instrumental
in awakening Galveston to its architectural patrimony.

Adjacent to the News Building are a string of residential
areas lining the north shore of Offatt's Bayou. At **9111
Teichman Road** (1995, Randall Porterfield Architects) is a
bayou house based on classic Texas coastal prototypes. At
8219 Teichman Road (1950, Charles L. Zwiener) is a
raised ranch-type house, a portent of the suburbanization of
Offatt's Bayou that began in the 1950s.

7711 Broadway   I–3
John's Oyster Resort
1928, Stowe & Stowe
The orange blush paint job, installed by a Houston
restaurateur, distracts from the unpretentious ambiance of
John's Oyster Resort. George and Elwood Stowe's Spanish
Mission detail was out of date when they designed John's for
John Lozica next to the Interurban's Oyster stop. But they
managed to spatialize a quintessential Gulf Coast feel in the
high-raised, stucco-faced building, with its big windows and
its rear dining porch, which overlooks Offatt's Bayou.

6801 Broadway   I–4
1963, Thomas M. Price
Before Galveston outgrew the Groesbeck town plan,
Galveston families established "camps" around the edge of
Offatt's Bayou as weekend retreats. Price's sleekly profiled
cottage, raised on an exposed concrete frame, succinctly

modernized the camp shack type.

Connecting Interstate 45 to the beach is Galveston's major north-south thoroughfare, **61st Street.** Despite the recent planting of palm trees and the fact that the street bridges Offatt's Bayou, 61st is a classic suburban strip. At 301 61st Street and Avenue R is the site of the Maceo brothers' famous roadhouse, the Hollywood Dinner Club (1926, R. R. Rapp). It burned in 1959 and was not rebuilt.

alvary Cemetery   **I–5**
Mary A. Oppermann Vault
885, N. J. Clayton

alvary Cemetery
Goggan Vault
884

Calvary Cemetery was acquired by Bishop Nicholas A. Gallagher between 1882 and 1883 to supplement Catholic Cemetery on Avenue K, which was beginning to fill up. It is now the sole spatial reminder that, until after the midpoint of the 20th century, this was a rustic landscape. The cemetery, which is entered off 65th Street, contains three High Victorian mortuary vaults that have managed to survive their isolated and exposed setting.

N. J. Clayton's magnificent, domed, High Victorian vault, built by the real estate investor Gustav Oppermann for his first wife, is the cemetery's outstanding work of architecture. It is detailed with crisp Italian Renaissance classical decor, which contrasts with the weathered cement plaster finish of the structure.

Across the lane, slightly to the north, is the burial place of **N. J. Clayton.** When Clayton died in 1916, his widow was so poor that she could not afford what she considered a proper gravestone. In 1983, historian and Clayton enthusiast Bob Nesbitt had the present headstone installed.

The **Goggan** family vault is finished in white-painted plaster. It is tempting to attribute the domed Victorian Gothic structure to Clayton, since he did work for various members of the Goggan family, but the attribution cannot be substantiated.

South of the Oppermann and Goggan vaults is the **Società Italiana di Mutuo Soccorso,** which is dated 1888. The central bay of the structure is a white-painted Victorian Gothic structure with a stepped dome.

1504 Driftwood Lane   **I–6**
1968, Ford, Powell & Carson
In the 1960s, Driftwood Lane became the preferred address of Galveston's elite, the successor to Broadway, Avenue O, and Caduceus Place. Houses on the north side of the street have frontage on Offatt's Bayou. This north-side house, designed by the San Antonio architects Ford, Powell & Carson, exemplifies the modern "Texas regional" house type that O'Neil Ford and his partners propagated in the 1960s. Counterthrust shed roofs establish the shifting center line of the house, which lies behind a self-effacing street front totally dedicated to the car. Walls of dun-colored brick provide privacy and contrast with the exposed-wood roof structure and wood infill panels. Scale, proportions, and detail have all been considered. Nearby are two modern houses designed in the 1960s by Ben J. Kotin & Tibor Beerman, the Clark W. Thompson House at **1616 Driftwood Lane** and the two-story house at **6808 Driftwood Lane.**

7202 Avenue N 1/2   **I–7**
Bayou Club
Date undetermined
Serving Galvestonians who don't have their own camps, this raised wooden building with a screened veranda represents the classic type of the camp shack. It is a type that has become endangered because of the desirability, and consequent rise in price, of bayou shore real estate, as is evident next door, the former site of the Kempner family camp.

2100 block 69th Street   **I-8**
Gymnasium and Auditorium
Island Elementary School (now Gladneo Parker
Elementary School)
1960, Thomas M. Price
Price's folded-plate roof structure, architecturally integrated
with the supporting columns, is the constituent feature of the
Island School gym. It originally served a school-on-stilts, built
with concrete lift-slab technology and designed by George
Pierce–Abel B. Pierce of Houston in association with O'Neil
Ford and Richard S. Colley (1954, demolished 1978).

65 Colony Park Circle   **I-9**
1974, Brian Hendricks
This French pavilion-like suburban house, designed by the
Beaumont architect Brian Hendricks for Mr. and Mrs.
Gene Wyatt, lies in the subdivision of Colony Park. Colony
Park was the site of Island Homes, the Housing Authority
of the City of Galveston's low-income project for white
families. After federal civil rights legislation was passed in
the mid-1960s outlawing racial segregation, the Housing
Authority depopulated Island Homes and sold its site for
redevelopment as an affluent, treeless, residential enclave.

63 Colony Park Circle   **I-10**
1977, S. I. Morris Associates
Eugene Aubry designed this austere, gable-roofed, brick-
planed house, which stands out amid the low ranch-house
rooflines of Colony Park. Among the other designed houses
in Colony Park are **3 Park Lane** (1972, P. M. Bolton
Associates) and **10 Dansby Court** (1977, Louis L. Oliver).

2886 Dominique Drive   **I-11**
1983, Louis L. Oliver & Tibor Beerman
Havre Lafitte is a typical middle-income Texas subdivision
of the 1960s: no trees, wall-to-wall ranch-type houses, and

the omnipresent texture of Mexican brick. It is a spatial
photocopy of Colony Park and Westwood. Exceptions to
the architectural rules are rare. In Havre Lafitte, most of the
exceptional houses are along the west shore of the artificially
made Lake Madeline. These include the remodeled ranch
house at **2946 Dominique Drive** (1987, Leslie Barry
Davidson), the house at **2930 Dominique Drive** (1972),
the Sol Druss House at **2922 Dominique Drive** (1966,
Louis L. Oliver), the Dr. Thomas S. Allen House at **2908
Dominique Drive** (1966, Todd Tackett Lacy; addition,
1987, Jack W. Morris), the Dr. Stephen L. Lewis House at
2902 Dominique Drive (1968), and, the most imposing,
the house at **2886 Dominique Drive.**

81st Street and Hope Boulevard   **I-12**
Moody Gardens
Visitor Center, IMAX 3D Theater, and Rainforest Pyramid
1992–93, Morris Architects
The Moody Gardens, the Moody Foundation's major project
of the 1980s and 1990s, is a 19th-century pleasure garden
reinterpreted as a late-20th-century ecological theme park.
Set on a 142-acre site along the south edge of Offatt's Bayou,
extracted from what had been the grounds of the World War
II–era Galveston Army Airbase (now Scholes Field
Municipal Airport), Moody Gardens combines a sequence of
landscaped outdoor recreational areas, a Convention and
Conference Center (1991, Morris Architects), and Hope
Therapy with the IMAX 3D theater and the Rainforest
Pyramid. The architecture of the Visitor Center–Theater
complex and the Convention Center aims to be lighthearted.
Their lyricism seems strained, however, and not entirely
persuasive. The dramatic Rainforest Pyramid is the most
architecturally assured work in the complex. Its 10-story
height makes it a striking landmark from across the island.
Yet inside, it recedes above the intensely planted tropical
tableaux that Moody Gardens has installed. Pete Ed Garrett,
Morris's designer, pays tribute to both I. M. Pei's glass
pyramid at the Louvre in Paris and Emilio Ambasz's Halsell
Conservatory in San Antonio in the shape and horticultural
content of the Rainforest Pyramid. John Kriegel, Moody
Gardens's staff horticulturist and a specialist in saline-tolerant
plantings in semitropical climates, is responsible for the
profuse landscape installations.
    As yet unrealized is the most awesome design vision for
Moody Gardens, which will give the complex world

tature. This is the **Gardens of Man,** designed by the great British architect and landscape architect Sir Geoffrey Jellicoe (1984–85). Jellicoe at first proposed an extraordinary series of gardens that would have covered most of the site. These were based on the epic poem "De rerum natura" by the classical Roman poet Lucretius and were to represent the history of the world from the perspective of plants. Because the expense was more than the Moody Foundation could sustain, Jellicoe produced a greatly reduced proposal for a linked series of gardens and landscapes to represent the history of garden design. These are scheduled to be installed in the final phase of Moody Gardens's development, in 2003.

Moody Gardens is a curious place. It is a secure controlled enclave, pristine and immaculate, overlaid with a veneer of education, therapy, and ecological consciousness. Yet it feels disconnected from, rather than engaged with, its site and the rest of Galveston.

12416 East Ventura Drive   I-14
1991, Carlos Jiménez

Situated at one edge of the small beach subdivision of Spanish Grant is this modest, purple-blue beach house designed by Carlos Jiménez. He minimally reinterpreted the Galveston beach house-on-stilts type to emphasize the profile of the small blue building against the expanse of sky and sea, which is so apparent outside the city.

700 Sydnor Lane   I-13
Galveston Island Municipal Golf Course Club House
1976, Louis L. Oliver & Tibor Beerman

Galveston's municipal golf course occupies acreage in a sector of town haphazardly laid out on the west shore of Sydnor Bayou. In this unpromising setting, Oliver & Beerman's Club House stands out as an accomplished work of architecture. A low-pitched, standing-seam metal roof shelters its components, which are organized in an L-plan configuration atop a planted berm. Yellow glazed-brick walls give the building a lilting tone and penetrate the deep shadows cast by the roof overhang.

Nearby, at **9902 Airway Lane,** is a tall, white-stucco-surfaced house facing Offatt's Bayou by Houston architect Tim Cisneros (1989).

Farther west along Stewart Road, west of Sweetwater Lake, one of the many bodies of water that penetrate the north shore of Galveston Island, is Eight Mile Road. Near the north end of Eight Mile Road is Sportsman Road, which contains an isolated string of houses facing Galveston Bay and backing up to island wetlands. At **12000 Sportsman Road** is a substantial, high-set house by the Houston architect Carlos Jiménez (1996). It is bent in plan to afford panoramic views across the bay to the Deer Islands, Tiki Island, and Texas City.

4228 San Domingo Court   I-15
1986, Ray Bailey Architects

Built to replace a house destroyed in Hurricane Alicia in 1983, this substantial house, located at Pirates Beach, makes a postmodern nod to older Galveston traditions in the exaggerated lattice arch that spans beneath the second-floor balcony facing the beach. The shape of the house and its rooftop cupola pay homage to the pre-Alicia house. These are identifying elements of a series of Galveston beach houses built by the client's professional associates. At **4203 San Domingo** is another beach house by Ray Bailey Architects.

4246 Sandpiper Court I-16

1986, W. O. Neuhaus Associates

Also located in Pirates Beach, this house by the Houston architect Bill Neuhaus features sharply planed geometries that rotate out in plan, and step-in in section, to respond to the curve of a cul-de-sac. Ray Bailey's first Galveston beach house is nearby at **4224 Spoonbill Court** (1979).

4211 Rum Bay Circle I-17

Far Niente

1995, Ray Bailey Architects

The Houston architect Ray Bailey is especially identified in Galveston with his beach and bay houses for Houston clients. This traffic-stopping house in Pirates Beach West appears at first glance to be an optical illusion, or the aftermath of an architectural head-on collision. Far Niente is, however, a spatial demonstration of the late-20th-century movement in American architecture called "deconstruction." The peculiarly angled wall and roof planes recharge the old Galveston penchant for exuberant eccentricity.

3504 Cross Bones Circle I-18

1991, W. O. Neuhaus Associates

On the bay side of the island, Pirates Cove was developed by George Mitchell on the former Sealy-Stewart ranch. Lake Como was dredged to become a basin for pleasure craft, which can sail into finger canals along which house sites cluster. At the end of one such street, Neuhaus produced a variation on the house he designed in Pirates Beach. Here, it is a taut planar front that faces the street, rather than the narrow end of the house. Neuhaus incorporated such Galvestonian touches as lattice screens and even a panel of

fish-scale shingles framing the deeply recessed entrance alcove.

Nearby, at **14055 Grambo Boulevard,** facing the golf course of the Galveston Country Club, is Houston architect Virginia Kelsey's abstraction of a raised Creole cottage of the Louisiana bayou country (1994).

3401 Muscatee Circle I-19

1983

This modern bay house is simple, yet very compelling, especially in the manipulation of solid and void relationships. A generously sized screened porch is elevated for views over tidal wetlands to Delehide Cove.

3425 Jolly Roger Circle I-20

1994, Natalye Appel

This striking bay house is long and tall, a picturesque accumulation of taut shapes that provides a strong spatial edge on its cul-de-sac street. The Houston architect Natalye

Appel deftly organized the house so that it seems poised between the street, on one side, and the network of narrow canals on the other. What she achieves is a kind of spatial density that makes the lanes and canals of Pirates Cove feel urban rather than blandly suburban, although the spontaneous character of the house gives it an air appropriate to its resort setting. Across the canal at **3412 Petit Circle** is a bay house by Ray Bailey Architects.

3824 Musket Lane   **I–21**
1990, Charles Tapley Associates

The Heffron House at 503 17th Street in the East End was the model for the water front of this bay house, designed by the Houston architect Charles Tapley. It represents a rare instance where modern resort architecture in Galveston invokes a bona-fide Galveston prototype. The house occupies an excitingly exposed location on the edge of Delehide Cove.

4520 Stewart Road   **I–22**
Isla Ranch House
1926, Atlee B. & Robert M. Ayres

The prolific San Antonio architects Robert Ayres and his father, Atlee, designed the core of this now much enlarged and altered house for Eugenia Taylor and George Sealy, Jr., on what was, in the 19th century, Marcus L. Mott's down-island ranch on the shore of Lake Como. From 1933 until 1944, the ranch was owned by Maco Stewart, founder of the Stewart Title Company, and, after the elder Stewart's death, by his son, Maco Stewart, Jr. Both expanded the Sealys' small house with multiple homemade additions. After Maco Stewart, Jr., gave the property to the University of Texas Medical Branch, the house became the residence of

UTMB's dean. Since 1967 it has been owned by George Mitchell's Mitchell Development Corporation.

Around the bend in Stewart Road is the **Mary Moody Northen Amphitheater,** built by the Moody Foundation for the production of outdoor musicals and now part of Galveston Island State Park (1977, P. M. Bolton Associates). **Galveston Island State Park** (entered at 13 1/2 Mile Road and Termini Road) occupies 2,000 acres of the Mott-Sealy-Stewart ranch and spans from Dana Cove and Carancahua Cove on Galveston Bay to the Gulf of Mexico. Most of the site is a nature preserve, but the beachfront has been developed for public recreation. Architectural improvements, including the Main Concession Building (1974), are the work of the Texas City architects Joseph Allen Hoover & Robert Edward Morgan.

Down island from the park is the city of Jamaica Beach, a resort development begun by the Jamaica Resort Corporation in the mid-1960s. Contrasting with the South Sea Islands Contemporary–style of its earliest houses is the bay house at **16716 Flamingo Way** (1996) by Lonnie Hoogeboom & Blair Satterfield of Houston.

18503 East DeVaca Lane   **I–23**
1986, Anthony E. Frederick

Elegant understatement and the Galveston beach house tend to be mutually exclusive categories. An exception is this house, designed by the Houston architect Anthony E. Frederick for a Galveston-born client in Indian Beach. Frederick adapted a Louisiana Creole raised prototype for this precisely composed, beautifully proportioned house. Its low-pitched hipped roof and dark green lattice screens are redolent of old Galveston. Note that the community tennis court in Indian Beach is walled with oleanders, in the best Caduceus Place manner.

18807 West DeVaca Lane   I–24

c. 1990

Like the beach house that Anthony Frederick designed on East DeVaca, this Indian Beach house relies on profile, proportion, and understatement to make its point. The way that the diagonal of the front entrance stair qualifies the symmetry of the house front subtly animates the architecture, in contrast to the exhibitionism that predominates in this and other affluent beach subdivisions. At **18903 West DeVaca Lane** is a cubic, white-stucco-faced beach house by the Galveston architect David Watson (1988).

19134 Kahala Drive   I–25

1994, Richard Fitzgerald & Partners

Richard Fitzgerald adapted, or, more precisely, abstracted, the beach house prototype at 4228 San Domingo Court in Pirates Beach for this calmly composed, gabled house with its lighthouse lantern.

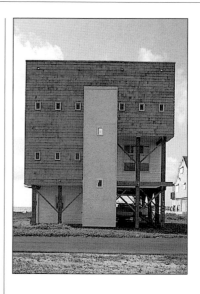

22609 Kennedy Drive   I–26

Highway House

1990, Natalye Appel

The first building that Natalye Appel designed when she went into independent practice was this beach house facing Termini Road in the Sea Isle subdivision. Because of its location, Appel called it the Highway House and conceived it as a series of buildings that changed in response to their surroundings. Therefore, the house is very different on its beach side. So articulately is this idea pursued that the small-scaled house is winsome without being cloying. Details such as the cabled balcony and stair rails are delicate without being overly refined; the interlocking volumes are thin but never fragile. Nearby at **22102** and **22106 Kennedy Drive** are two shingled houses, one green, the other blue, by Houston architect Burdette Keeland (1996).

Although buildings in Galveston exhibit great variety, most will fit within a basic type or typology (the more academic term), which is defined by the floor plan and shape. The following types are among those most frequently seen in Galveston.

Shotgun cottage (Commissary house)

A one-room-wide cottage with rooms arranged in file, one after the other. The narrow end of the house and entrance are on the street side. Three-room shotgun cottages are most common. Roofs are either gabled or hipped, and porches either attached or inset. In the South, this cottage type is associated with rental housing for low-income families. In Galveston pre-cut shotgun houses were dispensed for emergency housing through commissaries located in neighborhood wards after the 1900 hurricane – thus called commissary houses.

Front-gabled cottage

One or one-and-one-half story cottage, rectangular in shape, with the gable-end (and therefore, the narrow end of the house) turned toward the street. The interior floor plan sometimes contains a center hall flanked by two rooms, or, at other times, a side hall along a line of rooms—the placement of the main entrance reflects the floor plan. The house may be prefaced with an attached porch or inset veranda.

Side-gabled cottage with attached porch

One-story cottage, rectangular in shape, usually containing a center hall plan flanked by two rooms. Roof gables, which form an inverted V, are on the sides of the house. The main entrance is usually centered and protected by a porch that is attached to the building and not an integral structural element. The roof may have dormer windows giving the house an added half-story or attic space. These houses often have rear additions.

Gulf Coast cottage

One or one-and-one-half story cottage, usually with a center hall plan flanked by two rooms. The side-gabled roof may have dormer windows. The veranda is inset within the gabled roof, which is what distinguishes this house type from the side-gabled cottage with an attached porch. In other states along the Gulf of Mexico, the Gulf Coast cottage is sometimes called a Creole cottage.

I-house

Most often a two-story house with double front porches and a centrally placed main entrance. The term derives from the I-shape of the floor plan, which usually contains a center hall with one room to each side (and only one room deep). If the porches are attached to the house-front, it is a two-story version of the side-gabled cottage with attached porch. If the porch is inset beneath the roof, it is a two-story version of a Gulf Coast cottage.

Southern town house

A two-story house with double front porches, and a floor plan consisting of a side hall, entered from the street front, and running alongside a file of rooms. The front room usually has two windows opening onto the porch. The roofline tends to be low and may be hipped or gabled. This type of town house organization is associated with the London row house. In Southern cities, after the second quarter of the 19th century, such town houses were built as free-standing houses (rather than row houses), and prefaced with double verandas.

Italianate house

So-called after the Italianate style, popular in the middle decades of the 19th century. Characteristic features are: blocky, cubical units; low roofline; wide overhanging eaves supported by prominent, decorative brackets; projecting window bays; numerous porches and balustraded balconies; and paired or grouped windows. In Galveston, such houses often are a modified version of the side-hall plan with only one window facing the street front and a minimal front porch.

L-front (or L-plan) Victorian cottage

A picturesque cottage popular in the last two decades of the 19th century, in which a bay projects forward from one side of the street elevation with a porch recessed alongside the bay, thereby forming an L-figure in plan. Even if the house contains a central hall with rooms to either side, the house front appears asymmetrical. Most L-front houses are one-story, but there are two-story examples.

Corner store

A commercial building (usually a grocery store), built on the sidewalk lines at a street corner in a residential neighborhood. Galveston corner stores tend to be two-stories, rectangular or almost square in shape with a hip roof. Originally, most had a one-story canopy extending to the curbline that shaded the sidewalk and the entrance, which usually was set in a diagonal chamfer at the corner of the building. Traditionally, the grocer's family lived on the second floor.

Southern church

A gable-roofed rectangular building with a central door flanked by two windows (sometimes a pair of doors instead) on the narrow, gable-ended street front, and five windows on the long side walls. A cupola or steeple often is centered on the gable crest at the front of the building. Openings are frequently pointed.

Commercial loft building

A storehouse or warehouse building of brick perimeter bearing-wall construction built on the sidewalk line of the street as part of a row of buildings. Unless located on a corner lot, it has windows and doors in the front and rear walls only, with solid side walls. The upper floors and roof are supported on structural posts, so that the interiors can be flexibly partitioned. Ground-floor doors open directly to the sidewalk, which is usually covered by a canopy in front of the building.

Beach house

A resort house, built at the beach or on the bay. It is raised a full story above grade on tall pilings, which is its distinguishing characteristic. All buildings down island from the end of the Seawall lie in the flood plain and are legally required to have their first floors raised 14 feet above sea level. The resulting ground-floor space must remain open.

arcade A covered walk or space open at one or both ends and supported by arched openings.

architrave See entablature.

arcuated Arched in shape.

ashlar Squared and finished building stone.

baluster, balustrade (pl.) A short, vertical column supporting a railing; (pl.) a series of balusters and the railing connecting them.

bay The division of a wall by similar vertical elements such as windows. The repeated division of a building design used in describing the structure, such as a five-bay-wide house which means the house has five openings on the front facade.

bay window A window that projects beyond the main wall plane.

board and batten Vertical plank siding with joints covered by narrow wood strips.

bracket A supporting member, often decorative, placed under an architectural overhang such as a cornice.

buttress An abutting pier that strengthens a wall.

canopy A roofed member extending outward from a building and providing protective covering. In Galveston, also called a shed.

capital The top part of a column.

cartouche An ornamental panel or tablet often in the form of a scroll with an inscription.

casement window A window hinged on the side, opening its entire length.

chamfered Cut at a diagonal.

clapboard Narrow, horizontal, overlapping wood boards used to cover the exterior of buildings.

coping The capping of a wall to provide a finish as protection against weather.

corbel Successive rows of masonry extending beyond a building wall.

cornice The projecting member where the wall and roof meet. See entablature.

dormer window A window that projects through a pitched roof.

double leaf A pair as in a pair of doors.

eave Lower part of a sloping roof that projects beyond the wall.

entablature The horizontal member at the top of a column. It is composed of the architrave (bottom), frieze, and cornice (top).

facade The principal face or front of a building, or any side of a building that faces open space.

fanlight A semicircular window over a door.

fascia A long, flat horizontal band.

finial A crowning ornament.

frieze See entablature.

frontispiece Decorative porch or doorway on the front facade of a building.

gable The triangular shape of a building wall above eaves level and formed by two sloping roof planes.

gable roof A roof formed by two sloping sides and appearing as an inverted V.

gablet A diminutive gable, usually used as a decorative device.

gallery A roofed passageway extending along an exterior wall, often supported by arches on the outer side.

hip roof A four-sided sloping roof.

lintel A horizontal member spanning an opening.

loggia A passage or gallery, colonnaded on one or both sides.

louvered A series of overlapping, usually movable, horizontal slats set in a frame. Louvred shutters are the traditional protective covering for window openings in Galveston.

mansard roof A roof that is double pitched on all four sides, the lower pitch being longer and steeper.

modillion A bracket used in a series under the soffit of a cornice.

muntin The small bars of wood that hold the glass panes in a window or door.

ogee Double- or S-curved.

ogival Pointed.

open-gabled When the section between the two slopes of a gable is not covered by a wall.

oriel A projecting window that extends from a building above ground level. (A bay window begins at ground level.)

parapet A low, retaining wall at the edge of a roof, terrace, or porch.

pediment The triangular gable end of a roof with an obvious horizontal cornice at the base of the triangle.

pier An upright support for a building or bridge; the supports between arches in an arcade. In Galveston, the word "pier" also applies to the structures built out into the water on both the Bay and the Gulf sides of the island.

pilaster A flat pier or column that projects only slightly from the wall.

pitch The slope of a roof.

planar Flat.

plinth The plain square member on which a column rests.

porch A covered platform attached to a building usually with a separate roof, to shelter an entrance.

portal A large door or entrance, usually the main entrance to a building.

port-cochere A covered shelter for vehicles attached to a building and at an entrance doorway.

portico A covered entrance or porch with a roof supported by columns.

quatrefoil An ornamental figure composed of four lobes.

quoin Dressed stone or masonry at the corners of a building.

raised In Galveston, the term means that a building is not resting on a foundation but rather, has been raised off the ground and placed on brick piers or a wooden framework.

rusticated Made to look like stone.

scored A plaster or concrete surface incised to look like masonry.

sidelights A pair of narrow windows flanking a door.

sill The lowest horizontal member of a window or door.

soffit The finished underside of any component of a building such as a lintel, arch, or cornice.

spandrel The horizontal band in a wall beneath a window or a line of windows.

spatialize To express or represent spatially.

spindle A short, turned piece of woodwork.

terra cotta Cast and fired clay units.

transom An opening above a door or window that is usually sashed and hinged, the latter for ventilation.

turret A small tower.

typology The systematic classification of buildings by floor plans and shapes.

veneer A thin layer of one material applied over another material.

veranda A long one- or two-story covered porch, often partly enclosed.

vergeboard The board under the roof edge of a gable, often decorated.

vernacular Showing characteristics of a specific locale or region.

General reading

Alperin, Lynn M. *Custodians of the Coast: History of the United States Army Engineers at Galveston.* Galveston: Galveston District United States Army Corps of Engineers, 1977.

Barnstone, Howard. *The Galveston That Was.* Photographs by Henri Cartier-Bresson and Ezra Stoller. New York: Macmillan Company and the Museum of Fine Arts, 1966. Reprinted Houston: Rice University Press, 1994.

Barthelme, Donald. "I Bought a Little City," *The New Yorker*, 50 (11 November 1974), pp. 42-44. (A fictional short story about Galveston.)

Beasley, Ellen. *The Alleys and Back Buildings of Galveston.* Houston: Rice University Press, 1996.

Beasley, Ellen. "The Corner Store of Galveston: A Family's Residence, A Neighborhood's Parlor," in *Center: A Journal for Architecture in America.* Distributed by University of Texas Press, Vol. 8, 1993, pp. 62-71.

Brindley, Anne A, editor. *Historic Galveston Homes.* Galveston: Galveston Historical Society, 1951.

Chapman, John. "Galveston," *The Southwest Review*, 15 (Winter 1930), pp. 145-176.

Christensen, Roberta Marie. *Pioneers of West Galveston Island.* Austin: Nortex Press, 1992.

Darst, Elisabeth F. and Douglas R. Zwiener. *A Guide to Historic Galveston.* Galveston: privately printed, 1966.

Eisenhour, Virginia. *Galveston, A Different Place: A History and Guide.* Galveston: privately printed, 1983.

Fornell, Earl Wesley. *The Galveston Era: The Texas Crescent on the Eve of Secession.* Austin: University of Texas Press, 1961.

Fox, Stephen. "Broadway: Galveston, Texas," in *The Grand American Avenue, 1850-1920,* edited by Jan Cigliano and Sarah Bradford Landau. San Francisco: Pomegranate Artbooks, 1994.

Henson, Margaret Swett. *Samuel May Williams, Early Texas Entrepreneur.* College Station: Texas A & M University Press, 1976.

Hyman, Harold M. *Oleander Odyssey: The Kempners of Galveston, 1856-1980s.* College Station: Texas A & M University Press, 1990.

McComb, David G. *Galveston: A History.* Austin: University of Texas Press, 1986.

Nesbitt, Robert. *Bob's Galveston Island Reader.* Galveston: privately printed, 1985.

Payne, Richard and Geoffrey Leavenworth. *Historic Galveston.* Houston: Herring Press, 1985.

Turner, Elizabeth Hayes. "Women, Religion and Reform in Galveston, 1880-1920," in *Urban Texas: Politics and Development,* edited by Char Miller and Heywood T. Saunders. College Station: Texas A & M University Press, 1990, pp. 75-95.

Publications about Specific Places

Eisenhour, Virginia. *The Strand of Galveston.* Galveston: privately printed, 1973.

Freeman, Martha Doty and Sandra L. Hannum. *A History of Fortifications at Fort San Jacinto, Galveston Island, Texas.* Austin: Prewitt & Associates, 1991.

Hafertepe, Kenneth. *A History of Ashton Villa: A Family and Its House in Victorian Galveston.* Austin: Texas State Historical Association, 1991.

Henson, Margaret Swett. *The Samuel May Williams Home: The Life and Neighborhood of an Early Galveston Entrepreneur.* Austin: Texas State Historical Association, 1992.

Jellicoe, Geoffrey Alan. *The Landscape of Civilisation Created for the Moody Historical Gardens.* Northiam, East Sussex, U. K.: Garden Art Press, 1989.

Lehman, Donald J. *Lucky Landmark: A Study of a Design and Its Survival: The Galveston Customhouse, Post Office, and Court House of 1861.* Washington, D. C.: General Services Administration Public Buildings Section, 1973.

Pinckard, Jane and Rebecca. *Lest We Forget: The Open Gates.* Houston: privately printed, 1988.

University of Texas Medical Branch at Galveston, A Seventy-Five Year History by the Faculty and Staff. Austin: University of Texas Press, 1967.

Publications about Planning and Preservation

Cable, Carol. *Architecture and Planning in Galveston, Texas.* Monticello: Vance Bibliographics, 1981.

Cheek, Lawrence W. "Galveston Defies the Odds," *Historic Preservation,* 41 (September-October 1989), pp. 28-35.

Dillon, David. "The Marvelous Mitchells of Galveston, Texas," *Historic Preservation,* 47 (September-October 1995), pp. 64-71.

Longo, Gianni, Jean Tatge, and Lois Fishman. *What Makes Cities Liveable? Learning from Galveston.* New Brunswick: Institute for Environmental Action, 1983.

Urban Design International, 2 (July- August 1981), issue on Galveston, published in conjunction with the Third International Conference on Urban Design, held in Galveston, 28-31 October 1981.

The authors would like to express their gratitude to the many individuals and organizations that have made preparation and publication of this guidebook possible. Our personal thanks to Joal and John Donovan; Ed Eubanks; Burke Evans; Sally and Jack Wallace; Alice and Larry Wygant; and Mary Jane and Charles Zwiener.

A special acknowledgment to Zula Mae Beasley, who over the last few years has developed a far greater interest in and commitment to Galveston architecture than she ever thought she would have.

Two generous foundations have made the research and writing of this book possible: Anchorage Foundation of Texas: Anne Schlumberger Bohn, president; Pierre M. Schlumberger, Jody Blazek, Edwin A. Eubanks, C. Leroy Melcher III, Pierre S. Melcher, and Marc C. Melcher, board members; and the Harris and Eliza Kempner Fund: Lyda Ann Q. Thomas, chairman, Ann O. Hamilton, vice chairman, John T. Currie, secretary/treasurer, Hetta T. Kempner, I.H. Kempner III, Rabbi James Kessler, Barbara W. Sasser, Daniel K. Thorne, and Peter K. Thompson, M.D., trustees, and Elaine Perachio, executive director.

The following individuals and firms have been invaluable in gathering details and data: Linda Acosta, TAMU; Lynda Alexander, UTMB; Ann Anderson; Natalye Appel, AIA; Mary Faye Barnes, Galveston County Historical Commission; Howard Barnstone, FAIA; Mr. and Mrs. Tibor Beerman; Robert J. Beliveaux; Kenneth Bentsen, FAIA; Sadie Gwin A. Blackburn; Peter H. Brink; Leonora Brown, City of Galveston; Patrick H. Butler, III; John S. Chase, FAIA; Mary Clayton; Mrs. Nicholas J. Clayton, Jr.; Margaret Culbertson, librarian, Architecture Library, University of Houston; Maury Darst; Dan O'Donahoe; Margaret Dorrance, Moody Mansion & Museum; Julia Dunn, Rosenberg Library; Laura and Tom Eisenhour; Stephen Engblom; Eubanks/Bohn Associates; Mrs. Sidney C. Farmer, Jr.; John Ferguson; Ford, Powell & Carson; Galveston County Clerk's Office; Casey Edward Greene, Galveston and Texas History Center, Rosenberg Library; Diana Hall; Shelly Henley-Kelly, Rosenberg Library; Mrs. Henry W. Hoagland; Christopher Hutson; George O. Jackson, Jr.; Arthur Jones, FAIA; Marilyn Marshall Jones; Virginia W. Kelsey, AIA; Mr. and Mrs. James Kempner; Mr. and Mrs. I. H. Kempner, III; Mary L. Kurtz; Mrs. A. D. Lasell; Andrew A. Loomis; Mrs. Gus Loomis; Graham B. Luhn, AIA; Gwen Marcus; Ann Masel; E. Sinks McLarty, Jr., M.D.; Barry Moore, FAIA; Morris•Architects; Robert Morris; Robert Nesbitt; Ross Novelli; Bobbie Oldfield; Louis Lloyd Oliver AIA; Joseph K. Oppermann, AIA; Randy Pace; Anna Peebler, Rosenberg Library; W. Irving Phillips, FAIA; Mary Anne Piacentini; Jane Burton Pinckard; Thomas M. Price, AIA; Diana J. Rasmussen; Rice University: Brown Art & Architecture Library and Government Documents and Mircomaterials, Fondren Library; Carol Roark, Dallas Public Library; Mildred Robertson; Evelyn F. Rosenthal; Beverly Rudy; Elisabeth D. Runge; Sandy Sheehy; Kenneth Shelton; John Sieber; Edward Simmen; Dr. and Mrs. Ray L. Simmons; Mr. and Mrs. Louis Sklar; John F. Staub, FAIA; Don Suderman; The Rev. David Tarbet; Texas and Local History Component, Houston Metropolitan Research Center, Houston Public Library; Texas Historical Commission; Leonora K. Thompson; Nancy P. Thompson; Robert Tucker; Michael Tracy; Drexel Turner; University of Texas, Austin: Architectural Drawings Collection and Eugene C. Barker Texas History Research Center; Emily Whiteside; Evangeline Loessin Whorton; Donald E. Willett.

Production of this guidebook has been made possible through the dedication and expertise of many including Susan Bielstein, Barrie Scardino, Ryan Hess, Shelly Hagen, Chuck Jackson, and our editor, Mary Sieber, of Rice University Press; graphic designers Mark Judson, Jeff Davis, and Paul Hera of Judson Design; photograph production of Greg Nowicki and Dean Stern of Hot Flash; Betty A. Massey, David Bush, Kathleen Hink, Olivia Meyer, and Anna Mod of Galveston Historical Foundation; Lars Lerup, dean, School of Architecture, Rice University; Bruce Webb, dean, College of Architecture, University of Houston.

Photo Credits and Notations

Documentary photographs courtesy Rosenberg Library, pages 2, 4, 5, 6, 7, 8, 14, 15, 62, 63, 121, 132, 162, 163, 210, 226 and 239. The 1894 photographs on pages 4, 6, and 198 were published in *Art Work of Galveston,* (Chicago: The W.H. Parish Publishing Co., 1894).

The Museum of Fine Arts, Houston, page 9.

Photographs for all individual tour entries were taken in 1995 and 1996 except A–124 (1992) and B–83 (1990).

Quotation Sources

The Roemer quotation on page 5 is from Ferdinand Roemer, *Texas with Particular Reference to German Immigration and the Physical Appearance of the Country,* trans. Oswald Mueller (San Antonio: Standard Printing Co., 1935), p. 40.

The "sands upon our beach" quotation on page 5 is from *Galveston City Directory, for 1868-1869,* C.W. Marston, compiler (Galveston: Shaw & Blaylock, 1868), p. vii.

The Ferber quotation on page 8 is from Edna Ferber, *A Kind of Magic* (Garden City: Doubleday, 1963), p. 102.

The Eisenhour quotation on page 14 is from Virginia Eisenhour, *The Strand of Galveston* (Galveston: privately printed, 1973), p. 1.

Adams, Gayle, 67
Adams, Joe, 67
Adams Architects, 67
Adickes, David, 22
Adjmi, Morris, 18
Adoue, Bertrand, 75
Adoue, Fanny Kempner, 221
Adoue Playground, Louis, 94
Adriance, Henry Trueheart, 180
Adriance, John, 115, 146
Adriance, John, II, 218
Adriance family, 113
Affleck, T. D., 129
African Baptist Church, 162, 166
Agin, Stanka, 92
Aiken, Marcia Allen, 107
Ainslie, Richard C., 44
Akokisa Indians, 4
Alamo Elementary School, 217
Albertson, Charles, 157
Allen, A. C., 187
Allen, Alexander A., 107-8
Allen, Edward Rudge, 190
Allen, Dr. Thomas S., 244
Allen, Winifred, 193
Amateis, Louis, 51, 58
Ambasz, Emilio, 244
American Indemnity Company, 54
American Institute of Architects, 112
American National Bank, 147
American National Insurance Company, 22, 35-37,
    108, 221
Ansell, Walter C., 171
Appel, Natalye, 246, 248
Aramco blinds, 118, 188
Armour & Company Building, 21
Armstrong, Josephine, 181
Armstrong, William T., III, 181
Arnold, Isadore, 139
Aronsen, Edwin P., 117
Artillery Club, 186-87, 235
Aschoff, H. C. L., 78
Aschoff, Mrs. H. C. L., 78
Ashbel Smith Hall (UTMB), 121, 127-28
Ashton Villa, 14, 56-57, 68, 150, 184
Atcheson, Topeka & Santa Fe Railway, 18, 57
Atkinson, Simon, 25
Aubry, Eugene, 18, 34, 128, 230, 242, 244
Austin, Edward T., 70-71, 170
Austin, Stephen F., 58, 70, 186, 190
Austin Junior High School, Stephen F., 160
Autrey, Herbert S., 233
Ave Maria Hall, St. Mary's Hospital, 126
Avenue L Missionary Baptist Church, 162, 166
Aves, Dr. Frederick W., 52
Ayres, Atlee B., 247

Ayres, Robert M., 247
Ayres, Walter F., 97

Baden, Ida D., 190
Bader, August, 183
Bailey, Thomas E., 114
Bailey Architects, Ray, 27, 245-46
Baldwin, Matthias H., 46
Balinese Room, 215, 234
Ball, George, 19, 53-54, 94, 113, 138
Ball, Mrs. George, 98
Ball, Hutchings & Company, 19, 24, 98, 184
Ball, Sarah Catherine Perry, 54
Ball High School, 54, 92, 205, 217
Ballinger, Carrie Mather, 185
Ballinger, William P., 169, 185-86, 192
Ballinger, Mrs. William P., 169
Ballinger & Jack Building, 43
Ballinger family, 185-86
Barbin, Earl, 42
Barker, Carlotta Morris, 102
Barker, David V., 33, 102, 187
Barnes, Benjamin F., 79
Barnes Institute, 162, 166
Barnstone, Howard, 9, 34, 56, 112, 128, 147, 202, 242
Barthelme, Donald, 108, 174, 188, 235
Batterson, Mary J., 76
Battle of San Jacinto, 109
Batts, Clara G., 145
Baulard, Victor J., 32, 59
Baum, Max, 195
Bauss, Theodore, 88
Baylor University, 51
Bayou Club, 243
Beach Hotel, 227, 233
Beerman, Tibor, 23, 41, 51, 54, 94, 124, 143, 145,
    221-22, 235, 244-45
Beers, William F., 97
Beissner, Frederick W., 98-99
Beissner, Henry, 98, 204-5
Belding, W. G., 173
Bell, Gracey W., 95
Bell, Wayne, 222
Bellis, A. J., 181
Belo, A. H., 34
Belo & Company, A. H., 83
Bennison, Hugh, 35
Bentinck, Henry W., 105
Bentsen Associates, Kenneth, 124, 126
Berlocher, John, 22, 31
Bernheim, Jacob S., 103
Bessie (lighter), 151
Best, Charles, 146
Best, Max, 146
Bethel Church, 175
Bevil, Dr. Cooper P., 91, 192

Biehl, Carl C., 112, 185

Biehler, C. Leopold, 180

Bishop's Palace (Gresham House), 111-13, 115

Black, Atkinson & Vernooy, 25

Black, Sinclair, 25

Blaisdell & Emerson, 45

Blanton, Joseph Edwin, 219

Blaylock, Louis, 77

Bleicke, Joseph, 144

Block, Louis, 100

Blocker, Dr. Truman G., Jr., 142

Blocker, Dr. Virginia, 142

Blum, Hennie (Mrs. I. H. Kempner), 113

Blum, Henrietta (Mrs. Leon H. Blum), 177

Blum, Hyman, 30

Blum, Leon & H., 30, 72, 107

Blum, Leon H., 30, 177

Blum, Sylvain, 30, 112

Blum Hardware Company, 22, 87

Blum Monument, Henrietta, 177

Boddeker, J. A., 93

Boepple, William G., 174

Bohn, George, 71

Bollinger, Thomas E., 75

Bolton Associates, P. M., 244, 247

Bolton Estate Building, 19

Booker T. Theater, 40

Borden, Gail, 126, 190

Borden, Thomas H., 190

Bossom, Alfred C., 37

Bottomley, Wagner & White, 26

Bottomley, William Lawrence, 26

Bourdelle, Pierre, 109-10

Bowden, M. C., 66

Brick Wharf Saloon, 86

Brink, Peter H., 32

Brink, Susan Silverman, 18

Briscoe, Birdsall P., 114

Broadway Baptist Church, 172-73

Brock, Anthony, 174

Brockelman, Joseph, 106

Bromberg, Dr., 116

Brooks, Bradley, 59

Brooks & Barr, 124

Brooks Barr Graeber & White, 124, 126

Brown, Alfred, 79

Brown, James M., 31, 56-57, 142

Brown, Matilda, 142

Brown, Rebecca Ashton, 57

Brown & Company Building, J. S., 24

Bryan, Guy M., 186

Bryan, Ron, 46

Bryan family, 185, 186

Buccaneer Hotel, 233-34

Buckhart, John T., 232

Buechner, Marie, 140

Bulger, Charles W., 27, 30, 31, 33, 38, 42-43, 74, 86, 88, 97, 102, 107, 112, 115-16, 137, 139, 140, 174, 191, 193, 204

Bulger & Son, C. W., 172-73

Bullacher, John, 167

Bullacher, Rudolph, 157-58

Bunting, Rev. R. F., 47

Burke, Edward, 76

Burke, John, 76

Burke, Katharine, 76

Burke, Mike, 76

Burke & Brothers Grocery, J., 76

Burns, Fred, 187

Burns, Pat, 187

Burr, Lemuel, 107

Burroughs, James M., 151, 155

Burton, Mr. and Mrs. Miles K., 219

Busch, Adolphus, 203

Butler, Patrick H., III, 59

Bütterowe, Henry, 170

Byrne, Bishop Christopher, 106, 111

Byrnes, James W., 52

C. B. Comstock (dredgeboat), 151

Caduceus Place subdivision, 211, 219-20, 247

Calvary Cemetery, 243

Cameron, Allen E., 82

Cameron, Mary, 82

Campbell, Archibald R., 116

Cannady, Jackson & Ryan, 35

Cannady, William T., 35

Caravageli, Dr. and Mrs. Menelaus, 219

Carnes, Howard, 152

Carroll, Rucker T., 146

Carruthers, Dr. William S., 81

Cartier-Bresson, Henri, 9, 20, 33, 75, 114

Carver Theater, 40

Casa del Mar, 230

Casteel, Asbury H., 88

Castle District, 112-13

Catholic Building, 36-37

Catholic Cemetery, 243

Catterall, Fred W., 140

Caudill Rowlett Scott, 38

Causeway, 239, 242

Cecere, Gaetano, 109-110

Cedar Lawn subdivision, 211, 214-16, 218

Cedar Lawn Apartments, 214

Cedar Terrace, 204

Center for Transportation and Commerce, 18

Central Christian Church, 189

Central High School (1924), 166

Central High School (1954), 205-6

Central Hotel, 39, 41, 46

Central Methodist Church, 55

Central Middle School, 205

Central Park, 14-15, 52, 54-55, 217

Central Plaza, 42
Century of Progress Exposition, 110
Chapman, Annie, 137
Chapman, Willoughby J., 110
Chapman & Duffield Bar & Billiard Saloon, 42
Chase, John S., 41, 206
Cheesborough, E. R., 137
Cherry, Wilbur, 85, 173
Chisolm, Benjamin G., 56
Christ Church (Houston), 172
Cisneros, Tim, 245
Cisneros Architects, 18
City Beautiful movement, 58, 233
City Cemetery, 162, 177
City Hall (1847), 5
City Hall (1916), 58-59
City Hall (Dallas), 58
City Hall and Market House (1888), 37, 58
City Hospital, 121
City Market, 37
City Market House (1847), 5
City National Bank, 38, 41-42
City of Galveston, 28, 57, 84, 115, 168, 183, 232, 234, 238
Civil War, 5-6, 20, 24-25, 44, 47-49, 62, 66, 68, 108-09, 162, 166-67, 183, 191, 198-99
Clark, R. C., 21
Clark Hall, Bessie and Ben, 143
Clarke, Charles, 103-04
Clarke, Robert, 29
Clarke & Courts, 29-31
Classic Car Museum, 35, 36
Clayton, Mary, 234
Clayton, Nicholas J., 6, 9, 19-25, 29, 31, 33-34, 36-40, 42, 44, 46-49, 51-54, 57, 69, 70-75, 83, 86, 87, 94, 95, 98, 99, 100, 102, 105, 107, 110-15, 126-27, 138-39, 143-45, 150, 152, 163, 166, 172, 174-80, 183-84, 186, 190, 216, 227, 233-34, 243
Clayton, Mrs. Nicholas J., 174, 243
Clayton & Company, N. J., 19, 29, 31, 44, 52, 57, 98, 111, 113, 127, 143, 172, 179, 183-84, 190
Clayton & Lynch, 19, 24, 53, 69, 175
Cleveland, Charles L., 82
Clouser, John Henry, 169
Cluskey, Charles B., 45
Coca Cola Bottling Company, 208
Cohen, Abraham, 72, 95
Cohen, George S., 178, 186
Cohen, Dr. Henry, 52
Cohen, Robert I., 186
Cohen, Robert I., Jr., 186
Cohen, Robert I., III, 218
Cohen Community House, Henry, 52
Cohen Monument, Agnes Lord and Robert I., 178
Cokins, Nick M., 220
Colleraine, Edward A., 86, 87

Colley, Richard S., 244
Collins, Ira E., 158
Colored Free School, 166
Coltrin, Robert M., 113
Comegys, P. N., 19-20, 31, 38, 43
Commodore Motel, 232
Community College District Building, 230-31
Compton, Eugene H., 141
Compton Plumbing Company, 141
Concrete and Steel Engineering Company, 242
Congregation B'nai Israel Temple, 52, 185-86
Congregation Beth Jacob Synagogue, 143
Conness, William S., 139
Cook Industries, 202
Cooke, B. N., 82
Cooke, Henry C., 114
Cooke, Dr. Willard R., 219
Cooke & Company, H. C., 114
Cooley, Joseph F., 115, 222
Coon, Richard S., 100
Coppini, Pompeo, 223
Cordray, Thomas, 81
Cornell University, 129
Cortes, Henry, 170
Cosmopolitan Hotel, 32
Cotton Compress Workers, Inc. Building, 41
Cotton Concentration Company, 207-08, 219, 220
Cotton Exchange and Board of Trade Building, 34-35
Country Club, Galveston, 246
Court House, United States, 50
Courthouse, Galveston County, 14, 54
Courts, George M., 29
Cox, Frank, 45
Crain/Anderson Architects, 128
Crawford, A. C., 154
Craycroft, Mrs. George, 143-44
Cret, Paul P., 127
Crippled Children's Hospital, 125
Crockett Courts, 231
Croft, John J., Jr., 235
Cross, Thomas L., 185
Crow, Lewis & Wickenhoefer, 68, 112, 118, 128
Cruise Terminal, 28-29
Crystal Palace, 233
Cuney, N. Wright, 205
Cunningham, R. George, 26
Custom House (1861), 45-46, 50, 154
Custom House (1933), 26, 50, 214
Custom House (1937), 50

Dahl, George L., 127, 234
Dallas Morning News, 34
Danelly, Louisa B., 92
Dargan & Tobyn Building, 21-22
Darragh, Laura Leonard, 85
Darragh, John L., 39, 84-85

Davidson, Leslie Barry, 244

Davidson, Mr. and Mrs. Robert V., 186

Davie, J. P., 32, 89, 176

Davie Building, J. P., 32

Davie Vault, J. P., 176

Davis, Abraham, 89

Davis, B. R., 177

Davis, Drusilla, 188

Davis, Edmund J., 143

Davis, J. J., 55

Davis, Randall, 30

Davis, Sarah, 143

Davis, Waters S., 143

Davis, Mrs. Waters S., Jr., 53

Davis, Yetta, 94. *See also* Heidenheimer, Yetta

Davis Monument, B. R., 177

Day, Joseph P., 187

de Young, John, 53, 106, 180

Dealey, Thomas W., 83

Deats, James K., 146, 193

Debner, Theodore, 206

DeForest, James S., 46

Del Papa, Omero, 129

Delesdernier, George H., 67

Dell'Osso Shopping Center, 159

Dennis, Leland S., 220

Denver Resurvey, 210-11

DeWitt, Roscoe, 166

DeWitt & Lemmon, 54, 166

Dibbrell, William C., 174

Dickey, George E., 47, 75

Dickey & Helmich, 75, 99, 150

Dickson, S. R., 203

Dietzel, Arthur A., 174

Dignan, Lawrence P., 140

Dignan, Thomas S., 117, 118

Dignified Resignation Confederate memorial, 54

Dinsdale, Thomas B., 138

Diocese of Galveston, 106, 110, 111, 150

Diocese of Galveston Chancery Office Building, 106-7

Diocese of Galveston-Houston, 144, 214

Disbrow, Benjamin F., 153

Discovery Channel Store, 19

Dobbert, Tenie, 159

Dobbert family, 159

Doctors Clinic Building, 116

Doherty, Mike, 141

Doherty, Weez, 141

Dolson, Ben, Jr., 192

Dolson-Horn Furniture Company Warehouse, 35

Dominican Convent, 75

Dominican High School, 75

Dorfman, Eva, 194

Dorfman, Sadell, 194

Dormitory A, Texas A&M, Mitchell Campus (Galveston), 203

Drewa, Edward F., 183

Drewa, Sophie, 182-83

Drie, C., 2, 41, 55, 66-67, 84, 147

Dubie Building, 39

Duffin, Jack L., 50

Duhamel, E. J., 105, 176

Duhamel & Lawler, 32, 105, 176

Dunne, W. Scott, 48

Dyer, Dr. Alex A., 182

Eames & Young, 51

Earthman, Mr. and Mrs. James B., 43

East District School, 109

East End Historic District, 84, 97

East End Historical District Association, 63, 85

East End Historical District Association Park, 97

Easterwood & Easterwood, 51

Eaton, Rev. Benjamin, 53

Eaton, Stephen, 141

Eaton Memorial Chapel, 53

Edgewater Methodist Retirement Community, 233-34

Edwards, Charles, 109

Edwards, George, 109

Egert, John, 190

Eggers, Dr. George W. N., 220-21

Eggers & Higgins, 124-25

Eiband, Henry C., 108

Eiband, Joe G., 176, 216

Eiband Building, 43

1894 Grand Opera House, 45

Eimar, Henry, 171

Eisenfelder, Charles W., 195

Eisenhour, Virginia Ketchum, 14, 187

El Cortez Apartments, 52

El Mina Shrine Temple, 57

Eldridge, W. T., 202

Electric Service Company Building, 48

Elissa (tall ship), 27-28

Elks Club Building, 139

Ellisor Engineers, 36

Engberg, Arne G., 26, 204

Engelke, Charles, 154

Engelke Building, 39

Engine House #5 (fire station), 146

English Memorial Building, T. William, 46-47, 52

Enterprise meat market, 149

Episcopal Cemetery, 178-79

Episcopal Diocese of Texas, 180

Eubanks/Bohn Associates, 20-21, 22, 28, 31, 81

Evans, C. P., 114

Evans, Jack S., 222

Everett, Alexander B., 82, 93

Fadden, James, 19

Fadden, Rosa, 19

Fairchild, Cameron, 113, 163, 184, 188, 216, 218-21, 230, 233

Far-Mar-Co Export Grain Elevator, 202, 236

Far Niente, 246

Farmers Export Company, 202

Fash, Ronald D., 218

Favrot Fund, 84

Feagin, Joe R., 34

Fedder, Albert A., 195

Fellman Dry Goods Company, 43

Felt, Mrs. Charles F. W., 88

Ferber, Edna, 8, 184

Fields, Cato, 79

Findlay, James, 98

Fine, Joseph P., 93

Finger, Joseph, 29, 49-50

Finn, Alfred C., 48, 50, 215

Fire of 1869, 20, 21, 39

Fire of 1877, 24, 30, 34

Fire of 1885, 43, 45-46, 54, 56, 62-63, 71, 73, 75, 85, 89, 90, 98-99, 102-03, 114-15, 133, 145, 150, 152

Fire Station Number 3, 41

First Baptist Church, 51, 53, 57, 143, 166

First Church of Christ Scientist, 182

First Evangelical Lutheran Church, 50

First Hutchings-Sealy National Bank Building, 38

First Latin Assembly of God Church, 72-73

First Lutheran Church, 50

First Methodist Church, 56

First National Bank, 6, 23

First Presbyterian Church, 46-47, 52, 55, 98, 205

Fish Village, 128

Fisher, Dr. and Mrs. Frederick K., 150, 191

Fisherman's Wharf at Pier 22, 28

Fitzgerald & Partners, Richard, 248

Fivel, Madeline, 156

Flagship Hotel, 232-33

Flake, Adolph, 152, 171

Flake & Company, A., 39

Fleming, Bartholomew M., 166

Fleming, C. C. Pat, 190

Fletcher, Dr. William H., 216

Flood, George D., 95

Focke, Anita, 68

Focke, John, 138

Focke, John W., 193

Foley Brothers, 186

Ford, Benson, 69

Ford, O'Neil, 129, 167-68, 222, 243-44

Ford, Powell & Carson, 18-19, 21, 27-28, 30-32, 35, 124, 222, 234-35, 243

Ford & Rogers, 129

Fordtran homestead, 81

Fort Crockett, 211, 222, 227, 230-31

Fort San Jacinto, 93, 231, 236

Fort Travis, 231

Foster, James W., 191

Fowler, Charles, Jr., 182

Fowler & McVitie, 140

Fox, Christopher, 71, 96

Fox, George, Mr. and Mrs., 96

Fox, Louis F., Jr., 217

Frank Leslie's Illustrated Weekly, 34

Franklin, Joseph, 175

Franklin, Robert M., 152

Franzheim, Kenneth, 126

Fraser, Andrew C., 35, 48, 50, 118, 168, 214, 232, 233-34, 235

Frederich, William J., 95

Frederick, Anthony E., 247

Freeman Monument, David, 178

Frenkel, Adolph, 142

Freybe, Olympia, 42

Frosh Building, 21, 22

Fullen, Bill H., 24

Gaertner, Michael, 71

Gaertner & Watson, 54

Gage, Bard O., 192

Gaido, M. J., 217

Gaines, Nancy A., 136

Gallagher, Bishop Nicholas A., 37, 243

Galveston, City of, 28, 57, 84, 115, 168, 183, 232, 234, 238

Galveston, Henderson & San Antonio Railway Company, 204

Galveston, Houston & Henderson Railroad (GH&H), 28, 187, 198, 203-04, 242

Galveston, Houston & Northern Railway, 175

Galveston Air Base, 244

Galveston and Texas History Center, 51

Galveston Army Airbase, 244

Galveston Artillery Club, 186-87, 235

Galveston Arts Center, 6, 23

Galveston Bagging & Cordage Company, 206-7

Galveston Bank & Trust Company, 172

Galveston Bible Church, 46

Galveston Brewery, 203

Galveston Brewery Association, 203

Galveston Burns Institute, 124

Galveston Catholic School, 163, 180

Galveston Causeway, 239, 242

Galveston City Company, 4, 28, 54, 85, 167, 176, 187, 190, 191

Galveston City Hall (1847), 4

Galveston City Hall (1916), 58-59

Galveston City Hall and Market House (1888), 37, 58-59

Galveston City Hospital, 121

Galveston Coffee & Spice Company, 174

Galveston Cotton and Woolen Mills, 206-7

Galveston Cotton Exchange and Board of Trade Building, 34-35

Galveston Country Club, 246

Galveston County, 14, 38, 55, 70, 81, 242

Galveston County Community College District Building, 230-31

Galveston County Courthouse, 14, 54

Galveston County Cultural Arts Council, 23, 32, 45

Galveston County Health Department, 214

Galveston County Historical Museum, 37

Galveston County Parks and Recreation Building, 54-55

Galveston County Publishing Company Building, 242

Galveston Daily News, 20-21, 32-34, 38, 47, 66, 83, 102, 105, 111-12, 117, 136, 156, 173, 183, 242. *See also Galveston News*

Galveston Daily News Building, 242

Galveston Garden Club, 188

Galveston Garten-Verein, 163, 183

Galveston Gas Company, 203

Galveston Historical Foundation, 15, 21-22, 24, 26-27, 32, 36, 55, 57, 73, 76, 81-82, 84-85, 105, 127, 139, 144-45, 155, 157, 167, 170, 183, 187, 190-91

Galveston-Houston Electric Railway, 242

Galveston Ice & Cold Storage Company, 26

Galveston Insurance Board, 2

Galveston Island Municipal Golf Course Club House, 245

Galveston Island State Park, 247

Galveston Land & Improvement Company, 210-11

Galveston Model Dairy Building, 51

Galveston Municipal Pleasure Pier, 232-33

Galveston News, 85. *See also Galveston Daily News*

Galveston News Building, 34

Galveston Opera House-Hotel Grand, 45

Galveston Orphans Home, 151, 156, 188

Galveston Real Estate and Loan Association, 142

Galveston Seawall and Grade Raising Monument, 233

Galveston Seventh-day Adventist Church, 155

Galveston Ship Channel, 21

Galveston State Psychopathic Hospital, 126

Galveston That Was, The, 9, 20, 33, 42, 56, 75, 84, 112, 114, 242

Galveston Tidal Wave Monument, 223

Galveston Water & Electric Light Station, 204

Galveston Wharf Company, 28, 85, 114, 208

Galvestonian, The, 236

Galvez Hotel, 8

Garbade, Eiband & Company Buillding, 43

Garbade, W. L., 108

Garber, Dr., 116

Gardens of Man, 244-45

Gardner, Henry, 84

Garnett, Robert B., 89, 152, 170, 173, 175

Garrett, Dr. and Mrs. Lafayette, 171, 172

Garrett, Pete Ed, 244

Garten-Verein, 163, 183

General Services Administration, 45, 231

Gengler, Mrs. Emilia, 55

Gengler, Peter M., 70, 116

George, W. Eugene, Jr., 59

Geosciences and Maritime Studies, College of, 202-03

Geren, Preston M., 205, 217

German Methodist Episcopal Church, 155

Gethsemane Missionary Baptist Church, 196

Gilbert, C. S., 26, 207

Gilbert, Cass, 127

Gilbough, Frederick M., 181

Ginsberg & Associates, William, 242

Girardeau House, 115

Giraud, François, 47

Giraud, Theodore E., 47-48, 111

Glasco, Joe, 24, 104

Glenn, Dr. and Mrs. William L., Jr., 220

Globe Discount Center, 207

Goggan, John, 147

Goggan, Thomas, 87

Goggan Vault, 243

Gold, Herman H., 151

Goldstein, Henrietta, 103

Goldstein, Joseph, 102

Goldstein, Minnie, 103

Goldthwaite, Mr. and Mrs. Joseph G., 138, 173

Golemon & Rolfe, 41-42, 124, 126

Golf Course Club House, 245

Goodman, R. Wilbur, 216

Goodwin, Edwin J., Jr., 125

Gotsdiner Architects, 21

Grace Episcopal Church, 172, 180

Grace Episcopal Church Parish House, 172

Grade Raising Board, 137

Grand Opera House, 45

Grand Reef resort development, 236

Grand Southern Hotel, 34, 106

Grand Synagogue of Toledo (Spain), 111

Graugnard's Bakery Building, 148

Graves, Michael, 18, 21, 30, 236

Gray, Ann Miller, 30

Gray, John, 217

Greacen, Thomas E., II, 129

Great A & P Tea Company Building, 77-78

Great American Homes Awards, 187

Great Depression, 188, 233

Green, Lewis Sterling, 29, 43, 49, 87, 115

Green & Finger, 29, 49, 207

Greene, Herbert M., 127

Greene, LaRoche & Dahl, 127

Greene Co., Herbert M., 127

Greenleve, Block & Company, 20, 68

Green's Funeral Home, 204

Greenwall, Henry, 45

Greeson, John A., II, 41

Gresham, Esther (Mrs. W.B. Lockhart), 97

Gresham, Walter, 97, 106, 111, 113, 115, 152, 181, 184

Gresham, Mrs. Walter, 111

Gresham House. *See* Bishop's Palace

Griffin, William H., 95

Grillette, Loranzy, 216

Groesbeck, John D., 4-5, 54, 121, 176, 210-11, 214, 217, 219, 233, 238, 242

Gross, John Charles, 175
Grover, George W., 70
Grumbach, Nephtali, 86
Guaranty Federal Savings & Loan Association, 37
Gudman, Mrs. Hans, 188
Guinard, Mary Margaret, 221
Gulf, Colorado & Santa Fe Railway, 18, 28, 57, 181-82, 184, 188, 191
Gulf Breeze Apartments, 151
Gulf City Cotton Press, 206
Gulf Fisheries Company, 110
Gunter Hotel (San Antonio), 235
Gunther, Robert M., 106
Gustafson, Victor, 76
Gutheim, Frederick, 111

Haas, Otto, 36
Haas, Richard, 23-24
Haberman, Mr. and Mrs. Louis, 115
Hackbarth, Henry W., 104-5
Hackett, Greg, 116
Hadcock, Fred, 168
Haden, Dr. and Mrs. Henry C., 193
Hafertepe, Kenneth, 57
Hagelman, H. J., 90
Hagemann, John, 174-75
Hall Merriman, 28
Hall-Scott Buildings, 40
Halsell Conservatory (San Antonio), 244
Hamilton, B. O., 20
Hance, William B., 66
Hanna, John, 69
Hanretta Building, 29
Hanson, Edward P., 182
Harbor House, 27
Harbor Square, 27
Harbor View, 128
Harbor View Development Company, 128
Harbruck, Mary Carol, 222
Hardy Holzman Pfeiffer & Associates, 45
Harmony Club, 44, 48
Harmony Hall, 44, 48
Harper's Weekly, 111, 183
Harris, Bertha, 136
Harris, Brantly Mr. and Mrs., 219, 220
Harris, Charles A., 89
Harris, Fletcher, 220
Harris, Frances, 136
Harris, Joan, 216
Harris, John W., 150
Harris, Rosella, 136
Harris, Dr. Titus H., 112
Harris family, 185
Harrison, E. A., 18
Hartel, Fred, 138

Havre Lafitte subdivision, 244
Hawley, Harry, 143
Haywood, Norcell, 167
Haywood Jordan McCowan, 167
Hebrew Benevolent Society Cemetery, 177-78
Hedrick, Wyatt C., 126
Heffron, Isaac, 27, 74, 76, 247
Heidenheimer, Sampson, 33, 35, 106
Heidenheimer, Yetta, 89. See also Davis, Yetta
Heidenheimer & Company Building, 35
Heiman, Anton, 136
Heiner, Eugene T., 30, 33, 54
Helmbrecht, William C., 189, 221
Helmich, D. A., 75, 150
Henck, August J., 84, 106
Henck, Christian J., 91
Henck, Henry C., Jr., 157
Henderson, Dr. Edmond A., 236
Hendley Buildings, 14, 25-26, 32
Hendley Market, 26
Hendley Wall, 25-26
Hendricks, Brian, 244
Henningson, Durham & Richardson, 124
Henry, Melton, 22, 203
Henson, Margaret Swett, 191
Heritage Christian Academy, 146
Herolz, Robert, 184
Hertford, John, 116
Heye, Gustav, 77
Highway House, 248
Hildenbrand, Christian F., 185
Hildenbrand, Elise, 185
Hilger, Michael, 183
Hill, John J., 217
Hill & Company, C. D., 49, 58, 182, 186, 188
Hill Brothers, 235
Hill's Pier 19 Restaurant, 28
Hilton, Conrad N., 233
Hilton Hotels Corporation, 233
Hitchcock, L. M., Jr., 144
Hodson, John D., 73, 74
Hoesli, Bernard, 129
Hollywood Dinner Club, 215, 243
Holt, Charles A., 190
Homer, Arthur B., 80
Homer, Winslow, 80
Homrighaus, Christopher, 96
Hoogboom, Lonnie, 247
Hoover, Joseph Allen, 247
Horner & Wyatt, 202
Hotel Galvez, 173, 234-35
Hotel Grand, 45
Hotel Paso del Norte (El Paso), 235
Houlahan, William J., 43
Hourigan, John, 46, 142

House Building, T. W., 22
Housing and Urban Development, Department of, 57
Housing Authority, United States, 206
Housing Authority of the City of Galveston, 26, 151, 204, 206-07, 244
Houston, Sam, 58
Houston Ice & Brewing Company, 167
Houston Ship Channel, 8
Howard & Associates, Barry, 18
Huckins, Sarah, 143
Huddleston, Dr. William E., 214
Hudler, Herbert W., Jr., 129
Hughes, Robert J., 80-81
Hughes Building, 40
Hunter, Fred F., 93
Hunter, Joseph J., 173
Hurley, Charles W., 95-96
Hurricane *Alicia*, (1983), 32, 59, 187, 194, 234, 245
Hurricane *Carla*, (1961), 58, 180, 181, 233, 234
Hurricane of 1900. *See* Storm of 1900
Hurricane of 1915. *See* Storm of 1915
Hurtley, Sarah C., 175
Hutchings, John H., 19, 29, 183-85, 187
Hutchings, Mrs. John H., 182
Hutchings, Laura, 112
Hutchings, Mary Moody, 184
Hutchings, Minnie Knox (Mrs. John H.), 184
Hutchings, Robert K., 188
Hutchings, Robert M., 29
Hutchings, Sealy, 30, 184
Hutchings, Mr. and Mrs. Sealy, Jr., 184
Hutchings, Sealy & Co., 19, 88
Hutchings family, 185, 186
Hutchings-Sealy National Bank, 19, 23, 38, 188, 219

Iglesia Metodista Unida Zion, 71
Ikelheimer & Company Building, 44-45
Ilies, C. J. H., 48
Ilies-McKenzie Monument, Justine, 177
IMAX 3D Theater, 244
Immaculate Conception Church (New Orleans), 111
Imperial Sugar Company, 202
Improvement Loan & Trust Company Building, 44
Indian Beach subdivision, 247
International & Great Northern Railway (I&GN), 18, 203
International Longshoremen's Association Local Union 851 Building, 41
International Pageant of Pulchritude, 234
Interurban (Galveston-Houston Electric Railway), 239, 242
Isla Ranch House, 247
Island City Turf Exchange, 141
Island City Wood Working Company, 66
Island Community Center, 207
Island Elementary School, 243-44
Island Homes, 244

Islander East, 236
Ittner, William B., 54, 166

J. C. Penney Company, 43
Jack, Laura, 186
Jack, Thomas McKinney, Jr., 186
Jack family, 185
Jack Tar Court, 235
Jackson, James, 73
Jackson Building, 72-73
Jackson Square Building, 53-54
Jacobs, Barbara L., 83
Jacobs, Bernheim & Co., S., 104
Jahn, Helmut, 18
Jamaica Beach subdivision, 238-39, 247
Jamaica Resort Corporation, 238, 247
James, Mary, 79
Jameson, Rufus, 84
Jary, Mary Canales, 45, 59
Jean Lafitte Hotel, 48
Jellicoe, Sir Geoffrey, 244-45
Jessen Associates, 124
Jiménez, Carlos, 245
Jiménez, Brother Peter, SJ, 111
Jinkins, Dr. Julius L., 192
Jinkins, Dr. and Mrs. Wiley J., 184
Jockusch Building, 25
John's Oyster Resort, 242
Johnson, Adolph G., 190
Johnson, Bernard, 124
Johnson, Charles, 169
Johnson, Robert C., 66
Johnson, Walter L., 216
Johnston, Mary, 145
Johnston, Dr. McKenzie, 145
Jones, Edward C., 46-47
Jones, Jenkin Lloyd, 51
Jones, John M., 154
Jones & Baldwin, 46
Jordan, David C., 49
Jordan, Mary, 49
Jordan, Michael M., 49
Jordan Building, D. C. & M., 49
Jugenfeld & Company, E., 203
Juneman, Dorothea, 99, 100
Juneman, George, 99
Junior League of Galveston County, 23, 33
Justine Apartments, 48

Kahn, Gustav, 140
Kahn, Marvin, 221
Kane, Joseph J., 220
Kane Boiler Works, 220
Kauffman, Meyers & Company, 70
Kauffman, Runge & Company, 106

Kauffman & Runge, 33, 95
Keeland, Burdette, 248
Keiller Building, 127
Kelley, Dr. W. D., 88
Kelly, Frank, 217
Kelly, W. Frank, 156
Kelly Avenue Tenant Cottages, 169
Kelsey, Virginia, 245
Kelso, Alvin N., 216
Kelso, Walter A., 185
Kempner, Daniel W., 37, 181-82, 207, 235
Kempner, Eliza Seinsheimer, 114
Kempner, H., 37, 114, 152, 183
Kempner, Harris L., 221
Kempner, I. H., 112-13, 115, 152, 181, 202, 207, 235
Kempner, Stanley E., 183
Kempner family, 114, 202, 243
Kempner Park, 183, 184
Kennon, Paul A., Jr., 38
Ketchum family, 187
Killis Almond & Associates, 45, 59, 176, 188
King, Annie L., 174
Kirkham Hall, Emmett O., 202
Kirksey Architects, John, 235
Kirwin High School, 150
Kissinger, James H., 100
Kleberg, Marcellus E., 94
Klein, Irving R., 43, 221
Kleinecke House, 180
Knights of Columbus, 44
Koch, Augustus, 2, 41, 94
Koester, Louis R., 192
Koetter Tharp Cowell & Bartlett, 126
Kopperl Monument, Moritz, 178
Korn, Anton F., Jr., 68, 112, 118, 128, 185, 215
Kory, Charles I., 90
Kotin, Ben J., 41, 51, 54, 94, 143, 145, 186, 207, 221-22, 235
Kotin, Sol, 222, 235
Kotin & Associates, Ben J., 41, 185-86, 221
Kress & Company Building, S. H., 44
Kreuzberger, Frederick, 74
Kriegel, John, 68, 69, 244
Krohn, Charlotte, 149
Kruger, Adolf, 179
Kruger, Rudolph E., 74
Kuhn Memorial Pergola, Albert, 183

La King's Confectionery, 19-20
LaBarbera Store, Carmelo, 189
Labatt, Amelia, 188
Labatt, Henry J., 114
Ladd, Caroline Willis, 188
Ladies Aid Society House, 50
Laffite's Cove subdivision, 239
Lakeview Cemetery, 211, 223

Lalor Building, 39-40
Lancton, Augustine, 92
Landes, Henry A., 75, 99
Landry's Seafood House at the San Luis, 230
Lang, Clara, 23-24
Langbehn, Fred A., 235
Langbehn, J. Henry, 109, 184
Lange, August F., 138
Lasell, Mrs. A. D., 57
Lasker, Morris, 114, 146
Lasker Home for Homeless Children, 146
Lawrence, Dr. David H., 154
Laycock, Walter H., 193
Lazzari, Craig, 20, 69
Lazzari, Mary Clifford (Mrs. Craig), 69
Le Corbusier, 129
League, John Charles, 113-14
League, Mrs. John Charles, 53-54, 113
League, Mary Williams, 191
League, T. J., 191-92
League, T. M., 136
League, Thomas J., Jr., 191
League, Thomas M., 150
League Building, T. J., 21
League House, 62
Lee, Dr. George T., 219, 220
Lehman, Donald J., 45
Leinbach, F. George, 110
Lemmon, Mark, 126, 166, 222
Lenz, Conrad, 149
Levi Building, 40
Levin Hall, William C., 124, 126
Levy, Aaron, 87
Levy, Mrs. Abraham, 103
Levy, Adrian Felix, 150
Levy, Bernard, 150
Levy, Edward S., 97
Levy, Harry H., 193
Levy, Julian A., 221
Levy, Max, 115
Levy, Ruth, 221
Levy, Sam, 69
Levy, Sol L., 182
Levy & Brother, J., 44
Levy & Company, E. S., 42, 221
Levy Building, E. S., 38, 42, 45
Lewis, Dr. Stephen L., 244
Liberty Fish & Oyster Company, 28
Lindale Park, 128
Lindeberg, Harrie T., 219
Lindenberg, Professor Emil, 144
Little Theater of Galveston, 73
Live Oak Missionary Baptist Church, 167
Lloyd, Hermon, 217, 220
Lloyd Jones Brewer & Associates, 236
Locke, Henry, 94

ockhart, W. B., 97
ockwood & Andrews, 202
oebenstein, Julius, 155
one Star Brewing Company, 203
one Star Cotton Jammers of Texas, 41
one Star Property Management, 37
oomis, Gus, 215
oomis, Michael A., 214-16
oomis Construction Company, 129
ost Bayou Historic District, 133, 145-46, 149
ouvre (Paris), 244
oveless, I. E., 126
ovenberg, Isadore, 69, 94
owell, H., 28
ozica, John, 242
ucas, Thomas, 117
ucas Terrace, 117
ucretius, 245
uhn, Graham B., 33, 46, 59, 191
uth, Lawson, 76
ynch, Robert L. K., 20, 24
yon, James E., 232-33

Maas, Isabella Offenbach, 104
Maas, Max, 103-04
Macedonia Baptist Church, 168
Maceo, Edna, 215
Maceo, Rosario, 180, 214-15, 233-34, 243
Maceo, Sam, 214-17, 233-35, 243
Maceo's Grotto, 234
MacKenzie, H. Jordan, 48
Magale Building, 20
Magnolia Homes, 26
Magnolia Petroleum Building (Dallas), 37
Magnolia Petroleum Company, 134, 189
Makepeace & Co., C. R., 206
Makover Levy, 214
Malkin, Steve, 116
Mallory Building, 24
Mallory Line Warehouse, 28-29
Malloy & Sons Funeral Home, F. P., 176
Malone, Michael, 19
Mann, George E., 105
Manning & Company, J. F., 58
Mardi Gras, 18
Mardi Gras Arches, 18-19, 21, 30, 236
Mardi Gras Museum, 22
Marine Building, 35
Marschner, Charles F., 36, 170
Marschner Building, C. F., 36
Martin, Milton Foy, 129
Martin, Sydney, 173
Martin & Company Building, R. F., 40
Martingano, Michael, 71
Martini, Frederick, 68
Martini, Giosue "Sonny," 40, 221

Martini Theater, 48
Marwitz, Herman, 53, 175
Marwitz, Ida, 175
Marwitz & Company, H., 33-34
Marx, Louis, 104
Marx, Marx, 44
Marx & Blum Building, 31
Marx & Kempner, 23-24, 152
Mary Moody Northen Amphitheater, 247
Mary Moody Northen, Inc., 59
Mary Moody Northen Pavilion, 126
Masonic Temple, 44, 52
Masterson, Thomas W., 186
Mather, H. S., 98, 205
Mathes Group, 57
Mauran, Russell & Garden, 181
Mauran & Russell, 173, 234-35
Mayo, W. G., 157
McAfee & Duncan, 234
McBee, Silas, 172
McComb, David, 40
McConnell, J. R., 21-22, 27, 54, 214, 236
McCullough, John W., 219
McCullough family, 113
McDonald, James, 117
McDonald House, 221
McDonnell Building, 31-32
McEvilley, Thomas, 202
McHale, T. G., 179
McKenzie, Donald N., 27, 31, 46-48, 50, 52, 70, 102, 139, 146-47, 158, 176-77, 183, 215
McKim, Mead & White, 57, 103, 113, 179
McKinney, Liberty S., 92
McLean, Doug, 57
McLemore, Marcus C., 146
Meadows Foundation of Dallas, 84
Medical Arts Building, 35
Medical Building (now El Cortez Apartments), 52
Medical Department Building (UTMB), 121, 127-8
Medical Laboratory Building (UTMB), 127
Medical Research Building (UTMB), 126
Meenen, Simon J., 158
Mehos, John A., 128
Meininger, William, 86-87
Ménard, Medard, 92
Ménard, Michael B., 92, 162, 187, 188, 190, 191
Ménard, W. Kendall, 221
Ménard family, 113, 219
Ménard Memorial Tower, 176
Ménard Park, 206, 232
Mennike, Adolph, 154
Merchants and Planters Compress and Warehouse Company, 207
Merchants Mutual Insurance Company Building, 19-20
Mermaid Pier, 234
Merriman Holt, 31

Merritt, Warren F., 216

Messer, Sanguinet & Messer, 54

Methodist District Parsonage, 218

Methodist Homes for Older People, 233

Meyer, Emma, 86

Meyer, Gustave A., 150

Meyers, Mr. and Mrs. John H., 70

Michael, Elise C., 73, 110, 114

Michaelis, Edward R., 216

Michels, John F., 99

Migel, Sam, 56

Milam, Ben, 34, 115, 160, 206, 220-21, 235

Milde, Frederick, 154

Miller, A. Wilkins, 89-90

Miller, Samuel I., 182, 186

Miller, William R., 74

Miller-Herman Boarding House, 47

Mills, Ballinger, 185

Mills, Ballinger, Jr., 58, 184-85

Mills, Margaret Leonard (Mrs. Ballinger Mills, Jr.), 58, 184

Mills, Robert, 183, 184

Mills family, 185-86

Milroy, Earl R., 118

Miramar Courts, 232

Mistrot, Felix E., 189

Mistrot Brothers & Company, 31

Mitchell, Cynthia (Mrs. George), 18-19, 21-22, 27-28, 30-32, 35, 129, 235

Mitchell, George, 18-19, 21-22, 27-28, 30-32, 35, 129, 230, 235, 246, 247

Mitchell, Mardi J., 205

Mitchell Campus, Texas A&M University, 202-3

Mitchell Development Corporation, 247

Mobil Oil Corporation, 189

Model Laundry and Dry Cleaning Works, 216

Model Laundry & Dye Works Building, 49-50

Model Steam Bakery, 96

Möller, Jens, 101-3

Möller, Maud Wilson, 86, 101-3

Montgomery, James S., 172

Moody, Edna, 221

Moody, Libbie (Mrs. Clark W. Thompson), 215

Moody, Libbie Shearn (Mrs. W. L. Moody, Jr.), 59

Moody, Robert, 232

Moody, Shearn, 168, 215

Moody, Mrs. Shearn, 232

Moody, Shearn, Jr., 232

Moody, William L., 22, 150

Moody, William L., Jr., 22, 34, 35, 37-38, 43, 59, 113, 168, 214-15, 222, 232-33

Moody, William L., III, 214-15, 221

Moody Building, W. L., 22

Moody Center, 234

Moody Compress and Warehouse Company, 207

Moody Foundation, 18, 57, 233, 244-45, 247

Moody Gardens, 68, 238, 244-45

Moody Hall, 53

Moody House, Edgewater Methodist Retirement Community, 233-34

Moody Library, 124

Moody Mansion and Museum, 14, 59

Moody Medical Library Building, 124

Moody Memorial First United Methodist Church, 55, 218, 222-23

Moody Memorial Wing, 51

Moody National Bank, 38, 41-42, 187

Moore, Barry, 57, 68

Moore, Charles, 18

Moore, Harvin C., 217-18, 220

Moore, McKinney & Co., 103

Moore, Stratton & Company Building, 6, 23

Morgan, Nathan V., 108

Morgan, Robert Edward, 247

Morgan, William Manning, 193

Moro Castle, 21

Morris, Carlotta, 102

Morris, George W., 91

Morris, Jack W., 107, 244

Morris, Dr. Seth M., 55

Morris Architects, 230, 244

Morris Associates, S. I. 244

Morris★Aubrey Architects, 230

Morrissey, Martin P., 139

Moseley, Dr. Mack J., 170

Moser, Eliza, 46, 141, 142

Moser, John, 23, 24, 33-35, 183

Moser, John H., 141-42

Moser, Paula, 142

Moser, Peter, 142

Mosle & Company, H., 193

Mosquito Fleet, 28

Mott, Marcus L., 247

Mount Olive Missionary Baptist Church, 206

Mudrak, Rudolf, 172-73

Muller, Alfred, 37, 49, 53, 58, 72-73, 76, 84-85, 92, 97, 102-5, 116, 143-44, 147, 151-52, 156, 183, 193-94

Muller, Frederick William, 156

Mullican, David, 84, 141

Murdock, W. S., 50, 182, 206

Murdoch's Bath House, 8, 234

Murff, Luther, 140

Myrick, David B. T., 221

Nash, James P., 49

Nathan's, 43, 221

National Historic Landmark Districts, 9, 15, 18, 63, 71, 79, 97

National Hotel Company, 38, 234

National Hotels Corporation, 233, 235

National Maritime Union of America Building, 36

National Park Service, 30

National Register of Historic Places, 97

National Trust for Historic Preservation, 187

NationsBank Building, 38

NationsBank Galveston, 23

Nelson, Donald, 109

Nelson, John, 76

Nesbitt, Bob, 243

Nettleton, Daniel W., 158

Neuhaus & Taylor, 36, 232

Neuhaus Associates, W. O., 245-46

Neumann, August, 155

Neuwiller, Charles F., 71

Neuwiller Building, 71-72

New Orleans Exporting Company, 185

Newcomb, William J., 175

Newson, Alfred S., 100

Nicholls, George H., 140

Nichols, Ebenezer B., 25

Nichols Building, 25

Nichols-Byrne subdivision, 190

Niemeyer, Oscar, 236

Noble, Alfred, 227, 233

Noel, Judge and Mrs. James L., 45

Northen, E. C., 235

Northen, Mary Moody, 38, 59, 113, 126, 247

Nussbaum, Herman, 118

O'Brien, John, 111

O'Connell High School, 18, 180

O'Connell Senior Campus, 150

O'Rourke, Richard, 71

Oaks, The, 185

Ochsner, Jeffrey Karl, 27

Ochsner Associates, 27

Odin, Most Rev. John M., 47

Oehler, Charles H., 207

Oehler Building, 207

Offenbach, Jacques, 104

Ohmstede, Theodore, 72

Ohring, Robert, 68

Old Central Cultural Center, 166

Old City Cemetery, 176-77

Old Galveston Square, 22

Old Red (University of Texas Medical Department Building, 1891), 121, 127-28 See also Ashbel Smith Hall

Old Strand Emporium, 24

Oldfield, Mr. and Mrs. Robert E., 115

Oleander Homes, 206

Oliver, Louis Lloyd, 23, 54, 78, 112, 124, 126, 193, 232, 235, 244, 245

Oliver & Beerman, 232

One Moody Plaza, 36

Open Gates (Sealy House), 14, 57-59, 103, 113, 184

Opera Glass, The, 66

Opera House, See Galveston Opera House

Operation Church Street, 84

Oppermann, Gustav, 24, 243

Oppermann Building, 24

Oppermann Vault, Mary A., 243

Orlopp & Orlopp, 233

Ormond, Julian, 221

Ott, Charles S., 179

Ott Monument Works, 179

Otten, Brother Cornelius, SJ, 111

Our Lady of Guadalupe Catholic Church, 214

Overmire, T. J., 106

Page & Son, P. H., 124-25

Page Southerland Page, 124

Palace Club, 214

Pallais, D. H., 154

Palliser, Robert, 55, 153

Palm Terrace, 206

Palms Motel, 235

Panama Canal, 29

Panama Hotel, 29

Panic of 1873, 20, 47, 183

Panic of 1893, 30, 211

Papa, Omero Del, 129

Park, Frank A., 109

Park, Lynch & Company, 77

Park Apartments, 214

Parker Elementary School, Gladneo, 244

Parkland Apartments, 206

Parks and Recreation Building, Galveston County, 54-55

Parnell, C. G., 125

Parsons, Herbert L., 92

Patch, Alice, 80

Pauls, Louis, 220

Pauls, Mr. and Mrs. Louis, Jr., 129

Pautsch, L. W., 169

Pautsch, William, 99, 155

PBK Architects, 217

Pearce, John E., 186

Pearce and Wilder Building, 49

Peete, Rosa McD., 85

Pehoski, Joe, 22

Pei, I. M., 244

Pelli, César, 18

Penland, Sam M., 77

Penney Company, J. C., 43

Peoples Theater, 44

Peters, Augusta, 101

Peterson, A. Qvistgaard, 185

Peterson, Carolyn, 30

Pharmacology Building (UTMB), 124

Phelps & Dewees, 219

Phillips, W. Irving, Jr., 129, 230

Phoenix Bakery and Coffe House, 32
Physical Education Facility, (Texas A&M Mitchell Campus), 203
Pichard Monument, Athen V., 177
Pierce, Abel B., 244
Pierce, George, 244
Pierce Goodwin Alexander, 124
Pierce Goodwin Flanagan, 125
Pirates Beach subdivision, 239, 245-46, 248
Pirates Cove subdivision, 246
Pix, Charles H., 44
Pix Building, 44
Planning and Transportation Department, City of Galveston, 2
Platt, Charles A., 112, 118
Playground Courts, 235
Pleasure Pier, 232-33, 235
Polk, Lucius J., 169
Post Exchange and Gymnasium (Fort Crockett), 231
Post Hospital (Fort Crockett), 231
Postal Telegraph-Cable Company, 136
Pottier & Stymus, 59
Powell, Boone, 18, 21, 27, 30, 124
Powhatan House, 188
Predecki, Isadore, 141
Prendergast, George M., 151
Preservation Technology of Winston-Salem, North Carolina, 59
Preston, Calvin W., 93, 94
Prets, Frank W., 218
Prets Lumber Company, 218
Price, Thomas M., 26, 38, 50, 51, 94, 114, 125, 128-29, 145, 186-87, 204, 217, 219-20, 222, 232-36, 242-43
Public Housing Administration, 26
Public Works Administration, 160, 231
"Puerta Santa María" (Toledo, Spain), 111

Quick, John, 80
Quinn, Arthur W., 45, 109
Quinn, Lyda Kempner, 109

Railroad Museum (Center for Transportation and Commerce), 18
Rainbow Row, 55
Rainforest Pyramid, 244
Rakel, Albert, 72
Ralph, Julian, 111, 183
Randall, Dr. Edward, 127
Randall, Dr. and Mrs. Edward, Jr., 191-92
Randall family, 185
Randall Porterfield Architects, 242
Rapp, Raymond, Jr., 128, 180
Rapp, Raymond R., 26, 36, 47-48, 52, 59, 75, 106, 108, 110, 116, 118, 126, 143, 145, 150, 163, 173, 176, 180, 182, 184, 190, 204-6, 216-17, 219-21, 232, 243

Rapp & Associates, Raymond R., 42, 54, 58, 94, 128, 145, 150-51, 180
Rapp Fash Sundin, 54
Rapp Partners, 29
Rapp Tackett Fash, 37, 125, 202
Reading, Dr. Boyd, 219
Rectory, Sacred Heart Catholic Church, 110
Rectory, St. Patrick's Catholic Church, 176
Redlich, Mr. and Mrs. Nathan S., 104
Reedy Chapel African Methodist Episcopal Church, 56
Rees, Ernest A., 221
Rehm, Lawrence A., 216
Rehm, Lillian, 216
Reiswerg, Mr. and Mrs. Victor, 218
Renfert, Henry, 182
Reppen, William, 73
Residential Preservation Program, Galveston Historical Foundation, 84, 145, 155
Resolution Trust Corporation, 55
"Restricted District", 40
Rex Steam Laundry Company Building, 168
Reybaud, Edith, 145
Reymershoffer, Gustav, 76
Reymershoffer, John, 77
Reymershoffer Monument, J., 176-77
Reymershoffer's Sons Building, J., 32
Rhea, John S., 116
Rhind, J. Massey, 44, 51, 54, 94
Rice, Baulard & Company Building, 32
Rice, Joseph W., 32, 59
Rice Hotel (Houston), 235
Rice Institute (Houston), 53
Richardson, H. H., 45, 184
Ricke, Joseph, 83
Riedel, Herman, 147
Rieman Building, 205
Ripley, H. C., 227, 233
Rismiller, Ed, 128
River House (Manhattan), 26
Riviera Apartments, 118
Robert, Henry M., 227, 233
Robertson, Joseph A., 108
Robinowitz, Robert, 39
Robinson, John T., 82
Robinson, Willard B., 47
Robison, Maurice, 203
Robles, Eduardo, 27
Robsjohn-Gibbings, T. H., 215
Roemer, Agnes Moser, 142
Roemer, Dr. Ferdinand, 5
Roemer, John, 142
Roempke, Axel I., 95
Roensch, Bernard, 97
Rogers, Jerry, 129
Rogers, John S., 153

Rogers, Kate, 80

Rogers Building, J. D., 25

Ronald McDonald House, 67

Root, Joseph C., 223

Root, Sarah P., 88

Rosenberg, Henry, 25, 44-45, 51, 53-54, 58, 68-69, 94, 151, 166, 172, 193

Rosenberg, Mollie Macgill, 69, 172

Rosenberg Building, 20, 25

Rosenberg Colored Library, 166

Rosenberg Elementary School, 94

Rosenberg Estate, 151, 166

Rosenberg Fountains, 44-45, 51, 54, 94, 97

Rosenberg Free School, 94

Rosenberg Home for Aged Women, Letitia, 193-94

Rosenberg Library, 7, 51, 58, 68, 69, 138

Rossi, Aldo, 18, 113

Rossi, David, 167

Rourke, John M., 180

Rowe, Colin, 129

Royal Hotel, 31

Roystone, William H., 98, 99, 102

Rühl, Julius H., 106

Runge, Elisabeth D., 68

Runge, Henry, 22

Runge, Julius, 210

Runge, Louis H., 68, 76

S.S. Galveston Hotel Courts, 235

Saarinen, Eliel, 186

Sacred Heart Academy, 75

Sacred Heart Catholic Church (1904), 110, 111

Sacred Heart Catholic Church (Augusta, Georgia), 111

Sacred Heart Church (1892), 111

Sacred Heart School, 110

Saengerfest Park, 20-21

Sage, F. H., 85

St. Augustine's Church, 180

St. Germain Place, 44

St. John's Lutheran Church, 179

St. Joseph's Catholic Church, 50, 144

St. Joseph's Hospital (Houston), 126

St. Luke's Missionary Baptist Church, 148

St. Mary's Cathedral, 5, 47-48, 52, 111, 143

St. Mary's Cathedral Basilica, 47-48

St. Mary's Hospital, 126

St. Mary's University, 53, 110

St. Patrick's Catholic Church, 175-76

St. Patrick's School, 176

St. Paul's Methodist Church, 109, 116

Salisbury, Hiram A., 179

Salvation Army Chapel, 46

Salzmann, Numa, 43

Salzmann-Houlahan Building, 42-43

Sampson, Dr. Arthur F., 73

Sampson & Son, 28

Samuel May Williams Home, 191

Samuels, E., 55

San Antonio Museum of Art, 203

San Jacinto, Battle of, 109

San Jacinto Elementary School (1964), 2, 132, 145

San Jacinto School (1886), 145

San Luis Hotel and Condominium, 230

San Marino subdivision, 129

Sanborn Map & Publishing Company, 2, 155-56

Sandpiper Motel, 236

Sandusky, William H., 54, 190, 210

Sanguinet, Marshall R., 54

Sanguinet, Staats & Hedrick, 37

Sanson & Farrand, 22

Santa Ana, Antonio López de, 58

Santa Fe Building, 18, 29

Santa Fe Railway, 18

Saracco, John, Mr. and Mrs., 34

Sarna Family Housing, Ensign Frank (Fort Crockett), 231

Sarwold, Dr., 116

Sawyer, Mrs. John D., 87

Sawyer, William, 87

Sawyer, Mrs. William L., 66

Sayers, Governor Joseph D., 58

Scanlan, Kate, 42

Schadt, Lillian, 219

Schadt, Mrs. William, 219

Schelewa, Charles F., 138

Schiller, Charles, 196

Schmalm, Dell N., 169

Schmidt, Dr. Bernard A., 173

Schmidt, Frederick C., 49, 92

Schmidt, Louis, 159

Schmidt's Garden, 159

Schneider, George, 150

Schneider & Company Building, George, 24-25

Scholes Field Municipal Airport, 238, 244

School of Allied Health and Nursing (UTMB), 126-27

Schott, J. J., 114

Schulte, Henry, 91

Schulte, Theresa, 116

Schulte Building, 39

Schutte, Henry D., 91

Schwartz, Elliott, 18

Schwartz, Ivan, 18

Scott, John Z. H., 115

Scott, Mitchell L., 40-41

Scottish Rite Cathedral, 48-49

Scottish Rite Temple, 44

Scribner Library (Saratoga Springs), 124

Scull, Emily, 109

Scull, Horace, 109

Scull, Ralph A., 109

Sea Isle subdivision, 248

Seahorse Motel, 232, 233

Sealy, George, 19, 53, 57, 103, 113

Sealy, George, Jr., 208, 219, 230, 235, 247

Sealy, John, 19, 32, 51, 54, 57, 125, 177-78

Sealy, Mrs. John, 175, 177

Sealy, John H., 37, 51, 125, 189

Sealy, Magnolia Willis (Mrs. George Sealy), 53, 57, 59, 188-89

Sealy, Robert, 57, 59

Sealy & Smith Foundation, 69, 125, 219

Sealy & Smith Professional Building, 125-26

Sealy Children's Hospital, John, 124-25

Sealy family, 219, 246

Sealy Hospital, Jenny, 125

Sealy Hospital (1889), John, 113, 121, 128

Sealy Hospital (1953), John, 124-25

Sealy Hospital Tower (1978), John, 124-25

Sealy Hospital Trauma Center (1991), John, 124-25

Sealy House. *See Open Gates*

Sealy Monument, George, 179

Sealy Monument, John, 177, 178

Sealy Office Buildings, John, 19

Sealy Outpatient Clinic, John, 125

Seaman's Center, 35

Seaport Museum, 27-28

Seawall, 7, 8, 109, 148, 163, 226-27, 230, 232-36, 238

Seawall and Grade Raising Monument, Galveston, 233

Seeligson, George, 94-95

Seeligson, Henry A., 94

Seinsheimer, Eliza, 183

Seinsheimer, J. Fellman, 139, 181-82

Senechal Grocery Building, L. W., 90-91

Sergeant Building, 29

Serio, Sam S., 234

1700 Strand Building, 26-27

Seventh-day Adventist Church, Galveston, 155

Shannon, H. S., 235

Shaw, Michael W., 70, 96

Shearn, Libbie. *See* Moody, Libbie Shearn

Shearn, Libbie Rice, 59, 222

Shearn Moody Plaza, 18

Sherman, Sidney, 109

Sherman family, 219

Sherman Monument, Sidney, 109-10

Sherman Square-Louis Adoue Playground, 94

Sherwin & Overmire, 34

Shindler Interests, Jim, 236

Shriners Hospital for Crippled Children Galveston Burns Institute, 124

Silk Stocking Historic District, 132-33, 136

Silver Spray Bar, 142

Simon, Louis A., 50

Simpson, Dalbert, 18

Singleton, Dr. Albert O., 113

Sisters of Charity of the Incarnate Word, 126

622 Building, 54

Skidmore College (Sarasota Springs), 124

Skinner, William C., 107

Skinner-Girardeau House, 115

Skogland, Herbert, 128

Sloan, Samuel, 57

Smallwood, Robert C., 215

Smith, E. W., 143

Smith, George C. Mr. and Mrs., 136

Smith, J. Carroll, 106

Smith, Jennie Sealy, 125

Smith, John F., 56, 93, 171

Smith, R. Waverly, 51-52, 186, 189

Smith, Mrs. R. Waverly, 51-52

Smith, Dr. and Mrs. Y. C., Jr., 221

Smith Apartments, 136

Smith Building, J. Mayrant, 28

Smith Hall, Ashbel (UTMB), 121, 127

Smith Memorial Pavilion, J. Waverly, 124-25

Smith Yacht Club, Bob, 128

Smoky Row, 40

Socha, Julius, 52

Società Italiana di Mutuo Soccorrso, 243

Society for the Help of Homeless Children, 146

Sonia Apartments, 118

Sonnentheil, Jacob W., 101-2

Sonya's Beauty Shop, 72

South Shore Addition, 217

Southern Coffee Co., 141

Southern Ornamental Iron Works, 21

Southern Union Gas Company, 203

Southern Union Gas Company Building (1940), 59

Southwestern Telegraph and Telephone Company, 49

Spalding, Albert T., Jr., 153

Spalding family, 153

Spangler, Harry S., 137

Spanish-American War, 231

Spanish Grant subdivision, 245

Spence, Nathaniel A., 158

Spencer, Mr. and Mrs. John Hutchings, 141

Spiller, Dr. William F., 190

Spiritual True Church, 168

Stafford, Fred B., 26

Stafford, Fred T., 204, 206, 216

Staley, Earl, 45

Stanley, Paul W., 195

Star Drug Store, 42, 81

Star State Fire Company, 41

Staub, John F., 113, 142, 163, 182, 184-85, 189-90, 191-92, 221

Stavenhagen, Ernest, 75

Steffens, Dr. Ferdinand, 182

Steinbomer, Henry, 50

Steph, Patti, 57, 218

Stephens, Dr. Edward M. F., 192

Stephenson, William, 91

Stern, Morris, 105

Stevens, Clarence E., 139

Steward, Fred S., 52

Stewart, Maco, 33, 247

Stewart, Maco, Jr., 247

Stewart, Walter F., 74

Stewart family, 246

Stewart Title Building, 33

Stewart Title Company, 33, 247

Stirling, Dr. and Mrs. E. Hopkins, 129, 217

Stoller, Ezra, 9, 33, 75, 84, 114

Stone, Dr. Charles T., 215

Stone & Webster Engineering Corporation, 242

Storm of 1900, 7-8, 22-24, 31, 46, 51, 53, 59, 79, 93, 96,
    102-3, 105, 108-9, 111-12, 115-17, 127, 144, 146-47,
    151, 154, 159-60, 166, 176, 180, 183, 185, 193-94,
    196, 203-5, 211, 223, 226, 231, 234, 242

Storm of 1909, 234

Storm of 1915, 7, 234-35, 242

Stowe, Elwood E., 47, 52, 53, 242

Stowe, George B., 40, 44, 47, 52-53, 55-56, 73-74, 86,
    101-4, 137, 146, 150-51, 166, 169, 184, 186, 189, 242

Stowe & Stowe, 53, 181, 205, 219, 242

Strand Action Plan, 22

Strand Brewery, 21

Strand Historic District, 15, 18, 22, 24, 27

Strand Street Theatre, 31

Strand Surplus Center, 22

Strand Visitors Center, 26

Stringfellow, Henry M., 96

Stripling, Raiford, 57

Stubblefield, Joe, 183

Stubbs, Dr., 116

Stühmer, Henry, 166

Sturrock, Margaret, 48

Suderman, Charles T., 192

Sui Jen, 234

Sullivan, Tim, 139, 140

Sunlight Baptist Church, 172-73

Supreme Court of Texas, 43

Sutton Hall (Austin), 127

Swanson Hiester Wilson Boland, 236

Sweeney, Thomas H., 142-43

Swenson, Bailey A., 218

Swiff, Joseph, 181

Sydnor, John S., 188

Sydnor-Heidenheimer House, 105

Tabb, Mrs. W. G., 194

Tackett, Gerald, 37, 202

Taft Architects, 20, 22, 24-26, 29, 32, 105

Talfor, Mrs. M. F., 114

Tankersley, John, 205

Tanner Brothers, 166

Tapley Associates, Charles, 247

Tartt Building, 53

Taylor, David, 35, 36

Taylor, Eugenia, 230, 247

Taylor Classic Car Museum, David, 35-36

Telephone Building, 49

Temple B'nai Israel, 52

Texas A&M University at Galveston, 202-3, 230-31

Texas Bottling Work, 170

Texas Centennial Exposition, 110, 188

Texas Cotton Press, 137

Texas Department of Corrections Hospital, 124-25

Texas Gulf Construction Company, 216

Texas Heroes Monument, 58, 110, 223

Texas Ice Company, 171

Texas Portland Cement & Lime Company, 137

Texas Produce & Commission Co., 158

Texas Prudential Insurance Company, 54

Texas Revolution, 58, 110

Texas Seaport Museum, 27-28

Texas Star Flour Mills and Elevator, 27

Texas Transport and Terminal Company, 85

Thomas, Lyda Ann Q., 45

Thomas, Mr. and Mrs. M. W., 108

Thompson, Clark W., 43, 214-15

Thompson, Edward R., Jr., 57

Thompson, Edward Randall, 113

Thompson, J. J., 51

Thompson Basic Sciences Building (UTMB), Libbie
    Moody, 126

Thompson, Rhoda A., 51

Thompson, T. C., 106

Thompson Building, T. E., 38-39

Thompson Company Building, Clark W., 43

Thompson Flats, 38

Thorne, Daniel K., 23, 32

3D/International, 126

Tidal Wave Monument, 223

Tiffany Studios, 53

Tigerman, Stanley, 18

Tinterow, Henry, 87

Tobey, Nathaniel W., Jr., 23, 25, 28, 45, 56, 94, 178

Tobin & Rooney, 59

Todd Tacket Lacy, 244

Tokio Roller Skating Rink, 233

Torbert, Alfred C., 188

Torregrossa, Joseph A., 231

Tracy, Michael, 24, 202

Trader Vic's, 234

Trapp, George, 99

Treaccar, Joseph, 167

Treasure Isle Motel, 235

Tremont Hotel, 30

Tremont House, 30, 31

Tremont Opera House, 45

Trentham, H. Lee, 20, 113

Trentham, Mrs. H. Lee, 113

Trinity Baptist Church, 168

Trinity Episcopal Church, 52, 53, 143, 182

Trinity Episcopal Church Parish House, 53
Trube, J. C., 104, 105
Trube Building, 39-40
Trube family, 104
Truchard, Rev. Antony M., 143-44
Trueheart, Caroline, 115
Trueheart, Henry M., 79, 88, 105, 113, 210
Trueheart & Co., H. M., 9, 33
Trueheart family, 113, 219
Trueheart Presbyterian Church, Anne, 196
Tucker, Philip C., 191
Tuller, Amos B., 171
Tuller, Mrs. Amos B., 171
2100 Market Street Garage, 37
Tyndall, William H., 59, 139, 146, 188, 207

Union Depot, 28
United States Appraiser's Stores Building, 27
United States Army, 227, 230-32, 244
United States Coast Guard, 231
United States Court House, 50
United States Custom House (1861), 45-46, 50, 154
United States Custom House (1933), 26, 50
United States Custom House (1937), 50
United States Home Corporation, 230
United States Housing Authority, 206
United States Marine Hospital, 210, 214
United States National Bank Building, 37, 38
United States Navy, 232
United States Post Office, Custom House, and Court
    House, 50, 58
United States Postal Service, 46
United Way of Galveston, 36
University Hospital Clinics Building, John Sealy Hospital,
    124-25
University of Texas Medical Branch (UTMB), 26, 57, 59,
    67, 68, 69, 94, 112, 113, 121, 124-28, 142, 184, 192,
    214, 215, 219, 236, 247
University of Texas Medical Department, 121
University of the South, 172
Ursuline Academy (1895), 163, 180
Ursuline Academy (1964), 180
Ursuline Convent, 53, 163, 180
USO Building, 206-7, 232

Vaiani, Albert, 142
Vaiani & Company Building, A., 142
Variety Saloon, 40
Varnell, Joseph, 110, 217
Varnell Apartments, 110
Venturi & Rauch, 22, 24
Victoria Plaza (San Antonio), 151
Victorian Condo-Hotel, 230
Vidor, Charles, 90
Vidor, King, 90
Viollet-le-Duc, Eugène Emmanuel, 46

Wainwright, A. H., 150
Waldorf Apartments, 194
Walker, Christian, 156
Walker, John C., 150
Walker, Woodrow J., 214
Wallace, Jack, 26
Wallace, Sally B., 26, 57
Wallis, Landes & Company, 19, 158
Walter, Anna, 90
Walters, Matilda (Mollie), 41, 189
Wansker, Morris, 102
Waples Lumber Company Building, 204
Ware, Dancie Perugini, 18
Ware, F. & A. B., 53
Warner, Gustavus, 69
Warren, David B., 57
Washington Hotel, 32
Waters, Evy, 185
Waters, James, 67
Waters, James S., 81, 82, 86
Waterwall, 24
Watkin, William Ward, 53-54, 178
Watson, David, 26, 31-32, 36-37, 47, 55-56, 71, 128, 248
Waul, Thomas N., 174
Weary & Alford, 38
Wegner Brothers Building, 36-37, 39
Wehmeyer, Mathilda, 90
Wells, Clinton G., Jr., 142
Wenk, Jacob, 100
Werner Grocery Building, William, 84
Wesley Tabernacle United Methodist Church, 205
West, Dr. Hamilton A., 94
West District School, 109, 162
West End Bakery, 189
West End Evangelical Mission, See St. John's Lutheran
    Church
West Point Missionary Baptist Church, 168
Westerlage, John H., 66
Westmoor Addition, 218
Wetmore, James A., 214
White, Robert Leon, 125, 127
White, William R., 141
Whiteside, Emily, 32, 45
Whorton, Evangeline Loessin, 190
Widman & Walsh, 26
Wilde, Oscar, 99
Wilder, Gaston H., 80-81
Wilkens, Richard M., 112
Wilkens & Biehl, 112
Wilkinson, Dr. Cary H., 54-55
Williams, Bryan F., 219
Williams, Sally Trueheart, 113
Williams, Samuel May, 162, 190-91
Williams, Mrs. Samuel May, 191
Williams, Tennessee, 140

Williams, Williams & Williams, 215

Williamson, Richard P., 81

Willis, Ella, 173

Willis, Magnolia. *See* Sealy, Magnolia Willis

Willis, Narcissa Worsham, 59

Willis, P. J., 173

Willis, R. S., 57, 59

Willis & Brother, P. J., 173

Willis-Moody House. *See* Moody Mansion and Museum

Willis Vault, P. J., 178-79

Willis Vault, Short A., 178

Wilson, George, 189

Wilson, Hezekiah, 67

Wilson, Robert H., Jr., 103

Wilson, Will, 40

Wilson Vault, Mrs. F. A., 179

Windsor Court Apartments, 188

Winterbotham, Lillian Seeligson, 95

Wolfe, Joel B., 98

Wolfer, Christian, 152

Wolston, Wells & Vidor Warehouse, 28

Wood, E. S., 22

Wood & Perot, 57

Wood Building, E. S., 22

Woodlands Development Corporation, 230, 238-39

Woodmen of the World, Galveston Tidal Wave Monument, 223

Woolford, Joseph B., 104

Works Progress Administration, 231

World War I, 81, 183

World War II, 8, 121, 129, 217, 230-32, 234, 238, 244

Wren, Powhatan S., 117

Wright, Frank Lloyd, 51, 182

Wright Cuney Park, 207

Wright Cuney Park Recreation Building, 206

Wyatt, Mr. and Mrs. Gene, 244

Yacht Club, Bob Smith, 128

Yen, Dr. and Mrs. Moore, 129

Young, Ammi B., 45

YWCA Building, 53-54

Zempter, J. W., 194

Zimmermann, Louis, 89

Zion Lutheran Church, 71

Zwiener, Charles L., 35, 53-54, 94, 113, 145, 176, 216, 218-20, 242